Living American History II

Our Nation's Past Through Its Documents

William D. Young
Maple Woods Community College
Vincent A. Clark
Johnson County Community College

KENDALL/HUNT PUBLISHING COMPANY
4050 Westmark Drive Dubuque, Iowa 52002

ISBN 0-7872-7289-2

Printed in the United States of America
10 9 8 7 6 5 4 3 2

Contents

Preface

We created *Living American History: Our Nation's Past Through Its Documents* to supplement the usual text and lectures in a United States history survey course. The survey course, in fact any good United States history course, should provide insights and basic background on our historic past, encourage further exploration by students and promote critical thinking. Too often the survey fails to accomplish any of these goals, because instructors are forced to use a panoramic approach. Forced to sprint across hundreds of years in two sixteen-week courses, professors paint a picture of our past with broad strokes, seldom having time for detailed work.

As attempts to remedy this, instructors assign student book critiques, create special in-class projects and group discussions, and use handouts of articles or primary documents. We believe that using primary documents is one of the best ways to do this: it's even essential. We also believe that this new primary documents reader provides an excellent way to incorporate documents into your classes.

First, this is an exciting collection of documents, which will make history classes come alive. We want this collection to let you smell the gunpowder from battles, hear the laughter of children, listen to the cries of workers and feel the frustrations of people from all classes. These documents personalize American history. They help students connect with the past as they discover that earlier Americans had worries, hopes and dreams similar to their own.

Second, we wanted to give instructors one of the widest possible ranges of documents. In our own classes we have often thought, "I wish I could use several readers. Then I could have the students read all the documents I wanted." We have included materials from the entire spectrum of social and political history, from a diverse variety of people, from different ethnic groups, classes, races, regions and nationalities.

Third, this book will help students recognize issues from past points of view and learn to understand the past on its own terms. Doing these things help students think critically. Part of the critical thinking process requires students to confront the issues, themes and cultural debates from the past that often continue to this very day. These themes should be considered in every United States history course, since we have debated their meanings even before becoming independent.

Work and economic issues are a good example. How should work be rewarded, and who should determine the division of goods and services? Should everyone be rewarded equally for similar work? Does the value of goods derive from the labor producing them? How important is labor? Is there an absolute conflict between labor and capital?

Human needs are important as well. What role do families, organizations and communities play in United States history? Are they all part of what Americans define as the "good life"? Do men and women have the same needs, enjoy the same opportunities and rewards, or share the same experiences in our history? What do different groups of immigrants, ethnic and religious minorities, or anyone else have to do to belong in approved society? How do we determine what is more important, individual greed and accomplishment or the welfare and health of the entire community? How do we define community in the United States?

What is the relationship between individuals, citizenship and the state? What are the origins of our government, why was it formed and who formed it? Where does the government derive its power to rule? What rights do citizens have, and how do we know this? Do all Americans enjoy these same rights throughout time, and if not, why not? What is the relationship between liberty and order, between natural rights and property rights in United States history? If the government is supposed to provide order and justice for citizens, does this mean the same for everyone in society (e.g., slaves, women, white males, religious minorities, workers, students and the poor)? When and on what grounds should the people challenge the authority of the government?

What does all of this mean to me? How am I affected by America's past, by government actions and individual accomplishments, by both virtuous citizens and evildoers? How does the past explain the United States today? How do political and business leaders misuse and abuse history for their own purposes?

To the Instructor

How often do students tell you that history is boring, that it is their worst or least favorite subject? We hear that from freshmen, who describe high school history as nothing more than memorizing names, dates and treaties. As historians we know that is learning trivia, not real history. History is learning how to put information in proper perspective, to use documents and historic accounts to understand the past.

Each module of this reader is organized around an issue or event in United States history. Unlike some readers, we chose not to focus simply on problems in our past. For example, Module V examines the struggle to ratify the Constitution, focusing on the arguments and tactics used by both sides. Students learn that not everyone embraced the document, and that its ratification was not a sure thing. In Module XXI we take a closer look at the Cold War. Different views of the Marshall Plan, of Truman's firing of General MacArthur, and of McCarthyism force students to realize there is often not one simple answer or truth to the past.

Every module begins with an introduction to the topic, providing historical background and introducing the historical arguments over the issue. This is followed by clues on how to consider the evidence in the readings. Each document has its own introduction, with additional background on the material, the writer or speaker, and additional questions to help students focus on key issues.

At the end of each module is a worksheet, with a series of questions requiring students to apply the information in the documents. These are not simple fill-in-the-blank questions, but require some analysis. These worksheets are perforated so students may complete them and turn them in as assignments.

We included many different types of evidence in this book. Instructors who want a variety of materials will find presidential addresses, Congressional debates and hearings, personal diaries, formal speeches, musical lyrics, folk tales, advertisements, court cases, memoirs, personal letters, oral interviews, newspaper accounts and wartime propaganda. You will hear from religious and secular leaders, from the rich and the poor, from slaveowners and slaves, from our friends and our enemies, from land-hungry whites and Native Americans, from men and women, from business and labor, from those who favor a strong government and those who oppose it, from Yankees and Confederates. Some of the documents are important classics, such as John Winthrop's sermon on the *Arbella* and Roosevelt's "Day of Infamy" speech. Other selections have not been included in readers before and should be a refreshing look at new material. We made sure the documents vary in length as well. Sometimes small snippets suffice, but other times instructors want (and students need) complete documents to understand the author's intent. Because the documents often assume conflicting positions, students are forced to think like historians. Our nation's past is full of conflict: our ancestors did not agree on everything, so students can try to understand what they disagreed on and why. Common assumptions and popular myths that students grew up with are challenged as well. For example, while we take the Constitution for granted today, its passage was not a sure thing, nor was support for the new government anywhere near unanimous.

This reader and its contents may be used in a variety of ways. These documents can be the basis for classroom discussion and group projects. The authors write specific questions for their examinations and require students to use the documents to answer the questions. Instructors can compare materials in different chapters, to trace the development of attitudes across time. For example, does the obligation of all citizens to the health and well-being of their community demonstrated in Module

II continue throughout the rest of Volume I? Are there similarities in the attitudes expressed before the American Revolution in Module IV and during the Civil War in Module XII? Do the conservative appeals in Module XVIII on the 1920s resemble conservative appeals in Module XXVI? If you want other suggestions, feel free to contact the authors. We have suggestions for additional documents to use as well.

To the Student

What do you do in class when you need information or do not understand something? You usually raise your hand and ask a question. That is what historians do when they look at documents; they ask questions for the document to answer. You already do this too. Your class syllabus is a document. It contains key information about your course, insights into your instructor's thinking and values, and his expectations for you and the timing of the current semester. Ten instructors may teach the same course, and every syllabus will be different. Same course, but different ideas on how and what to teach. Learning to read any historical document is like reading your syllabus. It is important to ask the right questions and reach the correct conclusions, even in the face of conflicting arguments. What types of questions should you ask about each document? Consider the following.

- Who wrote the document? This means the name of the person and their position, because their experiences and position in life influence views expressed in the document. A slave and his owner will obviously view slavery differently. So consider what social status, specific group, religion or gender influences the information in the document. Also important to your understanding is the background information on the period covered in the module, information gained from your textbook and instructor.
- Who is the intended audience? Every document has a specific audience, and determining who the audience is also lets you understand the document better. Was this intended as a private letter between friends, with no holds or secrets between them? Was it private and personal, as in a diary? Was the document intended for public consumption, such as an editorial, letter to the editor, speech, autobiography or pamphlet? What story are they trying to tell? Sometimes the audience influences how the story is told. The writer includes certain details to inflame the audience, or leaves out bits of information he or she assumes the audience already knows. Knowing who the audience is helps you understand why the document was written, and also helps explain the form the document took, e.g., poem, diary. Was it intended to help win an election, or perhaps arouse the population into righteous indignation? Would all people accept or respond to the arguments in the same way as the intended audience?
- You also need to go beyond the facts you can observe from the document if you are going to think critically like a historian. Assuming the document intended to sway an audience at the other end, can you believe the information presented? Is the letter, diary, etc., believable? Can you accept the claims of slaveowners that slavery is the best life for African Americans? Can you accept the claims of Joseph McCarthy that over 200 communists were working in the State Department in 1950? Has the document been altered from its original form, so you are reading an altered version?
- What does the document tell you about American society at that time period? Documents reveal the way their authors think about politics, class structure, immigration and other issues. Does the choice of words reveal certain attitudes or biases? Are there covert messages being spread with the overt ones? Do you think the attitudes expressed in the document, or the lifestyle described, reflect the views and lives of everyone in American society at that time?
- What does this documents mean to you, a United States history student in the twenty-first century? What does this document tell you about who we are as a nation today, where our

values and ideas come from? How much have we changed? What events from the past directly affect you today? Using the skills you honed comparing arguments in the modules, can you dissect political arguments and advertisements today?

William D. Young
Social Sciences
Maple Woods Community College
2601 NE Barry Road
Kansas City, MO 64156
816/437-3332
youngw@maplewoods.cc.mo.os

Vincent A. Clark
Department of History
Johnson County Community College
12345 College Blvd.
Overland Park, KS 66210
913/469-8500
vclark@jccc.net

Acknowledgements

An enormous amount of time and labor is expended researching, gathering and editing documents for a reader like this one. William D. Young thanks the library staff at Maple Woods Community College, starting with Linda Wilson, who encouraged him that her staff liked a good challenge. Monica Cuen and Diane Christiansen are the Maple Woods Interlibrary Loan staff who met the challenge, with assistance from Ted Ostaszewski on the Penn Valley Community College campus. Steve Jansen, historian for the Douglas County (Kansas) Historical Society and Watkins Museum, located key items for Module XI. Larry Cox patiently listened to descriptions of this book, looked at materials, and gave freely from his 38 years of teaching experience. Without the help of all these individuals this book would not have been finished. Finally, William Young thanks his wife Michelle and sons Michael and Benjamin. As with other projects, they served as sounding boards to determine what made sense, and reminded him how much nicer life would be once the book was finished. Vincent A. Clark would like to thank Doreen Maronde, Director of the Humanities at Johnson County Community College, for providing a supportive environment for teaching, where many of these documents were tried out. He also thanks his children, Geoffrey, Elizabeth and Katherine for friendly support, questions and jokes while this project was under way. We both want to thank our editor, Jason Mills, for his enthusiasm for this project in the first place, and his unceasing reminders that we needed to finish the book before we could use it. At Kendall/Hunt headquarters, Stefani DeMoss also provided invaluable help in making this book appear. Colleen Zelinsky did yeoman's work tracking down permissions for the material included, sometimes with very little help on our end. Finally, we thank our students, who have been both inspirations and test subjects for these materials.

Module XIII

Reconstruction and Beyond: Old South, New South?

The fighting was over. The last Confederate armies had surrendered and troops from both sides could return home. The Old South was destroyed and four million slaves were free. But what comes next? After the guns fall silent how do you reunite the nation? There was little agreement in 1865, and historians have disagreed about Reconstruction ever since. When fighting a war you have heroes marching valiantly off to war, fighting and dying for their ideals. In the name of those ideals you can rally the civilian population as well, urging them to make sacrifices as great as the troops at the front. This is the heroic stuff; this is why people remember the Civil War, and raise monuments to fallen heroes. But you will find few monuments to Reconstruction, because people cannot agree on its goals or results. Where are the fallen heroes and hard fought successes?

The Civil War left three questions to be answered about the South. First, what was going to happen to all of the "traitors," those men who fought in Confederate armies or served in the government? Second, what would be the fate of the southern states: would they be treated as conquered provinces, colonies or old time equals? Third, what do the four million former slaves receive besides freedom? To answer these questions the government will pass numerous pieces of legislation. People North and South, Republicans and Democrats will disagree over what actions to take, whether force is justified, whether social change can be forced through legislation. In the end the South was treated quite mildly compared to the losers in other attempted revolutions. In most western nations the losers faced massive executions, land seizures and permanent loss of wealth and privileges. Despite myths about Reconstruction, the South was handled with kid gloves.

Bloody vengeance was not visited upon the traitors/southern patriots who fought in the Civil War. Despite Union soldiers singing "We'll Hang Jeff Davis from a Sour Apple Tree" as they marched south, he did not die. He went to jail for two years, and came out as a martyr. Robert E. Lee and other military leaders, who swore an oath to defend the United States when they were in the antebellum army, were never tried for treason, nor were they even arrested. The only rebel tried and executed was Henry Wirz, Commandant of Andersonville Prison. He was tried for war crimes, not treason.

The former Confederate states went through a formal process to regain their equal status in the American political system. This was not some massive Radical Reconstruction plot to foist rule by northern criminals ("carpetbaggers") and "black rule" upon a defenseless South, although that was the popular myth for years. Radical Republicans were never in charge of the northern government, and moderate Republicans held off formal action until violent acts, the murder of former Union soldiers, and southern refusal to renounce secession forced their hand. The Reconstruction Acts of 1867 set up a process for Federal control and law enforcement in the South, partial disenfranchisement of former Confederates, and assistance to the freedmen until the conquered states proved their loyalty. To do this required passing the 14th and 15th Amendments, renouncing both secession and the Confederacy's wartime debts, and eliminating the black codes restricting the rights of freedmen. During the years that Reconstruction governments controlled southern states they increased democracy by opening up most state offices for election, building schools for blacks and whites, stimulating industry and diversifying the southern economy. Despite later southern claims, these governments were controlled by white leaders, were no more corrupt than the southern "Redeemer" governments that replaced them, and actually improved the southern standard of living.

What of the freedmen? Former Confederate General Robert V. Richardson reflected the popular view when he declared, "The emancipated slaves own nothing, because nothing but freedom has been given to them." In the wake of emancipation many former slaves fled the plantations for towns and cities, where "freedom was free-er." Others went searching for wives and other family members sold in years past, and then took steps to legalize earlier marriages and living arrangements. African Americans had their own agenda, which called for political power and economic independence. This meant the right to vote and hold office, and the opportunity to hold land. Many former slaves realized, as did their former masters, that the right to vote is meaningless without economic independence. The Civil Rights Act of 1866 and the 14th and 15th Amendments helped achieve the goal of political rights, but economic successes were far fewer.

By 1877, southern whites regained control of the state governments, and for the rest of the century systematically eliminated the political and social advances African Americans had achieved because of the Civil War. Using a variety of illegal methods, whites disenfranchised black voters, segregated public facilities, partially re-enslaved blacks on the farms and former plantations and used massive violence to keep them in their "place."

Considering the Evidence in the Readings

The documents in this module provide firsthand accounts of the South during Reconstruction. As you learn what happened and how people were treated, consider what actions the federal government needed to take to protect the rights of all its citizens. This is what these reports and firsthand testimony are all about, giving the government information so it can act as needed. Be sure to trace the evolution of the South from the end of the war to the twentieth century and consider how much the region did or did not change.

Document 13.1 An Anonymous Journalist Describes the South in 1866

More than two hundred writers visited the South in the first fifteen years after the Civil War. Most worked for northern newspapers and journals, and were assigned to investigate southern conditions and report back to their readers. This meant primarily observing the lives of the freedmen and checking on the loyalty of the former Confederates. Some writers arrived hoping for a quick reconciliation between sections and reported back positively. Some came South expecting treason to still be rampant and sent back reports that the South required harsh treatment. Others hoped for the best, but were disappointed or alarmed by the attitudes and defiance of southern whites. The following report is from the *Atlantic Monthly* of February 1866. How does the author describe southern attitudes? Have they accepted the outcome of the war, or the supremacy of the national government? What is the attitude towards the former slaves or northern soldiers and officials? What action does this writer recommend?

I spent the months of September, October, and November, 1865, in the States of North Carolina, South Carolina, and Georgia. I travelled over more than half the stage and railway routes therein, visited a considerable number of towns and cities in each State, attended the so-called reconstruction conventions at Raleigh, Columbia, and Milledgeville, and had much conversation with many individuals of nearly all classes.

I was generally treated with civility, and occasionally with courteous cordiality. I judge, from the stories told me by various persons, that my reception was, on the whole, something better than that accorded to the majority of Northern men travelling in

From *Atlantic Monthly,* February 1866.

that section. Yet at one town in South Carolina, when I sought accommodations for two or three days at a boarding-house, I was asked by the woman in charge, "Are you a Yankee or a Southerner?" and when I answered, "Oh, a Yankee, of course," she responded, "No Yankee stops in this house!" and turned her back upon me and walked off. In another town in the same State I learned that I was the first Yankee who had been allowed to stop at the hotel since the close of the war. In one of the principal towns of Western North Carolina, the landlord of the hotel said to a customer, while he was settling his bill, that he would be glad to have him say a good word for the house to any of his friends; "but," added he, "you may tell all d—d Yankees I can git 'long jest as well, if they keep clar 'o me"; and when I asked if the Yankees were poor pay, or made him extra trouble, he answered, "I don't want 'em 'round. I ha'n't got no use for'em nohow." In another town in the same State, a landlord said to me, when I paid my two-days 'bill, that "no d—n Yankee" could have a bed in his house. In Georgia, I several times heard the people of my hotel expressing the hope that the passenger-train wouldn't bring any Yankees; and I have good reason for believing that I was quite often compelled to pay an extra price for accommodations because I was known to be from the North. In one town, several of us, passengers by an evening train, were solicited to go to a certain hotel; but the clerk declined to give me a room, when he learned that I was from Massachusetts, though I secured one after a time through the favor of a travelling acquaintance, who sharply rebuked the landlord.

It cannot be said that freedom of speech has been fully secured in either of these three States. Personally, I have very little cause of complaint, for my role was rather that of a listener than of a talker; but I met many persons who kindly cautioned me, that at such and such places, and in such and such company, it would be advisable to refrain from conversation on certain topics. Among the better class of people, resident in the cities and large towns, I found a fair degree of liberality of sentiment and courtesy of speech; but in travelling off the main railway-lines, and among the average of the population, any man of Northern opinions must use much circumspection of language; while in many counties of South Carolina and Georgia, the life of an avowed Northern radical would hardly be worth a straw but for the presence of the military. In Barnwell and Anderson districts, South Carolina, official records show the murder of over a dozen Union men in the months of August and September; and at Atlanta, a man told me, with a quiet chuckle, that in Carroll County, Georgia, there were "four d—n Yankees shot in the month of October." Any Union man, travelling in either of these two States, must expect to hear many very insulting words; and any Northern man is sure to find his principles despised, his people contemned, and himself subjected to much disagreeable contumely. There is everywhere extreme sensitiveness concerning the negro and his relations; and I neither found nor learned of any village, town, or city in which it would be safe for a man to express freely what are here, in the North, called very moderate views on that subject. Of course the war has not taught its full lesson, till even Mr. Wendell Phillips can go into Georgia and proclaim "The South Victorious."

I often had occasion to notice, both in Georgia and the Carolinas, the wide and pitiful difference between the residents of the cities and large towns and the residents of the country. There is no homogeneity, but everywhere a rigid spirit of caste. The longings of South Carolina are essentially monarchical rather than republican; even the common people have become so debauched in loyalty, that very many of them would readily accept the creation of orders of nobility. In Georgia there is something less of this spirit; but the upper classes continually assert their right to rule, and the middle and lower classes have no ability to free themselves. The whole structure of society is full of separating walls; and it will sadden the heart of any Northern man, who travels in either of these three States, to see how poor, and meagre, and narrow a thing life is to all the country people. Even with the best class of townsfolk it lacks very much of the depth and breadth and fruitfulness of our Northern life, while with these others it is hardly less materialistic than that of their own mules and horses.

Thus, Charleston has much intelligence, and considerable genuine culture; but go twenty miles away, and you are in the land of the barbarians. So, Raleigh is a city in which there is love of beauty, and interest in education; but the common people of the county are at least forty years behind the same class of people in Vermont. Moreover, in Macon are many fine residences, and the city may boast of its gentility and its respect for the nourishing elegancies of life; but a dozen miles out are large neighborhoods not yet half-civilized. The contrast between the inhabitants of the cities and those of the country is hardly less striking than that between the various classes constituting the body of the common people. Going from one county to another is frequently going into a foreign country. Travel continually brings novelty, but with that always came pain. Till all these hateful walls of caste are thrown down, we can have neither intelligent love of liberty, decent respect for justice, nor enlightened devotion to the idea of national unity. "Do men gather grapes of thorns, or figs of thistles?"

It has been the purpose of the ruling class, apparently, to build new barriers between themselves and the common people, rather than tear away any of those already existing. I think no one can understand the actual condition of the mass of whites in Georgia and the Carolinas, except by some daily contact with them. The injustice done to three fourths of them was hardly less than that done to all the blacks. There were two kinds of slavery, and negro slavery was only the more wicked and debasing than white slavery. Nine of every ten white men in South Carolina had almost as little to do with even State affairs as the negroes had. Men talk of plans of reconstruction;—that is the best plan which proposes to do most for the common people. Till civilization has been carried down into the homes and hearts of all classes, we shall have neither regard for humanity nor respect for the rights of the citizen. In many sections of all these States human life is quite as cheap as animal life. What a mental and moral condition does this indicate! Any plan of reconstruction is wrong that does not assure toleration of opinion, and the elevation of the common people to the consciousness that ours is a republican form of government. Whether they are technically in the Union or out of the Union, it is the national duty to deal with these States in such a manner as will most surely exalt the lower and middle classes of their inhabitants. The nation must teach them a knowledge of their own rights, while it also teaches them respect for its rights and the rights of man as man.

Stopping for two or three days in some back county, I was always seeming to have drifted away from the world which held Illinois and Ohio and Massachusetts. The difficulty in keeping connection with our civilization did not so much lie in the fact that the whole structure of daily life is unlike ours, nor in the other fact that I was forced to hear the Union and all loyal men reviled, as in the greater fact that the people are utterly without knowledge. There is everywhere a lack of intellectual activity. Schools, books, newspapers,—why, one may almost say there are none outside the cities and towns. The situation is horrible enough, when the full force of this fact is comprehended; yet there is a still lower deep,—there is small desire, even feeble longing, for schools and books and newspapers. The chief end of man seems to have been "to own a nigger." In the important town of Charlotte, North Carolina, I found a white man who owned the comfortable house in which he lived, who had a wife and three half-grown children, and yet had never taken a newspaper in his life. He thought they were handy for wrapping purposes, but he couldn't see why anybody wanted to bother with the reading of them. He knew some folks spent money for them, but he also knew a many houses where none had ever been seen. In that State I found several persons—whites, and not of the "clay-eater" class, either—who never had been inside a school-house, and who didn't mean to 'low their children to go inside one. In the upper part of South Carolina, I stopped one night at the house of a moderately well-to-do farmer who never had owned any book but a Testament, and that was given to him. When I expressed some surprise at this fact, he assured me that he was as well off as some other people thereabouts. Between Augusta and Milledgeville I rode in a stage-coach in which were two delegates of the Georgia Convention. When I said that I hoped the day would soon come in which school-houses would be as numerous in Georgia as in Massachusetts, one of them answered: "Well, I hope it'll never come,—popular education is all a d—n humbug in my judgment"; whereunto the other responded, "That's my opinion, too." These are exceptional cases, I am aware, but they truly index the situation of thousands of persons. It is this general ignorance, and this general indifference to knowledge, that make a Southern trip such wearisome work. You can touch the masses with few of the appeals by which we move our own people. There is very little aspiration for larger life; and, more than that, there is almost no opportunity for its attainment. That education is the stairway to a nobler existence is a fact which they either fail to comprehend or to which they are wholly indifferent.

Where there is such a spirit of caste, where the ruling class has a personal interest in fostering prejudice, where the masses are in such an inert condition, where ignorance so generally prevails, where there is so little ambition for improvement, where life is so hard and material in its tone, it is not strange to find much hatred and contempt. Ignorance is generally cruel, and frequently brutal. The political leaders of this people have apparently indoctrinated them with the notion that they are superior to any other class in the country. Hence there is usually very little effort to conceal the prevalent scorn of the Yankee,—this term being applied to the citizen of any Northern State. Any plan of reconstruction, is wrong that tends to leave these old leaders in power. A few of them give fruitful evidence of a change of heart,—by some means save these for the sore and troubled future; but for the others, the men who not only brought on the war, but ruined the mental and moral force of their people before unfurling the banner of rebellion,—for these there should never any more be place or countenance among honest and humane and patriotic people. When the nation gives them life, and a chance for its continuance, it shows all the magnanimity that humanity in such case can afford.

In North Carolina there is a great deal of something that calls itself Unionism; but I know nothing more like the apples of Sodom than most of this North Carolina Unionism. It is a cheat, a Will-o-the-wisp; and any man who trusts it will meet with overthrow. Its quality is shown in a hundred ways. An old farmer came into Raleigh to sell a little corn. I had some talk with him. He claimed that he had been a Union man from the beginning of the war, but he refused to take "greenback money" for his corn. In a town in the western part of the State I found a merchant who prided himself on the fact that he had always prophesied the downfall of the so-called Confederacy and had always desired the success of the Union arms; yet when I asked him why he did not vote in the election for delegates to the Convention, he answered, sneeringly,—"I shall not vote till you take away the military." The State Convention declared by a vote of ninety-four to nineteen that the Secession ordinance had always been null and void; and then faced squarely about, and, before the Presidential instructions were received, impliedly declared, by a vote of fifty-seven to fifty-three, in favor of paying the war debt incurred in supporting that ordinance! This action on these two point exactly exemplifies the quality of North Carolina Unionism. There may be, in the seed of loyalty, but woe to him who mistakes the germ for the ripened fruit! In all sections of the State I found abundant hatred of some leading or local Secessionist; but how full of promise for the new era of national life is the Unionism which rests only on this foundation?

In South Carolina there is very little pretence of loyalty. I believe I found less than fifty men who admitted any love for the Union. There is everywhere a passionate devotion to the State, and the common sentiment holds that man guilty of treason who prefers the United States to South Carolina. There is no occasion to wonder at the admiration of the people for Wade Hampton, for he is the very exemplar of their spirit,—of their proud and narrow and domineering spirit. "It is our duty," he says, in his letter of last November, "it is our duty to support the President of the United States so long as he manifests a disposition to restore all our rights as a sovereign State."

That sentence will forever stand as a model of cool arrogance, and yet it is in full accord with the spirit of the South-Carolinians. He continues:—"Above all, let us stand by our State,—all the sacred ties that bind us to her are intensified by her suffering and desolation. . . . It only remains for me, in bidding you farewell, to say, that, whenever the State needs my services, she has only to command, and I shall obey." The war has taught this people only that the physical force of the nation cannot be resisted. They will be obedient to the letter of the law, perhaps, but the whole current of their lives flows in direct antagonism to its spirit.

In Georgia there is something worse than sham Unionism or cold acquiescence in the issue of battle; it is the universally prevalent doctrine of the supremacy of the State. Even in South Carolina a few men stood up against the storm, and now claim credit for faith in dark days. In Georgia that man is hopelessly dead who doubted or faltered. The common sense of all classes pushes the necessity of allegiance to the State into the domain of morals as well as into that of politics; and he who did not "go with the State" in the Rebellion is held to have committed the unpardonable sin. At Macon I met a man who was one of the leading Unionists in the winter of 1860–1861. He told me how he suffered then for his hostility to Secession, and yet he added,—"I should have considered myself forever disgraced, if I hadn't heartily gone with the State, when she decided to fight." And Ben Hill, than whom there are but few more influential men in the State, advises the people after this fashion,—"I would vote for no man who could take the Congressional test-oath, because it is the highest evidence of infidelity to the people of the State." I believe it is the concurrent testimony of all careful travellers in Georgia, that there is everywhere only cold toleration for the idea of national sovereignty, very little hope for the future of the State as a member of the Federal Union, and scarcely any pride in the strength and glory and renown of the United States of America.

Much is said of the hypocrisy of the South. I found but little of it anywhere. The North-Carolinian calls himself a Unionist, but he makes no special pretence of love for the Union. He desires many favors, but he asks them generally on the ground that he hated the Secessionists.

He expects the nation to recognize rare virtue in that hatred, and hopes it may win for his State the restoration of her political rights; but he wears his mask of nationality so lightly that there is no difficulty in removing it. The South-Carolinian demands only something less than he did in the days before the war, but he offers no pleas of Unionism as a guaranty for the future. He rests his case on the assumption that he has fully acquiesced in the results of the war, and he honestly believes that he has so acquiesced. His confidence in South Carolina is so supreme that he fails to see how much the conflict meant. He walks by such light as he has, and cannot yet believe that Destiny has decreed his State a secondary place in the Union. The Georgian began by believing that rebellion in the interest of Slavery was honorable, and the result of the war has not changed his opinion. He is anxious for readmission to fellowship with New York and Pennsylvania and Connecticut, but he supports his application by no claim of community of interest with other States. His spirit is hard and uncompromising; he demands rights, but does not ask favors; and he is confident that Georgia is fully as important to the United States as they are to Georgia.

Complaint is made that the Southern people have recently elected military men to most of their local State offices. We do ourselves a wrong in making this complaint. I found it almost everywhere true in Georgia and the Carolinas the best citizens of to-day are the Confederate soldiers of yesterday. Of course, in many individual cases they are bitter and malignant; but in general the good of the Union, no less than the hope of the South, lies in the bearing of the men who were privates and minor officers in the armies of Lee and Johnston. It may not be pleasant to us to recognize this fact; but I am confident that we shall make sure progress toward securing domestic tranquillity and the general welfare, just in proportion as we act upon it. It should be kept in mind that comparatively few of those who won renown on the field were promoters of rebellion or secession. The original malcontents,—ah! where are they? Some of them at least are beyond interference in earthly affairs; others are in hopeless poverty and chilling neglect; others are struggling to mount once more the wave of popular favor. A few of these last have been successful,—to see that no more of them are so is a national duty. I count it an omen of good, when I find that one who bore himself gallantly as a soldier has received preferment. We cannot afford to quarrel on this ground; for, though their courage was for our wounding, their valor was the valor of Americans. The really bad feature of the situation with respect to the relations of these States to the General Government is, that there is not only very little loyalty in their people, but a great deal of stubborn antagonism, and some deliberate defiance. Further war in the field I do not deem among the possibilities. Be the leaders never so bloodthirsty, the common people have had enough of fighting. The bastard Unionism of North Carolina, the haughty and self-complacent State pride of South Carolina, the arrogant dogmatism and insolent assumption of Georgia,—how shall we build nationality on such foundations? That is the true plan of reconstruction which makes haste very slowly. It does not comport with the character of our Government to exact pledges of any State which are not exacted of all. The one sole needful condition is, that each State establish a republican form of government, whereby all civil rights at least shall be assured in their fullest extent to every citizen. The Union is no Union, unless there is equality of privileges among the States. When Georgia and the Carolinas establish this republican form of government, they will have brought themselves into harmony with the national will, and may justly demand readmission to their former political relations in the Union. Each State has some citizens, who, wiser than the great majority, comprehend the meaning of Southern defeat with praiseworthy insight. Seeing only individuals of this small class, a traveller might honestly conclude that the States were ready for self-government. Let not the nation commit the terrible mistake of acting on this conclusion. These men are the little leaven in the gross body politic of Southern communities. It is no time for passion or bitterness, and it does not become our manhood to do anything for revenge. Let us have peace and kindly feeling; yet, that our peace may be no sham or shallow affair, it is painfully essential that we keep these States awhile within national control, in order to aid the few wise and just men therein who are fighting the great fight with stubborn prejudice and hide-bound custom. Any plan of reconstruction is wrong which accepts forced submission as genuine loyalty, or even as cheerful acquiescence in the national desire and purpose.

Before the war, we heard continually of the love of the master for his slave, and the love of the slave for his master. There was also much talk to the effect that the negro lived in the midst of pleasant surroundings, and had no desire to change his situation. It was asserted that he delighted in a state of dependence, and throve on the universal favor of the whites. Some of this language we conjectured might be extravagant; but to the single fact that there was universal good-will between the two classes every Southern white person bore evidence.

So, too, in my late visit to Georgia and the Carolinas, they generally seemed anxious to convince me that the blacks had behaved well during the war,—had kept at their old tasks, had labored cheerfully and faithfully, had shown no disposition to lawlessness, and had rarely been guilty of acts of violence, even in sections where there were many women and children, and but few white men.

Yet I found everywhere now the most direct antagonism between the two classes. The whites charge generally that the negro is idle, and at the bottom of all local disturbances, and credit him with most of the vices and very few of the virtues of humanity. The negroes charge that the whites are revengeful, and intend to cheat the laboring class at every opportunity, and credit them with neither good purposes nor kindly hearts. This present and positive hostility of each class to the other is a fact that will sorely perplex any Northern man travelling in either of these States. One would say, that, if there had formerly been such pleasant relations between them, there ought now to be mutual sympathy and forbearance, instead of mutual distrust and antagonism. One would say, too, that self-interest, the common interest of capital and labor, ought to keep them in harmony; while the fact is, that this very interest appears to put them in an attitude of partial defiance toward each other. I believe the most charitable traveller must come to the conclusion, that the professed love of the whites for the blacks was mostly a monstrous sham or a downright false pretence. For myself, I judge that it was nothing less than an arrogant humbug.

The negro is no model of virtue or manliness. He loves idleness, he has little conception of right and wrong, and he is improvident to the last degree of childishness. He is a creature,—as some of our own people will do well to keep carefully in mind,—he is a creature just forcibly removed from slavery. The havoc of war has filled his heart with confused longings, and his ears with confused sounds of rights and privileges: it must be the nation's duty, for it cannot be left wholly to his late master, to help him to a clear understanding of these rights and privileges, and also to lay upon him a knowledge of his responsibilities. He is anxious to learn, and is very tractable in respect to minor matters; but we shall need almost infinite patience with him, for he comes very slowly to moral comprehensions.

Going into the States where I went,—and perhaps the fact is true also of the other Southern States,—going into Georgia and the Carolinas, and not keeping in mind the facts of yesterday, any man would almost be justified in concluding that the end and purpose in respect to this poor negro was his extermination. It is proclaimed everywhere that he will not work, that he cannot take care of himself, that he is a nuisance to society, that he lives by stealing, and that he is sure to die in a few months; and, truth to tell, the great body of the people, though one must not say intentionally, are doing all they can to make these assertions true. If it is not said that any considerable number wantonly abuse and outrage him, it must be said that they manifest a barbarous indifference to his fate, which just as surely drives him on to destruction as open cruelty would.

There are some men and a few women—and perhaps the number of these is greater than we of the North generally suppose—who really desire that the negro should now have his full rights as a human being. With the same proportion of this class of persons in a community of Northern constitution, it might be justly concluded that the whole community would soon join or acquiesce in the effort to secure for him at least a fair share of those rights. Unfortunately, however, in these Southern communities the opinion of such persons cannot have such weight as it would in ours. The spirit of caste, of which I have already spoken, is an element figuring largely against them in any contest involving principle,—an element of whose practical workings we here know very little. The walls between individuals and classes are so high and broad, that the men and women who recognize the negro's rights and privileges as a freeman are almost as far from the masses as we of the North are. Moreover, that any opinion savors of the "Yankee"—in other words, is new to the South—is a fact that even prevents its consideration by the great body of the people. Their inherent antagonism to everything from the North—an antagonism fostered and cunningly cultivated for half a century by the politicians in the interest of Slavery,—is something that no traveller can photograph, that no Northern man can understand, till he sees it with his own eyes, hears it with his own ears, and feels it by his own consciousness. That the full freedom of the negroes would be acknowledged at once is something we had no warrant for expecting. The old masters grant them nothing, except at the requirement of the nation,—as a military and political necessity; and any plan of reconstruction is wrong which proposes at once or in the immediate future to substitute free-will for this necessity.

Three-fourths of the people assume that the negro will not labor, except on compulsion; and the whole struggle between the whites on the one hand and the blacks on the other hand is a struggle for and against compulsion. The negro insists, very blindly perhaps, that he shall be free to come and go as he pleases; the white insists that he shall come and go only at the pleasure of his employer. The whites seem wholly unable to comprehend that freedom for the negro means the same thing as freedom for them. They readilly enough admit that the Government has made him free, but appear to believe that they still have the right to exercise over him the old control. It is partly their misfortune, and not wholly their fault, that they cannot understand the national intent, as expressed in the Emancipation Proclamation and the Constitutional Amendment. I did not anywhere find a man who could see that laws should be applicable to all persons alike; and hence even the best men hold that each State must have a negro code. They acknowledge the overthrow of the special servitude of man to man, but seek through these codes to establish the general servitude of man to the commonwealth. I had much talk with intelligent gentlemen in various sections, and particularly with such as I met during the conventions at Columbia and Milledgeville, upon this subject, and found such a state of feeling as warrants little hope that the present generation of negroes will see the day in which their race shall be amenable only to such laws as apply to the whites.

I think the freedmen divide themselves into four classes: one fourth recognizing, very clearly, the necessity of work, and going about it with cheerful diligence and wise forethought; one fourth comprehending that there must be labor, but needing considerable encouragement to follow it steadily; one fourth preferring idleness, but not specially averse to doing some job-work about the towns and cities; and one fourth avoiding labor as much as possible, and living by voluntary charity, persistent begging, or systematic pilfering. It is true, that thousands of the aggregate body of this people appear to have hoped, and perhaps believed, that freedom meant idleness; true too, that thousands are drifting about the country or loafing about the centres of population in a state of vagabondage. Yet of the hundreds with whom I talked, I found less than a score who seemed beyond hope of reformation. It is a cruel slander to say that the race will not work, except on compulsion. I made much inquiry, wherever I went, of great numbers of planters and other employers, and found but a very few cases in which it appeared that they had refused to labor reasonably well, when fairly treated and justly paid. Grudgingly admitted to any of the natural rights of man, despised alike by Unionists and Secessionists, wantonly outraged by many and meanly cheated by more of the old planters, receiving a hundred cuffs for one helping hand and a thousand curses for one kindly word,—they bear themselves toward their former masters very much as white men and women would under the same circumstances. True, by such deportment they unquestionably harm themselves; but consider of how little value life is from their stand-point. They grope in the darkness of this transition period, and rarely find any sure stay for the weary arm and the fainting heart. Their souls are filled with a great, but vague longing for freedom; they battle blindly with fate and circumstance for the unseen and uncomprehended, and seem to find every man's hand raised against them. What wonder that they fill the land with restlessness!

However unfavorable this exhibit of the negroes in respect to labor may appear, it is quite as good as can be made for the whites. I everywhere found a condition of affairs in this regard that astounded me. Idleness, not occupation, seemed the normal state. It is the boast of men and women alike, that they have never done an hour's work. The public mind is thoroughly debauched, and the general conscience is lifeless as the grave. I met hundreds of hale and vigorous young men who unblushingly owned to me that they had not earned a penny since the war closed. Nine tenths of the people must be taught that labor is even not debasing. It was pitiful enough to find so much idleness, but it was more pitiful to observe that it was likely to continue indefinitely. The war will not have borne proper fruit, if our peace does not speedily bring respect for labor, as well as respect for man. When we have secured one of these things, we shall have gone far toward securing the other; and when we have secured both, then indeed shall we have noble cause for glorying in our country,—true warrant for exulting that our flag floats over no slave.

Meantime, while we patiently and helpfully wait for the day in which "All men's good shall Be each man's rule, and Universal Peace Lie like a shaft of light across the land," there are at least five things for the nation to do: make haste slowly in the work of reconstruction; temper justice with mercy, but see to it that justice is not overborne; keep military control of these lately rebellious States, till they guaranty a republican form of government; scrutinize carefully the personal fitness of the men chosen therefrom as representatives in the Congress of the United States; and sustain therein some agency that shall stand between the whites and the blacks, and aid each class in coming to a proper understanding of its privileges and responsibilities.

Document 13.2 A Report from the Joint Committee on Reconstruction, June 20, 1866

In December 1865 Republicans in Congress voted to create a joint committee of fifteen (nine representatives and six senators) to create national reconstruction policy. Dominated by moderate members of the Republican party, this committee held hearings and solicited testimony from Freedman's Bureau agents, traveling correspondents, military commanders, and southern Unionists about growing hostility and violence in the South, violence aimed at undoing the results of the war. Based on the evidence presented the committee determined new laws were required to protect blacks, insure the loyalty of the South, and help the freedmen become productive citizens. The committee also looked into the recent elections in the South, where avowed disunionists and former Confederate leaders were elected to seats in Congress. At a time when blacks were denied chances to vote in the South, and the southern states had not yet renounced secession, were these elections valid?

A claim for the immediate admission of senators and representatives from the socalled Confederate States has been urged, which seems to your committee not to be founded either in reason or in law, and which cannot be passed without comment. Stated in a few words, it amounts to this: That inasmuch as the lately insurgent States had no legal right to separate themselves from the Union, they still retain their positions as States, and consequently the people thereof have a right to immediate representation in Congress without the imposition of any conditions whatever. . . . It has even been contended that until such admission all legislation affecting their interests is, if not unconstitutional, at least unjustifiable and oppressive.

It is believed by your Committee that these propositions are not only wholly untenable, but, if admitted would tend to the destruction of the government.

It must not be forgotten that the people of these States, without justification or excuse, rose in insurrection against the United States. They deliberately abolished their State governments so far as the same connected them politically with the Union. . . . They opened hostilities and levied war against the government. They continued this war for four years with the most determined and malignant spirit. . . . Whether legally and constititionally or not, they did, in fact, withdraw from the Union and made themselves subjects of another government of their own creation. And they only yielded when they were compelled by utter exhaustion to lay down their arms . . . expressing no regret, except that they had no longer the power to continue the desperate struggle.

It cannot, we think, be denied by any one, having tolerable acquaintance with public law, that the war thus waged was a civil war of the greatest magnitude. The people waging it were necessarily subject to all the rule which, by the law of nations, control a contest of that character, and to all the legitimate consequences following it. One of those consequences was that, within the limits prescribed by humanity, the conquered rebels were at the mercy of the conquerors. That a government thus outraged had a most perfect right to exact indemnity for the injuries done, and security against the recurrence of such outrages in the future, would seem too clear for dispute.

Your committee came to the consideration of the subject referred to them with the most anxious desire to ascertain what was the condition of the people of the States recently in insurrection, and what, if anything, was necessary to be done before restoring them to the full enjoyment of all their original privileges. It was undeniable that the war into which they had plunged the country had materially changed their relations to the people of the loyal States. Slavery had been abolished by constitutional amendment. A large proportion of the population had become, instead of mere chattels, free men and citizens. Through all the past struggle these had remained true and loyal, and had, in large numbers, fought on the side of the Union. It was impossible to abandon them, without securing them their rights as free men and citizens. . . . Hence it became important to inquire what could be done to secure their rights, civil and political. It was evident to your committee that adequate security could only be found in appropriate constitutional provisions. By an original provision of the Constitution, representation is based on the whole number of free persons in each State, and three-fifths of all other persons. When all become free, representation for all necessarily follows. As a consequence the inevitable effect of the rebellion would be to increase the political power of the insurrectionary States, whenever they should be allowed to resume their position as States of the Union. . . . It did not seem just or proper that all the political advantages derived from their becoming free should be confined to their former masters, who had fought against the Union, and withheld from themselves, who had always been loyal. . . . Doubts were entertained whether Congress had power, even under the amended Constitution, to prescribe the qualifications of voters in a State, or could act directly on the subject. It was doubtful . . . whether the States would consent to surrender a power they had always exercised, and to which they were attached. As the best if not the only method of surmounting the difficulty, and as eminently just and proper in itself, your committee came

Report from Joint Committee on Reconstruction, June 20, 1866.

to the conclusion that political power should be possessed in all the States exactly in proportion as the right of suffrage should be granted, without distinction of color or race. This it was thought would leave the whole question with the people of each State, holding out to all the advantage of increased political power as an inducement to allow all to participate in its exercise. Such a provision would be in its nature gentle and persuasive, and would lead, it was hoped, at no distant day, to an equal participation of all, without distinction, in all the rights and privileges of citizenship, thus affording a full and adequate protection to all classes of citizens, since all would have, through the ballot-box, the power of self-protection. . . .

With such evidence before them, it is the opinion of your committee

I. That the States lately in rebellion were, at the close of the war, disorganized communities, without civil government, and without constitutions or other forms, by virtue of which political relations could legally exist between them and the federal government.

II. That Congress cannot be expected to recognize as valid the election of representatives from disorganized communities, which, from the very nature of the case, were unable to present their claim to representation under those established and recognized rules, the observance of which has been hitherto required.

III. That Congress would not be justified in admitting such communities to a participation in the government of the country without first providing such constitutional or other guarantees as will tend to secure the civil rights of all citizens of the republic; a just equality of representation; protection against claims founded in rebellion and crime; a temporary restoration of the right of suffrage to those who had not actively participated in the efforts to destroy the Union and overthrow the government, and the exclusion from positions of public trust of, at least, a portion of those whose crimes have proved them to be enemies to the Union, and unworthy of public confidence.

Document 13.3 The Louisiana Black Code, 1865

One action that particularly disturbed northerners was the passage of "Black Codes" by the southern legislatures during 1865 and 1866. These codes were designed to regulate black behavior and restrict their rights. Codes segregated public facilities, prohibited inter-racial marriage, and excluded blacks from juries; all actions similar to some northern laws. But the codes also essentially reinvented slavery. Blacks could be declared vagrants and hired out to planters to pay off the court imposed fines. White courts could decide if under-aged blacks had adequate parental support; then apprentice the young freedmen to their former masters for an undetermined length of time. Consider the sections of the Louisiana Black Code printed below. This was one of the milder codes among southern states. What basic rights are blacks denied? Is this an attempt to overturn the results of the Civil War?

Sec. 1. *Be it ordained by the police jury of the parish of St. Landry,* That no negro shall be allowed to pass within the limits of said parish without special permit in writing from his employer. Whoever shall violate this provision shall pay a fine of two dollars and fifty cents, or in default thereof shall be forced to work four days on the public road, or suffer corporeal punishment as provided hereinafter. . . .

Sec. 3. . . . No negro shall be permitted to rent or keep a house within said parish. Any negro violating this provision shall be immediately ejected and compelled to find an employer; and any person who shall rent, or give the use of any house to any negro, in violation of this section, shall pay a fine of five dollars for each offence.

Sec. 4. . . . Every negro is required to be in the regular service of some white person, or former owner, who shall be held responsible for the conduct of said negro. But said employer or former owner may permit said negro to hire his own time by special permission in writing, which permission shall not extend over seven days at any one time. . . .

Louisiana Black Code, 1865.

Sec. 5. . . . No public meeting or congregations of negroes shall be allowed within said parish after sunset; but such public meetings and congregations may be held between the hours of sunrise and sunset, by the special permission in writing of the captain of patrol, within whose beat such meetings shall take place. . . .

Sec. 6. . . . No negro shall be permitted to preach, exhort, or otherwise declaim to congregations of colored people, without a special permission in writing from the president of the police jury. . . .

Sec. 7. . . . No negro who is not in the military service shall be allowed to carry fire-arms, or any kind of weapons, within the parish, without the special written permission of his employers, approved and endorsed by the nearest and most convenient chief of patrol. . . .

Sec. 8. . . . No negro shall sell, barter, or exchange any articles of merchandise or traffic within said parish without the special written permission of his employer, specifying the article of sale, barter or traffic. . . .

Sec. 9. . . . Any negro found drunk within the said parish shall pay a fine of five dollars, or in default thereof work five days on the public road, or suffer corporeal punishment as hereinafter provided.

Sec. 11. . . . It shall be the duty of every citizen to act as a police officer for the detection of offences and the apprehension of offenders, who shall be immediately handed over to the proper captain or chief of patrol.

Document 13.4 Petition from a Convention of Loyal African American Citizens, 1865

The former slaves realized that they had their freedom, but without federal protection they would not have much else. Vengeful southern whites could deny them (or take violently from them) food, shelter and almost every basic right. Gathering in conventions across the South, African Americans discussed the best way to protect their new freedoms, and many sent petitions into Congress. The following is a petition from a convention held in Alexandria, Virginia, August 2–5, 1865. What do they warn the national government about? Why do they need protection and aid? What actions do they recommend the national government take?

We, the undersigned members of a Convention of colored citizens of the State of Virginia, would respectfully represent that, although we have been held as slaves, and denied all recognition as a constituent of your nationality for almost the entire period of the duration of your Government, and that by *your permission* we have been denied either home or country, and deprived of the dearest rights of human nature: yet when you and our immediate oppressors met in deadly conflict upon the field of battle the one to destroy and the other to save your Government and nationality, *we*, with scarce an exception, in our inmost souls espoused your cause, and watched, and prayed, and waited, and labored for your success.

When the contest waxed long, and the result hung doubtfully, you appealed to us for help, and how well we answered is written in the rosters of the two hundred thousand colored troops now enrolled in your service; and as to our undying devotion to your cause, let the uniform acclamation of escaped prisoners, *"whenever we saw a black face we felt sure of a friend,"* answer.

Well, the war is over, the rebellion is "put down," and we are *declared* free! Four fifths of our enemies are paroled or amnestied, and the other fifth are being pardoned, and the President has, in his efforts at the reconstruction of the civil government of the States, late in rebellion, left us entirely at the mercy of these subjugated but unconverted rebels, in *everything* save the privilege of bringing us, our wives and little ones, to the auction block. . . . We *know* these men—know them *well*—and we assure you that, with the majority of them, loyalty is only **"lip deep,"** and that their professions of loyalty are used as a cover to the cherished design of getting restored to their former relations with the Federal Government, and then, by all sorts of "unfriendly legislation," to render the freedom you have given

---

Petition from a Convention of Loyal African American Citizens, 1865

us more intolerable than the slavery they intended for us.

We warn you in time that our only safety is in keeping them under Governors of the *military persuasion* until you have so amended the Federal Constitution that it will prohibit the States from making any distinction between citizens on account of race or color. In one word, the only salvation for us besides the power of the Government, is in the *possession of the ballot.* Give us this, and we will protect ourselves. . . . But, it is said we are ignorant. Admit it. Yet who denies we *know* a traitor from a loyal man, a gentleman from a rowdy, a friend from an enemy? The twelve thousand colored votes of the State of New York sent Governor Seymour home and Reuben E. Fenton to Albany. Did not they know who to vote for? . . . All we ask is an *equal chance* with the white traitors varnished and japanned with the oath of amnesty. Can you deny us this and still keep faith with us?

We are *"sheep in the midst of wolves,"* and nothing but the military arm of the Government prevents us and all the truly loyal white men from being driven from the land of our birth. Do not then, we beseech you, give to one of these "wayward sisters" the rights they abandoned and forfeited when they rebelled until you have secured our rights by the aforementioned amendment to the Constitution.

Trusting that you will not be deaf to the appeal herein made, nor unmindful of the warnings which the malignity of the rebels are constantly giving you, and that you will rise to the height of being just for the sake of justice, we remain yours for our flag, our country and humanity.

Document 13.5 The *Atlanta News* Calls for Whites to Use Brute Force

Southern whites resisted Congressional Reconstruction with violence. Violence was epidemic in the South from the late 1860s onward, but by the early 1870s whites made open appeals to use force. Newspapers, politicians and ministers all claimed this was the only way to "redeem" the South from northern and African American control. Besides brute force other methods of intimidation were used to discourage black voters and ostracize whites cooperating with Republican rule. Rifle clubs were formed to attack Reconstruction supporters, and the Ku Klux Klan and White Leagues stepped up open attacks on blacks. The following is the editorial appeal of a major newspaper, the *Atlanta News,* for increased violence in the cause of redeeming the South. On what basis does the editor call for such action?

Let there be White Leagues formed in every town, village and hamlet of the South, and let us organize for the great struggle which seems inevitable. If the October elections which are to be held at the North are favorable to the radicals, the time will have arrived for us to prepare for the very worst. The radicalism of the republican party must be met by the radicalism of white men. We have no war to make against the United States Government, but against the republican party our hate must be unquenchable, our war interminable and merciless. Fast fleeting away is the day of wordy protests and idle appeals to the magnanimity of the republican party. By brute force they are endeavoring to force us into acquiescence to their hideous programme. We have submitted long enough to indignities, and it is time to meet brute-force with brute-force. Every Southern State should swarm with White Leagues, and we should stand ready to act the moment Grant signs the civil-rights bill. It will not do to wait till radicalism has fettered us to the car of social equality before we make an effort to resist it. The signing of the bill will be a declaration of war against the southern whites. It is our duty to ourselves, it is our duty to our children, it is our duty to the white race whose prowess subdued the wilderness of this continent, whose civilization filled it with cities and towns and villages, whose mind gave it power and grandeur, and whose labor imparted to it prosperity, and whose love made peace and happiness dwell within its homes, to take the gage of battle the moment it is thrown down. If the white democrats of

From *Atlanta News,* 1870

the North are men, they will not stand idly by and see us borne down by northern radicals and half-barbarous negroes. But no matter what they may do, it is time for us to organize. We have been temporizing long enough. Let northern radicals understand that military supervision of southern elections and the civil-rights bill mean war, that war means bloodshed, and that we are terribly in earnest, and even they, fanatical as they are, may retrace their steps before it is too late.

Document 13.6 Personal Accounts of Ku Klux Klan Attacks

The oldest and best known of all the southern white supremacist organizations is the Ku Klux Klan (KKK). Originally organized to insure a steady labor supply on postwar plantations, the KKK moved on to other goals. Its night-riding, white hooded members enforced a code of behavior, visiting freed African Americans who acted or spoke "improperly" to whites. By the 1870s their primary goal was terrorizing black voters to reduce Republican votes in the South and allow Southern Democrats to regain control of the states. This terrorist organization murdered hundreds of voters and elected state officials to intimidate others not to vote. Following are three accounts of Klan activity. Note that the KKK attacked field hands, women and even members of state legislatures. What do the following accounts have in common? What response was needed by the federal government to combat these terrorist attacks?

Elias Hill is a remarkable character. He is crippled in both legs and arms, which are shriveled by rheumatism; he cannot walk; cannot help himself, has to be fed and cared for personally by others; was in early life a slave, whose freedom was purchased, his father buying his mother and getting Elias along with her, as a burden of which his master was glad to be rid. Stricken at seven years old with disease, he never was afterward able to walk, and he presents the appearance of a dwarf with the limbs of a child, the body of a man, and a finely developed intellectual head. He learned his letters and to read by calling the school children into the cabin as they passed, and also learned to write. He became a Baptist preacher, and after the war engaged in teaching colored children, and conducted the business correspondence of many of his colored neighbors. He is a man of blameless character, of unusual intelligence, speaks good English, and we put the story of his wrongs in his own language:

"On the night of the 5th of last May, after I had heard a great deal of what they had done in that neighborhood, they [the Ku Klux Klan] came. It was between 12 and 1 o'clock at night when I was awakened and heard the dogs barking, and something walking, very much like horses. . . . At last they came to my brother's door, which is in the same yard, and broke open the door and attacked his wife, and I heard her screaming and mourning. . . . At last I heard them have her in the yard. She was crying and the Ku-Klux were whipping her to make her tell where I lived. . . . Some one then hit my door. It flew open. One ran in the house, and stopping about the middle of the house, which is a small cabin, he turned around, as it seemed to me as I lay there awake, and said, 'Who's here?' Then I knew they would take me, and I answered, 'I am here.' He shouted for joy, as it seemed, 'Here he is! Here he is! We have found him!' and he threw the bedclothes off of me and caught me by one arm, while another man took me by the other and they carried me into the yard between the houses. . . . The first thing they asked me was, 'Who did the burning? Who burned our houses?'—gin-houses, dwelling-houses and such. Some had been burned in the neighborhood. I told them it was not me; I could not burn houses; it was unreasonable to ask me. Then they hit me with their fists, and said I did it, I ordered it. They went on asking me didn't I tell the black men to ravish all the white women. No, I answered them. They struck me again with their fists on my breast, and then they went on. . . .

"They pointed pistols at me all around my head once or twice, as if they were going to shoot me, telling me they were going to kill me; wasn't I ready to die, and willing to die? Didn't I preach? That they came to kill me—all the time pointing pistols at me. . . . One said 'G-d d—n it, hush!' He had a horsewhip, and he told me to pull up my shirt, and he hit me. He told me at every lick, 'Hold up your shirt.' I

Personal Accounts of Ku Klux Klan Attacks, 1870.

made a moan every time he cut with the horsewhip. I reckon he struck me eight cuts right on the hip bone; it was almost the only place he could hit my body, my legs are so short—all my limbs drawn up and withered away with pain. . . . They all had disguises on. I then thought they would not kill me. One of them then took a strap, and buckled it around my neck and said, 'Let's take him to the river and drown him . . .'

"They said 'Look here! Will you put a card in the paper next week like June Moore and Sol Hill?' They had been prevailed on to put a card in the paper to renounce all republicanism and never vote. I said, 'If I had the money to pay the expense, I could.' They said I could borrow, and gave me another lick. They asked me, 'Will you quit preaching?' I told them I did not know. I said that to save my life. They said I must stop the republican paper that was coming to Clay Hill. It has been only a few weeks since it stopped. The republican paper was then coming to me from Charleston. It came to my name. They said I must stop it, quit preaching, and put a card in the newspaper renouncing republicanism, and they would not kill me; but if I did not they would come back the next week and kill me."

Harriet Hernandez

Q: Did the Ku-Klux ever come to your house at any time?

A: Yes, sir; twice.

Q: Go on to the second time. . . .

A: They came in; I was lying in bed. Says he, "Come out here, sir; Come out here, sir!" They took me out of bed; they would not let me get out, but they took me up in their arms and toted me out—me and my daughter Lucy. He struck me on the forehead with a pistol, and here is the scar above my eye now. Says he, "Damn you, fall!" I fell. Says he, "Damn you, get up!" I got up. Says he, "Damn you, get over this fence!" And he kicked me over when I went to get over; and then he went to a brush pile, and they laid us right down there, both together. They laid us down twenty yards apart, I reckon. They had dragged and beat us along. They struck me right on the top of my head, and I thought they had killed me; and I said, "Lord o' mercy, don't, don't kill my child!" He gave me a lick on the head, and it liked to have killed me; I saw stars. He threw my arm over my head so I could not do anything with it for three weeks, and there are great knots on my wrist now.

Q: What did they say this was for?

A: They said, "You can tell your husband that when we see him we are going to kill him."

Q: Did they say why they wanted to kill him?

A: They said, "He voted the radical ticket, didn't he?" I said, "Yes, that very way."

Q: When did your husband get back after this whipping? He was not at home, was he?

A: He was lying out; he couldn't stay at home, bless your soul! . . .

Q: Has he been afraid for any length of time?

A: He has been afraid ever since last October. He has been lying out. He has not laid in the house ten nights since October.

Q: Is that the situation of the colored people down there to any extent?

A: That is the way they all have to do—men and women both.

Q: What are they afraid of?

A: Of being killed or whipped to death.

Q: What has made them afraid?

A: Because men that voted radical tickets they took the spite out on the women when they could get at them.

Q: How many colored people have been whipped in that neighborhood?

A: It is all of them, mighty near.

Testimony of Abram Colby (1872)

On the 29th of October 1869, they broke my door open, took me out of bed, took me to the woods and whipped me three hours or more and left me for dead. They said to me, "Do you think you will ever vote another damned radical ticket?" I said, "I will not tell you a lie." I supposed they would kill me anyhow. I said, "If there was an election tomorrow, I would vote the radical ticket." They set in and whipped me a thousand licks more, with sticks and straps that had buckles on the ends of them.

Q: What is the character of those men who were engaged in whipping you?

A: Some are first-class men in our town. One is a lawyer, one a doctor, and some are farmers. They had their pistols and they took me in my night-clothes and carried me from home. They hit me five thousand blows. I told President Grant the same that I tell you now. They told me to take off my shirt. I said, "I never do that for any man." My drawers fell down about my feet and they took hold of them and tripped me up. Then they pulled my shirt up over my head. They said I had voted for Grant and had carried the Negroes against them. About two days before they whipped me they offered me $5,000 to go with them and said they would pay me $2500 in cash if I would let another man go to the legislature in my place. I told them that I would not do it if they would give me all the county was worth.

The worst thing about the whole matter was this. My mother, wife and daughter were in the room when they came. My little daughter begged them not to carry me away They drew up a gun and actually frightened her to death. She never got over it until she died. That was the part that grieves me the most.

Q: How long before you recovered from the effects of this treatment?

A: I have never got over it yet. They broke something inside of me. I cannot do any work now, though I always made my living before in the barber-shop, hauling wood, &c.

Q: You spoke about being elected to the next legislature?

A: Yes, sir, but they run me off during the election. They swore they would kill me if I staid. The Saturday night before the election I went to church. When I got home they just peppered the house with shot and bullets.

Q: Did you make a general canvas there last fall?

A: No, sir. I was not allowed to. No man can make a free speech in my county. I do not believe it can be done anywhere in Georgia.

Q: You say no man can do it?

A: I mean no Republican, either white or colored.

Document 13.7 General Alfred Terry Testifies about Race Relations in Georgia

General Alfred Terry filed this official report to the Secretary of War in 1869. He discusses the deteriorating state of race relations, the increased intolerance and attacks by groups such as the KKK, and the overall attitude of the southern people. What does he propose as a government response? What justifications does Terry give for the use of force by the national government?

I have delayed making the report thus called for until the present time, in order that I might become acquainted with the condition of affairs in Georgia before expressing any opinion in regard to them. Now I have reluctantly come to the conclusion that the situation here demands the interposition of the national government, in order that life and property may be protected, freedom of speech and political action secured, and the rights and liberties of the freedmen maintained. This opinion is based upon complaints made to me, the reports of officers detailed to investigate alleged outrages, and upon the statements of many persons of respectability and high position from different parts of the State, in whose representations I must repose confidence; some of whom have given me information only under the pledge of secrecy, the state of affairs in their section being such that they feared the extreme of personal violence should it become known that they had been in communication with me.

In many parts of the State there is practically no government. The worst of crimes are committed, and no attempt is made to punish those who commit them. Murders have been and are frequent; the abuse in various ways of the blacks is too common to excite notice. There can be no doubt of the existence of numerous insurrectionary organizations known as "Ku-Klux Klans," who, shielded by their disguise, by the secrecy of their movements, and by the terror which they inspire, perpetrate crime with impunity. There is great reason to believe that in some cases local magistrates are in sympathy with the members of these organizations. In many places they are overawed by them and dare not attempt to punish them. To punish such offenders by civil proceedings would be a difficult task, even were magistrates in all cases disposed and had they the courage to do their duty, for the same influences which govern them equally affect juries and witnesses. A conversation which I have had with a wealthy planter, a gentleman of intelligence and education, and a political opponent of the present national administration, will illustrate this difficulty. While deploring the lamentable condition of affairs in the county in which he lives, he frankly admitted to me that, were the most worthless vagabond in the county to be charged with a crime against the person of a republican or a negro, neither he nor any other person of

Official Report to the Secretary of War, 1869.

property within the county would dare to refuse to give bail for the offender, nor would they dare to testify against him, whatever might be their knowledge of his guilt.

That very many of the crimes which have been committed have no political bearing I believe; that some of them were prompted by political animosity, and that most of the numerous outrages upon freedmen result from hostility to the race induced by their enfranchisement, I think cannot be controverted.

The same difficulties which beset the prosecution of criminals are encountered by negroes who seek redress for civil injuries in the local courts. Magistrates dare not do their duty toward them, and instances are not wanting where it has even been beyond the power of a magistrate to protect a negro plaintiff from violence in his own presence while engaged in the trial of his case. I desire it to be understood that in speaking of magistrates I in no degree refer to the judges of the superior courts; they are gentlemen of high character. I have every confidence that they will do their duty fearlessly and impartially, but it is to be observed that even they cannot control grand and petty juries; they cannot compel the former to indict, nor the latter to render unprejudiced verdicts.

The executive of the State would gladly interpose to give to all citizens the protection which is their right, but under the constitution and laws he has power neither to act directly in bringing offenders to justice nor to compel subordinate officers to do their duty. I do not suppose that the great majority of the people of the State, of either race, approve of the commission of these crimes. I believe that not only would they gladly see good order restored, peace and quiet maintained, and the law vindicated; but would lend their aid to secure these ends were they not controlled by their fears. Governed, however, by their apprehensions, and having no confidence that the civil authorities will afford them protection, in many counties they suffer these evils to exist without an effort to abate them, and meekly submit to the rule of the disorderly and criminal minority.

While I have been in command of the department I have endeavored to take no action which could not be justified by the letter of the law, even if Georgia should be held to be restored to its original relations to the general government. I have confined myself to giving support to the civil authorities and moving detachments of troops into some of the disturbed counties, where their presence would exert a good influence, and where they would be ready to act if properly called upon. I think that some good has in this way been accomplished, but the great evil has by no means been reached. As a department commander I can do no more; for whatever may be the status of Georgia, and whatever may be the powers which an officer assigned to command the third district created by the reconstruction acts would possess, it is only an officer so assigned who could exercise them; they are not vested in me by my assignment to the command of this department. Where, therefore, the civil authorities are in sympathy with or are overawed by those who commit crime, it is manifest that I am powerless. In this connection I respectfully call the special attention of the General commanding the army to the reports in regard to the attempt made in Warren County to secure the arrest and punishment of persons charged with crime, which are this day forwarded. It appears to me that the national honor is pledged to the protection of the loyalists and the freedmen of the South. I am well aware that the protection of persons and property is not ordinarily one of the functions of the national government, but when it is remembered that hostility to the supporters of the government is but a manifestation of hostility to the government itself, and that the prevailing prejudice against the blacks results from their emancipation—the act of the government—it would seem that such protection cannot be denied them if it be within the power of the government to give it. I know of no way in which such protection can be given in Georgia except by the exercise of the powers conferred on military commanders by the reconstruction acts.

Document 13.8 Black Life during Reconstruction

Not all freedmen were attacked, and life consisted of more than dodging white bullets. During the 1930s the New Deal's Federal Writers' Project sent interviewers out to collect firsthand biographies of the survivors of slavery and Reconstruction. Between 1936 and 1938 interviewers in seventeen states recorded the memories of thousands of former slaves. These materials left a record of daily life that went beyond contemporary newspaper accounts. In the two accounts that follow, what do the participants remember most about life? Is the Klan ever too far from their minds?

Mingo White

Interviewed at Burleson, Alabama
Interviewed by Levi D. Shelby, Jr.
Age when interviewed: 85–90

De day dat we got news dat we was free, Mr. White called us niggers to the house. He said: "You are all free, just as free as I am. Now go and get yourself somewhere to stick your heads."

Just as soon as he say dat, my mammy hollered out: "Dat's 'nough for a yearlin'." She struck out across de field to Mr Lee Osborn's to get a place for me and her to stay. He paid us seventy-five cents a day, fifty cents to her and two bits for me. He gave us our dinner along with de wages. After de crop was gathered for that year, me and my mammy cut and hauled wood for Mr. Osborn. Us left Mr. Osborn dat fall and went to Mr. John Rawlins. Us made a share-crop with him. Us'd pick two rows of cotton and he'd pick two rows. Us'd pull two rows of corn and he'd pull two rows of corn. He furnished us with rations and a place to stay. Us'd sell our cotton and open corn and pay Mr. John Rawlins for feedin' us. Den we moved with Mr. Hugh Nelson and made a sharecrop with him. We kept movin' and makin' sharecrops till us saved up 'nough money to rent us a place and make a crop for ourselves.

Us did right well at dis until de Ku Klux got so bad, us had to move back with Mr. Nelson for protection. De mens that took us in was Union men. Dey lived here in the South but dey taken us part in de slave business. De Ku Klux threat to whip Mr. Nelson, 'cause he took up for de niggers. Heap of nights we would hear of de Ku Klux comin' and leave home. Sometimes us was scared not to go and scared to go away from home.

One day I borrowed a gun from Ed Davis to go squirrel huntin'. When I taken de gun back I didn't unload it like I always been doin'. Dat night de Ku Klux called on Ed to whip him. When dey told him to open de door, he heard one of 'em say, "Shoot him time he gets de door open." "Well," he says to 'em, "Wait till I can light de lamp." Den he got de gun what I had left loaded, got down on his knee and stuck it through a log and pulld de trigger. He hit Newt Dobbs in de stomach and kilt him.

He couldn't stay round Burleson any more, so he come to Mr. Nelson and got 'nough money to get to Pine Bluff, Arkansas. The Ku Klux got bad sure 'nough den and went to killin' niggers and white folks, too.

Charles Davenport

Interviewed at Natchez, Mississippi
Interviewed by Edith Wyatt Moore
Age at interview: About 100

Like all de fool niggers o' dat time I was right smart bit by de freedom bug for awhile. It sounded powerful nice to be told: "You don't have to chop cotton no more. You can throw dat hoe down and go fishin' whensoever de notion strikes you. And you can roam 'round at night and court gals just as late as you please. Ain't no marster gwine to, say to you, 'Charlie, you's got to be back when de clock strikes nine.'"

I was fool 'nough to believe all dat kind o' stuff. But to tell de honest truth, most o' us didn't know ourselfs no better off. Freedom meant us could leave where us'd been born and bred, but it meant, too, dat us had to scratch for us ownselfs. Dem what left de old plantation seemed so all fired glad to get back dat I made up my mind to stay put. I stayed right with my white folks as long as I could.

My white folks talked plain to me. Dey say real sadlike, "Charlie, you's been a dependence, but now you can go if you is so desirous. But if you wants to stay with us you can sharecrop. Dey's a house for you and wood to keep you warm and a mule to work. We ain't got much cash, but dey's de land and you can count on havin' plenty o' victuals. Do just as you please."

When I looked at my marster and knowed he needed me, I pleased to stay. My marster never forced me to do nary thing about it.

Lord! Lord! I knows about de Kloo Kluxes. I knows a-plenty. Dey was sure 'nough devils a-walkin' de earth a-seekin' what dey could devour. Dey larruped de hide off de uppity niggers an' drove de white trash back where dey belonged.

Us niggers didn't have no secret meetin's. All us had was church meetin's in arbors out in de woods. De preachers would exhort us dat us was de chillen o' Israel in de wilderness an' de Lord done sent us to take dis land o' milk and honey. But how us gwine-a take land what's already been took?

I sure ain't never heard about no plantations bein' divided up, neither. I heard a lot o' yaller niggers spoutin' off how dey was gwine-a take over de white folks' land for back wages. Dem bucks just took all dey wages out in talk. 'Cause I ain't never seen no land divided up yet.

From *New Deal's Federal Writers' Project.*

In dem days nobody but niggers and "shawl-strap" folks voted. Quality folks didn't have nothin' to do with such truck. If dey hada wanted to de Yankees wouldn'ta let 'em. My old marster didn't vote and if anybody knowed what was what he did. Sense didn't count in dem days. It was powerful ticklish times and I let votin' alone. . . . [O]ne night a bunch o' uppity niggers went to a entertainment in Memorial Hall. Dey dressed deyselfs fit to kill and walked down de aisle and took seats in de very front. But just about time dey got good set down, de curtain dropped and de white folks rose up without a-sayin' a word. Dey marched out de buildin' with dey chins up and left dem niggers a-sittin' in a empty hall.

Dat's de way it happen every time a nigger tried to get too uppity. Dat night after de breakin' up o' dat entertainment, de Kloo Kluxes rode through de land. I heard dey grabbed every nigger what walked down dat aisle, but I ain't heard yet what dey done with 'em.

Document 13.9 Black Land Ownership and Sharecropping in the Postwar South

For most former slaves freedom meant owning and farming their own land, but this rarely happened in the postwar south. Approximately 80% of former slaves ended up as sharecroppers on land owned by whites, sometimes by their former masters. On the plus side, this provided them more autonomy than slavery did because they worked the land without a slave driver, and they could keep their wives out of the fields if they chose. It also bound them to the land and guaranteed perpetual poverty. The property owner provided the land, seed, livestock and farm implements, as well as credit to live on before harvest. The cropper provided the labor and received half of the crop in return, but then had to pay off his debts—if he ever could. The following are accounts of freed African Americans discussing their attempts to make a living through honest labor. What were they able to accomplish? Did they reach any sort of financial independence through their hard work? What obstacles stood in their way?

Henry Blake

After freedom, we worked on shares a while. Then, we rented. When we worked on shares, we couldn't make nothing—just over-alls, and something to eat. Half went to the white man, and you would destroy your half, if you weren't careful. A man that didn't know how to count would always lose. He might lose anyhow. The white folks didn't give no itemized statements. No, you just had to owe so much. No matter how good account you kept, you had to go by their account, and—now, brother, I'm telling you the truth about this—it's been that way for a long time. You had to take the white man's words and notes on everything. Anything you wanted you could get, if you were a good hand. If you didn't make no money, that's all right; they would advance you more. But you better not try to leave and get caught. They'd keep you in debt. They were sharp. Christmas come, you could take up twenty dollars in somethin'-to-eat and much as you wanted in whiskey. You could buy a gallon of whiskey—anything that kept you a slave. Because he was always right and you were always wrong, if there was a difference. If there was an argument, he would get mad and there would be a shooting take place.

Emanuel Fortune

They will not sell our people any land. They have no disposition to do so. They will sell a lot now and then in a town, but nothing of any importance.

Q: What could you get a pretty good farm for—how much an acre?

A: Generally from $10 to $15 an acre. Very poor people cannot afford that

Q: You can get it if you have the money?

A: They will not sell it in small quantities. I would have bought forty acres if the man would have sold me less than a whole tract. They hold it in

---

From *New Deal's Federal Writers' Project*.

that way so that colored people cannot buy it. The lands we cultivate generally are swamp or lowlands.

Q: Is there not plenty of other land to buy?

A: Not that is worth anything. I do not know of any Government land that will raise cotton.

Henry M. Turner

Q: You say that colored men employed in the country have not been able to get anything for their labor. Why is that?

A: During the year there is very little money paid to them and if they want to obtain provisions or clothing they are given an order on some store. At the end of the year these little bills are collected and however small a quantity of things have been taken, almost always the colored man is brought into debt. That is alleged as a reason why they should be bound to stay with their employers and work out what they say they owe them.

Q: A sort of practical peonage?

A: Yes, sir. Whenever there is fear that the laborer will go to work with someone else the following year, he is apt to come out $25 to $30 in debt and his employer calls upon him to work it out. There was a bill introduced the other day to make it a penal offense for a laborer to break his contract. For instance, a white man writes out a contract. He reads the contract to the black man and, of course, reads just what he pleases. When the black man takes it to somebody else and gets him to read it, it reads quite differently. Among other things there is a provision in the contract that he must not go to any political gathering or meeting. If he does, he will lose $5 for every day that he is absent, and yet he is to receive only $50 or $75 a year. Every day that he is sick, a dollar or a dollar and a half is to be deducted. The man may want to quit and work for some person else who will pay him better wages.

Q: The effect of the legislation would be to render the laborer practically a slave during the period of his contract?

A: Or else he would be liable to punishment by imprisonment. There is no doubt that they will pass some kind of law to that effect.

Q: With a view to harmonize the relations of labor and capital?

A: Yes, sir, that is the phrase.

Document 13.10 A Texas Shares Contract

Share cropping contracts usually spelled out clearly what the obligations of both parties were. Greater detail was given to the cropper's duties, including number of hours to work each day, extra work required beyond normal, and how debts are to be repaid. Some freedmen worked for wages instead of a share of the crops. The following shares contract provides a typical division of obligations and rewards. What is expected from each side?

Said _______ of the first part furthermore agrees to furnish the said Freedmen of the second part with good and sufficient quarters, _______ wholesome food, fuel, and such medical treatment as can be rendered by the person superintending the place. Said *J C Mitchell* of the 1st part in consideration of the faithful discharge of the duties assumed by the parties of the second part, does hereby agree to furnish *the freedmen* the necessary tools and implements for the cultivation of the land, and allow said Freedmen *one third* interest in the crops raised on said *plantation* by their labor. It is also mutually agreed that ten hours shall constitute a day's work, and if any labor in excess of ten hours per day is rendered it shall be paid for as extra labor. Said parties of the second part do furthermore agree to do all necessary work on Sundays or at night when it is for the protection of plantation or crops against destruction by storms, floods, fire or frost, provided always that such service shall be paid for as extra labor; extra labor to be paid for at the rate of one day's labor and one-half rations extra for each six hours work. Provided that our employer failing to comply with any part of this agreement, this contract shall be annulled; also provided, that should any of the parties of the second part leave said *plantation*

From *New Deal's Federal Writers' Project.*

without proper authority, or engage elsewhere, or neglect or refuse to work as herein agreed, they or any part of them so offending shall be liable to be discharged and forfeit all wages due up to that time.

Also Provided, that this Contract shall constitute the first lien upon all crops raised by the labor of said parties of the Second part.

Said J C Mitchell shall have power to make such rules and regulations necessary to the management of the plantation as are not inconsistent with the term of this contract; all lost time to [be] deducted from the one third interest in crop to the freedmen.

Document 13.11 Lynchings in the South

After Reconstruction southern whites steadily eroded the rights blacks had acquired after the war. Jim Crow laws regulated association between whites and blacks, enforced segregation, and restricted black job opportunities. A strict code of social etiquette was also in place, and blacks were expected to behave deferentially around whites at all time. This included removing hats, addressing whites as Mister or Ma'am, and bowing, behavior reminiscent of slavery's heyday. To enforce these laws and rules two types of justice systems were in place in the South: formal court systems and lynch mobs. Between 1889 and 1918, 2,522 African Americans were lynched, 50 of them women. They were hacked to death, burned alive or hanged. Some form of torture usually preceded death. While whites claimed lynching occurred for sexual offenses, most took place because blacks attempted to vote, argued with white men or were economically successful. Following are two examinations of lynching. The first is a report from the *Crisis* of the lynching of Samuel Petty in Leland, Mississippi, in 1914. Second is an article written by Mary Church Terrell of Washington D.C. criticizing the practice. What do the two accounts have in common? Why did lynchings take place according to white Americans? What are the real causes according to these accounts? Is this law and order, or racism run amuck?

The news spread like wildfire and in twenty minutes the entire white population was armed and headed for the cabin which was situated about a half mile from the depot, which is in the center of the town. I looked in every direction and could see men and mere boys, some not over 12 years old, carrying rifles, shotguns, pistols and, in fact, every imaginable thing that would shoot. They were acting as though there was an entire army of Negroes to be taken. The man who had killed the officer submitted to arrest by the mob, which by this time numbered about 400. Placing a rope around his neck he was led to the center of the town and in the presence of women and children they proceeded to hold a conference as to the kind of death that should be meted out to him. Some yelled to hang him; some to burn him alive. It was decided in a few minutes. Willing hands brought a large dry goods box, place it in the center of the street, in it was straw on which was poured a tub of oil; then the man was lifted with a rope around his neck and placed in this box head down, and then another tub of oil was poured over him. A man from the crowd deliberately lit a match and set fire to the living man. While in this position the flames shot up at great height. The crowd began to yell as the flames shot upward. In an instant the poor creature managed to lift himself out of the box, a mass of flames. He was fighting the flames with his hands in an effort to shield his face and eyes, and in this condition attempted to run. The crowd allowed him to run to the length of the rope, which was held by willing hands, until he reached a distance of about twenty feet; then a yell went up from the crowd to shoot. In an instant there were several hundred shots and the creature fell in his tracks. The crowd deliberately walked up to the prostrate form and shot the remainder of their guns into his lifeless body. With the flames still leaping into the air, he was pulled back into the fire that was now roaring with boxes and oil brought out of the different stores by men and boys. Every time they would throw on more oil and boxes the crowd would yell as though they were at a bull fight. Standing about fifty or seventy-five feet from the scene I could actually

From Crisis, 1914.

smell the flesh of the poor man as it was being burned. Not a voice was raised in the defense of the man. No one attempted to hide their identity. I looked into the faces of men whom I knew to be officers of the town lending a willing hand in the burning of this man. No wonder the coroner who held the inquest returned a verdict that the Negro came to his death "at the hands of an enraged mob unknown to the jury," because to get a jury in that town they had to get some who participated in the burning. I can never feel toward the white man as I have felt after seeing what I have attempted to describe. After burning the body into ashes the burned bones and ashes were buried in the edge of the street in front of a colored barber shop. May God forbid that any other living man will ever see a sight as I witnessed; this is the third Negro who has been killed in this vicinity in the last three weeks. The man burned was named Sam Pettie [sic], known by everybody to be quiet and inoffensive. I write this hoping you may get enough out of what I have tried to describe to tell your great number of readers what we are up against. To mention my name in connection with this would be equivalent to committing suicide.

Mary Church Terrell

Hanging, shooting and burning black men, women and children in the United States have become so common that such occurrences create but little sensation and evoke but slight comment now. . . . In the discussion of this subject, four mistakes are commonly made.

In the first place, it is a great mistake to suppose that rape is the real cause of lynching in the South.

Beginning with the Ku Klux Klan, the negro has been constantly subjected to some form of organized violence ever since he became free. It is easy to prove that rape is simply the pretext and not the cause of lynching. Statistics show that, out of every 100 negroes who are lynched, from 75–85 are not even accused of this crime, and many who are accused of it are innocent. . . .

In the second place, it is a mistake to suppose that the negro's desire for social equality sustains any relation whatsoever to the crime of rape. . . . It is safe to assert that, among the negroes who have been guilty of ravishing white women, not one had been taught that he was the equal of white people or had ever heard of social equality. . . . Negroes who have been educated in Northern institutions of learning with white men and women, and who for that reason might have learned the meaning of social equality and have acquired a taste for the same, neither assault white women nor commit other crimes, as a rule. . . . Strange as it may appear, illiterate negroes, who are the only ones contributing largely to the criminal class, are coddled and caressed by the South. To the educated, cultivated members of the race, they are held up as a bright and shining examples of what a really good negro should be. The dictionary is searched in vain by Southern gentlemen and gentlewomen for words sufficiently ornate and strong to express their admiration for a dear old "mammy" or a faithful old "uncle," who can neither read nor write, and who assure their white friends they would not if they could. On the other hand, no language is sufficiently caustic, bitter and severe, to express the disgust, hatred and scorn which Southern gentlemen feel for what is called the "New Issue," which, being interpreted, means negroes who aspire to knowledge and culture, and who have acquired a taste for the highest and best things in life. At the door of this "New Issue," the sins and shortcomings of the whole race are laid. This "New Issue" is beyond hope of redemption, we are told, because somebody, nobody knows who, has taught it to believe in social equality, something, nobody knows what. The alledged fear of social equality has always been used by the South to explain its unchristian treatment of the negro and to excuse its many crimes. . . . In the North, which is the only section that accords the negro the scrap of social equality enjoyed by him in the United States, he is rarely accused of rape. The only form of social equality ever attempted between the two races, and practised to any considerable extent, is that which was originated by the white masters of slave women, and which has been perpetuated by them and their descendants even unto the present day. . . . There is no more connection between social equality and lynching today than there was between social equality and slavery before the war, or than there is between social equality and the convict-lease system, or any other form of oppression to which the negro has uniformly been subjected in the South.

The third error on the subject of lynching consists of the widely circulated statement that the moral sensibilities of the best negroes in the United States are so stunted and dull, and the standard of morality among even the leaders of the race is so low, that they do not appreciate the enormity and heinousness of rape. . . . Only those who are densely ignorant of the standards and sentiments of the best negroes, or who wish willfully to misrepresent and maliciously slander a race already resting under burdens greater than it can bear, would accuse its thousands of reputable men and women of sympathizing with rapists, either black or white, or of condoning their crime. . . .

What, then is the cause of lynching? At the last analysis, it will be discovered that there are just two causes of lynching. In the first place, it is due to race hatred, the hatred of a stronger people toward a weaker who were once held as slaves. In the second place, it is due to the lawlessness so prevalent in the section where nine-tenths of the lynchings occur. . . .

Lynching is the aftermath of slavery. The white men who shoot negroes to death and flay them alive, and the white women who apply flaming torches to their oil-soaked bodies today, are the sons and daughters of women who had but little, if any, compassion on the race when it was enslaved. The men who lynch negroes today are, as a rule, the children of women who sat by their firesides happy and proud in the possession and affection of their own children, while they looked with unpitying eye and adamantine heart upon the anguish of slave mothers whose children had been sold away, when not overtaken by a sadder fate . . . It is impossible to comprehend the cause of the ferocity and barbarity which attend the average lynching-bee, without taking into account the brutalizing effect of slavery upon the people of the section where most of the lynchings occur. . . . It is too much to expect, perhaps, that the children of women who for generations looked upon the hardships and the degradation or their sisters of a darker hue with few if any ptotests, should have mercy and compassion upon the children of that oppressed race now. But what a tremendous influence for law and order, and what a mighty foc to mob violence Southern white women might be, if they would arise in the purity and power of their womanhood to implore their fathers, husbands and sons no longer to stain their hands with the black man's blood! . . . Whenever Southern white people discuss lynching, they are prone to slander the whole negro race. Not long ago, a Southern writer of great repute declared without qualification or reservation that "the crime of rape is well-nigh wholly confined to the negro race," and insisted that "negroes furnish most of the ravishers." These assertions are as unjust to the negro as they are unfounded in fact. According to statistics recently published, only one colored male in 100,000 over five years of age was accused of assault upon a white woman in the South in 1902, whereas one male out of every 20,000 over five years of age was charged with rape in Chicago during the same year. If these figures prove anything at all, they show that the men and boys in Chicago are many times more addicted to rape than are the negroes in the South. . . .

But even if the negro's morals were as loose and as lax as some claim them to be, and if his belief in the virtue of women were as slight as we are told, the South has nobody to blame but itself . . . Men do not gather grapes of thorns nor figs of thistles. Throughout their entire period of bondage, colored women were debauched by their masters. From the day they were liberated to the present time, prepossessing young colored girls have been considered the rightful prey of white gentlemen in the South, and they have been protected neither by public sentiment nor by law. In the South, the negro's home is not considered sacred by the superior race. White men are neither punished for invading it, not lynched for violating colored women and girls. . . .

How can lynching be extirpated in the United States? . . . Lynching can never be suppressed in the South, until the masses of ignorant white people in that section are educated and lifted to a higher moral plane. . . . Lynching cannot be suppressed in the South, until all classes of white people who dwell there . . . respect the rights of other human beings, no matter what may be the color of their skin . . . and learn a holy reverence for the law. . . .

Until there is a renaissance or popular belief in the principles of liberty and equality upon which this government was founded, lynching, the Convict-Lease System, the Disfranchisement Acts, the Jim Crow Car Laws, unjust discriminations in the professions and trades and similar atrocities will continue to dishearten and degrade the negro, and stain the fair name of the United States. For there can be no doubt that the greatest obstacle in the way of extirpating lynching is the general attitude of the public mind toward this unspeakable crime. The whole country seems tired of hearing about the black man's woes. The wrongs of the Irish, or the Armenians, of the Romanian and Russian Jews, or the exiles of Russia and of every other oppressed people upon the face of the globe, can arouse the sympathy and fire the indignation of the American public, while they seem to be all but indifferent to the murderous assaults upon the negroes in the South.

Document 13.12 Booker T. Washington: The Atlanta Compromise

How should African Americans act or behave to get ahead? Should they have to behave in a way to please whites? These themes are prominent in the famous speech made by Booker T. Washington in 1895. Washington was born a slave in 1856, earned a living and paid for his education through a series of menial jobs. His whole life was dedicated to hard work. A guiding force behind the Tuskegee Institute in Alabama, Washington argued blacks should learn basic skills to provide for themselves, and thus earn the respect of whites. In his Atlanta speech, what does he say blacks should do? What should they not push for, as that might offend whites? How do you think Southern whites responded to this speech? Is this a surrender of the rights promised in the 14th and 15th Amendments and won by the blood shed in Civil War?

Mr. President and Gentlemen of the Board of Directors and Citizens:

One-third of the population of the South is of the Negro race. No enterprise seeking the material, civil, or moral welfare of this section can disregard this element of our population and reach the highest success. I but convey to you, Mr. President and Directors, the sentiment of the masses of my race when I say that in no way have the value and manhood of the American Negro been more fittingly and generously recognized than by the managers of this magnificent Exposition at every stage of its progress. It is a recognition that will do more to cement the friendship of the two races than any occurrence since the dawn of our freedom.

Not only this, but the opportunity here afforded will awaken among us a new era of industrial progress. Ignorant and inexperienced, it is not strange that in the first years of our new life we began at the top instead of at the bottom; that a seat in Congress or the state legislature was more sought than real estate or industrial skill; that the political convention or stump speaking had more attractions than starting a dairy farm or truck garden.

A ship lost at sea for many days suddenly sighted a friendly vessel. From the mast of the unfortunate vessel was seen a signal, "Water, water; we die of thirst!" The answer from the friendly vessel at once came back, "Cast down your bucket where you are." A second time the signal, "Water, water; send us water!" ran up from the distressed vessel, and was answered, "Cast down your bucket where you are." And a third and fourth signal for water was answered, "Cast down your bucket where you are." The captain of the distressed vessel, at last heeding the injunction, cast down his bucket, and it came up full of fresh, sparkling water from the mouth of the Amazon River. To those of my race who depend on bettering their condition in a foreign land or who underestimate the importance of cultivating friendly relations with the Southern white man, who is their next-door neighbor, I would say: "Cast down your bucket where you are"—cast it down in making friends in every manly way of the people of all races by whom we are surrounded.

Cast it down in agriculture, mechanics, in commerce, in domestic service, and in the professions. And in this connection it is well to bear in mind that whatever other sins the South may be called to bear, when it comes to business, pure and simple, it is in the South that the Negro is given a man's chance in the commercial world, and in nothing is this Exposition more eloquent than in emphasizing this chance. Our greatest danger is that in the great leap from slavery to freedom we may overlook the fact that the masses of us are to live by the productions of our hands, and fail to keep in mind that we shall prosper in proportion as we learn to dignify and glorify common labour, and put brains and skill into the common occupations of life; shall prosper in proportion as we learn to draw the line between the superficial and the substantial, the ornamental gewgaws of life and the useful. No race can prosper till it learns that there is as much dignity in tilling a field as in writing a poem. It is at the bottom of life we must begin, and not at the top. Nor should we permit our grievances to overshadow our opportunities.

To those of the white race who look to the incoming of those of foreign birth and strange tongue and habits for the prosperity of the South, were I permitted I would repeat what I say to my own race, "Cast down your bucket where you are." Cast it down among the eight millions of Negroes whose habits you know, whose fidelity and love you have tested in days when to have proved treacherous meant the ruin of your firesides. Cast down your bucket among these people who have, without strikes and labour wars, tilled your fields, cleared your forests, builded your railroads and cities, and brought forth treasures from the bowels of the earth, and helped make possible this magnificent representation of the progress of the South. Casting down your bucket among my people, helping and encouraging them as you are doing on these grounds, and to education of head, hand, and heart, you will find

---

Booker T. Washington, 1895.

that they will buy your surplus land, make blossom the waste places in your fields, and run your factories. While doing this, you can be sure in the future, as in the past, that you and your families will be surrounded by the most patient, faithful, law-abiding, and unresentful people that the world has seen. As we have proved our loyalty to you in the past, in nursing your children, watching by the sick-bed of your mothers and fathers, and often following them with tear-dimmed eyes to their graves, so in the future, in our humble way, we shall stand by you with a devotion that no foreigner can approach, ready to lay down our lives, if need be, in defense of yours, interlacing our industrial, commercial, civil, and religious life with yours in a way that shall make the interests of both races one. In all things that are purely social we can be as separate as the fingers, yet one as the hand in all things essential to mutual progress.

There is no defense or security for any of us except in the highest intelligence and development of all. If anywhere there are efforts tending to curtail the fullest growth of the Negro, let these efforts be turned into stimulating, encouraging, and making him the most useful and intelligent citizen. Effort or means so invested will pay a thousand per cent interest. These efforts will be twice blessed—blessing him that gives and him that takes. There is no escape through law of man or God from the inevitable:

The laws of changeless justice bind Oppressor with oppressed;

And close as sin and suffering joined We march to fate abreast.

Nearly sixteen millions of hands will aid you in pulling the load upward, or they will pull against you the load downward. We shall constitute one-third and more of the ignorance and crime of the South, or one-third [of] its intelligence and progress; we shall contribute one-third to the business and industrial prosperity of the South, or we shall prove a veritable body of death, stagnating, depressing, retarding every effort to advance the body politic.

Gentlemen of the Exposition, as we present to you our humble effort at an exhibition of our progress, you must not expect overmuch. Starting thirty years ago with ownership here and there in a few quilts and pumpkins and chickens (gathered from miscellaneous sources), remember the path that has led from these to the inventions and production of agricultural implements, buggies, steam-engines, newspapers, books, statuary, carving, paintings, the management of drug stores and banks, has not been trodden without contact with thorns and thistles. While we take pride in what we exhibit as a result of our independent efforts, we do not for a moment forget that our part in this exhibition would fall far short of your expectations but for the constant help that has come to our educational life, not only from the Southern states, but especially from Northern philanthropists, who have made their gifts a constant stream of blessing and encouragement.

The wisest among my race understand that the agitation of questions of social equality is the extremest folly, and that progress in the enjoyment of all the privileges that will come to us must be the result of severe and constant struggle rather than of artificial forcing. No race that has anything to contribute to the markets of the world is long in any degree ostracized. It is important and right that all privileges of the law be ours, but it is vastly more important that we be prepared for the exercise of these privileges. The opportunity to earn a dollar in a factory just now is worth infinitely more than the opportunity to spend a dollar in an opera-house.

In conclusion, may I repeat that nothing in thirty years has given us more hope and encouragement, and drawn us so near to you of the white race, as this opportunity offered by the Exposition; and here bending, as it were, over the altar that represents the results of the struggles of your race and mine, both starting practically empty-handed three decades ago, I pledge that in your effort to work out the great and intricate problem which God has laid at the doors of the South, you shall have at all times the patient, sympathetic help of my race; only let this be constantly in mind, that, while from representations in these buildings of the product of field, of forest, of mine, of factory, letters, and art, much good will come, yet far above and beyond material benefits will be that higher good, that, let us pray God, will come, in a blotting out of sectional differences and racial animosities and suspicions, in a determination to administer absolute justice, in a willing obedience among all classes to the mandates of law. This, coupled with our material prosperity, will bring into our beloved South a new heaven and a new earth.

Module XIII
Worksheet and Questions

1. Using the documents in Module XIII, prove that most southerners never accepted losing the Civil War, or the idea that African Americans had rights. Demonstrate whether their attitudes improved or racism decreased at any time during Reconstruction or afterwards.

2. Assume the role of a northern civil rights activist testifying before Congress. Present a case for strict Reconstruction laws and the need for Federal troops in the South to enforce them. What laws and actions are necessary to protect southern blacks and white Republicans and why are they needed? How would your attitude change by the beginning of the twentieth century?

3. What rights did former slaves want to give real meaning to their new status as citizens? Why were these rights so important? Why did African Americans believe land ownership was just as important as political rights? Describe the life of the sharecropper. Is this really freedom or just another version of slavery?

4. There has just been a lynching in your rural Mississippi town. Justify this from a white point-of-view, not only the recent event but also how lynching is a white public ritual aimed at keeping blacks "in their place." Then explain the reality of lynching as a black resident in the same community. What are the real causes of lynching? Why do whites lie about the causes of the violence?

Differing Views of the Western Frontier

Introduction

Between the end of the Civil War and the beginning of the twentieth century, white Americans flooded into the Great Plains, the Rocky Mountain region, and the Pacific Coast. In doing so, they established U,S. control over the entire American continent. This process has subsequently become the source of the legends of the Old West, celebrated in popular music and Hollywood films, in which cowboy and pioneer heroes confronted and subdued Indians and other bad guys.

The reality is much more complex. The indigenous Indians, who fought to retain control of the region were, as most people now concede, much more than simply savage impediments to progress. And the white settlement of the West was also more than the story of heroic accomplishment. In this chapter we will look at contrasting views of life on the last geographic frontier by those who experienced it themselves. After reading these documents, you should be able to better make up your own mind about what life on the frontier was really like.

First, we will look at different interpretations of the Battle of Little Bighorn, the legendary clash in which the Sioux and their native allies defeated the Seventh Cavalry under General George Armstrong Custer. At the time of the battle most white America saw this event as a savage massacre of brave soldiers. Later observers have seen the Indians with more sympathy. In this chapter we will read the accounts of both Indian and white observers.

Many whites believed that Indians should seek to adapt by adopting white ways of life. Partly for that purpose the government set up schools for Indian children. These were often located in the East, far from the Western Indians' traditional homes. Their goal was to teach Indian children to behave as much like whites as possible. As a young Sioux girl, Zitkala-sa, whose white name became Gertrude Simmons Bonnin, looked forward to going to school in the East, but then endured years of unhappiness while getting an education there.

Finally, we examine the experience of white settlers on the Great Plains. In the last half of the nineteenth century, all sorts of people poured into this region in search of prosperous farmland of their own. Their experiences often proved difficult, as we read in letters by two young farm women, one an American-born woman from regions farther east, the other an immigrant from Sweden.

Observers of the Last Great Clash: the Battle of Little Bighorn

Document 14.1 A Sioux Woman's Account

The last great clash between massed Indians and whites was the Battle of Little Bighorn, where in 1876 the U.S. Seventh Cavalry under the command of General George Armstrong Custer was defeated in present-day Montana by Sioux and Cheyenne warriors led by Sitting Bull. For years white Americans viewed Custer and his troops as heroes and the battle, which occurred in the centennial year of U.S. independence, as a massacre. Obviously, there are two perspectives on this battle, and many white Americans have begun to view the Sioux and Cheyenne with more sympathy. This section contains the accounts of three observers of the battle, two Indian and one white. The account below contains the memories of an aging Sioux woman looking back from the 1930s. As you read it, think of how it might differ from other views you are familiar with. How does it differ from the view of the white observer printed below?

A Sioux Woman's Account

She-Walks-With-Her Shawl

Account given to Walter S. Campbell in 1931

I was born seventy-seven winters ago, near Grand River, [in present-day] South Dakota. My father, Slohan, was the bravest man among our people. Fifty-five years ago we packed our tents and went with other Indians to Peji-slawakpa (Greasy Grass). We were then living on the Standing Rock Indian Reservation. I belonged to Sitting Bull's band. They were great fighters. We called ourselves Hunkpapa. This means confederated bands. When I was still a young girl (about seventeen) I accompanied a Sioux war party which made war against the Crow Indians in Montana. My father went to war 70 times. He was wounded nearly a dozen times.

But I am going to tell you of the greatest battle. This was a fight against Pehin-hanska (General Custer). I was several miles from the Hunkpapa when I saw a cloud of dust rise beyond a ridge of bluffs in the east. The morning was hot and sultry. Several of us Indian girls were digging wild turnips. I was then 23 years old. We girls looked towards the camp and saw a warrior ride swiftly, shouting that the soldiers were only a few miles away and that the women and children including old men should run for the hills in an opposite direction.

I dropped the pointed ash stick which I had used in digging turnips and ran towards my tipi. I saw my father running towards the horses. When I got to my tent, mother told me that news was brought to her that my brother had been killed by the soldiers. My brother had gone early that morning in search for a horse that strayed from our herd. In a few moments we saw soldiers on horseback on a bluff just across the Greasy Grass (Little Big Horn) River. I knew that there would be a battle because I saw warriors getting their horses and tomahawks.

I heard Hawkman shout, Ho-ka-he! Ho-ka-he! (Charge.) The soldiers began firing into our camp. Then they ceased firing. I saw my father preparing to go to battle. I sang a death song for my brother who had been killed.

My heart was bad. Revenge! Revenge! For my brother's death. I thought of the death of my young brother, One Hawk. Brown Eagle, my brother's companion on that morning, had escaped and gave the alarm to the camp that the soldiers were coming. I ran to a nearby thicket and got my black horse. I painted my face with crimson and unbraided my black hair. I was mourning. I was a woman, but I was not afraid.

By this time the soldiers (Reno's men) were forming a battle line in the bottom about a half mile away. In another moment I heard a terrific volley of carbines. The bullets shattered the tipi poles. Women and children were running away from the gunfire. In the tumult I heard old men and women singing death songs for their warriors who were now ready to attack the soldiers. The chanting of death songs made me brave, although I was a woman. I saw a warrior adjusting his quiver and grasping his tomahawk. He started running towards his horse when he suddenly recoiled and dropped dead. He was killed near his tipi.

Warriors were given orders by Hawkman to mount their horses and follow the fringe of a forest and wait until commands were given to charge. The soldiers kept on firing. Some women were also killed. Horses and dogs too! The camp was in great commotion.

Father led my black horse up to me and I mounted. We galloped towards the soldiers. Other warriors joined in with us. When we were nearing the fringe of the woods, an order was given by Hawkman to charge. Ho-ka-he! Ho-ka-he! Charge! Charge! The warriors were now near the soldiers. The troopers were all on foot. They shot straight, because I saw our leader killed as he rode with his warriors.

The charge was so stubborn that the soldiers ran to their horses and, mounting them, rode swiftly towards the river. The Greasy Grass river was very deep. Their horses had to swim to get across. Some of the warriors rode into the water and tomahawked the soldiers. In the charge the Indians rode among the troopers and with tomahawks unhorsed several of them. The soldiers were very excited. Some of them shot into the air. The Indians chased the soldiers across the river and up over a bluff.

Then the warriors returned to the bottom where the first battle took place. We heard a commotion far down the valley. The warriors rode in a column of fives. They sang a victory song. Someone said that another body of soldiers were attacking the lower end of the village. I heard afterwards that the soldiers were under the command of Long Hair (Custer). With my father and other youthful warriors I rode in that direction.

We crossed the Greasy Grass below a beaver dam (the water is not so deep there) and came upon many horses. One soldier was holding the reins of eight or ten horses. An Indian waved his blanket and scared all the horses. They got away from the men (troopers). On the ridge just north of us I saw blue-clad men running up a ravine, firing as they ran.

The dust created from the stampeding horses and powder smoke made everything dark and black. Flashes from carbines could be seen. The valley was dense with powder smoke. I never heard such whooping and shouting. "There was never a better day to die," shouted Red Horse. In the battle I heard cries from troopers, but could not understand what they were saying. I do not speak English.

Long Hair's troopers were trapped in an enclosure. There were Indians everywhere. The Cheyennes attacked the soldiers from the north and Crow King from the South. The Sioux Indians encircled the troopers. Not one got away! The Sioux used tomahawks. It was not a massacre, but [a] hotly contested battle between two armed forces. Very few soldiers were mutilated, as oft has been said by the whites. Not a single soldier was burned at the stake. Sioux Indians do not torture their victims.

After the battle the Indians took all the equipment and horses belonging to the soldiers. The brave men who came to punish us that morning were defeated; but in the end, the Indians lost. We saw the body of Long Hair. Of course, we did not know who the soldiers were until an interpreter told us that the men came from Fort Lincoln, then [in] Dakota Territory. On the saddle blankets were the cross saber insignia and the letter seven.

The victorious warriors returned to the camp, as did the women and children who could see the battle from where they took refuge. Over sixty Indians were killed, and they were also brought back to the camp for scaffold burial. The Indians did not stage a victory dance that night. They were mourning for their own dead. . . .

Document 14.2 A Sioux Man's Account

The next Indian account is by a Sioux man, who was a warrior in the Battle of Little Bighorn. In what ways is his account similar to or different from that of She-Walks-With-Her Shawl, who did not actually fight in the battle?

A Sioux Man's Account

One Bull

I was in Sitting Bull's camp on [Little] Big Horn River, One Horn Band Hinkowoji [Minneconjou] Tepee. They were called that because they planted their gardens near the river. Itazipco (Without Bow, or Sans Arc) was another band. Ogalala was the Red Cloud band. Another band, Schiyeio, means Cheyenne. They were a different tribe, not Lakota. They were friends of Lakota.

Pili (Gall) had another band. All the different bands camped together. There were many other chiefs with their bands, Four Horn and Two Moon and many others. Whenever the chiefs held a council, they went to Sitting Bull's camp because he was a good medicine man.

Lakota and Cheyennes had gone to this camp to look after their buffalo and so young men and women could get acquainted. White men had driven our buffalo away from Lakota land. So we went where buffalo were to take care of them and keep white men away.

I was a strong young man 22 years old. On the day of the fight I was sitting in my tepee combing my hair. I don't know what time it was. About this time maybe (2:00 P.M.). Lakota had no watches in those days. I had just been out and picketed my horses and was back in my tepee. I saw a man named Fat Bear come running into camp, and he said soldiers were coming on the other side of the river and had killed a boy named Deeds, who went out to picket a horse. Then I came out of my tepee and saw soldiers running their horses toward our camp on same side of the river. We could hear lots of shooting. I went to [the] tepee of my uncle, Sitting Bull, and said I was going to go take part in the battle. He said, "Go ahead, they have already fired."

I had a rifle and plenty of shells, but I took that off and gave it to Sitting Bull, and he gave me a shield. Then I took the shield and my tomahawk and got on my horse and rode up to where the soldiers were attacking us. They were firing pretty heavy. They were all down near the river in the timber. Lakota were riding around fast and shooting at them. I rode up to some Lakota and said, "Let's all charge at once." I raised my tomahawk and said, "Wakontanka, help me so I do not sin but fight my battle." I started to charge. There were five Lakota riding behind me. We charged for some soldiers that were still fighting, and they ran to where their horses were in the timber. Then the soldiers all started for the river. I turned my horse and started that way too, and there was a man named Mato Wasbte (Pretty Bear) right behind me, and he and his horse were shot down. I followed the soldiers. They were running for the river. I killed two with my tomahawk. Then the soldiers got across the river. I came back to where Pretty Bear was and got him up on my horse. He was wounded and covered with blood. I started my horse toward the river where the soldiers were, trying to get across.

Then I let Pretty Bear get off my horse, and I went across the river after the soldiers. I killed one more of them with my tomahawk.

Then I saw four soldiers ahead of me running up the hill. I was just about to charge them when someone rode along beside me and said, "You better not go any farther. You are wounded." That was Sitting Bull. I was not wounded, but I was all covered with blood that got on me when I had Pretty Bear on my horse. So I did what Sitting Bull told me. Then Sitting Bull rode back, but I went on. Another Lakota went after these four soldiers. He had a rifle and shot one of them off his horse. One of the soldiers kept shooting back but without hitting us. The man that was with me was a Lakota, but I did not know who he was. Now the soldiers were getting together up on the hill, and we could see the other soldiers coming with the pack mules a long way off.

Then I went back across the river and rode down it a way; then I rode with the man who was shooting at the four soldiers, and we crossed the river again just east of Sitting Bull's camp. We saw a bunch of horsemen up on a hill to the north, and they were Lakotas. We rode up to them and I told them I had killed a lot of soldiers and showed them my tomahawk. Then I said I was going up and help kill Custer's soldiers, but Sitting Bull told me not to go so I didn't go but we rode up where we could see the Lakotas and Cheyennes killing Custer's men. They

---

From *Lakota and Cheyenne: Indian Views of the Great Sioux Way, 1876–1877*, edited by Jerome A. Greene, 1994 University of Oklahoma Press. Reprinted by permission.

had been shooting heavy, but the Indians charged them straight from the west and then some rode around them shooting, and the Indians were knocking them off their horses and killing them with tomahawks and clubs. THEY WERE ALL KILLED. There were a lot of Sioux killed. The others were picking them up on their horses and taking them back to camp.

Then we had a war dance all night, and in the morning we heard that the soldiers with the pack mules were up on the hill, and the Sioux started up after them. I went with Sitting Bull and volunteered to go help kill these soldiers, but Sitting Bull said no. So we watched the fight from a hill. I didn't have my rifle with me then, just my tomahawk. The Sioux surrounded them and they fought that way all day. The soldiers had ditches dug all around the hill. Then along towards sundown the Sioux broke camp and went to the mountains.

The Sioux did not take any prisoners that I know of. I didn't see any. I don't know how many Indians there were, but it was a very big band. Many bands together. The Indians had rifles with little short cartridges. I didn't use mine.

After the fight we all stayed in the Big Horn Mountains about ten days. After that they broke camp and went north following along the Tongue River. Then we went to the Little Missouri, and we found a place where there must have been some soldiers, for we found a lot of sacks of yellow corn piled up. Then some of the bands went one way and some went another. One little band went to Slim Buttes, and they were all killed by soldiers.

I was with Sitting Bull all the time we were in camp on the [Little] Big Horn and saw him during the battle. He was telling his men what to do. The first I knew of any soldiers was when they killed the boy who went to picket his horse across the river from Sitting Bull's camp. Before we broke camp that night, we saw the walking soldiers coming from down the river, but my uncle said, "We won't fight them. We have killed enough. We will go. . . ."

Document 14.3 An Account by One of Custer's Scouts

Reality is often complicated. The Great Sioux Wars, like many of the white-Indian conflicts before them, did not simply pit all white newcomers against all of the indigenous peoples of the region. The Indians themselves were composed of many peoples, and they responded in different ways to white society. Many sought to make use of the new situation to improve their own lives. Some attempted to use the whites against their traditional native enemies. Others intermarried. William Jackson, the source of the next account, was a mixed blood man, who served as a scout for Custer during this conflict. He therefore provides a singular view of the events at Little Bighorn.

The Battle of Little Big Horn, June 25–26, 1876

William Jackson

General [Lieutenant Colonel] Custer, with his Seventh Cavalry, a pack train carrying fifteen days' rations and extra cartridges, his own scouts, and six Crow scouts under John Bruyer [Mitch Bouer], from Gibbon's command, left the mouth of the Rosebud about noon, June 22d. My brother and I rode with an old friend of ours. Frank [Fred] Girard [Gerard], a man who had once been captured by Crazy Horse's band of Sioux, and had lived with them so long that he had acquired no little of their ways, and their religion.

On the third day, we struck the trail of the hostiles, the one that Reno had found several days before. And what a trail it was; a trail all of three hundred yards wide, and deeply worn by travois, and lodge-pole ends. We went into camp close to the trail, and, cooking our supper, we scouts counciled together about the outlook. All agreed that at least

---

From *Battles and Skirmishes of the Great Sioux War, 1876–1877*, edited by Jerome A. Greene, 1993 University of Oklahoma Press. Reprinted by permission.

fifteen hundred lodges of the enemy had made that broad trail. Said [the Arikara scout] Bloody Knife: "My friends, this big trail proves what we heard, that the Ogalalla, Minneconjou, Sans Arc, and Teton Sioux have left their agencies to join Sitting Bull and Crazy Horse; but I am sure that even this trail does not account for all that have left their agencies. There surely are other trails of them; and trails, too, of Cheyennes and Arapahoes."

"Many Yanktonnais and Assiniboin have answered Sitting Bull's call for help, and joined him," said Frank Girard.

"Yes. They too," Bloody Knife continued. "It is as I have told Long Hair: this gathering of the enemy tribes is too many for us. But he will not believe me. He is bound to lead us against them. They are not far away; just over this ridge, they are all encamped and waiting for us. Crazy Horse and Sitting Bull are not men-without-sense; they have their scouts out, and some of them surely have their eyes upon us. Well, to-morrow we are going to have a big fight, a losing fight. Myself, I know what is to happen to me; my sacred helper has given me warning that I am not to see the set of to-morrow's sun."

Sad words, those. They chilled us. I saw [scout] Charlie Reynolds nod agreement to them, and was chilled again when he said in a low voice: "I feel as he does: tomorrow will be the end for me, too. Any one who wants my little outfit of stuff"—pointing to his war sack—"can have it right now." He opened it, began passing out tobacco; a sewing-kit; several shirts and so on. Many refused the presents; those who accepted them did so with evident reluctance.

We had little appetite for our coffee and hardtack, and the meat that we were broiling. While we were eating, word was passed from mess to mess to put out the fires. That was quickly done, and soon afterward, Lieutenant [Charles A.] Varnum, who was in charge of the scouts, came over and said that it was General Custer's plan to attempt a surprise attack upon the camp of the enemy. The command was to rest until about midnight, and then again take the trail; some of us scouts, meantime, were to push on ahead and try to locate the camp.

Said Bloody Knife: "We cannot surprise the enemy! They are not crazy; without doubt their scouts have watched every move that we have made."

"Well, Bloody Knife, that is probably true, but we must try to surprise them, must we not?"

"Yes, o' course. We *try*!" he replied.

"Very well. We will go out in three parties: Bryer, you take two of your Crows and go forward on the right of the trail. Bloody Knife, you take the left of the trail, with two of your Rees. You Jackson boys, and you, Reynolds, come with me on the trail," ordered Varnum.

We saddled our horses, mounted, and struck out all together. We kept together for all of a mile, and then Bruyer and the Crows and Bloody knife and the Rees branched off and left us to follow the trail. We moved on cautiously, often stopping to listen for the barking of camp dogs in answer to the howling of the wolves, and to look for the red gleam of sparks from some sick one's lodge-fire. So we went on and on through the night, getting no sight or sound of the enemy. At dawn, the command overtook us, and Lieutenant Varnum reported to General Custer. There we rested and had some breakfast.

While we were eating, several of the packers rode swiftly up through the command to General Custer, and we soon learned that they had lost a box of hardtack off one of the mules, and, on going back, had found some Indians around it, stuffing the contents into their clothing. None could now doubt that the enemy had all along kept watch of our advance. With a grim laugh, Charlie Reynolds said to me: "I knew well enough that they had scouts ahead of us, but I didn't think that others would be trailing along to pick up stuff dropped by our careless packers."

Convinced at last that we could not possibly surprise the enemy, General Custer ordered a quick advance, with the scouts and himself in the lead. We had not gone far when Bloody Knife and his two Rees joined us, and reported that on the other side of the ridge they had found the day-old trail of many more of the enemy going toward the valley of the Little Bighorn.

On we went over the divide. We soon met John Bruyer and his two Crows. They were excited, and Bruyer said to Custer: "General, we have discovered the camp, down there on the Little Horn. It is a big one! Too big for you to tackle! Why, there are thousands and thousands of Sioux and Cheyennes down there."

For a momet the general stared at him, angrily, I thought, and then sternly replied: "I shall attack them! If you are afraid, Bruyer—"

"I guess I can go wherever you do," Bruyer quickly answered; and at that, the general turned back to the command, we following him. He had the bugler sound the officers' call, and the command rested while they got together, and Custer gave his orders for the attack upon the camp.

None of the scouts had been far in the lead, and they all came in. Rees and Crows and whites and Robert and I, we were a gathering of solemn faces. Speaking in English, and the sign language, too, so that all would understand Bruyer described the enemy camp. It was, he said, all of three miles long, and made up of hundreds and hundreds of lodges.

Above it and below and west of it were thousands and thousands of horses that were being close-herded. With his few riders, Long Hair had decided to attack the camp, and we were going to have a terrible fight; we should all take courage, fight hard, make our every shot a killer. He finished, and none spoke. But after a minute or two, Bloody Knife looked up and signed to Sun: "I shall not see you go down behind the mountains to-night." And at that I almost choked. I felt that he knew that his end was near, that there was no escaping it. I turned and looked the other way. I thought that my own end was near. I felt very sad.

The officers' council did not last long, and, when it ended, Lieutenant Varnum came hurrying to us scouts and said that the command was going to split up to make the attack on the camp, and that we were to go with Major Reno's column, down the trail of the hostiles that we had been following from the Rosebud. We were soon in the saddle and headed down a narrow valley toward the river.

Bruyer told us that the big camp of the enemy was well below the foot of the narrow valley and on the other side of the Little Bighorn. We crossed the river, turned straight down the valley, went down it for more than a mile, and saw some of the enemy reteating before our advance. A grove of timber in a bend below prevented our seeing their camp. As we neared the timber, we heard a single shot fired beyond it, and then the Indians began firing at us. We then went on, and, passing the timber, saw a great camp, and a horde of riders coming up from it to attack us. We all turned into the timber then, and got our horses into an old timber and brush dry channel of the river.

Within two minutes from the time that we left our horses, and climbed up the bank from them, we had a line of defense in the brush and out across toward the west bluff of the valley. Then came the rush of the enemy, all of five hundred well-mounted riders in all their war finery, eager to get at us. Their shots, their war-cries, the thunder of their horses' feet were deafening.

It was the intention of the enemy to charge straight through the center of our line, but, by the time they had come within fifty yards, we had shot so many of them that they swung out and went streaming past the other end of our line, lying low upon their horses and firing rapidly. The dust that their swift charge raised—the ground was very dry—almost choked us: it drifted upon us like a thick fog, and obscured the sun.

As the enemy were coming straight at our line, Robert, at my side in the brush, exclaimed, "Look! That one on the big white horse! He's Black Elk!"

So he was Black Elk, our enemy of the Round Butte and Fort Buford. We both fired at him, our shots apparently missing, but, just as he with the others was swerving off to flank us, he suddenly pitched head first from his horse, and Robert shouted to me: "I got him!"

Several hundred of the enemy went thundering past that outer end of our line, and, swinging in, began attack upon our rear; others were starting to cut us off from the river, and more and more arrivals from the camp swarmed in front of us. I thought that we were about to meet our end right there, every one of us. Then an officer ordered us in to our horses. By the time we got to them, we were entirely surrounded. As we mounted, a man right beside me fell dead out of his saddle. I saw Bloody Knife, Reynolds, and Girard all getting upon their horses. I saw Major Reno, hatless, a handkerchief tied around his head, getting up on his plunging horse. Waving his six-shooter, he shouted something that I couldn't hear, and led swiftly off, up out of the depression that we were in. We all swarmed after him, and headed back up the way that we had come, our intention being to recross the river and get up onto the bluffs, where we could make a stand. By this time hundreds more of the enemy had come up from the camp, and all together they swarmed in on us and a hand-to-hand fight with them began.

I saw numbers of our men dropping from their horses, saw horses falling, heard their awful neighs of fright and pain. Close ahead of me, Bloody Knife, and then Charlie Reynolds, went down, right there met the fate that they had foretold.

A big heavy-set Indian brushed up against me, tried to pull me out of the saddle, and I shot him. Then, right in front, a soldier's horse was shot from under him, and as I came up, he grasped my right stirrup and ran beside me. I had to check my horse so that he could keep up, and so began to lag behind. Numbers of Indians were passing on both sides of us, eager to get at the main body of the retreat. At last one of the passing Indians made a close shot at the soldier and killed him, and, as I gave my horse loose rein, Frank Girard came up on my left, and we rode on side by side. Ahead, there was now a solid body of Indians between us and the retreating, hard-pressed soldiers, and Girard shouted to me: "We can't go through them! Let's turn back!"

Indians were still coming on from the direction of the camp, and, as we wheeled off to the left, and then went quartering back toward the timber, several of them shot at us, but we finally got into thick, high brush, dismounted and tied our horses. Just then we saw some one coming toward us, and were about to fire at him when we discovered that he was Lieutenant [Charles C.] De Rudio. He told us that his horse had run away from him. As we stood there, listening to the heavy firing up on the river, we were joined by [Private] Thomas O'Neil, of Company G, also horseless.

Lieutenant De Rudio asked that Girard and I put our horses farther back in the brush, and then all four look for a hiding-place. We did that, and were soon lying in a small, round, sandy depression surrounded by brush, about twenty yards from the open flat, up which a few Indians were still hurrying from the camp below. We lay each of us facing a different direction.

The sound of the fighting up the river seemed to be farther and farther from us. We learned later that, after we were cut off from the retreat, the enemy, at least a thousand of them against Reno's one hundred, drove the troops down a steep bank into the river and began following them across it. On the other side was a very high, steep bank, and some of the troops managed to get up onto it and check the Indians until the remaining troops got up, when they all went to the top of the main bluffs and there made a stand, and were there joined by [Captain Frederick W.] Benteen and his three companies, and then by [Captain Thomas B.] MacDougall and the pack train. They then went north along the bluffs, to try to find General Custer's column and join it, but were driven back to the point from which they started.

Great numbers of the enemy now went down the flat in front of us, riding fast, and we heard heavy firing away down the valley and knew that they were fighting Custer there. The sun beat down upon us, and we began to suffer from heat and thirst. Women from the camp came up on horseback, on foot, and leading travois-horses, and began carrying off their dead and wounded, and stripping our dead of their clothing, and slashing their bodies. That was a tough sight. Said O'Neil: "That's the way they will cut us up if they get us."

"But does it matter what happens to our bodies after we die! The point is, we mustn't die!" Girard exclaimed.

As the day wore on, we suffered terribly from want of water. We seldom spoke to one another; just watched and suffered.

When night came, we decided to try to make our way to the remains of our column, several miles up the river, and on the bluffs on the opposite side. Girard and I were to ride our horses, the others walking close at our side. Then, if we were discovered, De Rudio and O'Neil were to drop down flat upon the ground, and we were to ride away, drawing the enemy after us.

We were no sooner out of the brush than we began to pass the bodies of the men and horses that had been killed along the line of Reno's retreat. The men had all been stripped of their clothing, and were so badly cut up that, try as I would, I could not force myself to see if my brother were one of the slain.

We went on to the river, coming to a halt at the edge of a bank dropping straight down to the water; on the other side, a high, black, very steep bank faced us. Close under us the current was swift but noiseless, and we doubted that it was fordable. O'Neil jumped in to ascertain the depth, went in almost to his neck and would have been carried downstream had he not seized some overhanging brush and drawn himself to footing closer in. He filled his hat with water and passed it up to De Rudio, who handed it to me. I drank every drop it contained and wanted more. After the hat had been filled and passed up again and again, De Rudio got down into the stream to test its current and depth, and soon agreed with O'Neil that it was too swift and deep for us to ford. We went on up the shore, looking for a place to cross.

Back of us, down the valley, the enemy had built many fires in the open, and were singing, dancing, and counting their *coups* around them. Ahead of us was black darkness, heavy silence. As we went on, our hearts became more and more heavy; we feared that all of the troops had been killed.

We came to a place where the river was rippling and murmuring, as water does over a shallow stony bed, and De Rudio urged that we attempt to ford it there. I saw Girard, close beside me, take his watch out—it was a valuable gold watch—hold it aloft; and then, in Sioux, he murmured: "Oh Powerful One, Day Maker! And you, people of the depths, this I sacrifice to you. Help us, I pray you, to cross safely here!" And with that, he tossed out the watch. We heard it splash into the water. "What were you saying—what was that splash?" De Rudio asked.

"Take hold of my horse's tail, I will lead in," Girard replied. In we went, slowly, feeling our way. Nowhere across was the water up to our horses' knees! When we reached the other shore I bit my lips hard to keep from laughing; all for nothing had been Girard's sacrifice to his gods.

Here on the other shore was high grass and thick brush. We went quartering up through it, and realized eventually that we were on an island. We found ourselves facing the main channel of the river. As no shots had been fired on the opposite bluffs since nightfall, we now believed that the remnant of Reno's troops had been killed up there, and, after some talk, decided to go up where we had crossed the river after separating from Custer and Benteen, and take the back trail for Powder River.

Girard led off up the island, with De Rudio at his side, and I followed with O'Neil on the left of my horse. We had not gone more than two hundred yards, when, from a clump of brush not far ahead, a deep voice demanded in Sioux: "Who are you!"

The sudden challenge almost stunned me. I saw De Rudio and O'Neil drop down into the waist-high grass, heard Girard reply, as he checked up his horse: "Just us few."

"And where are you going?"

"Out here a way," Girard calmly answered as he turned and rode back past me, saying: "Quick! We must draw them after us!"

We rode swiftly down the island for several hundred yards, saw that we were not pursued, and stopped, then heard a few shots up where we had left De Rudio and O'Neil, and a moment later heard the splashing of horses crossing the west channel of the river, and then the thudding of their feet as they went swiftly down the flat toward the enemy camp.

"Those Indians were pickets! Reno's outfit has not been wiped out; it is still on the bluffs on the other side," I said.

"Right you are!" Girard replied.

We knew that our friends had fired the shots and frightened that group of pickets so badly that they had left the island. We did not dare return to them, lest we should reveal their hiding-place to others of the enemy; all up and down the valley the brush might be full of them. We were ourselves in great danger, crashing through the brush with our horses, and decided that, if we were ever to rejoin the troops, we should have to do it on foot. We tied our horses in a dense growth of willows, left the island, and went on up the valley. Below, the Indians were still dancing and singing victory songs around their open fires.

A little way above the head of the island, we came to a very wide reach of the river that looked as though it was fordable, and decided to try it. As we were taking off our shoes and socks and trousers, I whispered to Girard: "If you had your watch now to sacrifice it—"

"I have given it; I have faith that we shall cross," he answered.

We waded in, each carrying a stick with which we prodded ahead for quicksand or sudden drop of the bottom. On the other side we ran up into the brush, put on our clothes, and, with rifles cocked and ready, started on. Moving cautiously, we began climbing a steep brush and timber slope. We had reached a height from which, looking down the valley, we could see the many dancing fires of the enemy, when I stepped upon a dry stick that broke with a loud snap.

Close above us, a Sioux said: "Spotted Elk, did you hear that?"

"Yes, Maybe a deer," came the reply, up off to our left.

"I am thirsty; let us go down to the river," said another picket, above on the right, and at that, Girard and I turned and went leaping down the slope. I stumbled and fell over a log and crashed into a clump of rose-brush.

Below me, still another picket cried out. "What is the trouble up there?"

"Something running; sounds like a bear," one off to my left replied.

As I sat up, I could no longer hear Girard, and did not know whether he had stopped or gone back to the river. There were Sioux below me, above me, probably others scattered all along the slopes running up to the bluffs. The one who had said that he was thirsty said, "Any one going to the river with me?"

None replied. I heard him go down the slope; after a time, go back up it. Then all was silent. Weakened by lack of sleep and food, I began to doze as I sat there in the brush, surrounded though I was by the enemy. My head would nod. I would lean over more and more until about to lose my balance, then straiten up with a jerk. After a time I realized that I had slept, for I felt refreshed. I opened my eyes and saw that day was coming. All was still quiet there on the slope and down in the valley. Then, in the half-light of the coming day, a number of shots were fired below. This aroused the pickets surrounding me. One of them cried out: "There are still a few soldiers alive down there!"

"Yes. But probably those shots ended them," said another.

"Let us go down and see," one to my left proposed.

"You know that Gall told us to stay up here until he comes to make the big attack," said another.

"Well, anyhow, we can go down to our horses, and be ready to join him when he comes with his many," still another proposed.

"Yes, yes. Let us do that," the others agreed, and I heard them coming down on each side of me. I crouched still lower in my little brush corral. One of them passed within fifteen feet of me, the tail of his war bonnet fluttering behind him. As they went, a few more shots were fired, down in the valley. I may as well explain right here what was taking place down there:

When Girard and I left De Rudio and O'Neil, they remained on the island. In the dim light of dawn, they saw a large number of riders going up the valley, made out that one of them was wearing buckskin clothes, were sure that they recognized him, and De Rudio shouted: "Tom Custer! Wait!"

The answer to that was forty or fifty shots that struck all around the two, strangely enough, not one of them taking effect. They ran, dodging this way and that way around the thick clump of brush, and finally, coming to a big jam of driftwood and brush, they dropped down in it, and none came to look for them there.

This was because, just at that time, heavy firing broke out on top of the bluffs, and the party that was searching for them hurried to cross the river and join in the daylight attack upon Reno's position. The hillside pickets who had gone down past me came hurrying up on their horses and passed on each side of my brush patch as they went on to get into the fight. The firing on the day before had been terrible, but this was far heavier. I concluded that Reno and Custer and Benteen had got their troops together, and were doing the best that they could against three thousand Sioux and Cheyennes. I did not have the slightest hope that they would last an hour, so great were the odds against them.

After a time, the firing slackened, died out, and I said to myself: "That settles it; the last ones of the troops have been killed." But soon the shooting broke out again, and I knew that it wasn't the end for them. Then, as the day wore on, and I knew by the sound of the firing that successive attacks upon the troops were being repulsed, I felt that they might hold their position until General Terry, with General Gibbon and his troops, could come to aid them. This was June 26th, the day that they were due to arrive here.

The day wore on. Now and then straggling riders passed up and down near my hiding-place. Late in the afternoon, I heard a commotion below, and, at some risk of discovery, I stood up to see what it was about: a multitude of people, countless bands of horses, were going up the valley. The women and children and old men were moving camp while their warriors continued to fight up on the bluffs. I could hear, more clearly than the firing above, the shrill voices of the women as they sang. They were happy, they were singing victory songs, but still the fighting was going on. I could not understand that. Where was victory for them when the fight was not ended? I worried about it. I got up again, and looked down into the valley: there were more people, more horses in the long broad column going up the valley, than I had ever seen together. I said to myself "Now I understand. Their warriors are so many that they know that they will wipe out the troops. They sing of the sure victory that their fighters are winning." I sank down in my hiding-place with heavy heart.

From that time I saw no more riders on the slope where I lay, and when, at nightfall, the firing entirely ceased, I decided that the last of the troops had been wiped out, and the victorious warriors had passed above me as they went to join their moving camp. Of the three men who had been with me the night before, I believed that De Rudio and O'Neil were dead, and that Girard was probably already on his way back to the Yellowstone. I decided to strike out for there, too. It would be useless for me to go out where the troops had made their last stand; I could not bury the dead, there would be no wounded for the to aid: Sioux and Cheyennes never left any wounded enemies on the field. Well, first I must have some water. I got up, stretched my numb legs, and started for the river.

Indians Attempt to Adjust to the New White World

Many whites in and out of the federal government believed that the best course for Indians was to abandon traditional Indian ways of living and learn to live like whites. By the 1870s this idea of assimilating Indians into white society had become the policy of the federal government. In 1874 Congress passed the Dawes Severalty Act, which divided tribal land into individual allotments, which Indians were then supposed to use for private family farms. Another aspect of this policy was education. Indians were encouraged to attend both private religious and government schools. These schools usually prohibited the Indians from following such traditional customs as wearing long hair and required them instead to adopt white customs.

Document 14.4 A Young Sioux Woman Goes East to School

On the surface, one of the Indians most successful in white education was Zitkala-sa, or Red Bird, a Sioux woman from the Yankton reservervation in what became the state of South Dakota. In the 1880s she left home to attend a Quaker school for Indian children in Wabash, Indiana. She stayed there for three years before going back home to the reservation. Four years later she returned and finished school. She later studied at Earlham College, a Quaker institution in Richmond, Indiana. Later, under her white name of Gerrtude Simmons Bonnin, she wrote a series of articles describing her life, which appeared in 1900 in the *Atlantic Monthly* magazine.

As you read this account, ask yourself what experiences at school she found difficult? Why, do you think, the school required them? What effect did they really have on her? What should the school have done?

A Young Sioux Woman Goes East to School

Zitkala-sa (Gertrude Simmons Bonnin)

The first turning away from the easy, natural flow of my life occurred in an early spring. It was in my eighth year, in the month of March, I afterward learned. At this age I knew but one language, and that was my mother's native tongue. . . .

"Mother, my friend Judewin is going home with the missionaries. She is going to a more beautiful country than ours; the palefaces told her so!" I said wistfully, wishing in my heart that I too might go.

Mother sat in a chair, and I was hanging on her knee. Within the last two seasons my big brother Dawee had returned from a three years' education in the East, and his coming back influenced my mother to take a farther step from her native way of living. First, it was a change from the buffalo skin to the white man's canvas that covered our wigwam. Now she had given up her wigwam of slender poles, to live, a foreigner, in a home of clumsy logs.

"Yes, my child, several others besides Judewin are going away with the palefaces. Your brother said the missionaries had inquired about his little sister," she said, watching my face very closely.

My heart thumped so hard against my breast, I wondered if she could hear it.

"Did he tell them to take me, mother?" I asked, fearing lest Dawee had forbidden the palefaces to see me, and my hope of going to Wonderland would be entirely blighted.

With a sad, slow smile, she answered: "There! I knew you were wishing to go, because Judewin has filled your ears with the white men's lies. Don't believe a word they say! Their words are sweet, but, my child, their deeds are bitter. You will cry for me, but they will not even soothe you. Stay with me, my little one! Your brother Dawee says that going East, away from your mother, is too hard an experience for his baby sister."

Thus my mother discouraged my curiosity about the lands beyond our eastern horizon; for it was not yet an ambition for Letters that was stirring me. But on the following day the missionaries did come to our very house. I spied them coming up the footpath leading to our cottage. A third man was with them, but he was not my brother Dawee. It was another, a young interpreter, a paleface who had a smattering of the Indian language. I was ready to run out to meet them, but I did not dare to displease my mother. With great glee, I jumped up and down on our ground floor. I begged my mother to open the door, that they would be sure to come to us. Alas! They came, they saw, and they conquered!

Judewin had told the of the great tree where grew red, red apples; and how we could reach out our hands and pick all the red apples we could eat. I had never seen apple trees. I had never tasted more than a dozen red apples in my life; and when I heard of the orchards of the East, I was eager to roam among them. The missionaries smiled into my eyes, and patted my head. I wondered how mother could say such hard words against them.

"Mother, ask them if little girls may have all the red apples they want, when they go East," I whispered aloud in my excitement.

The interpreter heard me, and answered: "Yes, little girl, the nice red apples are for those who pick them; and you will have a ride on the iron horse if you go with these good people."

I had never seen a train, and he knew it.

"Mother, I'm going East! I like big red apples, and I want to ride on the iron horse! Mother, say yes!" I pleaded.

My mother said nothing. The missionaries waited in silence; and my eyes began to blur with tears, though I struggled to choke them back. The

---

From *Atlantic Monthly*, Vol. LXXXV, February 1900.

corners of my mouth twitched, and my mother saw me.

"I am not ready to give you any word," she said to then. "Tomorrow I shall send you my answer by my son."

With this they left us. Alone with my mother, I yielded to my tears, and cried aloud, shaking my head so as not to hear what she was saying to me. This was the first time I had ever been so unwilling to give up my own desire that I refused to hearken to my mother's voice.

There was a solemn silence in our home that night. Before I went to bed I begged the Great Spirit to make my mother willing I should go with the missionaries.

The next morning came, and my mother called me to her side. "My daughter, do you still persist in wishing to leave your mother?" she asked.

"Oh, mother, it is not that I wish to leave you, but I want to see the wonderful Eastern land," I answered.

My dear old aunt came to our house that morning, and I heard her say, "Let her try it."

I hoped that, as usual, my aunt was pleading on my side. My brother Dawee came for mother's decision. I dropped my play, and crept close to my aunt.

"Yes, Dawee, my daughter, though she does not understand what it all means, is anxious to go. She will need an education when she is grown, for then there will be fewer real Dakotas, and many more palefaces: This tearing her away, so young, from her mother is necessary, if I would have her an educated woman. The palefaces, who owe us a large debt for stolen lands, have begun to pay a tardy justice in offering some education to our children. But I know my daughter must suffer keenly in this experiment. For her sake, I dread to tell you my reply to the missionaries. Go, tell them that they may take my little daughter, and that the Great Spirit shall not fail to reward them according to their hearts." . . .

The Cutting of My Long Hair

The first day in the land of apples was a bitter-cold one; for the snow still covered the ground, and the trees were bare. A large bell rang for breakfast, its loud metallic voice crashing through the belfry overhead and into our sensitive ears. The annoying clatter of shoes on bare floors gave us no peace. The constant clash of harsh noises, with an undercurrent of many voices murmuring an unknown tongue, made a bedlam within which I was securely tied. And though my spirit tore itself in struggling for its lost freedom, all was useless.

A paleface woman, with white hair, came up after us. We were placed in a line of girls who were marching into the dining room. These were Indian girls, in stiff shoes and closely clinging dresses. The small girls wore sleeved aprons and shingled hair. As I walked noiselessly in my soft moccasins, I felt like sinking to the floor, for my blanket had been stripped from my shoulders. I looked hard at the Indian girls, who seemed not to care that they were even more immodestly dressed than I, in their tightly fitting clothes. While we marched in, the boys entered at an opposite door. I watched for the three young braves who came in our party. I spied them in the rear ranks, looking as uncomfortable as I felt.

A small bell was tapped, and each of the pupils drew a chair from under the table. Supposing this act meant they were to be seated, I pulled out mine and at once slipped into it from one side. But when I turned my head, I saw that I was the only one seated, and all the rest at our table remained standing. Just as I began to rise, looking shyly around to see how chairs were to be used, a second bell was sounded. All were seated at last, and I had to crawl back into my chair again. I heard a man's voice at one end of the hall, and I looked around to see him. But all the others hung their heads over their plates. As I glanced at the long chain of tables, I caught the eyes of a paleface woman upon me. Immediately I dropped my eyes, wondering why I was so keenly watched by the strange woman. The man ceased his mutterings, and then a third bell was tapped. Every one picked up his knife and fork and began eating. I began crying instead, for by this time I was afraid to venture anything more.

But this eating by formula was not the hardest trial in that first day. Late in the morning, my friend Judewin gave me a terrible warning. Judewin knew a few words of English; and she had overhead the paleface woman talk about cutting our long, heavy hair. Our mothers had taught us that only unskilled warriors who were captured had their hair shingled by the enemy. Among our people, short hair was worn by mourners, and shingled hair by cowards!

We discussed our fate some moments, and when Judewin said, "We have to submit, because they are strong," I rebelled.

"No, I will not submit! I will struggle first!" I answered.

I watched my chance, and when no one noticed I disappeared. I crept up the stairs as quietly as I could in my squeaking shoes—my moccasins had been exchanged for shoes. Along the hall I passed, without knowing whither I was going. Turning aside to an open door, I found a large room with three white beds in it. The windows were covered with dark green curtains, which made the room very dim.

Thankful that no one was there, I directed my steps toward the corner farthest from the door. On my hands and knees I crawled under the bed, and cuddled myself in the dark corner.

From my hiding place I peered out, shuddering with fear whenever I heard footsteps near by. Though in the hall loud voices were calling my name, and I knew that even Judewin was searching for me, I did not open my mouth to answer. Then the steps were quickened and the voices became excited. The sounds came nearer and nearer. Women and girls entered the room. I held my breath and watched them open closet doors and peep behind large trunks. Some one threw up the curtains, and the room was filled with sudden light. What caused them to stoop and look under the bed I do not know. I remember being dragged out, though I resisted by kicking and scratching wildly. In spite of myself, I was carried downstairs and tied fast in a chair.

I cried aloud, shaking my head all the while until I felt the cold blades of the scissors against my neck, and heard them gnaw off one of my thick braids. Then I lost my spirit. Since the day I was taken from my mother I had suffered extreme indignities. People had stared at me. I had been tossed about in the air like a wooden puppet. And now my long hair was shingled like a coward's! In my anguish I moaned for my mother, but no one came to comfort me. Not a soul reasoned quietly with me, as my own mother used to do; for now I was only one of many little animals driven by a herder.

Iron Routine

A loud-clamoring bell awakened us at half past six in the cold winter mornings. From happy dreams of Western rolling lands and unlassoed freedom we tumbled out upon chilly bare floors back again into a paleface day. We had short time to jump into our shoes and clothes, and wet our eyes with icy water, before a small hand bell was vigorously rung for roll call. . . .

A paleface woman, with a yellow-covered roll book open on her arm and a gnawed pencil in her hand, appeared at the door. Her small, tired face was coldly lighted with a pair of large gray eyes. . . .

Relentlessly her pencil black-marked our daily records if we were not present to respond to our names, and no chum of ours had done it successfully for us. No matter if a dull headache or the painful cough of slow consumption had delayed the absentee, there was only time enough to mark the tardiness. It was next to impossible to leave the iron routine after the civilizing machine had once begun its day's buzzing; and as it was inbred in me to suffer in silence rather than to appeal to the ears of one whose open eyes could not see my pain, I have many times trudged in the day's harness heavy-footed, like a dumb sick brute. . . .

I grew bitter, and censured the woman for cruel neglect of our physical ills. I despised the pencils that moved automatically, and the one teaspoon which dealt out, from a large bottle, healing to a row of variously ailing Indian children. I blamed the hard-working, well-meaning, ignorant woman who was inculcating in our hearts her superstitious ideas. Though I was sullen in all my little troubles, as soon as I felt better I was ready again to smile upon the cruel woman. Within a week I was again actively testing the chains which tightly bound my individuality like a mummy for burial. . . .

Incurring My Mother's Displeasure

In the second journey to the East I had not come without some precautions. I had a secret interview with one of our best medicine men, and when I left his wigwam, I carried securely in my sleeve a tiny bunch of magic roots. This possession assured me of friends wherever I should go. So absolutely did I believe in its charms that I wore it through all the school routine for more than a year. Then, before I lost my faith in the dead roots, I lost the little buckskin bag containing all my good luck.

At the close of this second term of three years I was the proud owner of my first diploma. The following autumn I ventured upon a college career against my mother's will.

I had written for her approval, but in her reply I found no encouragement. She called my notice to her neighbors' children, who had completed their education in three years. They had returned to their homes, and were then talking English with the frontier settlers. Her few words hinted that I had better give up my slow attempt to learn the white man's ways, and be content to roam over the prairies and find my living upon wild roots. I silenced her by deliberate disobedience.

Thus, homeless and heavy-hearted, I began anew my life among strangers. As I hid myself in my little room in the college dormitory, away from the scornful and yet curious eyes of the students, I pined for sympathy. Often I wept in secret, wishing I had gone West, to be nourished by my mother's love, instead of remaining among a cold race whose hearts were frozen hard with prejudice.

During the fall and winter seasons I scarcely had a real friend, though by that time several of my classmates were courteous to me at a safe distance. . . .

. . . I appeared as the college representative in [an oratorical] contest. This time the competition was among orators from different colleges in our state. It was held at the state capital, in one of the largest opera houses.

Here again was a strong prejudice against my people. In the evening, as the great audience filled the house, the student bodies began warring among themselves. Fortunately, I was spared witnessing any of the noisy wrangling before the contest began. The slurs against the Indian that stained the lips of our opponents were already burning like a dry fever within my breast.

But after the orations were delivered a deeper burn awaited me. There, before that vast ocean of eyes, some college rowdies threw out a large white flag, with a drawing of a most forlorn Indian girl on it. Under this they had printed in bold black letters words that ridiculed the college which was represented by a "squaw." Such worse than barbarian rudeness embittered me. While we waited for the verdict of the judges, I gleamed fiercely upon the throngs of palefaces. My teeth were hard set, as I saw the white flag still floating insolently in the air.

Then anxiously we watched the man carry toward the stage the envelope containing the final decision.

There were two prizes given, that night, and one of them was mine!

The evil spirit laughed within me when the white flag dropped out of sight, and the hands which furled it hung limp in defeat.

Leaving the crowd as quickly as possible, I was soon in my room. The rest of the night I sat in an armchair and gazed into the crackling fire. I laughed no more in triumph when thus alone. The little taste of victory did not satisfy a hunger in my heart. In my mind I saw my mother far away on the Western plains, and she was holding a charge against me.

Retrospection

Leaving my mother, I returned to the school in the East. As months passed over me, I slowly comprehended that the large army of white teachers in Indian schools had a larger missionary creed than I had suspected.

It was one which included self-preservation quite as much as Indian education. When I saw an opium-eater holding a position as teacher of Indians, I did not understand what good was expected, until a Christian in power replied that this pumpkin-colored creature had a feeble mother to support. An inebriate paleface sat stupid in a doctor's chair, while Indian patients carried their ailments to untimely graves, because his fair wife was dependent upon him for her daily food. . . .

My illness, which prevented the conclusion of my college course, together with my mother's stories of the encroaching frontier settlers, left me in no mood to strain my eyes in searching for latent good in my white co-workers. At this stage of my own evolution, I was ready to curse men of small capacity for being the dwarfs their God had made them. In the process of my education I had lost all consciousness of the nature world about me. Thus, when a hidden rage took me to the small white-walled prison which I then called my room, I unknowingly turned away from my one salvation.

Alone in my room, I sat like the petrified Indian woman of whom my mother used to tell me. I wished my heart's burdens would turn me to unfeeling stone. But alive, in my tomb, I was destitute!

For the white man's papers I had given up my faith in the Great Spirit. For these same papers I had forgotten the healing in trees and brooks. On account of my mother's simple view of life, and my lack of any, I gave her up, also. I made no friends among the race of people I loathed. Like a slender tree, I had been uprooted from my mother, nature, and God. I was shorn of my branches, which had waved in sympathy and love for home and friends. The natural coat of bark which had protected my oversensitive nature was scraped off to the very quick.

Now a cold bare pole, I seemed to be planted in a strange earth. Still, I seemed to hope a day would come when my mute aching head, reared upward to the sky, would flash a zigzag lightning across the heavens. With this dream of vent for a long-pent consciousness, I walked again amid the crowds.

At last, one weary day in the schoolroom, a new idea presented itself to me. It was a new way of solving the problem of my inner self. I liked it. Thus I resigned my position as teacher; and now I am in an Eastern city, following the long course of study I have set for myself. Now, as I look back upon the recent past, I see it from a distance, as a whole. I remember how, from morning till evening, many specimens of civilized peoples visited the Indian school. The city folks with canes and eyeglasses, the countrymen with sunburnt cheeks and clumsy feet, forgot their relative social ranks in an ignorant curiosity. Both sorts of these Christian palefaces were alike astounded at seeing the children of savage warriors so docile and industrious.

In answers to their shallow inquiries they received the students' sample work to look upon. Examining the neatly figured pages, and gazing upon the Indian girls and boys bending over their books, the white visitors walked out of the schoolhouse well satisfied; they were educating the children of the red man! They were paying a liberal fee to the government employees in whose able hands lay the small forest of Indian timber.

In this fashion many have passed idly through the Indian schools during the last decade, afterward to boast of their charity to the North American Indian. But few there are who have paused to question whether real life or long-standing death lies beneath this semblance of civilization.

The Farmers' Frontier

During the last half of the nineteenth century, immigrants poured into the United States. Many settled in growing cities; many others moved to agricultural regions hoping to acquire farms of their own. By this time the farming frontier had moved west to the Great Plains, where farmers found challenges far different from regions farther east.

The plains had few trees, and the lack of wood was hard for settlers who had moved from heavily wooded areas in the eastern United States or Europe. Wood for fences, houses, and other buildings had to be brought in. As a result, many settlers lived first in sod houses, constructed of chunks of soil held together by the grass which had grown in it. Many also found the countryside bleak and lonely.

Rainfall was also unreliable as well. Droughts often drastically reduced or destroyed crops. Insects, especially grasshoppers, often swept across the plains, destroying crops and gardens. In the two selections below settlers describe their experiences while settling on the plains of Kansas.

Document 14.5 Letter from a Kansas Pioneer Woman

Although life on the Great Plains was hard, the young woman who wrote this letter from Morton County, in western Kansas, tried to maintain her optimism.

Letter from a Kansas Pioneer Woman

I am writing in my far western home, the one I love best. Let me describe it to you. It is what we call in Morton County a dugout. Ours is dug four feet down, and has a frame part about five feet high on top of the ground. It is 12x20 inside, with a whitewashed ceiling and a canvas partition. . . .

It is hard work to come west to make a home. . . . I'll tell you how we manage: there are four of us. My husband and two little boys . . . and myself comprise our family. This year everything was a failure in this country. Everybody left that could, but we have a few cattle and enough corn stalks to keep them alive till grass comes. Some mornings there would be fourteen wagons going east, but they are not all gone, for we are here yet. Last spring everything was fine; good prospects for plenty in the fall; but the hot winds came and the rain did not. Out of the eighty acres of spring crops we planted we got nothing but corn stalks, not an ear of corn or a kernel for the seed. We may be thankful for the stalks, as some did not even get stalks. We are 47 miles from the railroad and the only way to get a living is to freight. It takes four days to go to the railroad and back with a load. My man has gone for a load now. While he is gone I take care of thirteen head of cattle, two pigs, one colt, and milk four cows, do my house work, make lace and crazy patch. This morning I sawed a new stove-pipe hole through the roof and put up a tin to run the pipe out through.

The boys are at school. I sleep with a double-barreled shot-gun loaded in the closet and a revolver handy. My nearest neighbor is one mile northeast. . . . It is hard work, hard work, I tell you, and little pay. We have already had a bitter touch of winter. It began by raining. . . . Then the snow came and the wind with it, and for four days and nights kept snowing and blowing.

Through it all stock had to be looked after and run under shelter. When they get out in a storm they drift with the wind, and get lost, often killed. Times are hard but I am generous and when you come out west just stay awhile at our dug-out.

You shall have pancakes and meat grease for breakfast—maybe a little coffee. Light bread for dinner, and mush and milk for supper the year round, with occasionally a young jack-rabbit fried with some milk gravy.

Document 14.6 Immigrants on the Farm Frontier (1870–1874)

In 1870 Swedish immigrants Ida Lindgren and her family arrived near the town of Manhattan, Kansas, hoping to begin farming. The letters she wrote reveal her feelings about this new land, much different from what she was familiar with. What are her perceptions of her life on the frontier? How do Lindgren's perceptions compare with how you have previously seen the West portrayed?

Immigrants on the Farm Frontier (1870–1874)

Ida Lindgren

15 May 1870

What shall I say? Why has the Lord brought us here? Oh, I feel so oppressed, so unhappy! Two whole days it took us to get here and they were not the least trying part of our travels. We sat on boards in the work wagon, packed in so tightly that we could not move a foot, and we drove across endless, endless prairies, on narrow roads; no, not roads, tracks like those in the fields at home when they harvested grain. No forest but only a few trees which grow along the rivers and creeks. And then here and there you see a homestead and pass a little settlement. The closer we came to Lake Sibley the more desolate the country seemed and the roads were altogether frightful, almost trackless. When we finally saw Lake Sibley, at twelve o'clock at night, it consisted of four houses, two larger ones and two small, very small, as well as two under construction. The rooms Albinson had written he wished to rent us were not available but we were quartered here in Albinson's attic. The attic is divided into three rooms but with no doors; I have hung up a sheet in front of our "door." When I immediately asked, after we arrived, to go up with the children and put them to bed, there was no table, no chair, no bed, nothing, and there we were to stay! I set the candle on the floor, sat down beside it, took the children in my lap and burst into tears. I feel about to do so now too, I cannot really pull myself together and the Albinsons appear quite uncomfortable every time they see me. The Indians are not so far away from here, I can understand, and all the men you see coming by, riding or driving wagons, are armed with revolvers and long carbines, and look like highway robbers. . . .

Gustaf is out with Magnus and Albinson to look at the land he bought and to see if there is any that Magnus would like to have. . . .

5 January 1871

. . . I must tell you about our Christmas! On "Little Christmas Eve," Sylvan (he had been in Chicago but came here to celebrate Christmas with us) and Tekla Littorin (she is employed four miles on the other side of Manhattan) arrived; then we all went over to Magnus and his family for Christmas

---

From *Letters from the Promised Land: Swedes in America, 1840–1914*, edited by H. Arnold Barton. Reprinted by permission of University of Minnesota Press, 1975.

Eve. They had everything so fine and cozy, three rooms downstairs and the attic all in order, and a Christmas tree of green cedar with candles and bonbons and apples on it, and the coffee table set, so it was really Christmas-like, and because of that I could not tear my thoughts away from you and from my old home and the tears kept welling up! . . . Then we had a few Christmas presents, the finest was a rocking chair which Magnus and his family gave us. From Gustaf I got two serving dishes, since we had none before, from Olga a rolling pin for cookies and three dozen clothespins to hang up wet clothes with when you do laundry, from Hugo a pair of woolen mittens, from Littorin a knitting bag, from Hedenskog material for a little sofa which we have made for the children to sleep on, from Carlson a pair of fire tongs.

I gave Magnus and the family a sofa cover, which I sewed last summer to exhibit, and a couple of pictures of Gustaf Vasa which we had with us. Hugo gave them a pair of drinking glasses and Olga gave Magnus a pipe pouch and Johanna clothespins like those I got. Helge had himself sewn a little lamp mat for them. I gave Gustaf a pair of real coarse, strong gloves for working, and Olga, Hugo, and Helge had gotten together to buy him a hat. Olga and Hugo had earned the money themselves that they used for Christmas presents.

After we had eaten our rice pudding and Christmas cookies, we sang a few hymns and "Hosianna," and then we broke up, though we all slept there, all the bachelors in the attic, Magnus and family in the kitchen, Gustaf, the younger children, and myself in the bedroom, and Olga, Tekla, and their hired girl in the parlor.

We stayed until the morning after the second day of Christmas and then we went home. Tekla, Ida, and Anna stayed on there, and so instead we took their hired girl and their hired man to help us slaughter our pig, which we were to have for New Year's, when Magnus and his family were to come to us. After we had finished with the slaughtering, I got started with laundry while we had Johanna's hired girl here, for it had been so cold that we had not been able to do any washing for some weeks, so now we had so much laundry. Washing is the worst work I have to do, for my hands can't take it and they have been so miserable, swollen and raw, that all the knuckles bled, but now it is better. . . .

All my menfolk are out in the woods today to cut fence rails; they took lunch with them so I don't know how long they will be away. . . . Now, dear Mamma, I will end for today, for I must tidy up a little here in the room before they come back from the woods, since it is Twelfth Night, and then I must skin two small hares for this evening. . . .

9 February 1871

. . . Magnus was here for a while this morning, so I can send greetings from them. They are well, but their hired girl has left so that Johanna now has to do everything herself, as I do. With the difference, however, that they are only two plus their hired man, while we are ten to bake and cook and wash up for every day, and worst of all, to wash clothes for. There is not much time for me to sit and do any handwork. America may be good in many respects, but certainly not for having servants. For no matter how good they may be in Sweden, as soon as they reach America's free soil, they become far from good and want instead to be gentlemen and ladies themselves, and would rather be waited on than wait on others. It is hard to get used to this, and therefore I think it is better to be one's own maid, though one gets awfully tired sometimes in both the back and legs. And my hands will not really accustom themselves to these tasks; they are sometimes roses, sometimes burrs, but never lilies smooth as satin. . . .

18 October 1871

. . . I was alone at home with the younger children, for Hugo had ridden over to Lindesfrid in the morning to help with the corn picking there, and around noon there was such a smell and smoke from burnt grass that I immediately suspected there was a prairie fire somewhere. Suddenly the smoke was so thick and ashes flew around (it was blowing up a real storm and the wind lay this way), that I couldn't see the nearest hills. I believed then that the fire was right upon us, so I ran in and gathered up the silver and Gustaf's watch and a little money all in a bundle, and put Anna on my arm and took Ida by the hand and ran through the woods down to the river. Oh, Mamma, how my heart pounded! I felt I could do nothing else, alone as I was with my little ones, for I believed that with the force with which the fire was moving today, it would go across the cornfield and set off all six haystacks and then there would be no saving the house. And then the woods were close by and there are now so many dry leaves that I felt there was no safety there. No, only in the river; there must I fly; if the fire should come so close to us I would take both children in my arms and go as far out into the water as I could: that was what I thought.

But first we sat down on the bank; Anna did not understand the danger, but Ida cried so bitterly that I had to try to calm her, fearful as I was myself. I told them, "We should pray to the Lord that He protect us." And so I prayed as well as I could, and the children repeated after me, and last of all we prayed for rain—for it had now been dry for several months and everything was so dried out that the fire could range freely, and no autumn grain could be sowed either until rain came. We sat there a couple of hours; once I took water in a spoon to drink but could not for it was black with ash that had flown here. When I thought the smoke had become less, I had the children sit where they were and I went up onto a rise to look.

Behold, there stood our house and home and the six haystacks unharmed, but a few that were out in the field and were intended for the owner were burned up, and the fire flamed on the other side on the hills and dales. We then went home, and when we came in, we fell on our knees and thanked the Lord who had protected us and our house and home. A little while later Hugo came: they had seen the fire coming toward us, and Gustaf had sent him to help me, and a half hour or hour later Lindgren came himself, for all danger was far from past. I now felt so calm and glad, but they had to be out with water and rags with others to fight the fire until late at night, when all danger was over here. How far the fire later continued, we don't know, but many, many people had their hay burned up, and we also had two small stacks at Lindesfrid that were lost. At Magnus's no hay burned but a section of fence. . . .

25 August 1874

. . . We have not had rain since the beginning of June, and then with this heat and often strong winds as well, you can imagine how everything has dried out. There has also been a general lamentation and fear for the coming year. We have gotten a fair amount of wheat, rye, and oats, for they are ready so early, but no one here will get corn or potatoes. We have a few summer potatoes, but many don't even have that, and we thought and hoped we would get a good crop of other potatoes, but will evidently get none. Instead of selling the oats and part of the rye as we had expected, we must now use them for the livestock, since there was no corn. We are glad we have the oats (for many don't have any and must feed wheat to the stock) and had hoped to have the corn leaves to add to the fodder. But then one fine day there came millions, trillions of grasshoppers in great clouds, hiding the sun, and coming down onto the fields, eating up everything that was still there, the leaves on the trees, peaches, grapes, cucumbers, onions, cabbage, everything, everything. Only the peach stones still hung on the trees, showing what had once been there.

They are not the kind of grasshoppers we see in Sweden but are large, grayish ones. Now most of them have moved southward, to devastate other areas, since there was nothing more to consume here. Certainly it is sad and distressing and depressing for body and soul to find that no matter how hard one drudges and works, one still has nothing, less than nothing.

Don't you think, Mamma, that I could bear a little bit of success? I think myself that I could well manage a little, but the Lord sees best what we need, and therefore He daily strikes and humiliates us, now in one way, now in another. But still He has not crushed our stubborn hearts. As burdened as I feel, my heart is still not weighed down; it still rises up from time to time.

Module XIV

Questions for Study and Critical Thinking

1. According to She-Walks-With-Her-Shawl, who started the Battle of Little Big Horn?

2. What does she say about charges that the battle was a massacre? That the Sioux tortured the soldiers?

3. In what ways does One Bull's account agree or disagree with that of She-Walks-With-Her-Shawl?

4. On what points does Offley's account agree with those of She-Walks-With-Her-Shawl and One Bull? How do the accounts differ?

5. What do you think really happened?

6. What aspects of white education made Red Bird (Zitkala-sa) unhappy?

7. Was there anything about the school that could have been changed to make education there a good experience for Indian children?

8. If you had been in charge of government policy during this time, what would you change in Indian education?

9. How does the young woman in Morton County, Kansas portray her life on the frontier?

10. How does this portrayal compare with your previous image of frontier life?

11. What problems did the Lindgrens face in Kansas?

12. What was Ida Lindgren's overall feeling about her life in Kansas?

13. Is the view presented in these letters similar or different from what you have previously thought about life on the frontier? In what ways?

Module XV

Work and Workers in the Age of Big Business

Introduction

What was it like to be a worker in the age of Andrew Carnegie and J.P. Morgan? Were working conditions good or bad? How were workers treated? Were conditions improving? What did workers say about their work and lives?

To answer these questions, we have several kinds of sources. First, there are statistics. These can give us hard facts about workers' wages, the cost of living (which we can then compare with their wages), and the number of accidents resulting in death and injury. These sources might be called objective evidence because they present hard facts. Then there is subjective evidence, which tells us how people felt. How, for example, did workers themselves feel about their conditions. Did they think they were improving?

Finally, people in different positions often have different perspectives about what is happening. Not only can we look at what workers thought; we can also look at how bosses saw the situation. In this period we see the first management consultants, who tried to advise businessmen on how to conduct their business. What did they advise? And what effect did their advice have on bosses and workers?

In this chapter we will look at each of these kinds of sources. As you read them, ask yourself, What does this tell me about what it was like to be a worker during this time?

Document 15.1 Wages of Iron and Steel Workers

The table below shows the wages of iron and steel workers. In order to compare wages over any period of time, you must make sure you are comparing the same type of thing. Here, one of the variables is the state from which the wages were reported. What state or states should you use to make a comparison across the whole period?

In the period 1865–1900 these wages fluctuated, often dramatically. What caused these fluctuations? Do wages increase over the whole period, do they decline or do they remain steady?

Table 15.1

Wages in the Iron and Steel Industry, 1858–1900

Furnace keepers, pig-iron blast furnaces, 1858–1900, by year and state

Year	State	Sex	Average hours per week	Rate per day (dollars) Lowest, highest, average
1858	Pennsylvania	M	(1)	1.70–1.70–1.70
1859	Pennsylvania	M	(1)	1.67–1.67–1.67
1860	Pennsylvania	M	(1)	1.85–1.85–1.85
1861	Pennsylvania	M	(1)	1.90–1.90–1.90
1862	Pennsylvania	M	(1)	1.68–1.68–1.68
1863	Pennsylvania	M	(1)	1.90–1.90–1.90
1864	Pennsylvania	M	(1)	2.70–2.70–2.70
1865	Pennsylvania	M	(1)	2.49–2.49–2.49
1866	Pennsylvania	M	(1)	2.41–2.41–2.41
1867	Pennsylvania	M	(1)	2.53–2.53–2.53
1868	Pennsylvania	M	(1)	2.53–2.53–2.53
1869	Pennsylvania	M	(1)	2.77–2.77–2.77
1870	Pennsylvania	M	(1)	2.77–2.77–2.77
1871	Pennsylvania	M	(1)	2.78–2.78–2.78
1872	Pennsylvania	M	(1)	3.15–3.15–3.15
1873	Pennsylvania	M	(1)	2.58–3.27–2.81
1874	Pennsylvania	M	(1)	1.25–4.00–1.94
1875	Pennsylvania	M	(1)	1.60–1.94–1.71
1876	Pennsylvania	M	(1)	.85–2.37–1.67
1877	Ohio	M	60–84–77	.86–1.90–1.32
	Pennsylvania	M	(1)	1.56–1.5–1.56
1878	Ohio	M	(1)	.86–1.75–1.37
	Pennsylvania	M	67–84–8	2.79–2.25–1.36
1879	Ohio	M	(1)	.86–2.80–1.51
	Pennsylvania	M	84–84–8	4.79–2.50–1.59
1880	Ohio	M	70–84–77	1.00–2.65–1.65
	Pennsylvania	M	84–84–84	1.78–1.90–1.84
1882	Pennsylvania	M	84–84–84	1.90–2.00–1.95
1883	Pennsylvania	M	(1)	2.25–2.25–2.25
1884	Michigan	M	(1)	1.85–1.85–1.85
	New Jersey	M	70–84–80	1.59–2.53–1.82
	Ohio	M	(1)	1.00–2.25–1.64

US Department of Labor, Bureau of Labor Statistics.

United States Department of Labor, Bureau of Labor Statistics, *History of* Wages in the United States from Colonial Times to 1928, Revision of Bulletin No. 499 (Washington, D.C., 1934), pp. 247–248.

Year	State	Sex	Average hours per week	Rate per day (dollars) Lowest, highest, average
	Pennsylvania	M	(1)	2.25–2.25–2.25
	Indiana	M	70–70–70	1.8–1.85–1.85
	Maryland	M	84–84–84	1.50–1.50–1.50
	New York	M	84–84–84	1.67–1.85–1.79
	Ohio	M	72–84–84	1.35–2.00–1.64
1885	Indiana	M	70–70–70	1.85–1.85–1.85
	Maryland	M	84–84–84	1.50–1.50–1.50
	New York	M	84–84–84	1.67–1.85–1.79
	Ohio	M	72–84–84	1.35–2.00–1.64
	Pennsylvania	M	84–84–84	1.80–2.25–2.02
	Tennessee	M	84–84–84	1.80–1.80–1.80
	Virginia	M	84–84–84	1.50–2.30–1.93
1886	Pennsylvania	M	(1)	2.05–2.05–2.05
1887	Ohio	M	70–84–74	1.40–2.25–1.91
	Pennsylvania	M	84–84–84	2.10–2.25–2.18
	Wisconsin	M	(1)	3.10–3.10–3.10
1888	Illinois	M	84–84–84	3.25–3.25–3.25
	Michigan	M	84–84–84	1.80–2.00–1.90
	New York	M	70–84–75	1.88–2.15–1.98
	Ohio	M	84–84–84	2.40–2.40–2.40
	Pennsylvania	M	84–84–84	1.85–2.25–2.04
	Tennessee	M	(1)	1.85–1.85–1.85
	Virginia	M	84–84–84	1.40–2.00–1.67
	West Virginia	M	84–84–84	2.40–2.40–2.40
1889	Alabama	M	84–84–84	1.25–2.00–1.89
	Georgia	M	84–84–84	1.65–1.65–1.65
	Illinois	M	84–84–84	3.10–3.25–3.21
	Indiana	M	84–84–84	1.70–1.70–1.70
	Maryland	M	72–72–72	1.58–1.58–1.58
	Michigan	M	84–84–84	2.00–2.00–2.00
	Missouri	M	84–84–84	1.70–1.70–1.70
	New York	M	84–84–84	1.85–2.15–1.98
	Ohio	M	84–84–84	1.80–2.50–2.07
	Pennsylvania	M	56–84–83	1.08–3.00–1.91
	Tennessee	M	77–84–82	1.75–2.00–1.89
	Virginia	M	84–84–84	1.50–2.00–1.83
	West Virginia	M	84–84–84	1.65–2.40–2.01
	Pennsylvania	M	84–84–84	1.90–2.25–2.02
	Wisconsin	M	84–84–84	3.00–3.00–3.00
1890	Alabama	M	84–84–84	2.00–2.00–2.00
	New York	M	(1)	2.00–2.00–2.00
	Ohio	M	72–84–76	1.00–2.30–1.43
1891	New York	M	(1)	1.75–2.20–1.93
	Pennsylvania	M	(1)	2.00–2.00–2.00
1892	Ohio	M	58–84–72	1.00–3.00–1.69

Year	State	Sex	Average hours per week	Rate per day (dollars) Lowest, highest, average
	Pennsylvania	M	(1)	2.25–2.25–2.25
1893	New Jersey	M	84–84–84	1.75–1.75–1.75
1895	Ohio	M	84–84–84	.75–2.25–1.70
1896	Pennsylvania	M	84–84–84	1.68–1.69–1.69
1897	Ohio	(1)	84–84–84	.75–2.20–1.50
	Pennsylvania	M	(1)	2.00–2.10–2.06
1898	Pennsylvania	M	(1)	2.10–2.20–2.17
1899	Alabama	M	84–84–84	1.75–1.85–1.82
	Pennsylvania	M	(1)	2.40–2.50–2.47
	Alabama	M	84–84–84	1.80–1.85–1.83

Document 15.2 Price Indexes, 1866–1890

Another important factor in standards of living is prices. The price indexes below show the prices of important commodities in each year and a composite figure for all prices. The index shows the prices as a percentage of the price in 1914, rather than in dollars. So a number over 100 means a price higher than in 1914, while a number under 100 means a lower price. Is the general trend of prices up or down? Why?

Price Indexes, 1866–1890

(1910–14 = 100)

Year	All commodities	Farm products	Foods products	Hides and leather products	Textile	Fuel and Lighting
1890	82	71	86	74	103	72
1889	81	67	79	80	99	71
1888	86	75	86	86	98	72
1887	85	71	86	92	98	70
1886	82	68	78	101	100	70
1885	85	72	84	105	105	72
1884	93	82	93	111	109	77
1883	101	87	103	107	116	89
1882	108	99	114	108	119	92
1881	103	89	106	109	119	91
1880	100	80	96	113	128	92

US Bureau of the Census.

Historical Statistics of the United States: Colonial Times to 1957 (Washington, D.C.: Bureau of the Census, 1960), p. 115.

Year	All commodities	Farm products	Foods products	Hides and leather products	Textile	Fuel and Lighting
1879	90	72	90	100	114	80
1878	91	72	93	95	115	93
1877	106	89	115	109	125	108
1876	110	89	113	104	138	127
1875	118	99	120	123	141	128
1874	126	102	126	128	151	135
1873	133	103	122	132	175	148
1872	136	108	121	130	177	153
1871	130	102	130	126	170	152
1870	135	112	139	128	179	134
1869	151	128	154	134	194	166
1868	158	138	171	126	197	149
1867	162	133	167	132	220	144
1866	174	140	173	146	245	160

Metal and metal products	Building materials	Chemicals and drugs	House furnishing goods	Spirits	Miscellaneous
123	84	90	91	—	89
116	81	101	94	74	80
121	80	103	94	80	73
119	81	97	92	77	75
110	82	99	94	79	74
109	81	100	99	79	78
124	84	105	105	81	78
144	85	110	110	83	93
157	88	114	109	80	93
150	83	120	109	81	90
166	81	120	117	83	91
134	74	120	105	82	90
126	72	127	109	82	88
141	80	136	118	86	95
157	84	140	123	86	98
175	90	149	134	88	98
194	101	176	149	78	111
243	106	181	160	75	115
257	107	175	159	73	125
203	102	177	154	74	120
200	101	199	164	78	128
227	110	227	178	86	136
225	116	204	178	117	153
248	120	229	196	146	162
278	128	283	220	154	170

Documnet 15.3 Workers' Views

Another kind of evidence comes from workers' own testimony. This is, of course, subjective, but it can provide us with much different and richer information than statistics.

A Miner's Story (1902)

Thomas O'Donnell

I am thirty-five years old, married, the father of four children, and have lived in the coal region all my life. Twenty-three of these years have been spent working in and around the mines. My father was a miner. He died ten years ago from "miners' asthma" [black lung disease].

Three of my brothers are miners; none of us had any opportunities to acquire an education. We were sent to school (such a school as there was in those days) until we were about twelve years of age, and then we were put into the screen room of a breaker to pick slate. From there we went inside the mines as driver boys. As we grew stronger we were taken on as laborers, where we served until able to call ourselves miners. We were given work in the breasts and gangways. There were five of us boys. One lies in the cemetery—fifty tons of top rock dropped on him. He was killed three weeks after he got his job as a miner—a month before he was to be married.

In the fifteen years I have worked as a miner I have earned the average rate of wages any of us coal heavers get. To-day I am little better off than when I started to do for myself. I have $100 on hand; I am not in debt; I hope to be able to weather the strike without going hungry.

I am only one of the hundreds you see on the street every day. The muscles on my arms are no harder, the callous on my palms no deeper than my neighbors' whose entire life has been spent in the coal region. By years I am only thirty-five. But look at the marks on my body; look at the lines of worriment on my forehead; see the gray hairs on my head and in my mustache; take my general appearance, and you'll think I'm ten years older.

You need not wonder why. Day in and day out, from Monday morning to Saturday evening, between the rising and the setting of the sun, I am in the underground workings of the coal mines. From the seams water trickles into the ditches along the gangways; if not water, it is the gas which hurls us to eternity and the props and timbers to a chaos.

Our daily life is not a pleasant one. When we put on our oil soaked suit in the morning we can't guess all the dangers which threaten our lives. We walk sometimes miles to the place—to the man way or traveling way, or to the mouth of the shaft on top of the slope. And then we enter the darkened chambers of the mines. On our right and on our left we see the logs that keep up the top and support the sides which may crush us into shapeless masses, as they have done to many of our comrades.

We get old quickly. Powder, smoke, after-damp, bad air—all combine to bring furrows to our faces and asthma to our lungs. I did not strike because I wanted to; I struck because I had to. A miner—the same as any other workman—must earn fair living wages, or he can't live. And it is not how much you get that counts. It is how much what you get will buy. I have gone through it all, and I think my case is a good sample.

I was married in 1890, when I was 23 years old—quite a bit above the age when we miner boys get into double harness. The woman I married is like myself. She was born beneath the shadow of a dirt bank; her chances for school weren't any better than mine; but she did have to learn how to keep house on a certain amount of money. After we paid the preacher for tying the knot we had just $185 in cash, good health and the good wishes of many friends to start us off.

Our cash was exhausted in buying furniture for housekeeping. In 1890 work was not so plentiful, and by the time our first baby came there was room for much doubt as to how we would pull out. Low wages, and not much over half time in those years, made us hustle. In 1890–91, from June to May, I earned $368.72. That represented eleven months' work, or an average of $33.52 per month. Our rent

---

From *Independent 54*, June 12, 1902.

was $10 per month; store not less than $20. And then I had my oil suits and gum boots to pay for. The result was that after the first year and a half of our married life we were in debt. Not much, of course, and not as much as many of my neighbors, men of larger families, and some who made less money, or in whose case there had been sickness or accident or death. These are all things which a miner must provide for.

I have had fairly good work since I was married. I made the average of what we contract miners are paid; but, as I said before, I am not much better off than when I started.

In 1896 my wife was sick eleven weeks. The doctor came to my house almost every day. He charged me $20 for his services. There was medicine to buy. I paid the drug store $18 in that time. Her mother nursed her, and we kept a girl in the kitchen at $1.50 a week, which cost me $15 for ten weeks, besides the additional living expenses.

In 1897, just a year afterward, I had a severer trial. And mind, in those years, we were only working about half time. But in the fall of that year one of my brothers struck a gas feeder. There was a terrible explosion. He was hurled downward in the breast and covered with the rush of coal and rock. I was working only three breasts away from him and for a moment was unable to realize what had occurred. Myself and a hundred others were soon at work, however, and in a short while we found him, horribly burned over his whole body, his laborer dead alongside of him.

He was my brother. He was single and had been boarding. He had no home of his own. I didn't want him taken to the hospital, so I directed the driver of the ambulance to take him to my house. Besides being burned, his right arm and left leg were broken, and he was hurt internally. The doctors—there were two at the house when we got there—said he would die. But he didn't. He is living and a miner today. But he lay in bed fourteen weeks, and was unable to work for seven weeks after he got out of bed. He had no money when he was hurt except the amount represented by his pay. All of the expenses for doctors, medicine, extra help and his living were borne by me, except $25, which another brother gave me. The last one had none to give. Poor work, low wages and a sickly woman for a wife had kept him scratching for his own family.

It is nonsense to say I was not compelled to keep him, that I could have sent him to a hospital or the almshouse. We are American citizens and we don't go to hospitals and poorhouses. . . .

Document 15.4 Part of the Working Class

Rose Pastor Stokes was a Jewish immigrant, born in Poland in 1979. With her mother she later emigrated to England and then to the United States. As a girl in Cleveland, she worked as a cigar maker–an experience that shaped her viewpoint. Later as a young woman she became a journalist in New York City, writing for the *Jewish Daily News,* which was published in Yiddish and English. She supported all of the major strikes of the period. In a storybook episode, she married James Graham Phelps Stokes, a political activist and also a member of one of New York's wealthiest and most socially prominent families. When the United States entered World War I, Stokes, like some other radicals, opposed the war. She also became one of the founding members of the U.S. Communist Party.

Part of the Working Class

Rose Pastor Stokes

Our lives were like our neighbors' lives. The Installment man came Monday mornings. There was not always the dollar to give him. We would take the money from the bread we needed, to pay for the blankets we needed as much. The same blankets, in the store, were half the price. All the neighbors knew it. My mother discovered it for herself. She raged against the Installment Robbers. "But how many poor workers are there who can buy for cash? Yes! That's why these leeches can drain our blood on the Installment Plan!"

[My stepfather] loved my mother. He would have given her the moon and stars for playthings had he been able. The least he could bear to let her have were the few cheap new things he was paying on. His work kept him driving his horse and wagon about the city—often, in the avenues of the wealthy. Sometimes he'd be called into the homes of the rich to cart away old magazines, or bottles, or rags, or old plumbing material, or discarded what-not. He knew the beautiful things the rich lived with.

My step-father's gains were uncertain. Some days he'd clear two or three or three and a half dollars. On other days there would be no gains at all. There would even be losses through a bad "buy." Or he would be cheated in the sale of his load. On such days the horse had to get his feed as when he salvaged two or three dollars from his labor. I brought home little enough, that first winter: between one and two dollars a week, at first. After that, from two and a half to three and a half dollars a week; and toward the end of the winter nearer four.

Food became so scarce in our cupboard that we almost measured out every square inch of bread. There was nothing left for clothing and shoes. I wore mine till the snow and slush came through. I had often to sit all day at my bench with icy feet in wet leather.

I was working ten or eleven hours a day [at cigar making] with swift, sure hands. Mr. Wertheim had said, one morning: "Rose Pastor, you're the quickest and best worker in the shop!" I didn't know or think how much I was earning for Mr. Wertheim, but I knew I was getting hunger and cold for my portion.

All winter long I wore the gingham dress and thin jacket. Every morning of that winter, when my mother tucked my lunch of bread and milk and an apple—or orange—or banana—newspaper-wrapped under my arm and opened the door to let me out into the icy dawn, I felt the agony that tugged at her mother-heart. "Walk fast," she would always say, "walk as fast as you can, Rosalie. Remember, it is better to walk fast in the cold."

After the long day in the stogie factory, and after supper and the chores for mother, there was my book—there were Lamb's *Tales*—the magic of words. . . . Before the kitchen stove, when the house was asleep, I'd throw off my shoes, thaw out the icy tissues that bit all day into my consciousness, and lose myself in the loves and losses, the sorrows and joys, the gore-dripping tragedies and gay comedies of kings and queens, lords and ladies of olden times. I read and re-read the "Tales" with never-flagging interest. But (and this is perhaps a noteworthy fact) with complete detachment. Not then, nor later, when I read Shakespeare in the text did I ever, for even a fleeting moment identify myself with the people of Shakespeare's dramas. The rich lords and ladies, the ruling kings and queens of whom the supreme dramatist wrote in such noble strain, were alien to me. They moved in a different world. On the other hand, there lurked in my heart an undefined feeling of resentment over the fact that his clowns were always poor folk. He seemed never to draw a poor man save to make him an object of ridicule. Instinctively, I identified myself with his poor.

At the end of winter I had quit the shop under the viaduct, and Spring found me in Mr. Brudno's "factory." Mr. Brudno ran what cigar makers in Ohio called a "buckeye." A "buckeye" is a cigar "factory" in a private home. In other words, it was a sweat shop.

In the three small rooms that comprised Mr. Brudno's stogie "factory" were a dozen scattered benches. Of the dozen workers at the bench not counting strippers, bookers, and packers, six were Brudno's very own: four sons and two daughters. Several others were blood-relations—first cousins;

---

and still another was a distant connection by marriage. The remaining few were "outsiders"; young girls and boys and I came to fill the last unoccupied bench.

Mr. Brudno was a picturesque patriarch, with his long black beard, and his tall black skull-cap. He had come from the old country with a little money (not acquired through toil, rumor had it) and was determined to get rich quick in America. With money and six grown children, and the persuasive need of his poverty-stricken relatives and compatriots here and in the old world, he had an undoubted advantage over the rest of us. He put his children to work, and drew in his poor relations. In this godless America he would give them plenty of work in a shop where the Sabbath was kept holy! It was his strength, for they would work in no shop where the Sabbath was not kept holy. Their learner's period to be stretched out far beyond the usual time limit, thus adding much to his profits. The "outsiders" were young children. He hired them and drove them, and kept reducing their pay:

He would go about the "buckeye" dreaming aloud . . . This was his first sweatshop. By-and-bye he'd have a bigger place—a real stogie factory with dozens of new workers. His children would do all the work of foremen and watchers, and work at the bench too. Soon there would be a big factory building all his own. . . .

In the six years, off and on, that I worked for Mr. Brudno, his dream grew to reality. He did everything a boss could do to make his dream come true. Beginning in a little "buckeye," he soon moved to an enormous loft, where the dozen benches he started with, were many times multiplied. There his factory hummed with the industry of boys and girls, of men, women, and young children. The stripping and the bunch-making were concentrated in one end of the vast room where the rolling was done. The raw material was unpacked and sorted, the drying, storing, and other processes carried on in another room. Driven by Mr. Brudno and our own need, we piled up stogies rapidly. Brudno paid miserably little for our labor, and always complained that we were getting too much. But before long, he was able to rear a factory building of his own, on a very desirable site on Broadway. It was of red brick—and several stories high. There he drove us harder than ever, and in time added another story to his Broadway structure. Now he was a big "manufacturer"; he strutted about and watched us manufacture.

When the "buckeye" moved to the big loft and became a factory, Mr. Brudno announced a cut. The stogie-rollers were getting fourteen cents a hundred. Now it would be thirteen. We took the cut in silence. We were for the most part poor little child slaves, timid and unorganized. The thought of union never occurred to us. There was no strength in us or behind us. It was each one by his lone self. Not one of us would have ventured to pit his little self against the boss. We merely looked into one another's faces. No words. But each had the same thought in mind: Now there would be less of something that was already scarce: Bread, milk, or coal. Mr. Brudno owned the factory and we were his workers. Nothing could be done about it. So we raced some more . . . and still more, and more!

It never occurred to me that I was being used by the boss to set the pace in his stogie factory. . . . And that one cut would follow another, as our speed increased. . . .

A cut came the week that the new baby came.

"Rosalie!"

My step-father's voice, tense and unnatural with excitement, shook me out of sleep.

I heard my mother's shriek piercing the deep night, and rushed into the room next to mine.

"Mother! Oh, my mother!" What could be wrong with my mother?

My step-father rushed after me, and snatched me out of the room.

"Rosalie, run to the midwife! Say she's to come right away. Mother's giving birth. Quick!"

"Giving birth?" A new baby coming! . . . Out into the dark, chill, deserted streets I went, shoes unbuttoned, hair loose in the wind, feet flying. . . .

It was hard enough to scrape together the ten dollars for the midwife. To get help for the two weeks of confinement was out of the question. For those two weeks, after shop, I did the work at home. There was no water in the flat on Liberal Street. I had to carry pails of water from the pump in the yard to fill the wash tubs upstairs and take the water down to spill. How heavy the sheets were, and how hard to rub clean! . . . Every day of the two weeks, I washed: Diapers, sheets, other "linens," carrying water up and down, up and down, till all was washed and rinsed, and the white things hanging out on the line in the yard.

Something was in the air. Not only at Brudno's, but everywhere. Our little world of working fathers, dependent mothers, and young bread-winners was tense with an apprehension never felt before.

We were always hanging over a precipice. But now we felt that something was going to break; that the precarious bit of shale we called "life" to which we clung in such desperation would give way; and that we—all of us—with our poverty and our crust of bread, would go crashing down to disaster! This was the beginning of the crisis of 1893.

My step-father, though no worker in a factory, felt the effects of the crisis along with the rest of our class. His horse and wagon now carried fewer and of the loads that gave a precarious living. At the week's end, after all was paid—feed and stall for the horse and shed-rent for the wagon—he would find only four or five dollars clear.

He worked harder now and cleared less. He would bring his diminishing loads to the warehouses, and get smaller return for them with every passing day. A deep depression settled upon him.

My own work too fell off. Most of the workers at Brudno's were sent home. A few were kept on part-time. These were the quickest and best workers—the most profitable to him in busy season—the boss preferred not to lose them. He pretended to be generous in keeping us on the payroll.

The three or three-and-a-half dollars I brought, when added to the miserable little that my poor step-father was able to bring in, spelled deeper need for us.

Mr. Brudno was often in a genial mood now, but not too often. Frequently he was morose; at times, vindictive. His black skull-cap announced the mood. If he came through the swinging doors with the cap to his right or left ear we expected taciturnity or jest. If the cap sat against the back of his skull we looked for trouble. Then no work he examined was good enough for him. He would go from rack to rack, picking up handfuls of stogies. A mis-roll or two, a head or two badly sealed; a slight unevenness in length would call forth a violent fit of temper. He would hurl curses at the workers, break and twist the stogies out of shape, and throw them into the drawer of waste cuttings! A morning's work gone to the scrap-pile!

The most intolerable fines were inflicted upon us. For example, the leaf tobacco in which we rolled our "bunches" was often so rotted that we were forced to re-roll our stogies several times, each time removing the worthless piece to try another. Or, the leaf would be so badly worm-eaten we could not cover a third of the required number of stogies. This bad stock retarded the work. It meant rolling two or three hundred less in a day; it meant beside[s], unusual effort; increased care and anxiety; and a nervous strain that sent us home trembling from head to feet. Yet for this stock Mr. Brudno demanded the same standard of workmanship and the same number of stogies to the pound that was set for the finest leaf tobacco, and docked us heavily for the inescapable failure. When we opened our slim pay envelopes, we would often find from fifty cents to one dollar and fifty cents deducted, out of a possible five dollars When driven too hard, some one of us would venture to complain in a timid voice: "But look at this stock, Mr. Brudno. How can you expect the same work out of such rotten leaf tobacco? See this and this and this!—and look at the holes in these. . . . Look! look! I just brought this pound from the stripping room. We can't do the impossible!"

"Well, what's wrong with this stock anyway? A little hole, here and there; that's nothing. Rotten? That ain't rotten. You pull too hard, so it tears. Don't pull, or you'll go home."

"Ask your own sons and daughters; they'll tell you what sort of stock it is."

But if he ever asked them we were not told. The fines were taken out of our pay, often without any previous warning; and those who complained too disrespectfully were "fired."

If a period of good stock followed, we would race madly. Now is the time to make up for the bad weeks! If then we succeeded—if we increased our speed and turned out a few hundred stogies more than usual at the week's end, Mr. Brudno would announce a reduction of a cent or two on the hundred. Before these attacks we were helpless sheep. We knew nothing of organizing protest. A few of us dreamed. . . . But nothing came of our dreams.

Brudno's shop, however, was to have a strike—a curious strike confined to his relatives. One morning, at daybreak, I was roused by a sharp rap at our door. It was Lyoti, one of that group of blood relations whom Brudno drew from the old country with tales of work and freedom, in a shop that kept the Sabbath holy.

"I came to beg you please, not to go back to the shop, this morning!" he said, "We are on strike."

"We? Who?"

"The boss's relations," he explained. "We can't do the special work he gives us to do, and live on the pay. It is impossible."

I roused my sleeping mother. The children woke. They ran or toddled to the door of the tiny frame house on Orange Street where we now lived, halfnaked; sleepy, yet curious.

I kissed my mother, kissed each child in turn, and forgot for the moment that our father, in despair, had left home the week before and had not been heard from since. A strike at Brudno's shop! Every outraged feeling in me broke into exultant rebellion.

"I'll stay out even if we starve altogether! Eh, Mamele?" My mother kissed me and nodded assent. There were shadows as we contemplated the children. "But a strike is a strike," said my mother. And Lyoti explained, "If we win, you win too. If we win, the boss will not dare to press you harder than he is already pressing you. He will not dare to take another cent off the hundred from anybody."

My first strike—a sympathy strike! I visited workers in their homes that early morning and got them to stay out. I picketed the shop. Lyoti turned to me for many strike activities. I did as directed and

drew in others. At the end of some ten or twelve days the men returned in triumph. The boss had yielded to their demands, and the rest of us who appeared to have gained nothing, felt stronger—even a bit audacious in the presence of the boss. The old timidity never again quite overcame any of us—for was he not beaten in our sight?

With the monopoly of the newly-invented suction machine, by which a worker could turn out many times the number of cigars made by skilled hand labor, the Cigar Trust came into existence. It was spreading westward from New York. It needed workers to operate the new machines. A Mr. Young, foreman at Baer's, had shown off my skill, economy of motion, and economical use of material, to visiting buyers and "manufacturers." Mr. Young it was who was now engaged by the trust to start their Cleveland factory, and who, in turn, engaged me to learn the suction-machine method, and to teach it to other workers. Soon I was given charge of an entire floor, at fifteen dollars a week.

But my job lasted only a few weeks. A Mr. Weiss, vice-president of the newly-formed trust, was making a tour of inspection of their factories, and came to Cleveland. Early one morning the elderly superintendent of the building stopped me on my way up to the loft: "I'm sorry, Miss Pastor, but you can't go up to the suction-room." His words were like a blow. I could only stammer: "Why-why-what have I done?" "Mr. Weiss was here," said the superintendent. "He opened your desk, and found a book." Yes, I understood. I had been reading a book, Vandervelde's *Collectivism.* I went back to the bench where, by terrific driving, I earned between six and seven dollars a week. But the lesson in the antagonism between Capital and Labor sank deep.

I remained a "socialist by instinct." However, within the limited franchise for women I voted for socialist candidates (for school offices) when I became of voting age and went about with the vague notion that some day, in some way, we workers would abolish wage-slavery. When the local political boss, who had a saloon on Orange Street, asked me to "vote Democrat," I proudly announced that I was a socialist and would vote for socialist candidates only. Although friends had warned me that "without this man's good-will no good can come to anybody in the entire neighborhood."

An attempt was made to organize several of the stogie factories. We hired a little hall, got the workers to attend several times; speeches were made; the group held together. But when we applied for membership in the Cigar Makers Union, we were told by the American Federation of Labor that there was no room in the union for unskilled workers.

Document 15.5 Management Documents

The rise of big business meant significant changes in how people worked. It also led to new problems for those running the industries. They had to learn how to organize their companies and how to manage the workers—who were much more numerous than had ever worked for one enterprise before. In addition, they had to defend themselves against charges that they mistreated their employees. In response to these new conditions, people claiming expertise in business began to write about management. This chapter contains excerpts from two books on the subject. The first is by Marshall Kirkman, devoted specifically to railroads, the first big business in the United States. The second is by Frederick Taylor, a pioneer in attempting to study efficiency and one of the most influential people in the world of business at the time.

These documents may reveal a number of things. They are certainly, of course, the opinions of the management consultants who wrote them. Since people bought these books, they may also show us how businessmen attempted to run their businesses. And they may also give us some idea of what it was like to work in factories of the period.

The Science of Railways

Marshall Kirkman

Subordination is a cardinal principle of organized labor—subordination to the employer, subordination to each other according to rank and natural precedence. It is based upon a just conception of the rights of men in their relation to property. All men, however, are entitled to justice and humane treatment.

The discipline of corporate forces is as absolute as that of a man of war. Obedience to superior authority is unqualified. It is, however, the privilege and duty of every subordinate in emergencies, when an order is given, to make such suggestions as the circumstances of the case demand. Here his responsibility ends, except in criminal cases.

An order once given, must be obeyed. Absolutism such as this involves grave responsibilities. It presupposes skill, accurate knowledge and appreciation.

In the administrative department of carriers lack of discipline breeds insubordination, idleness and extravagance. It engenders kindred evils in the operating department, with the added element of danger.

It is necessary that the forces of a railroad should possess esprit de corps, coupled with interest, intelligence and courage that no event can deaden or divert.

While the discipline of corporate life is as absolute as that of an army, there is this difference between them: army life destroys the individuality of all below the rank of officer; corporate life intensifies the personality of subordinates by recognition and promotion. Everyone knows that promotion will follow intelligence, faithfulness and industry. The officers of railroads are drawn from the ranks. It is therefore for the interests of such corporations to build up the intelligence and morale of subordinates; to strengthen the force by careful selection and cultivation. Individuals should be taught to think and act for themselves in all cases where discretion can safely be allowed. They will thus be taught self reliance, and the exercise of prudence and good judgment. . . .

In general, that form of organization is best for corporate property that enforces the most minute responsibility and offers the greatest encouragement to those who work for it; that enables a company to know the measure of faithfulness and capacity of its servants; that rewards the trustworthy and takes cognizance of the derelict. . . .

It is probable that many labor associations have, at the bottom, a belief that the employer does not properly regard the interests of his employee. This belief is false. But in order to dispel it and in doing so break up such combinations as are subversive of the employee's interest, railways must actively interest themselves in the concerns of those who work for them. Their interests are jeopardized, not because they have been disregardful but because their employees believed they have. This erroneous impression the owner must correct if he would not have foreign and unfriendly agents meddling in his affairs. There are two ways in which corporations may and do manifest their interest in those who work for them. In America it is done by kindly treatment, the payment of high wages, continued service, promotion, and by making the employee self reliant and independent. In many countries wages are unavoidably low, and so corporations eke out their efforts by small annuities and distress funds, and by special interest in the sicknesses, discomforts and forebodings of those who work for them.

The vicissitudes of corporate service require a paternal form of government. The owner must be the father. Failure to recognize this will aggravate the growth of unfriendly labor associations. . . .

In general, employees are safer in the hands of the employer than in those of anyone else. His interest is permanent, material and fatherly. The conception of the employer by those who work for him must be broad and charitable. Nothing is attainable without this. Employees must not be quick to believe they are treated unjustly, are overlooked or forgotten. They must be governed by reason. They must accept the conditions of life as they are. They must go ahead sturdily and cheerfully, believing that if they comprehend their business and are active in the discharge of it, their services will be recognized. They must also appreciate this truth, that those who are preferred are, on the whole, worthy of it. That

---

The Science of Railways, World Railway Publishing Company, 1896.

while there are exceptions to the rule, they are unworthy of regard. Disappointed men, instead of repining, must seek by renewed zeal and attachment the recognition they desire. They must not seek, in such emergencies, through combinations, or otherwise, to force what they cannot peaceably attain. . . .

Unflagging industry and continual study is the only road to preferment. All others are makeshift, temporary and incomplete. When men do not progress as fast as they think they should, let them work and study the harder; do more and better work. There is no other road to preferment. . . .

Document 15.6 The Principles of Scientific Management

The Principles of Scientific Management

Frederick Taylor

The principal object of management should be to secure the maximum prosperity for the employer, coupled with the maximum prosperity for each employee. . . .

The majority of . . . men believe that the fundamental interests of employees and employers are necessarily antagonistic. Scientific management, on the contrary, has for its very foundation the firm conviction that the true interests of the two are one and the same; that prosperity for the employer cannot exist through a long term of years unless it is accompanied by prosperity for the employee, and vice versa; and that it is possible to give the workman what he most wants—high wages—and the employer what he wants—a low labor cost—for his manufactures. . . .

No one can be found who will deny that in the case of any single individual the greatest prosperity can exist only when that individual has reached his highest state of efficiency; that is, when he is turning out his largest daily output.

The truth of this fact is also perfectly clear in the case of two men working together. To illustrate: if you and your workman have become so skillful that you and he together are making two pairs of shoes in a day, while your competitor and his workman are making only one pair, it is clear that after selling your two pairs of shoes you can pay your workman much higher wages than your competitor who produces only one pair of shoes is able to pay his man, and that there will still be enough money left over for you to have a larger profit than your competitor. . . .

When the same workman returns to work on the following day, instead of using every effort to turn out the largest possible amount of work, in a majority of the cases this man deliberately plans to do as little as he safely can—to turn out far less work than he is well able to do—in many instances to do not more than one-third to one-half of a proper day's work. And in fact if he were to do his best to turn out his largest possible day's work, he would be abused by his fellow-workers for so doing, even more than if he had proved himself a "quitter" in sport. Underworking, that is, deliberately working slowly so as to avoid doing a full day's work, "soldiering," as it is called in this country, "hanging it out," as it is called in England, "ca' cannie," as it is called in Scotland, is almost universal in industrial establishments, and prevails also to a large extent in the building trades; and the writer asserts without fear of contradiction that this constitutes the greatest evil with which the working-people of both England and America are now afflicted. . . .

There is no question that the tendency of the average man (in all walks of life) is toward working at a slow, easy gait, and that it is only after a good deal of thought and observation on his part or as a result of example, conscience, or external pressure that he takes a more rapid pace. . . .

. . . considerable space will later in this paper be devoted to illustrating the great gain, both to employers and employees, which results from the substitution of scientific for rule-of-thumb methods in even the smallest details of the work of every trade. The enormous saving of time and therefore increase in the output which it is possible to effect through

---

The Principles of Scientific Management, 1911.

eliminating unnecessary motions and substituting fast for slow and inefficient motions for the men working in any of our trades can be fully realized only after one has personally seen the improvement which results from a thorough motion and time study, made by a competent man.

To explain briefly, owing to the fact that the workmen in all of our trades have been taught the details of their work by observation of those immediately around them, there are many different ways in common use for doing the same thing, perhaps forty, fifty, or a hundred ways of doing each act in each trade, and for the same reason there is a great variety in the implements used for each class of work. Now, among the various methods and implements used in each element of each trade there is always one method and one implement which is quicker and better than any of the rest. And this one best method and best implement can only be discovered or developed through a scientific study and analysis of all of the methods and implements in use, together with accurate, minute, motion and time study. This involves the gradual substitution of science for rule of thumb throughout the mechanic arts.

This paper will show that the underlying philosophy of all of the old systems of management in common use makes it imperative that each workman shall be left with the final responsibility for doing his job practically as he thinks best, with comparatively little help and advice from the management. And it will also show that because of this isolation of workmen, it is in most cases impossible for the men working under these systems to do their work in accordance with the rules and laws of a science or art, even where one exists.

The writer asserts as a general principle (and he proposes to give illustrations tending to prove the fact later in this paper) that in almost all of the mechanic arts the science which underlies each act of each workman is so great and amounts to so much that the workman who is best suited to actually doing the work is incapable of fully understanding this science, without the guidance and help of those who are working with him or over him, either through lack of education or through insufficient mental capacity. . . .

Under the old type of management success depends almost entirely upon getting the "initiative" of the workmen, and it is indeed a rare case in which this initiative is really attained. Under scientific management the "initiative" of the workmen (that is, their hard work, their good-will, and their ingenuity) is obtained with absolute uniformity and to a greater extent than is possible under the old system; and in addition to this improvement on the part of the men, the managers assume new burdens, new duties, and responsibilities never dreamed of in the past. The managers assume, for instance, the burden of gathering together all of the traditional knowledge which in the past has been possessed by the workmen and then of classifying, tabulating, and reducing this knowledge to rules, laws, and formulæ which are immensely helpful to the workmen in doing their daily work. . . .

. . . The philosophy of the management of "initiative and incentive" makes it necessary for each workman to bear almost the entire responsibility for the general plan as well as for each detail of his work, and in many cases for his implements as well. In addition to this he must do all of the actual physical labor. The development of a science, on the other hand, involves the establishment of many rules, laws, and formulæ which replace the judgment of the individual workman and which can be effectively used only after having been systematically recorded, indexed, etc. The practical use of scientific data also calls for a room in which to keep the books, records, etc., and a desk for the planner to work at. Thus all of the planning which under the old system was done by the workman, as a result of his personal experience, must of necessity under the new system be done by the management in accordance with the laws of the science; because even if the workman was well suited to the development and use of scientific data, it would be physically impossible for him to work at his machine and at a desk at the same time. It is also clear that in most cases one type of man is needed to plan ahead and an entirely different type to execute the work. . . .

The Bethlehem Steel Company had five blast furnaces, the product of which had been handled by a pig-iron gang for many years. . . .

We found that this gang were loading on the average about 12 1/2 long tons per man per day. We were surprised to find, after studying the matter, that a first-class pig-iron handler ought to handle between 47 and 48 long tons per day, instead of 12 1/2 tons. This task seemed to us so very large that we were obliged to go over our work several times before we were absolutely sure that we were right. Once we were sure, however, that 47 tons was a proper day's work for a first-class pig-iron handler, the task which faced us as managers under the modern scientific plan was clearly before us. It was our duty to see that the 80,000 tons of pig iron was loaded on to the cars at the rate of 47 tons per man per day, in place of 12 1/2 tons, at which rate the work was then being done. And it was further our duty to see that this work was done without bringing on a strike among the men, without any quarrel with the men, and to see that the men were happier and better contented when loading at the new rate of 47 tons than they were when loading at the old rate of 12 1/2 tons.

Our first step was the scientific selection of the workman. In dealing with workmen under this type of management, it is an inflexible rule to talk to and deal with only one man at a time, since each workman has his own special abilities and limitations, and since we are not dealing with men in masses, but are trying to develop each individual man to his highest state of efficiency and prosperity. Our first step was to find the proper workman to begin with. We therefore carefully watched and studied these 75 men for three or four days, at the end of which time we had picked out four men who appeared to be physically able to handle pig iron at the rate of 47 tons per day. A careful study was then made of each of these men. We looked up their history as far back as practicable and thorough inquiries were made as to the character, habits, and the ambition of each of them. Finally we selected one from among the four as the most likely man to start with. He was a little Pennsylvania Dutchman who had been observed to trot back home for a mile or so after his work in the evening about as fresh as he was when he came trotting down to work in the morning. We found that upon wages of $1.15 a day he had succeeded in buying a small plot of ground, and that he was engaged in putting up the walls of a little house for himself in the morning before starting to work and at night after leaving. He also had the reputation of being exceedingly "close," that is, of placing a very high value on a dollar. As one man whom we talked to about him said, "A penny looks about the size of a cart-wheel to him." This man we will call Schmidt.

The task before us, then, narrowed itself down to getting Schmidt to handle 47 tons of pig iron per day and making him glad to do it. This was done as follows. Schmidt was called out from among the gang of pig-iron handlers and talked to somewhat in this way:

"Schmidt, are you a high-priced man?"

"Vell, I don't know vat you mean."

"Oh yes, you do. What I want to know is whether you are a high-priced man or not."

"Vell, I don't know vat you mean."

"Oh, come now, you answer my questions. What I want to find out is whether you are a high-priced man or one of these cheap fellows here. What I want to find out is whether you want to earn $1.85 a day or whether you are satisfied with $1.15, just the same as all those cheap fellows are getting."

"Did I vant $1.85 a day? Vas dot a high-priced man? Vell, yes, I vas a high-priced man."

"Oh, you're aggravating me. Of course you want $1.85 a day every one wants it! You know perfectly well that that has very little to do with your being a high-priced man. For goodness' sake answer my questions, and don't waste any more of my time. Now come over here. You see that pile of pig iron?"

"Yes."

"You see that car?"

"Yes."

"Well, if you are a high-priced man, you will load that pig iron on that car to-morrow for $1.85. Now do wake up and answer my question. Tell me whether you are a high-priced man or not."

"Vell—did I got $1.85 for loading dot pig iron on dot car to-morrow?"

"Yes, of course you do, and you get $1.85 for loading a pile like that every day right through the year. That is what a high-priced man does, and you know it just as well as I do."

"Vell, dot's all right. I could load dot pig iron on the car to-morrow for $1.85, and I get it every day, don't I?"

"Certainly you do—certainly you do."

"Vell, den, I vas a high-priced man."

"Now, hold on, hold on. You know just as well as I do that a high-priced man has to do exactly as he's told from morning till night. You have seen this man here before, haven't you?"

"No, I never saw him."

"Well, if you are a high-priced man, you will do exactly as this man tells you to-morrow, from morning till night. When he tells you to pick up a pig and walk, you pick it up and you walk, and when he tells you to sit down and rest, you sit down. You do that right straight through the day. And what's more, no back talk. Now a high-priced man does just what he's told to do, and no back talk. Do you understand that? When this man tells you to walk, you walk; when he tells you to sit down, you sit down, and you don't talk back at him. Now you come on to work here to-morrow morning and I'll know before night whether you are really a high-priced man or not."

This seems to be rather rough talk. And indeed it would be if applied to an educated mechanic, or even an intelligent laborer. With a man of the mentally sluggish type of Schmidt it is appropriate and not unkind, since it is effective in fixing his attention on the high wages which he wants and away from what, if it were called to his attention, he probably would consider impossibly hard work.

What would Schmidt's answer be if he were talked to in a manner which is usual under the management of "initiative and incentive"? say, as follows:

"Now, Schmidt, you are a first-class pig-iron handler and know your business well. You have been handling at the rate of 12 1/2 tons per day. I have given considerable study to handling pig iron, and feel sure that you could do a much larger day's work than you have been doing. Now don't you think that if you really tried you could handle 47 tons of pig iron per day, instead of 12 1/2 tons?"

What do you think Schmidt's answer would be to this? . . .

Schmidt started to work, and all day long, and at regular intervals, was told by the man who stood over him with a watch, "Now pick up a pig and walk. Now sit down and rest. Now walk—now rest," etc. He worked when he was told to work, and rested when he was told to rest, and at half-past five in the afternoon had his 47 1/2 tons loaded on the car. And he practically never failed to work at this pace and do the task that was set him during the three years that the writer was at Bethlehem. And throughout this time he averaged a little more than $1.85 per day, whereas before he had never received over $1.15 per day, which was the ruling rate of wages at that time in Bethlehem. That is, he received 60 percent higher wages than were paid to other men who were not working on task work. One man after another was picked out and trained to handle pig iron at the rate of 47 1/2 tons per day until all of the pig iron was handled at this rate, and the men were receiving 60 percent more wages than other workmen around them.

The writer has given above a brief description of three of the four elements which constitute the essence of scientific management: first, the careful selection of the workman, and, second and third, the method of first inducing and then training and helping the workman to work according to the scientific method. Nothing has as yet been said about the science of handling pig iron. The writer trusts, however, that before leaving this illustration the reader will be thoroughly convinced that there is a science of handling pig iron, and further that this science amounts to so much that the man who is suited to handle pig iron cannot possibly understand it, nor even work in accordance with the laws of this science, without the help of those who are over him.

Module XV
Questions for Study and Critical Thinking

1. At the end of the period are wages of coal miners higher, lower, or the same than at the beginning of this period?

2. What is the general trend of wages over the period shown in the table? How do you determine the trend?

3. What are the fluctuations in wages during this period? What, do you think, caused these fluctuations?

4. In using the price indexes, what commodity or group of commodities is most useful to follow?

5. In what years do prices fluctuate? In those years which directions do they go? How much do they fluctuate? Based on your knowledge of the history of this period, why are they moving in those directions in those years?

6. What is the general trend of prices? How do prices at the end of the period compare with those at the beginning? Why do you think that is?

7. Taking into consideration both wages and prices, are workers better or worse off at the end of the period?

8. In the accounts of working conditions written by Thomas O'Donnell and Rose Pastor Stokes what do these workers say about conditions of their work and lives?

9. Do you think Rose Pastor Stokes's political positions influenced her description of her life? If so, where do you see this influence?

10. According to Kirkman, what is the basic principle of railroad work? What organization does Kirkman see as the model for modern business organizations? What does he say are the differences? Do you agree with Kirkman?

11. How do you compare this with the way people worked before the rise of big business? How does it compare with American political values? Is there a conflict?

12. What effect, do you think, would the application of Kirkman's ideas have on workers? Would you like to work in an organization run that way?

13. In *The Principles of Scientific Management* what benefit does Taylor believe his scientific management will produce for workers? What benefit will it produce for a company's owners?

14. What, according to Taylor, is wrong with the way most workmen were working in his day? How should methods of work be determined (according to Taylor)?

15. In Taylor's system, what happens to the judgment and initiative of the individual workman? In your opinion, is this a positive or a negative change?

16. What is Taylor's attitude toward the Pennsylvania Dutch man called Schmidt? How does he talk to him? What do you think of that attitude and the way he talked to the workman? Was he correct that this approach was necessary?

17. What effect would the application of Taylor's ideas have on workers' morale? Why?

18. After looking at all of these different kinds of evidence, what general conclusions can you make about work between the Civil War and the beginning of the twentieth century? What was it like to be a worker in that period? What was the economic condition of workers? Was it getting better or worse? Which documents provide that information? On the subjective side, how did workers feel about their work and lives? How do you think companies operated according to the ideas in the management documents would affect workers? Finally, how many of the characteristics of work in the late nineteenth century are still applicable today?

Module XVI

The Cities and Their People

Introduction

In the years following the Civil War the United States suddenly became a land of cities. Chicago, for example, grew from 100,000 in 1860 to one million in 1900. And New York grew from one million in 1860 to three million at the turn of the century. These cities were magnets for immigrants who flooded into the United States. By 1890, 87 percent of Chicago's population was foreign born, and other cities also had high percentages of immigrants. After 1890 more and more of these immigrants came from southern and eastern Europe. Polish, Russian, and Hungarian Jews; Poles, Czechs, Slovaks, Serbians, Italians, and Greeks joined the stream of immigrants pouring into Boston, New York, Cleveland, Chicago, and other industrial cities. Their arrival caused different reactions among those already in the country. Often poorer than the older immigrants and sometimes illiterate, these people, often referred to as "new immigrants," appeared different than longer-settled groups. As you will read in the documents below, some observers found them a great asset to the country; others found their presence and numbers profoundly disturbing and proposed limiting their immigration.

Immigrants

Document 16.1 Restriction of Immigration (1896)

Traditionally, the United States welcomed immigrants and had few legal limitations on immigration. Until the 1920s the only restrictions were laws barring those with certain health problems. With the influx of large numbers of new immigrants in the late nineteenth century, however, demands for legislation restricting immigration increased. In 1896 Francis A. Walker published the following article in the *Atlantic Monthly* magazine, a voice of respectable opinion. This selection begins with Walker summarizing his argument that immigration is unnecessary for population growth (which he thought was good).

As you read, ask yourself, what are Walker's arguments for restricting immigration? How valid are these arguments? Has subsequent history borne them out? How do they compare with current arguments for immigration limitation?

Restriction of Immigration (1896)

Francis A. Walker

Let social and economic conditions remain as they were, and population will go on increasing from year to year, and from decade to decade, with a regularity little short of the marvelous. Let social and economic conditions change, and population instantly responds. The arrival in the United States, between 1830 and 1840, and thereafter increasingly, of large numbers of degraded peasantry created for the first time in this country distinct social classes, and produced an alteration of economic relations which could not fail powerfully to affect population. The appearance of vast numbers of men, foreign in birth and often in language, with a poorer standard of living, with habits repellent to our native people, of an industrial grade suited only to the lowest kind of manual labor, was exactly such a cause as by any student of population would be expected to affect profoundly the growth of the native population. Americans shrank alike from the social contact and the economic competition thus created. They became increasingly unwilling to bring forth sons and daughters who should be obliged to compete in the market for labor and in the walks of life with those whom they did not recognize as of their own grade and condition. . . .

The second opinion regarding the immigration of the past, with which it seems well to deal before proceeding to the positive argument of the case, is that, whether desirable on other accounts or not, foreign immigration prior to 1860 was necessary in order to supply the country with a laboring class which should be able and willing to perform the lowest kind of work required in the upbuilding of our industrial and social structure, especially the making of railroads and canals. The opinion which has been cited constitutes, perhaps, the best example known to me of that putting the cart before the horse which is so commonly seen in sociological inquiry. When was it that native Americans first refused to do the lowest kinds of manual labor? I answer, When the foreigner came. Did the foreigner come because the native American refused longer to perform any kind of manual labor? No; the American refused because the foreigner came. Through all our early history, Americans, from Governor Winthrop, through Jonathan Edwards, to Ralph Waldo Emerson, had done every sort of work which was required for the comfort of their families and for the upbuilding of the state, and had not been ashamed. They called nothing common or unclean which needed to be done for their own good or for the good of all. But when the country was flooded with ignorant and unskilled foreigners, who could do nothing but the lowest kind of labor, Americans instinctively shrank from the contact and the competition thus offered to them. So long as manual labor, in whatever field, was to be done by all, each in his place, there was no revolt at it; but when working on railroads and canals became the sign of a want of education and of a low social condition, our own people gave it up, and left it to those who were able to do that, and nothing better.

We have of late had a very curious demonstration of the entire fallacy of the popular mode of reasoning on this subject, due to the arrival of a still lower laboring class. Within a few years Harper's Weekly had an article in which the editor, after admitting that the Italians who have recently come in such vast numbers to our shores do not constitute a desirable element of the population, either socially or politically, yet claimed that it was a highly providential arrangement, since the Irish, who formerly did all the work of the country in the way of ditching and trenching, were now standing aside. We have only to meet the argument thus in its second generation, so to speak, to see the complete fallacy of such reasoning. Does the Italian come because the Irishman refuses to work in ditches and trenches, in gangs; or has the Irishman taken this position because the Italian has come? The latter is undoubtedly the truth; and if the administrators of Baron Hirsch's estate send to us two millions of Russian Jews, we shall soon find the Italians standing on their dignity, and deeming themselves too good to work on streets and sewers and railroads. But meanwhile, what of the republic? what of the American standard of living? what of the American rate of wages?

All that sort of reasoning about the necessity of having a mean kind of man to do a mean kind of

---

Atlantic Monthly, June, 1896.

work is greatly to be suspected. It is not possible to have a man who is too good to do any kind of work which the welfare of his family and of the community requires to be done. So long as we were left to increase out of the loins of our people such a sentiment as that we are now commenting upon made no appearance in American life. It is much to be doubted whether any material growth which is to be secured only by the degradation of our citizenship is a national gain, even from the most materialistic point of view.

Let us now inquire what are the changes in our general conditions which seem to demand a revision of the opinion and policy heretofore held regarding immigration. Three of these are subjective, affecting our capability of easily and safely taking care of a large and tumultuous access of foreigners; the fourth is objective, and concerns the character of the immigration now directed upon our shores. Time will serve for only a rapid characterization.

First, we have the important fact of the complete exhaustion of the free public lands of the United States. Fifty years ago, thirty years ago, vast tracts of arable land were open to every person arriving on our shores, under the Preemption Act, or later, the Homestead Act. A good farm of one hundred and sixty acres could be had at the minimum price of $1.25 an acre, or for merely the fees of registration. Under these circumstances it was a very simple matter to dispose of a large immigration. To-day there is not a good farm within the limits of the United States which is to be had under either of these acts. The wild and tumultuous scenes which attended the opening to settlement of the Territory of Oklahoma, a few years ago, and, a little later, of the so-called Cherokee Strip, testify eloquently to the vast change in our national conditions in this respect. This is not to say that more people cannot and will not, sooner or later, with more or less of care and pains and effort, be placed upon the land of the United States; but it does of itself alone show how vastly the difficulty of providing for immigration has increased. The immigrant must now buy his farm from a second hand, and he must pay the price which the value of the land for agricultural purposes determines. In the case of ninety-five out of a hundred immigrants, this necessity puts an immediate occupation of the soil out of the question.

A second change in our national condition, which importantly affects our capability of taking care of large numbers of ignorant and unskilled foreigners, is the fall of agricultural prices which has gone on steadily since 1873. It is not of the slightest consequence to inquire into the causes of this fall, whether we refer it to the competition of Argentina and of India or the appreciation of gold. We are interested only in the fact. There has been a great reduction in the cost of producing crops in some favored regions where steam-ploughs and steam-reaping, steam-threshing, and steam-sacking machines can be employed; but there has been no reduction in the cost of producing crops upon the ordinary American farm at all corresponding to the reduction in the price of the produce. It is a necessary consequence of this that the ability to employ a large number of uneducated and unskilled hands in agriculture has greatly diminished.

Still a third cause which may be indicated, perhaps more important than either of those thus far mentioned, is found in the fact that we have now a labor problem. We in the United States have been wont to pride ourselves greatly upon our so easily maintaining peace and keeping the social order unimpaired. We have, partly from a reasonable patriotic pride, partly also from something like Phariseeism, been much given to pointing at our European cousins, and boasting superiority over them in this respect. Our self-gratulation has been largely due to overlooking social differences between us and them. That boasted superiority has been owing mainly, not to our institutions, but to our more favorable conditions. There is no country of Europe which has not for a long time had a labor problem; that is, which has not so largely exploited its own natural resources, and which has not a labor supply so nearly meeting the demands of the market at their fullest, that hard times and periods of industrial depression have brought a serious strain through extensive non-employment of labor. From this evil condition we have, until recently, happily been free. During the last few years, however, we have ourselves come under the shadow of this evil, in spite of our magnificent natural resources. We know what it is to have even intelligent and skilled labor unemployed through considerable periods of time. This change of conditions is likely to bring some abatement to our national pride. No longer is it a matter of course that every industrious and temperate man can find work in the United States. And it is to be remembered that, of all nations, we are the one which is least qualified to deal with a labor problem. We have not the machinery, we have not the army, we have not the police, we have not the traditions and instincts, for dealing with such a matter, as the great railroad and other strikes of the last few years have shown.

I have spoken of three changes in the national condition, all subjective, which greatly affect our capability of dealing with a large and tumultuous immigration. There is a fourth, which is objective. It concerns the character of the foreigners now resorting to our shores. Fifty, even thirty years ago, there was a rightful presumption regarding the average immigrant that he was among the most enterprising, thrifty, alert, adventurous, and courageous of the community from which he came. It required no small energy, prudence, forethought, and pains to conduct the inquiries relating to his migration, to accumulate the necessary means, and to find his way across the Atlantic. To-day the presumption is completely reversed. So thoroughly has the continent of Europe been crossed by railways, so effectively has the business of emigration there been exploited, so much have the rates of railroad fares and ocean passage been reduced, that it is now among the least thrifty and prosperous members of any European community that the emigration agent finds his best recruiting-ground. The care and pains required have been reduced to a minimum; while the agent of the Red Star Line or the White Star Line is everywhere at hand, to suggest migration to those who are not getting on well at home. The intending emigrants are looked after from the moment they are locked into the cars in their native villages until they stretch themselves upon the floors of the buildings on Ellis Island, in New York. Illustrations of the ease and facility with which this Pipe Line Immigration is now carried on might be given in profusion. So broad and smooth is the channel, there is no reason why every foul and stagnant pool of population in Europe, which no breath of intellectual industrial life has stirred for ages, should not be decanted upon our soil. Hard times here may momentarily check the flow; but it will not be permanently stopped so long as any difference of economic level exists between our population and that of the most degraded communities abroad.

But it is not alone that the presumption regarding the immigrant of today is so widely different from that which existed regarding the immigrant of thirty or fifty years ago. The immigrant of the former time came almost exclusively from western and northern Europe. We have now tapped great reservoirs of population then almost unknown to the passenger lists of our arriving vessels. Only a short time ago, the immigrants from southern Italy, Hungary, Austria, and Russia together made up hardly more than one per cent of our immigration. To-day the proportion has risen to something like forty per cent, and threatens soon to become fifty or sixty per cent, or even more. The entrance into our political, social, and industrial life of such vast masses of peasantry, degraded below our utmost conceptions, is a matter which no intelligent patriot can look upon without the gravest apprehension and alarm. These people have no history behind them which is of a nature to give encouragement. They have none of the inherited instincts and tendencies which made it comparatively easy to deal with the immigration of the olden time. They are beaten men from beaten races; representing the worst failures in the struggle for existence. Centuries are against them, as centuries were on the side of those who formerly came to us. They have none of the ideas and aptitudes which fit men to take up readily and easily the problem of self-care and self-government, such as belong to those who are descended from the tribes that met under the oak-trees of old Germany to make laws and choose chieftains. Their habits of life, again, are of the most revolting kind. Read the description given by Mr. Riis of the police driving from the garbage dumps the miserable beings who try to burrow in those depths of unutterable filth and slime in order that they may eat and sleep there! Was it in cement like this that the foundations of our republic were laid? What effects must be produced upon our social standards, and upon the ambitions and aspirations of our people, by a contact so foul and loathsome? The influence upon the American rate of wages of a competition like this cannot fail to be injurious and even disastrous. Already it has been seriously felt in the tobacco manufacture, in the clothing trade, and in many forms of mining industry; and unless this access of vast numbers of unskilled workmen of the lowest type, in a market already fully supplied with labor, shall be checked, it cannot fail to go on from bad to worse, in breaking down the standard which has been maintained with so much care and at so much cost. The competition of paupers is far more telling and more killing the competition of pauper-made goods. Degraded labor in the slums of foreign cities may be prejudicial to intelligent, ambitious, self-respecting labor here; but it does not threaten half so much evil as does degraded labor in the garrets of our native cities.

Finally, the present situation is most menacing to our peace and political safety. In all the social and industrial disorders of this country since 1877, the foreign elements have proved themselves the ready tools of demagogues in defying the law, in destroying property, and in working violence. A learned clergyman who mingled with the socialistic mob which, two years ago, threatened the State House and the governor of Massachusetts, told me that during the entire disturbance he heard no word spoken in any language which he knew—either in English, in German, or in French. There may be those who can contemplate the addition to our population of vast numbers of persons having no inherited instincts of self-government and respect for law; knowing no restraint upon their own passions but the club of the policeman or the bayonet of the soldier; forming communities, by the tens of thousands, in which only foreign tongues are spoken, and into which can steal no influence from our free institutions and from popular discussion. But I confess to being far less optimistic. I have conversed with one of the highest officers of the United States army and with one of the highest officers of the civil government regarding the state of affairs which existed during the summer of 1894; and the revelations they made of facts not generally known, going to show how the ship of state grazed along its whole side upon the rocks, were enough to appall the most sanguine American, the most hearty believer in free government. Have we the right to expose the republic to any increase of the dangers from this source which now so manifestly threaten our peace and safety?

For it is never to be forgotten that self-defense is the first law of nature and of nations. If that man who careth not for his own household is worse than an infidel, the nation which permits its institutions to be endangered by any cause which can fairly be removed is guilty not less in Christian than in natural law. Charity begins at home; and while the people of the United States have gladly offered an asylum to millions upon millions of the distressed and unfortunate of other lands and climes, they have no right to carry their hospitality one step beyond the line where American institutions, the American rate of wages, the American standard of living, are brought into serious peril. All the good the United States could do by offering indiscriminate hospitality to a few millions more of European peasants, whose places at home will, within another generation, be filled by others as miserable as themselves, would not compensate for any permanent injury done to our republic. Our highest duty to charity and to humanity is to make this great experiment, here, of free laws and educated labor, the most triumphant success that can possibly be attained. In this way we shall do far more for Europe than by allowing its city slums and its vast stagnant reservoirs of degraded peasantry to be drained off upon our soil. Within the decade between 1880 and 1890 five and quarter millions of foreigners entered our ports! No nation in human history ever undertook to deal with such masses of alien population. That man must be a sentimentalist and an optimist beyond all bounds of reason who believes that we can take such a load upon the national stomach without a failure of assimilation, and without great danger to the health and life of the nation. For one, I believe it is time that we should take a rest, and give our social, political, and industrial system some chance to recuperate. The problems which so sternly confront us to-day are serious enough without being complicated and aggravated by the addition of some millions of Hungarians, Bohemians, Poles, south Italians, and Russian Jews.

Document 16.2 Russian Jews as Desirable Immigrants

The new immigrants arriving in the United States often encountered suspicion and hostility, among them Jews from eastern Europe, especially Russia. They encountered not only the general antipathy to the new immigrant with what seemed like peculiar ways of dressing and behaving, but often anti-Semitism as well. The writer Ida M. Van Etten, however, took a different view and in this article particularly praises Russian Jews.

Russian Jews as Desirable Immigrants

Ida M. Van Etten

Most men, if asked what class immigrants they considered the least desirable, would answer, the Russian Jews. There is a preconceived idea that because most of the Russian Jews are dirty, cannot speak the English language, and live closely crowded in unwholesome, ill-smelling tenement quarters, they therefore form an objectionable part of our population. To these causes there might be added that

---

Forum, 15, 1893.

vague, indefinite phrase that they do not assimilate with other people. Thus even those who are willing enough to admit our indebtedness to immigration in the past object to Jewish immigrants, saying that the character of our immigrants is not what it was twenty years ago, forgetting that twenty years ago the prejudice against Irish immigrants was as strong and unreasoning as that which now exists against Jewish immigrants. Persons who have once accepted the idea of the Russian Jews, by habitually thinking of them as constituting the lowest dregs of population and by living far removed from any possible contact with them, harden this opinion into a fixed conviction and shut out further inquiry. Although the Russian Jews have now for several years taken an active part in the industrial, intellectual, and civil life of New York, few of its citizens know anything of this earnest, intelligent, and intensely interesting people.

It would clear away many misleading theories to remember that it is not the condition in which the immigrant comes that determines his usefulness, but the power that he shows to rise above his condition; and if the ability to rise superior to adverse conditions be a proof of strength of character, we must concede that the Russian Jew possesses this quality in no mean degree. Centuries of persecution and oppression tend to develop extreme traits of character, some most commendable, others not so praiseworthy. These people possess all the faults of an oppressed people, but they have also the heroic virtues fostered by their oppression. The Russian Jew seems to possess a dual character; to be the best of men and the worst, to practice the meanest vices and the most exalted virtues. He is suspicious, ungrateful, and often treacherous alike to friend and foe, qualities naturally fostered by centuries of tyranny and repression. But on the other hand he possesses, in large measure, the qualities which will inevitably make him a notable figure in the social and political evolution of any country of which he becomes a citizen. From an intimate knowledge of these people, I maintain that they are in many important respects among our most desirable immigrants.

The great influx of Russian and Polish Jews to the United States which resulted from their rigorous religious persecution by the Russian government began in 1881 and, with but slight interruption, has continued ever since. It is estimated that there are now more than two hundred thousand of them in that portion of New York City east of the Bowery and extending from Houston to Division streets. The history of the Jews has the eminent quality of being interesting at any point it may be taken up, and this Jewish settlement is no exception, for it is as full of interest as the history of the forefathers of these people.

Coming to America in great and unorganized masses, usually penniless, ignorant of the language, manners and customs of the country, unfamiliar with its industrial conditions, and compelled by their necessities to accept any wages offered to them, they undoubtedly formed the most serious menace to wages with which the American working men had had to contend. In many trades they replaced the miserably paid women by still cheaper labor, while their willingness to work for sixteen or eighteen hours a day rendered them still more obnoxious to American working men and women. There were other reasons why the Russian Jew was in the lowest industrial ranks and under the worst possible economic conditions. He had come from a country which is yet industrially undeveloped. He was, therefore, obliged to accept work in those industries that were most nearly like those in which he was engaged at home. These are obviously the sewing trades, which in Russia and in America are in about the same stage of development and which have the added advantage of requiring but little physical strength.

Entering in large numbers in the various sewing trades, they, especially in the early eighties, did reduce wages and degrade the conditions of life in these trades. During the years 1881 to 1888 wages in the trades principally filled by the Russian Jews rarely rose above five or six dollars a week, while the hours ranged from sixteen to eighteen, and in the busy season often much longer. I have seen cloakmakers working in the sweaters' shops* on the East Side at one or two o'clock in the morning, and members of the Cloak-makers' Union testify that before the formation of the union twenty hours was by no means an uncommon work-day. In fact, there seemed to be no limit to the extent of a day's work, except the limit of physical endurance. The conditions under which these people worked are almost indescribable to one who has never seen a sweater's den. The over-crowding and over-work, the filth and the squalor, and the horrible sanitary surroundings make a picture which must be seen to be understood. Factory laws and the regulations of the Board of Health were entirely ignored. Factory and sanitary inspectors were rare visitors in the sweaters' territory at this time, and it would be hard to picture the misery and suffering of these people, who in fleeing from the persecution of the Czar of Russia had fallen

*sweatshops

under the iron rule of a multitude of little industrial czars. They had fled from unbearable Old World conditions to sweaters' dens and tenement-houses where human beings are packed more closely than in any other quarter of the globe—a density of three hundred and seventy-four thousand persons to the square mile. In Russia they ate black bread, but they had at least plenty of pure air. In New York also they ate black bread, but they ate it in a poisonous atmosphere. But they have since come, through their efforts to better their condition, to experience more fully the advantages of the larger freedom of American institutions. Here they have had, at least, the right of free meeting for the purposes of agitation and organization.

Although demoralized by their manner of living and working, they showed a quick understanding of the power and advantages of organization and of combination. Their first efforts were feeble and unavailing and were viewed with contempt by their employers. But in 1887 there appeared a new element among the Jews; for then was issued by the Russian government the famous circular that reduced the number of Hebrew students who might enter the colleges and universities of Russia to so small a percentage that it really amounted to a proscription of them. Many of these, together with other refugees—chiefly political exiles—joined the stream of emigration which had already set toward America. It is to the coming of this class that the labor organizations of the Jewish workingmen in New York owe much of their radical and progressive character. The place which the Russian student holds among his own people is unique. Coming here as poor as the poorest immigrant, he is compelled to live in the same quarter and is often obliged to earn his living at the same trade as the most ignorant. Many of the cloak-makers of the East Side are exiled Russian students; in fact, most of the Russian Jewish students have served an apprenticeship at the sewing machine. This necessity brings them into closest touch and sympathy with the working classes. These earnest, intelligent, radical students became organizers of trades unions, editors, speakers, students of law and of medicine in New York colleges, but always and primarily they are agitators for higher social conditions. While American workingmen are prone to look with distrust upon educated men who take up their cause, the Jewish workingmen, with the great respect they have for learning, welcome the educated and acknowledge their leadership.

These zealous Russian students eagerly threw themselves into the movement for the relief of their oppressed countrymen. With this impetus the organization of the Jewish trades was carried on zealously. In 1889–90 the struggle for better social conditions became known to the outside world. The cloak-makers' union, consisting of seven or eight thousand members, was among the first organized. In no other had the sweating system been carried to such extremes. The wages of a work-day of from sixteen to eighteen hours often failed to supply the necessaries of their miserable existence. Immediately following their thorough organization came their long and memorable struggle for better wages, shorter hours, and more humane conditions of labor—a struggle undertaken and carried on for three months, without a dollar in the treasury of the union, and finally won, "because," as one of the members said, "the cloak-makers knew how to starve."

I remember going from house to house during the last fearful days of the strike and seeing men gaunt from hunger, women and little children unable to stand from want and exhaustion, with the threat of eviction hanging over their heads, and still I heard not one word of complaint, not to speak of surrender to the "boss." Nothing could have better illustrated the peculiar powers of the Jewish character than the patient endurance that marked the whole progress of this struggle for living wages.

The cloak-makers won, and it is even yet difficult to estimate the great advantage that their victory brought to the whole Jewish working class. The first result was the organization of the principal Jewish trades, especially the different clothing trades, and, more important still, the sweating system had received its first substantial set-back in New York. Organization soon spread to the other cities and large centres of industry; so that now in almost every large city of the United States there exist numerous labor organizations of Jewish working men and women. These organizations become a significant contribution to our civilization when we consider that they stand in every case for higher wages, a shorter work-day, and better conditions, and that they signify therefore a greater intelligence, a better education, and a higher culture of the working classes. In good measure have the Russian Jews compensated for the temporary depression of economic conditions brought about by their first experience here.

We are not in possession of accurate figures which would give us an exact knowledge of the increase in wages, and, more important still, the diminution of hours brought about by these organizations and their subsequent victories, but the Report of the New York State Bureau of Labor Statistics for 1890 shows that the increase of wages was more than $500,000 for the few months remaining in 1890 after the settlement of the strikes. I know that in some cases the wages of week-workers were doubled, while the decrease in hours in those trades where overwork had been a crime against the moral and physical nature of the worker were even more advantageous. The number of workmen engaged in such strikes as concerned wages alone was more than eleven thousand. The exposure of the horrors of the sweating system was one of the important results of these strikes, and it led to the passage of the Factory Act of March 9, 1892, which, if enforced, would practically abolish the system in New York.

Thus, although the Jewish immigrants were for a short time a disturbing factor in the trades in which they competed with native working men and women, they have by their organizations placed those very trades upon higher economic plan than they had previously occupied, while the shortening of work-hours brought about by the same means has created a greatly increased demand for labor in these industries. In fact, the competition of immigrants has, during the recent discussion of immigration, been very much exaggerated. Even a very slight reduction in the hours of a day's work would easily abolish the competition caused by immigration. And it is a significant fact that in the most progressive labor organizations of the country the leading element is of foreign birth, and nearly without exception all successful movements for reducing the hours of labor—the greatest and most effective aim of organized labor—can be traced directly to the leadership of immigrants. So these latter, even from the standpoint of conservative trade unions, in the long run repay tenfold to the labor movement whatever injury they may have done during the first years of their residence here. At any rate, when we consider the enormous reduction in hours effected by these Jewish organizations (in shirt-making alone the length of the working-day five years ago was fourteen hours, and it is now ten hours), it seems to me that we must concede that the Russian Jews have fairly created their own place in American industries. For example, twenty years ago nine-tenths of all the cloaks used in this country were imported, but nine-tenths have been made here since the beginning of the large immigration of Russian Jews. Many other industries which have been established here would have been impossible without the accession of foreign working people.

The Jewish workmen having effected a thorough and far-reaching organization in their respective crafts, did not stop there. The work of organization and education still goes steadily on. At an early stage in their organization they recognized the value of a federation of labor unions to secure the real and permanent success of organized labor. The United Hebrew Trades was formed in 1888—a central body composed of delegates from all the organized Hebrew trades in New York. One year after its organization it numbered about twenty-five organizations, representing more than ten thousand members. Every trade holds its own separate meeting, usually once a week, and these numerous trade gatherings are one of the important features of East Side life in New York. It is true that the number in the Jewish labor organizations varies, as in all trade unions. But among the organized Hebrew trades a temporary defeat in an economic struggle acts only as a slight check to their growth and progress, while a total rout of their forces is followed by an immediate rally. Such a thing as a complete paralysis of zeal and effort after defeat is unknown in Hebrew labor organizations. This again is due to the peculiar qualities of the Jewish character.

The Russian Jews are naturally radicals on all social questions. They have come from a country which represents to them only tyranny and oppression, and social questions have a deep, absorbing, and personal interest to them. Another fact that increases the radicalism of the educated Jews is that, not being an abiding people, they have no strong prejudices in favor of any established party. Thus from the force of circumstances as well as by natural inclination they find their natural and congenial place among the ultra-radical workingmen. Thousands of the disciples of Karl Marx may be found among the organized Jewish workingmen. Their intense desire to study and to discuss social questions I have never seen equalled. Scores of great agitation meetings are held weekly on the East Side. A few weeks ago a meeting called to discuss immigration was attended by over six thousand persons, while thousands were unable to obtain admission. A similar call for a meeting issued to native American or to Irish workingmen would probably have brought but a few hundreds.

Almost the first impulse of those who have a cause to champion is to seek the powerful aid of the press, and the Jews quickly recognized this power. In the face of apparently insurmountable obstacles, Russian students with a following chiefly of the underpaid employees of "sweaters"* succeeded in founding and maintaining a weekly labor paper of a high order of literary excellence—the "Arbeiter Zeitung" [*The Workers' Newspaper*], which has exerted great influence in the struggles of the Jewish workingmen. This newspaper is the centre of an agitation which represents great energy and self-denial on the

---

*owners of sweatshops

part of its promoters. The editor is a young Russian student who is a remarkable orator in both the Jewish and English languages. Anyone who has heard his speeches at the immense meetings which are often held by the Jews in Cooper Union would not be surprised at his influence over them. He was one of the most prominent figures at the recent International Labor Congress in Brussels, where he made an address on the social and industrial condition of the Jewish working class in Europe and America.

The records of the public schools show that the attendance of the Jewish children is more regular than the attendance of the children of any other class and that their standard of scholarship is higher. No sacrifice is considered too great by the Hebrew father and mother to keep their children at school as long as possible. A Jew who cannot read and write his own language at least is the exception. An educational restriction on immigration would have no appreciable effect in excluding Russian Jews.

The Jews are a temperate people, and the saloon is not likely to become an element in their social or political life. Instead of beer or strong alcoholic liquors, they drink enormous quantities of tea and coffee. Coffee-houses are numerous on the East Side and serve as the gathering-places of the Jewish working men and women. A glass of tea with lemon is served with a thin Russian cake for ten cents, and this refreshment, so dear to a Russian, is therefore within the means of the poorest artisan or student. Every night from ten to twelve these coffee-houses are crowded with students and workingmen, many of whom drop in from the numerous trade and agitation meetings which are nightly held in the Jewish quarter. The recreations of a people are commonly the truest indication of their real character. The frequenters of these dingy little coffee-houses are men rough and uncouth in appearance, poorly dressed and often dirty and unkempt, but a lady or a scholar would find nothing offensive in their conversation. They discuss trade matters, political economy, philosophy, the works of Karl Marx, Kropotkine [sic], Tolstoi, Tchernychewsky, and Zola. Almost any Jewish workingman you might chance to meet in these circles would be able to discuss intelligently these authors and their works. This undoubtedly due to the student influence which so largely predominates in their gatherings. These coffee-houses are often the scene of conversations and discussions which would do credit to a much more ambitious field.

Here, too, you meet the real actors in those Russian tragedies whose ending is usually in far off Siberia. I remember sitting one evening at a table in one of these coffee-houses, with a young Russian Jew whom I had sometimes met at labor meetings. He was reading a letter. When he had finished he turned to me and said, "It is from my sister in Siberia." When I asked him for what crime she had been sent there, he answered quietly but with a tone of bitter hate in his voice, "Because she studied and taught the others why we were so miserable in Russia." He then told me his sister's sad story. She was graduated at one of the gymnasiums [elite high schools preparing students for the university] at the age of sixteen with great honors. She and her brother became revolutionists and for two years devoted themselves to teaching the peasants and others revolutionary doctrines. It became known to the Russian government, and without warning, even without seeing her family, she was sent to Siberia for eighteen years. Her brother escaped to this country. Eight years of her sentence have now passed, and she is allowed, at stated intervals, to write to her friends. He added in a hopeless sort of way, "She has ten years more; she will not live out her sentence." Such stories are only too common on the East Side. Contrast the coffee-houses of the Jews with similar gatherings of American or Irish workingmen in what they call their recreations, and you will understand why the student sociology looks with greater hope to the Russian Jews.

Jewish immigration is free from the objection, so commonly urged against immigration in general, that it increases crime and pauperism. The Jewish quarter in New York, although more densely populated than any other tenement-house district, is rarely the scene of serious brawls or disturbances. Few policemen are to be seen here and these find but little demand for their services. The records of police courts are remarkably free from Jewish names. This is principally owing to their temperate habits, while their strong domestic virtues, their love of their wives and children, prevent family troubles whose settlement forms so large a part of the work of civil court and police justices. Statistics show that during the last few years, when Jewish immigration has so greatly increased, crime among this nationality has not shown a corresponding increase.

The whole number of Jewish prisoners in New York State is 360. This remarkably small number, in a State which contains so large a Jewish population, is a conclusive proof of their law-abiding character. In Sing Sing out of a total of 1,600 prisoners there are only 72 Jews, and of these 19 are Americans, leaving only 53 foreign-born. In Clinton prison among 900 there are 25 Jewish prisoners; in Auburn there are 36 Jews among 1,100 convicts. In the workhouse on Blackwell's Island, out of 1,100 inmates, there are only five Jews. The superintendent of the workhouse says that a Jew is seldom brought back a second time. There has never been a Jewish woman in the workhouse. In the penitentiary at Albany there are only two Jews among 700 prisoners. There is one Jewish prisoner in each of the penitentiaries of Syracuse, Rochester, and Buffalo. It is also a fact worthy of attention, that most of these prisoners have been convicted of petty crimes, into which they have been led by gambling practices. The Russian Jews are not addicted to this vice in their own country, but have acquired it in this country by the freedom with which pool rooms and policy-shops are allowed to flourish in our large cities, in open defiance of existing laws for their suppression.

The Russian Jews come here under the worst possible economic conditions, and are probably the poorest immigrants who land at Ellis Island; a property qualification would operate to keep out most of them; still it is a well-known fact that fewer Jews become recipients of either public or private charity than persons of any other nationality. This should be heeded by those who think to improve the character of our immigration by the imposition of a property tax. For many years there were only two Jews in the almshouse on Blackwell's Island, but in 1892, out of a total of 2,170, there were 11 Jews, five men and six women. Among the 1,000 patients at Charity Hospital there are usually from 12 to 15 Jewish patients.

The business instinct of the Jew, the money-getting faculty, is popularly supposed to be much stronger than in other races. But this is owing to the conditions under which they have lived. By their exclusion from nearly all other occupations they have been forced to become almost entirely a trading and commercial class, and this has abnormally stimulated their business faculties as well as developed the traits of character which have rendered them most objectionable and offensive in popular estimation. As employers of labor they are neither better nor worse than other employers. The rich Jew, like the rich Christian, invariably buys his labor at the cheapest possible rates. If there should seem to be a greater tendency on the part of the Jewish manufacturer to exploit the worker, it is usually due to his lower conception of the standard of living. The Jew who here becomes the employer of labor has been obliged, perhaps, as a workman in Europe to live upon two or three dollars a week, and therefore it seems to him perfectly proper and just that his workmen and women should conform to the same standard of living.

A strong point in favor of the Russian Jewish immigrants is the fact that they come here with the intention of becoming permanent citizens of the United States. They alone, perhaps, of all the immigrants who come to America are free from any endearing ties and associations which would, at any future time, draw them back to the land of their birth. Russia has not been a kind fatherland to the Jews. For good or for ill their fortunes are irrevocably cast with us. They and their descendants are destined to become a permanent factor in our national life.

The statement that they do not assimilate with our people and our institutions usually means in its last analysis that they do not become a part of the corrupt political institutions in the large cities where they live. This want of assimilation is generally more noticeable among the educated and intelligent immigrants than among the other classes. The truth is the Russian Jews have eagerly taken advantage of all our best and most progressive institutions. The Jews have been for so many generations excluded from all participation in the governments under which they have lived that we should naturally expect to find them disinclined and unfitted to take part in political affairs. But their past history does not show this to have been the case. In the countries where they have been allowed to take an active part in the conduct of government, as in France, England, and Germany, there are many eminent states men of Jewish birth. In England, Disraeli, notwithstanding seemingly insurmountable barriers of race, religion, and social prejudice, became the idolized leader of a Tory aristocracy, while in Germany Ferdinand Lassalle was the trusted teacher and leader of the working-class political movement. They are, as yet, too new in America to have become a political power, but their intelligent interest in all the public questions of the day, as shown by their discussions and reading, indicates that the presence of Jews in our national affairs is a matter of not distant date.

Politically, the Jews possess many characteristics of the best citizens. Their respect and desire for education make them most unlikely to follow an ignorant demagogue, while for a still deeper and more radical reason they make an enlightened selfishness their standard of all political worth. The centuries during which every conscious and unconscious tendency of the governments under which they lived has been to make their individual and race advancement their single object, have developed traits of character most unfavorable to that blind partisanship which is requisite for the successful carrying out of the objects of political organizations like Tammany Hall. The education given by the modern labor movement has, in a great degree, transformed their race-feeling into a class-feeling, and they now look with zeal to the advancement of the working people, in whose elevation they recognize that their hope for the future lies. The one or two Jewish political demagogues who strive to create a following on the East Side have met with doubtful success. In fact, there does not exist a more unpromising field in New York for the political trickster than the Jewish quarter of the city. Their cold, critical analysis of political nostrums is most disheartening to the district-leaders of Tammany Hall. Unlike most native or Irish voters, they are proof against the blandishments of the campaign orator and the fascinations of the torchlight procession and brass band. The great mass of Russian Jews are not yet naturalized, but of those who are the vast majority voted last year with the Socialist Labor party.

Document 16.3 How the Other Half Lives

One of the best-known accounts of the lives of the poor was *How the Other Half Lives* by Jacob Riis, a Danish-American writer and photographer. Riis's account and photographs of life in New York tenements shocked many middle-class Americans. Riis has been accused of sensationalization in his portrayal of tenement life. Do you think this is true? Why? What are the main ideas emerging from Riis's portrayal?

How the Other Half Lives

Jacob Riis

When once I asked the agent of a notorious Fourth Ward alley how many people might be living in it I was told: One hundred and forty families, one hundred Irish, thirty-eight Italian, and two that spoke the German tongue. Barring the agent herself, there was not a native-born individual in the court. The answer was characteristic of the cosmopolitan character of lower New York, very nearly so of the whole of it, wherever it runs to alleys and courts. One may find for the asking an Italian, a German, a French, African, Spanish, Bohemian, Russian, Scandinavian, Jewish, and Chinese colony. Even the Arab, who peddles "holy earth" from the Battery as a direct importation from Jerusalem, has his exclusive preserves at the lower end of Washington Street. The one thing you shall vainly ask for in the chief city of America is a distinctively American community. There is none; certainly not among the tenements. Where have they gone to, the old inhabitants? I put the question to one who might fairly be presumed to be of the number, since I had found him sighing for the "good old days" when the legend "no Irish need apply" was familiar in the advertising columns of the newspapers. He looked at me with a puzzled air. "I don't know," he said. "I wish I did. Some went to California in '49, some to the war and never came back. The rest, I expect, have gone to heaven, or somewhere. I don't see them 'round here."

Whatever the merit of the good man's conjectures, his eyes did not deceive him. They are not here. In their place has come this queer conglomerate mass of heterogeneous elements, ever striving and working like whiskey and water in one glass, and with the like result: final union and a prevailing taint of whiskey. The once unwelcome Irishman has been followed in his turn by the Italian, the Russian Jew, and the Chinaman, and has himself taken a hand at opposition, quite as bitter and quite as ineffectual, against these later hordes. Wherever these have gone they have crowded him out, possessing the block, the street, the ward with their denser swarms. But the Irishman's revenge is complete. Victorious in defeat over his recent as over his more ancient foe, the one who opposed his coming no less than the one who drove him out, he dictates to both their politics, and, secure in possession of the offices, returns the native his greeting with interest, while collecting the rents of the Italian whose house he has bought with the profits of his saloon. As a landlord he is picturesquely autocratic. An amusing instance of his methods came under my notice while writing these lines. An inspector of the Health Department found an Italian family paying a man with a Celtic name

From *How the Other Half Lives*, New York: Charles Scribner's Sons, 1890.

twenty-five dollars a month for three small rooms in a ramshackle rear tenement—more than twice what they were worth—and expressed his astonishment to the tenant, an ignorant Sicilian laborer. He replied that he had once asked the landlord to reduce the rent, but he would not do it.

"Well! What did he say?" asked the inspector.

"'Damma, man!' he said; 'if you speaka thata way to me, I fira you and your things in the streeta.'" And the frightened Italian paid the rent.

In justice to the Irish landlord it must be said that like an apt pupil he was merely showing forth the result of the schooling he had received, re-enacting, in his own way, the scheme of the tenements. It is only his frankness that shocks. The Irishman does not naturally take kindly to tenement life, though with characteristic versatility he adapts himself to its conditions at once. It does violence, nevertheless, to the best that is in him, and for that very reason of all who come within its sphere soonest corrupts him. The result is a sediment, the product of more than a generation in the city's slums, that, as distinguished from the larger body of his class, justly ranks at the foot of tenement dwellers, the so-called "low Irish."

It is not to be assumed, of course, that the whole body of the population living in the tenements, of which New Yorkers are in the habit of speaking vaguely as "the poor," or even the larger part of it, is to be classed as vicious or as poor in the sense of verging on beggary.

New York's wage-earners have no other place to live, more is the pity. They are truly poor for having no better homes; waxing poorer in purse as the exorbitant rents to which they are tied, as ever was serf to soil, keep rising. The wonder is that they are not all corrupted, and speedily, by their surroundings. If, on the contrary, there be a steady working up, if not out of the slough, the fact is a powerful argument for the optimist's belief that the world is, after all, growing better, not worse, and would go far toward disarming apprehension, were it not for the steadier growth of the sediment of the slums and its constant menace. Such an impulse toward better things there certainly is. The German rag-picker of thirty years ago, quite as low in the scale as his Italian successor, is the thrifty tradesman or prosperous farmer of to-day.

The Italian scavenger of our time is fast graduating into exclusive control of the corner fruit-stands, while his black-eyed boy monopolizes the boot-blacking industry in which a few years ago he was an intruder. The Irish hod-carrier in the second generation has become a bricklayer, if not the Alderman of his ward, while the Chinese coolie is in almost exclusive possession of the laundry business. The reason is obvious. The poorest immigrant comes here with the purpose and ambition to better himself and, given half a chance, might be reasonably expected to make the most of it. To the false plea that he prefers the squalid houses in which his kind are housed there could be no better answer. The truth is, his half chance has too long been wanting, and for the bad result he has been unjustly blamed.

As emigration from east to west follows the latitude, so does the foreign influx in New York distribute itself along certain well-defined lines that waver and break only under the stronger pressure of a more gregarious race or the encroachments of inexorable business. A feeling of dependence upon mutual effort, natural to strangers in a strange land, unacquainted with its language and customs, sufficiently accounts for this.

The Irishman is the true cosmopolitan immigrant. All-pervading, he shares his lodging with perfect impartiality with the Italian, the Greek, and the "Dutchman," yielding only to sheer force of numbers, and objects equally to them all. A map of the city, colored to designate nationalities, would show more stripes than on the skin of a zebra, and more colors than any rainbow.

The city on such a map would fall into two great halves, green for the Irish prevailing in the West Side tenement districts, and blue for the Germans on the East Side. But intermingled with these ground colors would be an odd variety of tints that would give the whole the appearance of an extraordinary crazy-quilt. From down in the Sixth Ward, upon the site of the old Collect Pond that in the days of the fathers drained the hills which are no more, the red of the Italian would be seen forcing its way northward along the line of Mulberry Street to the quarter of the French purple on Bleecker Street and South Fifth Avenue, to lose itself and reappear, after a lapse of miles, in the "Little Italy" of Harlem, east of Second Avenue. Dashes of red, sharply defined, would be seen strung through the Annexed District, northward to the city line. On the West Side the red would be seen over-running the old Africa of Thompson Street, pushing the black of the negro rapidly uptown, against querulous but unavailing protests, occupying his home, his church, his trade and all, with merciless impartiality. There is a church in Mulberry Street that has stood for two generations as a sort of milestone of these migrations. Built originally for the worship of staid New Yorkers of the "old stock," it was engulfed by the colored tide, when the draft-riots drove the negroes out of reach of Cherry Street and the Five Points. Within the past decade the advance wave of the Italian onset reached it, and to-day the arms of United Italy adorn its front. The negroes have made a stand at several points along Seventh and Eighth

Avenues; but their main body, still pursued by the Italian foe, is on the march yet, and the black mark will be found overshadowing to-day many blocks on the East Side, with One Hundredth Street as the centre, where colonies of them have settled recently.

Hardly less aggressive than the Italian, the Russian and Polish Jew, having over-run the district between Rivington and Division Streets, east of the Bowery, to the point of suffocation, is filling the tenements of the old Seventh Ward to the river front, and disputing with the Italian every foot of available space in the back alleys of Mulberry Street. The two races, differing hopelessly in much, have this in common: they carry their slums with them wherever they go, if allowed to do it. Little Italy already rivals its parent, the "Bend," in foulness. Other nationalities that begin at the bottom make a fresh start when crowded up the ladder. Happily both are manageable, the one by rabbinical, the other by the civil law. Between the dull gray of the Jew, his favorite color, and the Italian red, would be seen squeezed in on the map a sharp streak of yellow, marking the narrow boundaries of Chinatown. Dovetailed in with the German population, the poor but thrifty Bohemian might be picked out by the sombre hue of his life as of his philosophy, struggling against heavy odds in the big human bee-hives of the East Side. Colonies of his people extend northward, with long lapses of space, from below the Cooper Institute more than three miles. The Bohemian is the only foreigner with any considerable representation in the city who counts no wealthy man of his race, none who has not to work hard for a living, or has got beyond the reach of the tenement.

Down near the Battery the West Side emerald would be soiled by a dirty stain, spreading rapidly like a splash of ink on a sheet of blotting paper, headquarters of the Arab tribe, that in a single year has swelled from the original dozen to twelve hundred, intent, every mother's son, on trade and barter. Dots and dashes of color here and there would show where the Finnish sailors worship their djumala (God), the Greek pedlars the ancient name of their race, and the Swiss the goddess of thrift. And so on to the end of the long register, all toiling together in the galling fetters of the tenement. Were the question raised who makes the most of life thus mortgaged, who resists most stubbornly its levelling tendency—knows how to drag even the barracks upward a part of the way at least toward the ideal plane of the home—the palm must be unhesitatingly awarded the Teuton. The Italian and the poor Jew rise only by compulsion. The Chinaman does not rise at all; here, as at home, he simply remains stationary. The Irishman's genius runs to public affairs rather than domestic life; wherever he is mustered in force the saloon is the gorgeous centre of political activity. The German struggles vainly to learn his trick; his Teutonic wit is too heavy, and the political ladder he raises from his saloon usually too short or too clumsy to reach the desired goal. The best part of his life is lived at home, and he makes himself a home independent of the surroundings, giving the lie to the saying, unhappily become a maxim of social truth, that pauperism and drunkenness naturally grow in the tenements. He makes the most of his tenement, and it should be added that whenever and as soon as he can save up money enough, he gets out and never crosses the threshold of one again.

Document 16.4 From A *Bintel Brief*

In 1906, the *Jewish Daily Forward*, a Yiddish language newspaper in New York City, began the column "Bintel Brief," which gave advice in response to readers' letters. The Yiddish title means "a bundle of letters." Abraham Cahan, editor of the newspaper, produced the column. The letters reveal practical problems among Jewish immigrants, mostly from Eastern Europe, as they adapted to life in the United States. What problems of Jewish immigrants do you see these letters revealing? What values does Cahan show in his answers?

From A *Bintel Brief*

Abraham Cahan

{1906}

Worthy Editor,

We are a small family who recently came to the "Golden Land." My husband my boy and I are together, and our daughter lives in another city.

I had opened a grocery store here, but soon lost all my money. In Europe we were in business; we had people working for us and paid them well. In short, there we made a good living but here we are badly off.

My husband became a peddler. The "pleasure" of knocking on doors and ringing bells cannot be known by anyone but a peddler. If anybody does buy anything "on time," a lot of the money is lost, because there are some people who never intend to pay. In addition, my husband has trouble because he has a beard, and because of the beard he gets beaten up by the hoodlums.

Also we have problems with our boy, who throws money around. He works every day till late at night in a grocery for three dollars a week. I watch over him and give him the best because I'm sorry that he has to work so hard. But he costs me plenty and he borrows money from everybody. He has many friends and owes them all money. I get more and more worried as he takes here and borrows there. All my talking doesn't help. I am afraid to chase him away from home because he might get worse among strangers. I want to point out that he is well versed in Russian and Hebrew and he is not a child any more, but his behavior is not that of an intelligent adult.

I don't know what to do. My husband argues that he doesn't want to continue peddling. He doesn't want to shave off his beard, and it's not fitting for such a man to do so. The boy wants to go to his sister, but that's a twenty-five dollar fare. What can I do? I beg you for a suggestion.

Your Constant reader,
F L.

Answer:

Since her husband doesn't earn a living anyway, it would be advisable for all three of them to move to the city where the daughter is living. As for the beard, we feel that if the man is religious and the beard is dear to him because the Jewish law does not allow him to shave it off, it's up to him to decide. But if he is not religious, and the beard interferes with his earnings, it should be sacrificed.

{1906}

Dear Editor,

For a long time I worked in a shop with a Gentile girl, and we began to go out together and fell in love. We agreed that I would remain a Jew and she a Christian. But after we had been married for a year, I realized that it would not work.

I began to notice that whenever one of my Jewish friends comes to the house, she is displeased. Worse yet, when she sees me reading a Jewish newspaper her face changes color. She says nothing, but I can see that she has changed. I feel that she is very unhappy with me, though I know she loves me. She will soon become a mother, and she is more dependent on me than ever.

She used to be quite liberal, but lately she is being drawn back to the Christian religion. She gets up early Sunday mornings, runs to church and comes home with eyes swollen from crying. When we pass a church now and then, she trembles.

Dear Editor, advise me what to do now. I could never convert, and there's no hope for me to keep her from going to church. What can we do now?

Thankfully,
A Reader

Answer:

Unfortunately, we often hear of such tragedies, which stem from marriages between people of different worlds. It's possible that if this couple were

---

From *A Bintel Brief*, Letters to the Editor from 1906–1911.

to move to a Jewish neighborhood, the young man might have more influence on his wife. . . .

{1906}

Dear Editor,

I am a girl from Galicia and in the shop where I work I sit near a Russian Jew with whom I was always on good terms. Why should one worker resent another?

But once, in a short debate, he stated that all Galicians were no good. When I asked him to repeat it, he answered that he wouldn't retract a word, and that he wished all Galician Jews dead.

I was naturally not silent in the face of such a nasty expression. He maintained that only Russian Jews are fine and intelligent. According to him, the Galitzianer are inhuman savages, and he had the right to speak of them so badly.

Dear Editor, does he really have a right to say this? Have the Galician Jews not sent enough money for the unfortunate sufferers of the pogroms in Russia? When a Gentile speaks badly of Jews, it's immediately printed in the newspapers and discussed hotly everywhere. But that a Jew should express himself so about his own brothers is nothing? Does he have a right? Are Galicians really so bad? And does he, the Russian, remain fine and intelligent in spite of such expressions?

As a reader of your worthy newspaper, I hope you will print my letter and give your opinion.

With thanks in advance,
B. M.

Answer:

The Galician Jews are just as good and bad as people from other lands. If the Galicians must be ashamed of the foolish and evil ones among them, then the Russians, too, must hide their heads in shame because among them there is such an idiot as the acquaintance of our letter writer. . . .

{1907}

Worthy Editor,

I am eighteen years old and a machinist by trade. During the past year I suffered a great deal, just because I am a Jew.

It is common knowledge that my trade is run mainly by the Gentiles and, working among the Gentiles, I have seen things that cast a dark shadow on the American labor scene. Just listen:

I worked in a shop in a small town in New Jersey, with twenty Gentiles. There was one other Jew besides me, and both of us endured the greatest hardships. That we were insulted goes without saying. At times we were even beaten up. We work in an area where there are many factories, and once, when we were leaving the shop, a group of workers fell on us like hoodlums and beat us. To top it off, we and one of our attackers were arrested. The hoodlum was let out on bail, but we, beaten and bleeding, had to stay in jail. At the trial, they fined the hoodlum eight dollars and let him go free.

After that I went to work on a job in Brooklyn. As soon as they found out that I was a Jew they began to torment me so that I had to leave the place. I have already worked at many places, and I either have to leave, voluntarily, or they fire me because I am a Jew.

Till now, I was alone and didn't care. At this trade you can make good wages, and I had enough. But now I've brought my parents over, and of course I have to support them.

Lately I've been working on one job for three months and I would be satisfied, but the worm of anti-Semitism is beginning to eat at my bones again. I go to work in the morning as to Gehenna,* and I run away at night as from a fire. It's impossible to talk to them because they are common boors, so-called "American sports." I have already tried in various ways, but the only way to deal with them is with a strong fist. But I am too weak and there are too many.

Perhaps you can help me in this matter. I know it is not an easy problem.

Your reader,
E. H.

Answer:

In the answer, the Jewish machinist is advised to appeal to the United Hebrew Trades and ask them to intercede for him and bring up charges before the Machinists Union about this persecution. His attention is also drawn to the fact that there are Gentile factories where Jews and Gentiles work together and get along well with each other.

Finally it is noted that people will have to work long and hard before this senseless racial hatred can be completely uprooted. . . .

{1907}

*Gehenna: hell

Worthy Editor,

I was born in America and my parents gave me a good education. I studied Yiddish and Hebrew, finished high school, completed a course in bookkeeping and got a good job. I have many friends, and several boys have already proposed to me.

Recently I went to visit my parents' home in Russian Poland. My mother's family in Europe had invited my parents to a wedding, but instead of going themselves, they sent me. I stayed at my grandmother's with an aunt and uncle and had a good time. Our European family, like my parents, are quite well off and they treated me well. They indulged me in everything and I stayed with them six months.

It was lively in the town. There were many organizations and clubs and they all accepted me warmly, looked up to me—after all, I was a citizen of the free land, America. Among the social leaders of the community was an intelligent young man, a friend of my uncle's, who took me to various gatherings and affairs.

He was very attentive, and after a short while he declared his love for me in a long letter. I had noticed that he was not indifferent to me, and I liked him as well. I looked up to him and respected him, as did all the townsfolk. My family became aware of it, and when they spoke to me about him, I could see they thought it was a good match.

He was handsome, clever, educated, a good talker and charmed me, but I didn't give him a definite answer. As my love for him grew, however, I wrote to my parents about him, and then we became officially engaged.

A few months later we both went to my parents in the States and they received him like their own son. My bridegroom immediately began to learn English and tried to adjust to the new life. Yet when I introduced him to my friends they looked at him with disappointment. "This 'greenhorn' is your fiance?" they asked. I told them what a big role he played in his town, how everyone respected him, but they looked at me as if I were crazy and scoffed at my words.

At first I thought, Let them laugh, when they get better acquainted with him they'll talk differently. In time, though, I was affected by their talk and began to think, like them, that he really was a "greenhorn" and acted like one.

In short, my love for him is cooling off gradually. I'm suffering terribly because my feelings for him are changing. In Europe, where everyone admired him and all the girls envied me, he looked different. But, here, I see before me another person.

I haven't the courage to tell him, and I can't even talk about it to my parents. He still loves me with all his heart, and I don't know what to do. I choke it all up inside myself, and I beg you to help me with advice in my desperate situation.

Respectfully,
A Worried Reader

Answer:

The writer would make a grave mistake if she were to separate from her bridegroom now. She must not lose her common sense and be influenced by the foolish opinions of her friends who divided the world into "greenhorns" and real Americans.

We can assure the writer that her bridegroom will learn English quickly. He will know American history and literature as well as her friends do, and be a better American than they. She should be proud of his love and laugh at those who call him "greenhorn." . . .

{1907}

Dear Editor,

Since I do not want my conscience to bother me, I ask you to decide whether a married woman has the right to go to school two evenings a week. My husband thinks I have no right to do this.

I admit that I cannot be satisfied to be just a wife and mother. I am still young and I want to learn and enjoy life. My children and my house are not neglected, but I go to evening high school twice a week. My husband is not pleased and when I come home at night and ring the bell, he lets me stand outside a long time intentionally, and doesn't hurry to open the door.

Now he has announced a new decision. Because I send out the laundry to be done, it seems to him that I have too much time for myself, even enough to go to school. So from now on he will count out every penny for anything I have to buy for the house, so I will not be able to send out the laundry any more. And when I have to do the work myself there won't be any time left for such "foolishness" as going to school. I told him that I'm willing to do my own washing but that I would still be able to find time for study.

When I am alone with my thoughts, I feel I may not be right. Perhaps I should not go to school. I want to say that my husband is an intelligent man and he wanted to marry a woman who was educated. The fact that he is intelligent makes me more annoyed with him. He is in favor of the emancipation of women, yet in real life he acts contrary to his beliefs.

Awaiting your opinion on this, I remain,

Your reader,
The Discontented Wife

Answer:

Since this man is intelligent and an adherent of the women's emancipation movement, he is scolded severely in the answer for wanting to keep his wife so enslaved. Also the opinion is expressed that the wife absolutely has the right to go to school two evenings a week. . . .

{1911}

Dear Editor,

I plead with you to open your illustrious newspaper and take in my "Bintel Brief" in which I write about my great suffering.

A long gloomy year, three hundred and sixty-five days, have gone by since I left my home and am alone on the lonely road of life. Oh, my poor dear parents, how saddened they were at my leaving. The leave-taking, their seeing me on my way, was like a silent funeral.

There was no shaking of the alms box, there was no grave digging and no sawing of boards, but I, myself, put on the white shirt that was wet with my mother's tears, took my pillow, and climbed into the wagon. Accompanying me was a quiet choked wail from my parents and friends.

The wheels of the wagon rolled farther and farther away. My mother and father wept for their son, then turned with heavy hearts to the empty house. They did not sit shive [a period of mourning] even though they had lost a child.

I came to America and became a painter. My great love for Hebrew, for Russian, all of my other knowledge was smeared with paint. During the year that I have been here I have had some good periods, but I am not happy, because I have no interest in anything. My homesickness and loneliness darken my life.

Ah, home, my beloved home. My heart is heavy for my parents whom I left behind. I want to run back, but I am powerless. I am a coward, because I know that I have to serve under "Fonie" [the Czar] for three years. I am lonely in my homesickness and I beg you to be my counsel as to how to act.

Respectfully,
V.A.

Answer:

The answer states that almost all immigrants yearn deeply for dear ones and home at first. They are compared with plants that are transplanted to new ground. At first it seems that they are withering, but in time most of them revive and take root in the new earth.

The advice to this young man is that he must not consider going home, but try to take root here. He should try to overcome all these emotions and strive to make something of himself so that in time he will be able to bring his parents here.

Document 16.5 Strenuous Life of the Tammany District Leader

The Life and Thoughts of a Tammany District Leader

William L. Riordan

Honest Graft and Dishonest Graft

Everybody is talkin' these days about Tammany men growin' rich on graft, but nobody thinks of drawin' the distinction between honest graft and dishonest graft. There's all the difference in the world between the two. Yes, many of our men have grown rich in politics. I have myself. I've made a big fortune out of the game, and I'm gettin' richer every day, but I've not gone in for dishonest graft—blackmailin'

From *Plunkitt of Tammany Hall: Plain Talk and Practical Politics*, 1905.

gamblers, saloonkeepers, disorderly people, etc.—and neither has any of the men who have made big fortunes in politics.

There's an honest graft, and I'm an example of how it works. I might sum up the whole thing by sayin': "I seen me opportunities and I took 'em."

Just let me explain by examples. My party's in power in the city, and it's goin' to undertake a lot of public improvements. Well, I'm tipped off, say, that they're going to lay out a new park at a certain place.

I see my opportunity and I take it. I go to that place and I buy up all the land I can in the neighborhood. Then the board of this or that makes its plan public, and there is a rush to get my land, which nobody cared particular for before.

Ain't it perfectly honest to charge a good price and make a profit on my investment and foresight? Of course, it is. Well, that's honest graft.

Or supposin' it's a new bridge they're goin' to build. I get tipped off and I buy as much property as I can that has to be taken for approaches. I sell at my own price later on and drop some more money in the bank.

Wouldn't you? It's just like lookin' ahead in Wall Street or in the coffee or cotton market. It's honest graft, and I'm lookin' for it every day in the year. I will tell you frankly that I've got a good lot of it, too.

I'll tell you of one case. They were goin' to fix up a big park, no matter where. I got on to it, and went lookin' about for land in that neighborhood.

I could get nothin' at a bargain but a big piece of swamp, but I took it fast enough and held on to it. What turned out was just what I counted on. They couldn't make the park complete without Plunkitt's swamp, and they had to pay a good price for it. Anything dishonest in that?

Up in the watershed I made some money, too. I bought up several bits of land there some years ago and made a pretty good guess that they would be bought up for water purposes later by the city.

Somehow, I always guessed about right, and shouldn't I enjoy the profit of my foresight? It was rather amusin' when the condemnation commissioners came along and found piece after piece of the land in the name of George Plunkitt of the Fifteenth Assembly District, New York City. They wondered how I knew just what to buy. The answer is—I seen my opportunity and I took it. I haven't confined myself to land; anything that pays is in my line.

For instance, the city is repavin' a street and has several hundred thousand old granite blocks to sell. I am on hand to buy, and I know just what they are worth.

How? Never mind that. I had a sort of monopoly of this business for a while, but once a newspaper tried to do me. It got some outside men to come over from Brooklyn and New Jersey to bid against me.

Was I done? Not much. I went to each of the men and said: "How many of these 250,000 stones do you want?" One said 20,000, and another wanted 15,000, and other wanted 10,000. I said: "All right, let me bid for the lot, and I'll give each of you all you want for nothin'."

They agreed, of course. Then the auctioneer yelled: "How much am I bid for these 250,000 fine pavin' stones?"

"Two dollars and fifty cents," says I.

"Two dollars and fifty cents!" screamed the auctioneer. "Oh, that's a joke! Give me a real bid."

He found the bid was real enough. My rivals stood silent. I got the lot for $2.50 and gave them their share. That's how the attempt to do Plunkitt ended, and that's how all such attempts end.

I've told you how I got rich by honest graft. Now, let me tell you that most politicians who are accused of robbin' the city get rich the same way.

They didn't steal a dollar from the city treasury. They just seen their opportunities and took them. That is why, when a reform administration comes in and spends a half million dollars in tryin' to find the public robberies they talked about in the campaign, they don't find them.

The books are always all right. The money in the city treasury is all right. Everything is all right. All they can show is that the Tammany heads of departments looked after their friends, within the law, and gave them what opportunities they could to make honest graft. Now, let me tell you that's never goin' to hurt Tammany with the people. Every good man looks after his friends, and any man who doesn't isn't likely to be popular. If I have a good thing to hand out in private life, I give it to a friend. Why shouldn't I do the same in public life?

Another kind of honest graft. Tammany has raised a good many salaries. There was an awful howl by the reformers, but don't you know that Tammany gains ten votes for every one it lost by salary raisin'?

The Wall Street banker thinks it shameful to raise a department clerk's salary from $1500 to $1800 a year, but every man who draws a salary himself says: "That's all right. I wish it was me." And he feels very much like votin' the Tammany ticket on election day, just out of sympathy.

Tammany was beat in 1901 because the people were deceived into believin' that it worked dishonest graft. They didn't draw a distinction between dishonest and honest graft, but they saw that some Tammany men grew rich, and supposed they had been robbin' the city treasury or levyin' blackmail on disorderly houses, or workin' in with the gamblers and lawbreakers.

As a matter of policy, if nothing else, why should the Tammany leaders go into such dirty business, when there is so much honest graft lyin' around when they are in power? Did you ever consider that?

Now, in conclusion, I want to say that I don't own a dishonest dollar. If my worst enemy was given the job of writin' my epitaph when I'm gone, he couldn't do more than write:

"George W. Plunkitt. He Seen His Opportunities, and He Took 'Em."

Strenuous Life of the Tammany District Leader

NOTE: This chapter is based on exacts from Plunkitt's Diary and on my daily observation of the work of the district leader.—W.L.R.

The life of the Tammany district leader is strenuous. To his work is due the wonderful recuperative power of the organization.

One year it goes down in defeat and the prediction is made that it will never again raise its head. The district leader, undaunted by defeat, collects his scattered forces, organizes them as only Tammany knows how to organize, and in a little while the organization is as strong as ever.

No other politician in New York or elsewhere is exactly like the Tammany district leader or works as he does. As a rule, he has no business or occupation other than politics. He plays politics every day and night in the year, and his headquarters bears the inscription, "Never closed."

Everybody in the district knows him. Everybody knows where to find him, and nearly everybody goes to him for assistance of one sort or another, especially the poor of the tenements.

He is always obliging. He will go to the police courts to put in a good word for the "drunks and disorderlies" or pay their fines, if a good word is not effective. He will attend christenings, weddings, and funerals. He will feed the hungry and help bury the dead.

A philanthropist? Not at all. He is playing politics all the time.

Brought up in Tammany Hall, he has learned how to reach the hearts of the great mass of voters. He does not bother about reaching their heads. It is his belief that arguments and campaign literature have never gained votes.

He seeks direct contact with the people, does them good turns when he can, and relies on their not forgetting him on election day. His heart is always in his work, too, for his subsistence depends on its results.

If he holds his district and Tammany is in power, he is amply rewarded by a good office and the opportunities that go with it. What these opportunities are has been shown by the quick rise to wealth of so many Tammany district leaders. With the examples before him of Richard Croker, once leader of the Twentieth District; John F. Carroll, formerly leader of the Twenty-ninth; Timothy ("Dry Dollar") Sullivan, late leader of the Sixth, and many others, he can always look forward to riches and ease while he is going through the drudgery of his daily routine.

This is a record of a day's work by Plunkitt:

2 A.M.: Aroused from sleep by the ringing of his doorbell; went to the door and found a bartender, who asked him to go to the police station and bail out a saloonkeeper who had been arrested for violating the excise law. Furnished bail and returned to bed at three o'clock.

6 A.M.: Awakened by fire engines passing his house. Hastened to the scene of the fire, according to the custom of the Tammany district leaders, to give assistance to the fire sufferers, if needed. Met several of his election district captains who are always under orders to look out for fires, which are considered great vote-getters. Found several tenants who had been burned out, took them to a hotel, supplied them with clothes, fed them, and arranged temporary quarters for them until they could rent and furnish new apartments.

8:30 A.M.: Went to the police court to look after his constituents. Found six "drunks." Secured the discharge of four by a timely word with the judge, and paid the fines of two.

9 A.M.: Appeared in the Municipal District Court. Directed one of his district captains to act as counsel for a widow against whom dispossess proceedings had been instituted and obtained an extension of time. Paid the rent of a poor family about to be dispossessed and gave them a dollar for food.

11 A.M.: At home again. Found four men waiting for him. One had been discharged by the Metropolitan Railway Company for neglect of duty, and wanted the district leader to fix things. Another wanted a job on the road. The third sought a place on the Subway and the fourth, a plumber, was looking for work with the Consolidated Gas Company. The district leader spent nearly three hours fixing things for the four men, and succeeded in each case.

3 P.M.: Attended the funeral of an Italian as far as the ferry. Hurried back to make his appearance at the funeral of a Hebrew constituent. Went conspicu-

ously to the front both in the Catholic church and the synagogue, and later attended the Hebrew confirmation ceremonies in the synagogue.

7 P.M.: Went to district headquarters and presided over a meeting of election district captains. Each captain submitted a list of all the voters in his district, reported on their attitude toward Tammany, suggested who might be won over and how they could be won, told who were in need, and who were in trouble of any kind and the best way to reach them. District leader took notes and gave orders.

8 P.M.: Went to a church fair. Took chances on everything, bought ice cream for the young girls and the children. Kissed the little ones, flattered their mothers and took their fathers out for something down at the corner.

9 P.M.: At the clubhouse again. Spent $10 on tickets for a church excursion and promised a subscription for a new church bell. Bought tickets for a baseball game to be played by two nines from his district. Listened to the complaints of a dozen pushcart peddlers who said they were persecuted by the police and assured them he would go to Police Headquarters in the morning and see about it.

10:30 P.M.: Attended a Hebrew wedding reception and dance. Had previously sent a handsome wedding present to the bride.

12 P.M.: In bed.

That is the actual record of one day in the life of Plunkitt. He does some of the same things every day, but his life is not so monotonous as to be wearisome.

Sometimes the work of a district leader is exciting, especially if he happens to have a rival who intends to make a contest for the leadership at the primaries. In that case, he is even more alert, tries to reach the fires before his rival, sends out runners to look for "drunks and disorderlies" at the police stations, and keeps a very close watch on the obituary columns of the newspapers.

A few years ago there was a bitter contest for the Tammany leadership of the Ninth District between John C. Sheehan and Frank J. Goodwin. Both had had long experience in Tammany politics and both understood every move of the game.

Every morning their agents went to their respective headquarters before seven o'clock and read through the death notices in all the morning papers. If they found that anybody in the district had died, they rushed to the homes of their principals with the information and then there was a race to the house of the deceased to offer condolences, and, if the family were poor, something more substantial.

On the day of the funeral there was another contest. Each faction tried to surpass the other in the number and appearance of the carriages it sent to the funeral, and more than once they almost came to blows at the church or in the cemetery.

On one occasion the Goodwinites played a trick on their adversaries which has since been imitated in other districts. A well-known liquor dealer who had a considerable following died, and both Sheehan and Goodwin were eager to become his political heir by making a big showing at the funeral.

Goodwin managed to catch the enemy napping. He went to all the livery stables in the district, hired all the carriages for the day, and gave orders to two hundred of his men to be on hand as mourners.

Sheehan had never had any trouble about getting all the carriages that he wanted, so he let the matter go until the night before the funeral. Then he found that he could not hire a carriage in the district.

He called his district committee together in a hurry and explained the situation to them. He could get all the vehicles he needed in the adjoining district, he said, but if he did that, Goodwin would rouse the voters of the Ninth by declaring that he (Sheehan) had patronized foreign industries.

Finally, it was decided that there was nothing to do but to go over to Sixth Avenue and Broadway for carriages. Sheehan made a fine turnout at the funeral, but the deceased was hardly in his grave before Goodwin raised the cry of "Protection to home industries," and denounced his rival for patronizing livery-stable keepers outside of his district. The cry had its effect in the primary campaign. At all events, Goodwin was elected leader.

A recent contest for the leadership of the Second District illustrated further the strenuous work of the Tammany district leaders. The contestants were Patrick Divver, who had managed the district for years, and Thomas F. Foley.

Both were particularly anxious to secure the large Italian vote. They not only attended all the Italian christenings and funerals, but also kept a close lookout for the marriages in order to be on hand with wedding presents.

At first, each had his own reporter in the Italian quarter to keep track of the marriages. Later, Foley conceived a better plan. He hired a man to stay all day at the City Hall marriage bureau, where most Italian couples go through the civil ceremony, and telephone to him at his saloon when anything was doing at the bureau.

Foley had a number of presents ready for use and, whenever he received a telephone message from his man, he hastened to the City Hall with a ring or a watch or a piece of silver and handed it to the bride with his congratulations. As a consequence, when Divver got the news and went to the home of the couple with his present, he always found that Foley had been ahead of him. Toward the end of the campaign, Divver also stationed a man at the marriage bureau and then there were daily foot races and fights between the two heelers.

Sometimes the rivals came into conflict at the deathbed. One night a poor Italian peddler died in Roosevelt Street. The news reached Divver and Foley about the same time, and as they knew the family of the man was destitute, each went to an undertaker and brought him to the Roosevelt Street tenement.

The rivals and the undertakers met at the house and an altercation ensued. After much discussion the Divver undertaker was selected. Foley had more carriages at the funeral, however, and he further impressed the Italian voters by paying the widow's rent for a month, and sending her half a ton of coal and a barrel of flour.

The rivals were put on their mettle toward the end of the campaign by the wedding of a daughter of one of the original Cohens of the Baxter Street region. The Hebrew vote in the district is nearly as large as the Italian vote, and Divver and Foley set out to capture the Cohens and their friends.

They stayed up nights thinking what they would give the bride. Neither knew how much the other was prepared to spend on a wedding present, or what form it would take; so spies were employed by both sides to keep watch on the jewelry stores, and the jewelers of the district were bribed by each side to impart the desired information.

At last Foley heard that Divver had purchased a set of silver knives, forks and spoons. He at once bought a duplicate set and added a silver tea service. When the presents were displayed at the home of the bride, Divver was not in a pleasant mood and he charged his jeweler with treachery. It may be added that Foley won at the primaries.

One of the fixed duties of a Tammany district leader is to give two outings every summer, one for the men of his district and the other for the women and children, and a beefsteak dinner and a ball every winter. The scene of the outings is, usually, one of the groves along the Sound.

The ambition of the district leader on these occasions is to demonstrate that his men have broken all records in the matter of eating and drinking. He gives out the exact number of pounds of beef, poultry, butter, etc., that they have consumed and professes to know how many potatoes and ears of corn have been served.

According to his figures, the average eating record of each man at the outing is about ten pounds of beef, two or three chickens, a pound of butter, a half peck of potatoes, and two dozen ears of corn. The drinking records, as given out, are still more phenomenal. For some reason, not yet explained, the district leader thinks that his popularity will be greatly increased if he can show that his followers can eat and drink more than the followers of any other district leader.

The same idea governs the beefsteak dinners in the winter. It matters not what sort of steak is served or how it is cooked; the district leader considers only the question of quantity, and when he excels all others in this particular, he feels, somehow, that he is a bigger man and deserves more patronage than his associates in the Tammany Executive Committee.

As to the balls, they are the events of the winter in the extreme East Side and West Side society. Mamie and Maggie and Jennie prepare for them months in advance, and their young men save up for the occasion just as they save for the summer trips to Coney Island.

The district leader is in his glory at the opening of the ball. He leads the cotillion with the prettiest woman present—his wife, if he has one, permitting—and spends almost the whole night shaking hands with his constituents. The ball costs him a pretty penny, but he has found that the investment pays.

By these means the Tammany district leader reaches out into the homes of his district, keeps watch not only on the men, but also on the women and children; knows their needs, their likes and dislikes, their troubles and their hopes, and places himself in a position to use his knowledge for the benefit of his organization and himself. Is it any wonder that scandals do not permanently disable Tammany and that it speedily recovers from what seems to be crushing defeat?

Module XIV

Questions for Study and Critical Thinking

1. In his article, "Restriction of Immigration," what arguments does Francis A. Walker make for limiting immigration?

2. How valid are these arguments? Has subsequent history borne them out? How do they compare with current arguments for immigration limitation? Are there other, better arguments now for restricting immigration?

3. What are Van Etten's main points?

4. What virtues does Van Etten see in Russian Jews?

5. What ideas emerge from Riis's portrayal of tenement life?

6. How accurate do you think Riis's accounts are. Why?

7. In the *Bintel Brief*, what problems in their daily lives do Jewish immigrants reveal?

8. What values does Cahan demonstrate in his answers?

9. What distinction did Plunkitt make between "honest" and "dishonest" graft?

10. What do you think of that distinction? How is Plunkitt different from politicians today? In what ways is he similar?

Module XVII

The First World War: "Over There" and Here at Home

Introduction

For the United States, the First World War represented a novel experience. For the first time the United States was involved in a conflict with American troops fighting in Europe. This development evoked mixed emotions among Americans. President Woodrow Wilson sought to frame the issue in moral terms. For him the war was a struggle against militarism and for democracy, ultimately a "war to end war" itself. Some Americans, however, opposed the war. Some were German-Americans who saw it as a blatant attempt to aid Great Britain; others were isolationists who opposed American entanglements in morally dubious European affairs, and still others were political radicals who saw it as a fight between the rich exploiters of the working class.

Compared to the major European combatants–who fought with huge losses of life for four long years—the American involvement was relatively brief. While European soldiers on the Western Front suffered the misery and astronomical casualties of trench warfare, American soldiers, in their brief experience in Europe often saw the war as a great adventure. Of course, the American Expeditionary Force suffered injuries and deaths. American accounts of the war, therefore, reflect the mixture of light and shadow experienced by American troops.

For the United States, like the other countries involved, the First World War was total war. Unlike premodern wars, modern total war meant the mobilization not just of the army but of the whole society. Conscription exposed most young men to army service; the government attempted to synchronize the whole economy to provide maximum efficiency for the war effort; and both the government and private groups used propaganda to secure maximum public support for the war. Not only was support enlisted through propaganda, but both the government and private agencies, like the Boy Scouts, sought to suppress opposition to the war. Congress passed two bills that outlawed, among other things, "any language intended to bring the form of government . . . or the Constitution . . . or the military or naval forces . . . or the flag . . . of the United States into contempt, scorn, contumely, or disrepute. "It declared that any person would be in violation of the law who" shall wilfully display the flag of any foreign enemy, or shall wilfully . . . urge, incite, or advocate any curtailment of production in this country of any thing or things . . . necessary or essential to the prosecution of the war . . . and whoever shall wilfully advocate, teach, defend, or suggest the doing of any of the acts or things in this section enumerated and whoever shall by word or act support or favor the cause of any country with which the United States is at war or by word or act oppose the cause of the United States therein."

In this module, we will look at American experiences both in the European theater and at home in the U.S. As we do so, try to put yourself in the shoes of the American soldiers and nurses in Europe and those of Americans at home. Further, think about the policy issues involved in the war. Did the goals of the war, as articulated by leaders of the government such as President Wilson, justify the suffering you will read about? Were attempts to limit attacks on the government's war policy justified? Why, or why not?

Document 17.1 Life in the Trenches

Louis Felix Ranlett was a Harvard undergraduate when he entered the army. In 1927 he wrote a book in which he described his experience as an American soldier in the First World War. In this excerpt he describes fighting in the summer of 1918.

Life in the Trenches

Louis Felix Ranlett

Suddenly the dugout, deep underground though it was, trembled and shook as a ship might striking a rock; a heavy crust of dirt, from the bunks above, fell in my face, and the rat that had been exploring along the beam close by plumped on his back beside my head, writhed for a moment, squirmed over onto his feet, and darted off screeching. An all-enveloping blanket of heavy, rumbling sound fell about the dugout, and the roar of bursting shells outside merged in one grand clamor that hurled every occupant of the tiny space instantly into stunned wakefulness.

"What is it? What is it?" someone called in a strained, pleading voice, for he, like the rest of us, was too startled to understand. "An earthquake?"

"No! A barrage! Get dressed! Put 'em on!"

Each man started fumbling with his shoes and leggings, working in hurried helplessness.

I can only tell how I felt, but I believe that my comrades all experienced the same sensations. My whole body trembled convulsively as in a violent chill, my knees shook, my fingers and hands moved purposelessly. I seemed deprived of strength, almost of power to control my limbs, as a man struggling against a monster in a dream. I was afraid—and I admit it shamelessly, as every one of my comrades did—scared "into jelly." It was not the fear of any specific injury that I experienced, just an overpowering sense of the terrible unusual, the unknown that might happen. My voice was, can I say, staring, strained, unnatural—high-pitched and helpless.

I crammed on my helmet and grabbed my rifle, with bayonet fixed, from its nail on the wall. The others finally got themselves together, literally, and sat on the edge of their bunks talking rapidly and aimlessly, without listening to each other, to conceal their fear. The candles were burning low, and as we noticed it we whiffed out all but one to preserve them, for we were suddenly struck by an additional terror of being left in darkness.

Norton, the gas sentinel, with more courage than the rest of us, perhaps because he could see what was going on, remained silent at his post inside the dugout door, until, as he told me later, he saw, in the dim light made by the moon behind thin clouds, a gray haze settling down the steps above him. He stuck his head inside and remarked in an almost matter-of-fact way, "Gas, boys, gas!" He ducked inside, rolling down the double blankets, and hurried to the other door which he closed likewise. Since the stovepipe was already plugged, this made the dugout supposedly gas-proof, but we were taking no chances with the most dreaded of weapons.

We bounced off our helmets, dove into our masks, which had been close tied under our chins for the last four days, and then fumbled on the floor again for the suddenly discarded headgear. The masks shut us off from everything even more than the terrific sound which still eddied about us, and instinctively seeking contact with each other we drew in around the one candle where it sputtered on the edge of the bunk. I held two fingers together against it to measure the length, and wondered how many more minutes it could hold out. As it shrank and flickered, we crowded closer together.

Looking out through the steamed eye-pieces of the mask I saw a sight that instantly reminded me of some of the pictures of Captain Nemo and his faithful followers gathered about some treasure chest on the sea bottom. Just at the edge of the little circle of light ranged a row of huge staring eyes in black, pointed faces from the snouts of which a shaking pipe led down into the darkness. The mud-colored helmets hid the men's foreheads. Only their ears, white and large, projected out on either side of the

---

From *Let's Go! The Story of A.S. no. 2448602*, Houghton Mifflin Company, 1927.

weird mask faces. Conversation was reduced to a mere series of gurgles.

Sergeant Loffman had alone remained lying on the bunk in almost his characteristically undisturbed and somnolent state. Finally out of the recesses of his mask he called, "Load up your pockets with these shells!"

The crowd attacked the pile of French cartridges and divided them rapidly. The idea was good in that it kept the men busy and hence helped to reduce their fear, but had no other value, for the shells would fit only the auto-rifles of which there was not one in the dugout.

A half-hour went by, and finally, to my infinite relief, I heard Straight's voice outside.

"Ranlett, are you there?" he called.

"Yes."

"Come on out."

I pushed aside the blankets and found him at the top of the steps.

"Take your mask off, it's all safe now," he said. I obeyed.

"Get 'em all out quick! Stand to!" he cried when I was free of the mask.

I jumped down the steps, shouting, "Take 'em off, boys! It's all right. Come on out!"

"Go on out," called Loffman in his usual nonchalant tone of voice. A few of the men stepped out warily, and when they found that the racket had greatly diminished tried to persuade the rest to follow. All, however, still wore their masks.

"It's safe!" I called, rushing in. "I've got mine off."

When those inside saw me alive without a mask, some of their courage returned and, snatching off their face-pieces, they tumbled out, but balked at ascending the steps, for the shells were still bursting, though not in full chorus.

Lieutenant Bishop, his mask dangling from its satchel and his face pale but covered with sweat, was suddenly seen standing on the trench parados, a smoking automatic in his hand.

The sight brought courage with the thought, "If he can get away with it up there, I'm safe enough here," and each man hurried confidently to his post in the trenches. Thus by an exhibition of thoughtless, and what some would call foolhardy, courage, the lieutenant instantly transformed us all from scared creatures into fighting men. It was a lesson in leadership which I shall not forget, and for which he deserves much credit, though he maintained later that his only purpose in exposing himself was to see whether the Boches [Germans] were coming, and that he had fired his automatic merely to make sure it would work.

"Come out to Duffy's with me," shouted Straight. "I've been everywhere else. Zitto was hit. Plane flew along the trench and bullet came through the shelter roof. Got him in the back. He's patched up now and down at the station."

I hurried along behind him. In a depression we smelled a strong breath of gas and plunged into our masks again. Almost trotting through the dark trench in the steamed mask was like running in a dream. Straight had been on the move ever since the barrage started while I had been safe in the dugout, and now he was nearly overcome by exhaustion, the heat of his mask, and its pressure on his temples. He sat down on the fire step while I bathed his face around the edge of his mask with water from my canteen, until he could proceed. At last we reached Duffy's post which had been beyond the concentration of fire and found his crew, scared like the rest of us, but very thankful to know that the platoon was not wiped out leaving them alone in their isolated position.

Gradually the noise died down, and at last, an hour after it had begun, was suddenly cut off like the din of a shop at the closing gong. The Boches did not come over against us.

At six o'clock a horribly pale Frenchman, spitting green slime, almost speechless, and gasping frantically for every breath, struggled into our trench looking for the dugout where his sergeant had stayed with our lieutenant for the first night. He brought the news that the dugout we had given up that evening had been directly hit by a big shell, that his *sous-lieutenant* had been killed, and that all the platoon were casualties by gas or by the collapse of their shelter. The sergeant, assuring us that the barrage, of many caliber shells and all types of projector and shell gas, had been worse than any concentration of fire he had seen even at Verdun, hurried off to his mates, apparently little excited at their reported fate, though we could not help remarking on our good fortune in having changed dugouts.

By eight o'clock the two men from our platoon who had been gassed were carried to the dressing-station and a new schedule of watches was put into effect, with the resumption of the old quiet of trench life. At eight-thirty sad news came from the rear. The company kitchen had been struck by the first shell of the barrage, which had gone clean through the roof of the *abri,* ruining the stove and destroying all the provisions. The reserve platoon had suffered several gas casualties; one of the cooks was gassed to death through a failure to get the elastics of his mask untangled from the mouthpiece and several others were so badly affected that they died later. Lieutenant Miles's platoon, in the exposed trench of our former night position, suffered about twenty-five casualties by gas and fragments of H.E. (high explosive), several men being killed outright; and Sergeant Mitchell's platoon fared only a little better. It had been a severe first time under fire.

We later learned that the barrage had fallen for an hour upon the whole front of the Seventy-Seventh Division, which served to conceal the true purpose of the Boches. One of the front-line platoons of 'A' Company, about a half-mile to our left, directly in front of Badonviller, was surrounded by a box barrage which cut it off from the rear. A line of skirmishers advanced on its front, drawing the fire of the terrified men, so that a platoon column of enemy crept in on either flank unobserved and attacked with terrible success, taking several prisoners, killing many, and breaking up the whole platoon.

But none of these happenings touched us so much at the time—such was our already well-developed military callousness—as the fact that we should have no hot breakfast. The emergency ration proved its worth, everybody drawing a half-box of biscuits from the supply, so that life was made tolerable, but we missed our hot coffee and beans.

During the morning three more members of the platoon complained of gassing and were taken to the first-aid station. Just as the last of these men was removed, Corporal Nolan, always a nervous and depressed man, who had been becoming more and more silent and white-faced ever since the terrible night ordeal in the exposed trench, when the cold fingers of fear had clutched at all, seemed suddenly changed. He leaped up from his post and began running about the trench, tapping his companions as if in a game of tag. His eyes strained forward curiously in their sockets, his fingers twitched rapidly, and he jabbered incoherently. Loffman, who was near, grappled with him, and others came to his assistance to restrain the madman, overcome by shell shock and fear. We laid him upon a stretcher and held him down, while Lieutenant Bishop tried to quiet him.

"Don't you recognize me, Tom! Tom!—answer!"

Tom writhed on, frothing at the mouth.

"Be quiet, Tom! Keep still."

It was like a person soothing a crying child. Gradually Nolan became still and could be carried away.

I obtained an empty stretcher and putting it on the parapet where I should be undisturbed and could have plenty of fresh air, made up my two days' sleep in two hours.

That afternoon we made elaborate preparations in apprehension of an attack during the coming night, distributing much ammunition from the ammunition dugout and laying all the auto-rifles carefully. A new kitchen was installed at the P.C., and by supper the succession of luxurious meals was resumed. At one noon meal we had baked kidney beans, steak, boiled potatoes, coffee, cabbage, hot cakes, bread, rice pudding, and corn syrup. Our rationing in the trenches was more hearty, varied, and wholly satisfying than it had been at any time since we left Camp Upton, and was in every way a success. Sweets were supplied us in abundance in the form of syrup. Gallon cans of the pleasant syrup stood in every dugout, for we had more than we could use at any one meal. Candles, which were ordinarily issued with the ration, were, however, scarce when they were most needed, and matches were counted more carefully than franc pieces, so that we had to get on with a minimum of light.

Though food was abundant, water, which had to be carried just like food, was comparatively scarce. One was fortunate if he got a canteen full a day for all purposes: drinking, washing, and cleaning his mess kit. The kits were more often scoured with mud and wiped with paper than washed, and each man's small dishtowel became even more grease-encrusted than usual. There was hardly any water for toilet purposes; I shaved once during the week, using as a shaving-mug my canteen cup from which I ordinarily drank my coffee or ate my rice pudding, and washing my face and hands from the same cup full. Many of the men used coffee for shaving, both because it was hot acid [and] because it was more abundant than plain water. The order which made clear that a cake of issue soap was all that was necessary to keep one's uniform free from spots "under all conditions" could not have contemplated such a scarcity.

On Tuesday we continued our preparations for a warm reception. My training in map-sketching served me in good stead, for I was able to make a map of the sector to aid us in laying the lines of fire, and to serve as a guide to the platoon which should relieve us. The machine-gun company moved a gun into our position, and a night patrol was sent out to examine the area in front of us.

Wednesday night at eleven, when my turn to sleep was up, I scrambled from the bench in the mess shelter where I slept on my back on the single board, wedged in between the wall and the legs of the table, and began my rounds in the trenches. Way out in the long, unguarded section of line between Eulert's and Duffy's posts I saw the nodding line of helmets of the French visiting patrol coming toward me in the half-moonlight. Since safety demanded that we halt all persons passing through the trench, whether we thought we knew them or not, I halted and raised the loaded automatic which I was carrying in my hand, in welcome. The leading sergeant stopped at my tensely whispered "Halt!"

"Give the countersign."

"*Comment* [What]?"

"The password."

"*Pas comprend* [Don't understand]."

I was getting worried, and could not think of what to say next. Hah! I made a wild guess.

"*Le mot de passe.*"

"*Ah! Oui!—*" he burst out delightedly, but stopped, for he had been drinking and was not wholly steady. He did not know the password.

This was bad. Perhaps I had really stopped a German patrol. What should I do? There was my automatic, but I was alone and a dark line of figures stretched away around the traverse beyond the sergeant, who was now fumbling in his coat with one hand and with the other scratching his head under the edge of his tilted helmet as if to stimulate thought.

I waited. At last he found the object of his search—a piece of paper with the list of the daily passwords for the week. He picked out the right one and gave it to me—*"Chalöns!"* What a relief! . . .

Friday evening, a week after we had entered the line, came the word that we were to go into reserve. Saul, who had been through the *boyau* to the P.C. many times, was to guide us out after dark. At ten o'clock the first members of the relief arrived, under Sergeant Kimball, and I set out with a party for the rear. Saul became confused in the dark at the first trench crossing and gave up helplessly.

"Let me take it," I said, forcing my way to the head of the column. I had not been down that particular trench, but, having mapped our platoon sector and having seen the other end of the *boyau* at the P.C., thought I could lead the crowd out.

As I proceeded, clamors of protest arose behind:

"You'll get us into the Boche lines!—We've gone twice the distance already!—Stop and wait.—Go ahead yourself and find out whether you are right!"

I did not heed them, and in ten minutes, though it seemed an hour, we came out at the P.C. dugout and were assigned to an *abri* in the roadside, where we lit our candles and began reading the inscriptions left by the Iowa troops of the Forty-Second Division.

The relief was completed at eleven o'clock and we had just settled down with a gas sentinel near the big bell, for what we hoped might be our first good sleep in a week, when the inevitable happened. Hooper, the first sergeant, appeared at the door. "Hi, Ranlett, pick out a detail to carry coffee." I had the usual unpleasant job of trying to decide who had done the least work lately and would consequently be in line for assignment to the detail. Jolly little Corporal Lorier and five men "drew the unlucky numbers" and went out on a hard round. . . .

On Saturday night, June 29th, ten days after we had entered the front-line position, the company was relieved. At eleven o'clock, in the utter blackness of an overcast night, we took the road in section columns of twos with single connecting files at twenty-five-yard intervals between them. I was marching alone in this capacity, the rattle and bang of my equipment being the only sound that broke the stillness, when the low hum of a distant Boche plane struck my ears. It grew louder and louder, evidently approaching, but the plane was entirely invisible in the gloom. Suddenly a long stream of sparkling fire shot out of the night ahead and curved crackling to earth in short bursts. Fritz was peppering the road with tracer bullets. We dove for the grass ditch at the side, now that we knew where he was, for a mass of men on the white surface of the road would show clearly from above, while against the dark hue of the grass they would be hidden. Ahead of us and approaching swiftly darted the fearful stream of fire accompanied by the pulsing roar of the motor, but in an instant, directly over our heads, the thunder of another plane burst out and the hanging wheels of the night terror that had stolen up on us with motor shut off, under the diversion created by his comrade, appeared barely skirting the tree-tops.

He opened fire with a rush, the whizzing, flaming bullets spattering the hard surface of the road and dislodging bits of stone in the wreckage of the house against which I was crouching. On he swept—and as the stream of fire disappeared in the dark again, no one stirred.

Five minutes passed, but the planes did not return. I breathed again.

"Hi! Did he get you?" called Duffy, running up from behind.

"No. They went into the rocks there."

"Gee! He fired at you!"

"No!"

"He did. I saw it."

"Well, I was here. I ought to know."

"Lucky kid. Too close for me. He didn't miss any of us by much. Some stunt. Nice fellow."

Document 17.2 Reminiscences of an American Nurse

Helen T. Burrey was a nurse from Pittsburgh, Pennsylvania. She volunteered to serve in the war and was given the rank of Reserve Nurse in the Army Nurse Corps. Sent to France, she was assigned to U.S. Army Base Hospital No. 27 and then to army hospital trains. Her account is from the official history of the Red Cross posted on the Internet by her daughter.

Reminiscences of an American Nurse

Helen T. Burrey, Reserve Nurse, Army Nurse Corps

Base Hospital 27, located at Angers, France, received the first official order dated July 14, 1917, to supply Army nurses for this service. Until this time, the Medical Corps attached to hospital trains were caring for the wounded. Through Miss Blanche Rulon, chief nurse of Base Hospital 27, Edna Cooper, Grace O'Donnell and I were detailed to Hospital Train 57.

When told that we were to leave the next day to board this train, which was then stationed at Port Boulet, France, we were certainly filled with a spirit of adventure. We arrived at Port Boulet July 15, found our train and made ourselves known to the commanding officer, Captain Goodwin, who had knowledge of our coming. He received us very kindly and immediately showed us to our quarters.

We were agreeably surprised at the modern equipment. In our coach there were three compartments, which consisted of a dining room and two sleeping rooms and a lavatory (triangular in shape), containing a small wash bowl and commode. The sleeping rooms were made up of a private room, consisting of one berth and a wardrobe, and a second room, which contained a lower berth and an upper berth. Of course, we all wanted the private room, but since it could not be private among three, we resolved to take "turns about" and rotate from upper berth to private room. The rule was one week in the private room and the next week in the lower berth and the third week in the upper berth. As we had five months of this life, we had plenty of time for the private room. The dining room, which was also used as a living room, contained a table and two chairs and a side seat fitted to the wall. . . .

The rest of the train consisted of sixteen coaches, including one infectious car, which carried eighteen beds; one staff car, which carried eight beds; one kitchen and sitting sick officers' car, which carried three beds and twenty seats; eight ordinary lying ward cars, which carried 288 beds; one pharmacy car; one infectious-case sitting car, which carried fifty-six seats and fourteen upper berths; one kitchen and mess car with three beds for cooks; one personnel car with thirty beds; and one train crew and store car; the total capacity of the train was thus 400 beds.

Each moving hospital was equipped with electric lights, steam heat, electric fans, lavatories, and racks for personal belongings, and even ash trays for the patients' indulgence. There were eight ordinary ward cars for patients containing thirty-six beds arranged in tiers of three. These could easily be converted into seats to accommodate patients who were able to sit up; they could also be used for stretchers in emergency cases or folded against the sides of the coach when the cars required cleaning. . . .

Our first trip was to evacuate patients from different hospitals who were able to be moved to a point of embarkation for the United States. Since we were the first nurses, Colonel Howard Clark, who was then in charge of the train service, made the first trip to these different hospitals; this was also the first trip for transporting badly wounded patients from the hospitals near the front to the hospitals near the point of embarkation.

We started July 17, passed through Tours, Bourges, Nevers, Dijon, Chaumont, Neufchateau, Contrexville, Toul and Savenay, stopping at several base hospitals and filling our train with wounded

---

From the *History of American Red Cross Nursing*, Macmillan Company, 1922. Also appears on website maintained by Helen Burrey Brown's daughter, Mary Murphy, murphy56@bellatlantic.net.

who were to be taken to Base Hospital No. 8 at Savenay. After seeing our work, Colonel Clark congratulated us and recommended that all the trains be supplied with three nurses.

We worked day and night with those patients; the pathetic condition of our boys who were very badly wounded made us realize that being wounded was hard enough to bear, without the jolts, noise and dirt connected with traveling on a train. These patients were in our care for two nights and three days before they were loaded at Base Hospital No. 8. I remember two patients who had broken backs and had horrible bed sores. You can picture the special care such a case would require, but our time with each patient was limited and we gave the best attention possible. We also had many patients who had amputations of legs, or arms, and many other wounds that caused much pain and constant attention from doctors and nurses.

One of the chief discomforts which we noticed that the patients met was caused by the tightening of bandages due to the restless position of the patient and by the moving and stopping of the train. This condition was also aggravated by the infected wounds and the patients were constantly calling for relief from the bandages. . . .

During the drive at Chateau-Thierry a great number of the hospital trains were mobilized at Pantin, a suburb of Paris, for duty into Chateau-Thierry. From Paris to Chateau-Thierry was about three hours ride, and 27 was ordered to make the trip. The train was sent to evacuate patients from hospital No. 7, a mobile unit. These patients had received first aid; major operations were cared for. Some had hardly [recovered] from their anesthetic, and most of them were in a pitiable state.

In the station and surrounding it were litters covered with boys; mud-splattered and torn were the uniforms they wore. They were patiently waiting to be to be taken; they did not care where but some place where they could be given proper care. After we received our train load, about 400 patients, one of the things that bothered both patients and nurses most were the countless numbers of flies that infested our train. The odors from the wounds that had no care cannot be described but shall live in the memory of the nurses and orderlies. We made three trips to Chateau-Thierry.

The third one was to a small town outside of Chateau-Thierry. It was after dark when we got there and we immediately started to load our train with patients that had been gassed. At the height of our work, we had an alarm of the enemy airplanes, which meant all lights out, and we had to work in the dark, getting as many patients under shelter as possible. We loaded our train without keeping count of the patients that could walk. After the train pulled out and we got to a place of safety, the lights were turned on, and we found we had patients everywhere, in the berths, on the seats, and crowded in the aisle. . . .

To get to a certain base hospital, which was in a mountainous district, the train had to be divided; the engine could not pull the entire train up the mountain. We got no instructions as to the splitting of the train, so it was just luck that all the nurses were not in one part of the train. I found myself on one half of the train, garaged in a railroad yard with about two hundred patients; the other half with two nurses was starting up the hill. While they were gone, an engine was attached by mistake to our train, and soon we were rapidly moving away. We traveled about eight hours before we finally found the rest of our train. We were surely happy to see them again, for they happened to have the supply and the kitchen car.

When the train was empty, and we were moving, the scenery and the wonderful views of France thrilled us, but when the train stopped, we were garaged in some railroad yard. We might stay there an hour or maybe two days before our train was ordered to move. You can picture the average train yard in America; picture it in France in war times!

When we nurses would get off the train to stretch our legs, we were greatly amused at ourselves. We felt like three geese walking along, for we noticed we trailed one another. Did you ever see geese walking, one in the lead and the others following? We used to do that till we realized we were not on the train any longer but out in the street, and then we would chuckle to ourselves. Our reason for doing this was that the aisle in the train was so narrow that we had to walk single file.

Document 17.3 The Espionage Act, May 16, 1918

In May, 1917, two months after Congress had responded to President Wilson's message by declaring war on Germany, it passed the Espionage Act, which outlawed actions and even statements against military policies or draft laws. A year later, in May 1918, Congress passed another bill, elaborating on the restrictions already enacted. The crucial provisions of this second bill are shown below. Notice what actions are prohibited and what the penalties are.

The Espionage Act, May 16, 1918

Be it enacted, That section three of the Act . . . approved June 15, 1917, be . . . amended so as to read as follows:

SEC. 3. Whoever, when the United States is at war, shall wilfully make or convey false reports or false statements with intent to interfere with the operation or success of the military or naval forces of the United States, or to promote the success of its enemies, or shall wilfully make or convey false reports, or false statements, or say or do anything except by way of bona fide and not disloyal advice to an investor . . . with intent to obstruct the sale by the United States of bonds . . . or the making of loans by or to the United States, or whoever, when the United States is at war, shall wilfully cause . . . or incite . . . insubordination, disloyalty, mutiny, or refusal of duty, in the military or naval forces of the United States, or shall wilfully obstruct . . . the recruiting or enlistment service of the United States, and whoever, when the United States is at war, shall wilfully utter, print, write, or publish any disloyal, profane, scurrilous, or abusive language about the form of government of the United States, or the Constitution of the United States, or the military or naval forces of the United States, or the flag . . . or the uniform of the Army or Navy of the United States, or any language intended to bring the form of government . . . or the Constitution . . . or the military or naval forces . . . or the flag . . . of the United States into contempt, scorn, contumely, or disrepute . . . or shall wilfully display the flag of any foreign enemy, or shall wilfully . . . urge, incite, or advocate any curtailment of production in this country of any thing or things . . . necessary or essential to the prosecution of the war . . . and whoever shall wilfully advocate, teach, defend, or suggest the doing of any of the acts or things in this section enumerated and whoever shall by word or act support or favor the cause of any country with which the United States is at war or by word or act oppose the cause of the United States therein, shall be punished by a fine of not more than $10,000 or imprisonment for not more than twenty years, or both.

Document 17.4 In Defense of Free Speech in Wartime

Across the country supporters of the war whipped up hostility to those who opposed it or were suspected of doing so. Those attacked ranged from ordinary people who spoke German in public to Senators and Representatives. In August, Senator Robert La Follette of Wisconsin, a prominent Progressive and member of the Republican party, defended the right of Americans to free speech in opposing the war and government policies. Here in part is Senator La Follette's speech:

The Espionage Act, May 16, 1918.

In Defense of Free Speech in Wartime

Senator Robert LaFollette

Speech in the U.S. Senate, October 6, 1917

Mr. President:

Six Members of the Senate and fifty Members of the House voted against the declaration of war. Immediately there was let loose upon those Senators and Representatives a flood of invective and abuse from newspapers and individuals who had been clamoring for war, unequaled, I believe, in history of civilized society.

Prior to the declaration of war every man who had ventured to oppose our entrance into it had been condemned as a coward or worse, and even the President had by no means been immune from these attacks.

Since the declaration of war the triumphant war press has pursued those Senators and Representatives who voted against war with malicious falsehood and recklessly libelous attacks, going to the extreme limit of charging them with treason against their country.

This campaign of libel and character assassination directed against the Members of Congress who opposed our entrance into the war has been continued down to the present hour, and I have upon my desk newspaper clippings, some of them libels upon me alone, some directed as well against other Senators who voted in opposition to the declaration of war. One of these newspaper reports most widely circulated represents a Federal judge in the state of Texas as saying, in a charge to a grand jury—I read the article as it appeared in the newspaper and the headline with which it is introduced:

[LaFollette picks up newspaper and reads aloud.]

DISTRICT JUDGE WOULD LIKE TO TAKE SHOT AT TRAITORS IN CONGRESS

(A.P.) Houston, Texas, Oct. 1 Judge Waller T. Burns, of the United States district court, in charging a Federal grand jury at the beginning of the October term today, after calling by name Senators Stone of Missouri, Hardwick of Georgia, Vardaman of Mississippi, Gronna of North Dakota, Gore of Oklahoma, and LaFollette of Wisconsin, said: "If I had a wish, I would wish that you men had jurisdiction to return bills of indictment against these men. They ought to be tried promptly and fairly, and I believe this court could administer the law fairly; but I have a conviction, as strong as life, that this country should stand them up against an adobe wall tomorrow and give them what they deserve. If any man deserves death, it is a traitor. I wish that I could pay for the ammunition. I would like to attend the execution, and if I were in the firing squad I would not want to be the marksman who had the blank shell." . . .

If this newspaper clipping were a single or exceptional instance of lawless defamation, I should not trouble the Senate with a reference to it. But, Mr. President, it is not.

In this mass of newspaper clippings which I have here upon my desk, and which I shall not trouble the Senate to read unless it is desired, I find other Senators, as well as myself, accused of the highest crimes of which any man can be guilty—treason and disloyalty—and, sir, accused not only with no evidence to support the accusation, but without the suggestion that such evidence anywhere exists. It is not claimed that Senators who opposed the declaration of war have since that time acted with any concerted purpose either regarding war measures or any others. They have voted according to their individual opinions . . .

I am aware, Mr. President, that in pursuance of this campaign of vilification and attempted intimidation, requests from various individuals and certain organizations have been submitted to the Senate for my expulsion from this body and that such requests have been referred to and considered by one of the committees of the Senate.

Speech in the Senate in Defense of Free Speech in Wartime, Senator Robert LaFollette.

If I alone had been made the victim of these attacks, I should not take one moment of the Senate's time for their consideration, and I believe that other Senators who have been unjustly and unfairly assailed, as I have been, hold the same attitude upon this that I do. Neither the clamor of the mob nor the voice of power will ever turn me by the breadth of a hair from the course I mark out for myself, guided by such knowledge as I can obtain and controlled and directed by a solemn conviction of right and duty.

The purpose of this campaign [is] to throw the country into a state of terror, to coerce public opinion, to stifle criticism, and suppress discussion.

But, sir, it is not alone Members of Congress that the war party in this country has sought to intimidate. The mandate seems to have gone forth to the sovereign people of this country that they must be silent while those things are being done by their Government which most vitally concern their well-being, their happiness, and their lives. Today and for weeks past honest and law-abiding citizens of this country are being terrorized and outraged in their rights by those sworn to uphold the laws and protect the rights of the people. I have in my possession numerous affidavits establishing the fact that people are being unlawfully arrested, thrown into jail, held incommunicado for days, only to be eventually discharged without ever having been taken into court, because they have committed no crime. Private residences are being invaded, loyal citizens of undoubted integrity and probity arrested, cross-examined, and the most sacred constitutional rights guaranteed to every American citizen are being violated.

It appears to be the purpose of those conducting this campaign to throw the country into a state of terror, to coerce public opinion, to stifle criticism, and suppress discussion of the great issues involved in this war.

I think all men recognize that in time of war the citizen surrenders some rights for the common good which he is entitled to enjoy in time of peace. But sir, the right to control their own Government according to constitutional forms is not one of the rights that the citizens of this country are called upon to surrender in time of war.

Rather in time of war the citizen must be more alert to the preservation of his right to control his Government. He must be most watchful of the encroachment of the military upon the civil power. He must beware of those precedents in support of arbitrary action by administration officials which, excused on the plea of necessity in war time, become the fixed rule when the necessity has passed and normal conditions have been restored.

More than all, the citizen and his representative in Congress in time of war must maintain his right of free speech. More than in times of peace it is necessary that the channels for free public discussion of governmental policies shall be open and unclogged. I believe, Mr. President, that I am now touching upon the most important question in this country today—and that is the right of the citizens of this country and their representatives in Congress to discuss in an orderly way frankly and publicly and without fear, from the platform and through the press, every important phase of this war; its abuses, and manner in which it should be conducted, and the terms upon which peace should be made. The belief which is becoming widespread in this land that this most fundamental right is being denied to the citizens of this country is a fact, the tremendous significance of which those in authority have not yet begun to appreciate. I am contending, Mr. President, for the great fundamental right of the sovereign people of this country to make their voice heard and have that voice heeded upon the great questions arising out of this war, including not only how the war shall be prosecuted but the conditions upon which it may be terminated with a due regard for the rights and the honor of this Nation and the interests of humanity.

I am contending for this right because the exercise of it is necessary to the welfare, to the existence, of this Government, to the successful conduct of this war, and to a peace which shall be enduring for the best interest of this country.

Suppose success attends the attempt to stifle all discussion of the issues of this war, all discussions of the terms upon which it should be concluded, all discussion of the objects and purposes to be accomplished by it, and concede the demand of the war-mad press and war extremists that they monopolize the right of public utterance upon these questions unchallenged, what think you would be the consequences to this country not only during the war but after the war?

It is no answer to say that when the war is over the citizen may once more resume his rights and feel some security in his liberty and his person. As I have already tried to point out, now is precisely the time when the country needs the counsel of all its citizens. In time of war even more than in time of peace, whether citizens happen to agree with ruling administration or not, these precious fundamental personal rights—free speech, free press, and right of assemblage so explicitly and emphatically guaranteed by the Constitution should be maintained inviolable. There is no rebellion in the land, no martial law, no courts are closed, no legal processes suspended, and there is no threat even of invasion.

But more than this, if every preparation for war can be made the excuse for destroying free speech and a free press and the right of the people to assemble together for peaceful discussion, then we may well despair of ever again finding ourselves for a long period in a state of peace. . . . The destruction of rights now occurring will be pointed to then as precedents for a still further invasion of the rights of the citizen. . . .

Mr. President, our Government, above all others, is founded on the right of the people freely to discuss all matters pertaining to their Government, in war not less than in peace . . . How can that popular will express itself between elections except by meetings, by speeches, publications, by petitions, and by addresses to the representatives of the people? Any man who seeks to set limit upon those rights, whether in war or peace, aims a blow at the most vital part of our Government. And then as the time for election approaches and the official is called to account for his stewardship—not a day, not a week, not a month, before the election, but a year or more before it, if people choose—they must have the right to the freest possible discussion of every question upon which their representative has acted, of the merits of every measure he has supported or opposed, of every vote he has cast and every speech that he has made. And before this great fundamental right every other must, if necessary, give way for in no other manner can representative government be preserved.

Document 17.5 An Attack on the War

Despite the laws limiting dissent passed by Congress, Eugene Debs, leader of the Socialist Party and previous candidate for president, continued to attack the war vigorously and the government, as did other socialists, many of whom were prosecuted and imprisoned by the federal government. In June 1918 Debs gave the following speech in Canton, Ohio, after visiting three Socialists who had been imprisoned for criticizing the war. In September of the same year, Debs himself was convicted of ten counts of violating the Sedition Act and sentenced to ten years in prison.

An Attack on the War

Eugene Debs

Canton, Ohio, June 16, 1918

To speak for labor; to plead the cause of the men and women and children who toil; to serve the working class, has always been to me a high privilege; a duty of love. I have just returned from a visit over yonder [jail], where three of our most loyal comrades are paying the penalty for their devotion to the cause of the working class. They have come to realize, as many of us have, that it is extremely dangerous to exercise the constitutional right of free speech in a country fighting to make democracy safe in the world.

I realize that, in speaking to you this afternoon, there are certain limitations placed upon the right of free speech. I must be exceedingly careful, prudent, as to what I say, and even more careful and prudent as to how I say it. I may not be able to say all I think; but I am not going to say anything that I do not think. I would rather a thousand times be a free soul in jail than to be a sycophant and coward in the streets. They may put those boys in jail—and some of the rest of us in jail—but they can not put the Socialist movement in jail. Those prison bars separate their bodies from ours, but their souls are here this afternoon. They are simply paying the penalty that all men have paid in all the ages of history for standing erect, and seeking to pave the way to better conditions for mankind.

If it had not been for the men and women who, in the past have had the moral courage to go to jail, we would still be in the jungles . . .

An Attack on the War, Canton, Ohio, Eugene Debs, June 16, 1918.

If you go to the city of Washington, and you examine the pages of the Congressional Directory, you will find that almost all of those corporation lawyers and cowardly politicians, members of Congress, and misrepresentatives of the masses—you will find that almost all of them claim, in glowing terms, that they have risen from the ranks to eminence and distinction. I am very glad I cannot make that claim for myself. I would be ashamed to admit that I had risen from the ranks. When I rise it will be with the ranks, and not from the ranks. . . .

They who have been reading the capitalist newspapers realize what a capacity [they] have for lying. . . . They know all about the Socialist Party, the Socialist movement, except what is true . . .

Are we opposed to Prussian militarism?* Why, we have been fighting it since the day the Socialist movement was born; and we are going to continue to fight it, day and night, until is wiped from the face of the earth. . . .

But before I proceed along this line, let me recall a little history, in which I think we are all interested . . .

You remember that at the close of Theodore Roosevelt's second term as President, he went over to Africa to make war on some of his ancestors.** You remember that, at the close of his expedition, he visited the capitals of Europe, and that he was wined and dined, dignified and glorified by all the Kaisers and Czars and Emperors of the Old World. He visited Potsdam*** while the Kaiser was there, and, according to the accounts published in the American newspapers, he and the Kaiser were soon on the most familiar terms. They were hilariously intimate with each other, and slapped each other on the back. After Roosevelt had reviewed the Kaiser's troops, according to the same accounts, he became enthusiastic over the Kaiser's legions and said: "If I had that kind of an army, I could conquer the world!" He knew the Kaiser then just as well as he knows him now. He knew that he was the Kaiser, the "Beast of Berlin".**** And yet, he permitted himself to be entertained by that Beast of Berlin; had his feet under the mahogany of the Beast of Berlin; was cheek by jowl with the Beast of Berlin. And while Roosevelt was being entertained royally by the German Kaiser, that same Kaiser was putting the leaders of the Socialist Party in jail for fighting the Kaiser and the Junkers+ of Germany. Roosevelt was the guest of honor in the White House of the Kaiser while the Socialists were in the jails of the Kaiser for fighting the Kaiser. Who then was fighting for democracy? Roosevelt? Roosevelt, who was honored by the Kaiser, or the Socialists who were in jail by order of the Kaiser?

"Birds of a feather flock together."

. . . Now, after being the guest of Emperor [Kaiser=Emperor] Wilhelm, the Beast of Berlin, he comes back to this country, and wants you to send ten million men over there to kill the Kaiser, to murder his former friend and pal. Rather queer, isn't it? And yet, he is the patriot, and we are the traitors. I challenge you to find a Socialist anywhere on the face of the earth who was ever the guest of the Beast of Berlin, except as an inmate of his prison.

A little more history along the same line. I have a distinct recollection of it. It occurred fifteen years ago when Prince Henry [the Kaiser's brother] came here. All of our plutocracy, all of the wealthy representatives living along Fifth Avenue—all, all of them—threw their palace doors wide open and received Prince Henry with open arms. But they were not satisfied with this; they got down and groveled in the dust at his feet. Our plutocracy—women and men alike—vied with each other to lick the boots of Prince Henry, the brother and representative of the Beast of Berlin. And still our plutocracy, our Junkers, would have us believe that all the Junkers are confined to Germany. It is precisely because we refuse to believe this that they brand us as disloyalists. They want our eyes focused on the Junkers in Berlin so that we will not see those within our own borders. . . .

To whom do the Wall Street Junkers in our country marry their daughters? After they have wrung their countless millions from your sweat, your agony and your life's blood, in a time of war as in a time of peace, they invest these untold millions in the purchase of titles of broken-down aristocrats, such as princes, dukes, counts and other parasites and no-accounts. Would they be satisfied to wed their daughters to honest working men? To real democrats? Oh, no! They scour the markets of Europe for vampires who are titled and nothing else. And they swap their millions for the titles, so that

---

*The U.S. and its allies maintained German militarism was the enemy. Prussia was the largest state in Germany.

**This is a joke. Roosevelt was on a big-game hunting expedition.

***A town outside Berlin, where the German Kaiser had several palaces.

****A name American propaganda called the Kaiser.

+Prussian aristocrats, who had a great influence in the German government.

matrimony with them becomes literally a matter of money.

These are the gentry who are today wrapped up in the American flag, who shout their claim from the housetops that they are the only patriots, and who have their magnifying glasses in hand, scanning the country for evidence of disloyalty, eager to apply the brand of treason to men who dare to even whisper their opposition to Junker rule in the United States. . . .

Who appoints our federal judges? The people? In all the history of the country, the working class have never named a federal judge. There are hundreds of these judges and every solitary one holds his position, his tenure, through the influence and power of corporate capital. The corporations and trusts dictate their appointment. And when they go to the bench, they go, not to serve the people, but to serve the interests that place them and keep them where they are. . . .

Why, the other day, by a vote of five to four, a kind of craps—[Debs acts like he's rolling dice] "come seven, come 'leven"—[the Supreme Court] declared the child labor law unconstitutional, a law secured after twenty years of education and agitation on the part of all kinds of people And yet, by a majority of one, the Supreme Court—a body of corporation lawyers, with just one exception—wiped that law from the statute books, and this in our so-called democracy, so that we may continue to grind the flesh and blood and bones of puny little children into profits for the Junkers of Wall Street! And this in a country that boasts of fighting to make the world safe for democracy? The history of this country is being written in the blood of the childhood the industrial lords have murdered.

These are not palatable truths to them. They do not like to hear them; and what is more, they do not want you to hear them. And that is why they brand us as undesirable citizens, and as disloyalists and traitors. If we were actual traitors—traitors to the people and to their welfare and progress—we would be regarded as eminently respectable citizens of the republic; we would hold high office, have princely incomes, and ride in limousines; and we would be pointed out as the elect who have succeeded in life in honorable pursuit, and worthy of emulation by the youth of the land. It is precisely because we are disloyal to the traitors that we are loyal to the people of this nation!

. . . Some years ago I was to speak at Warren in this state. It happened to be at the time that President McKinley was assassinated. In common with all others I deplored that tragic event. There is not a Socialist who would have been guilty of that crime. We do not attack individuals. We do not seek to avenge ourselves upon those opposed to our faith. We have no fight with individuals as such. We are capable of pitying those who hate us. We do not hate them; we know better; we would freely give them a cup of water if they needed it.

Module XVII
Questions for Study and Critical Thinking

1. What are the major events described by Louis Felix Ranlett?

2. What are the principal feelings described by Ranlett?

3. Does Ranlett have a position on the war? If so, what is it?

4. What are the major events described by Helen Bury?

5. What is the dominant feeling about the war that can be derived from Bury's account?

6. How is Bury's description of the war different from or similar to Ranlett's?

7. What actions does the Espionage Act prohibit? List them all. According to this act, do statements have to be untruthful to be illegal?

8. Do you believe that during wartime the government should prohibit speech against the Constitution, the U.S. system of government, government policies, the war itself, conscription, or specific military actions? Why, or why not?

9. What violations of freedom of speech did Senator La Follette allege took place?

10. What arguments might be made in favor of suppressing freedom of speech during wartime? Do you agree with those arguments? Why or why not?

11. Do you agree with La Follette that broad freedom of speech must be preserved in wartime.?

12. What does Debs say that violates the Espionage Act?

13. Was Congress right in prohibiting such speech?

14. Why was Eugene Debs opposed to the war? Was he, in your opinion, correct?

Module XVIII

The New Era: Life and Culture in the 1920s

Introduction

When people think of the 1920s, they often think of Flappers, jazz, Prohibition, and speakeasies. They might also think of President Calvin ("Silent Cal") Coolidge and perhaps of exuberant business growth, of widespread and wild speculation in the stock market, and the Crash of 1929.

The Twenties were, in fact, a period in which the modern corporation and its ethos dominated the culture. Coolidge, president for much of the decade, expressed a common view of that period when he reportedly said, "The business of America is business." Two of the documents in this chapter deal with the power of the business ethos.

Cities were centers of business, and the 1920s was the first decade in which a majority of the population lived in urban areas. The cities were also the site of the flamboyant cultural expressions of this era.

To many people the new era was profoundly disturbing. Many believed it was a time to defend what they thought were the values and ethnic composition of an older American society. Banning the sale of alcoholic beverages, long popular among rural and non-immigrant communities, was one way to do this. Prohibition by Constitutional amendment and federal law existed throughout the decade. Many also supported curtailing unrestricted immigration, especially from newer sources, such as Italy, Poland, and Russia. In the mid-1920s Congress enacted two laws to accomplish this. All of these measures were controversial. Several documents present arguments in the debates over these measures.

As these documents show, the 1920s were more than ten years of fun and games. They were a period of intense conflict and debate. If you had lived then, what side would you have taken? What were the arguments on either side? Which were more persuasive?

Document 18.1 Big Ideas from Big Business

The glorification of business reached a peak in the writings of Edward Purinton, a prolific writer on business subjects during the 1920s. As you read this selection, try to determine the main ideas and evaluate them.

Big Ideas from Big Business

Edward Purinton

Among the nations of the earth today America stands for one idea: Business. . . . For in this fact lies, potentially, the salvation of the world.

Through business, properly conceived, managed and conducted, the human race is finally to be redeemed. How and why a man works foretells what he will do, think, have, give and be. And real salvation is in doing, thinking, having, giving and being—not in sermonizing and theorizing. . . .

What is the finest game? Business. The soundest science? Business. The truest art? Business. The fullest education? Business. The fairest opportunity? Business. The cleanest philanthropy? Business. The sanest religion? Business.

You may not agree. That is because you judge business by the crude, mean, stupid, false imitation of business that happens to be located near you.

The finest game is business. The rewards are for everybody, and all can win. There are no favorites—Providence always crowns the career of the man who is worthy. And in this game there is no "luck"—you have the fun of taking chances but the sobriety of guaranteeing certainties. The speed and size of your winnings are for you alone to determine; you needn't wait for the other fellow in the game—it is always your move. And your slogan is not "Down the Other Fellow!" but rather "Beat Your Own Record!" or "Do It Better Today!" or "Make Every Job a Masterpiece!" The great sportsmen of the world are the great business men. . . .

The fullest education is business. A proper blend of study, work and life is essential to advancement. The whole man is educated. Human nature itself is the open book that all business men study; and the mastery of a page of this educates you more than the memorizing of a dusty tome from a library shelf. In the school of business, moreover, you teach yourself and learn most from your own mistakes. What you learn here you live out, the only real test.

The fairest opportunity is business. You can find more, better, quicker chances to get ahead in a large business house than anywhere else on earth. The biographies of champion business men show how they climbed, and how you can climb. Recognition of better work, of keener and quicker thought, of deeper and finer feeling, is gladly offered by the men higher up, with early promotion the rule for the man who justifies it. There is, and can be, no such thing as buried talent in a modern business organization.

The cleanest philanthropy is business. By "clean" philanthropy I mean that devoid of graft, inefficiency and professionalism, also of condolence, hysterics and paternalism. Nearly everything that goes by the name of Charity was born a triplet, the other two members of the trio being Frailty and Cruelty. Not so in the welfare departments of leading corporations. Savings and loan funds; pension and insurance provisions; health precautions, instructions and safeguards; medical attention and hospital care; libraries, lectures and classes; musical, athletic and social features of all kinds; recreational facilities and financial opportunities—these types of "charitable institutions" for employees add to the worker's self-respect, self-knowledge and self-improvement, by making him an active partner in the welfare program, a producer of benefits for his employer and associates quite as much as a recipient of bounty from the company. I wish every "charity" organization would send its officials to school to the heads of the welfare departments of the big corporations; the charity would mostly be transformed into capability, and the minimum of irreducible charity left would not be called by that name.

The sanest religion is business. Any relationship that forces a man to follow the Golden Rule rightfully belongs amid the ceremonials of the church. A great business enterprise includes and presupposes this relationship. I have seen more Christianity to the square inch as a regular part of the office equipment of famous corporation presidents than may ordinarily be found on Sunday in a verbalized but not vitalized church congregation. A man is not wholly religious until he is better on weekdays than he is on Sunday. The only ripened fruits of creeds are deeds. You can fool your preacher with a silky sprout or a wormy semblance of character, but you

---

From *The Independent*, 105, April 16, 1921.

can't fool your employer. I would make every business house a consultation bureau for the guidance of the church whose members were employees of the house. . . .

Document 18.2 The Man Nobody Knows

The son of a Protestant minister, Bruce Barton was a founder of one of America's largest advertising agencies. With General Mills as a client, Barton invented the character of Betty Crocker. He also wrote inspirational books and articles, served in Congress, and was the long-time head of Batten, Barton, Durstine, and Osborn, the agency he helped found. In an effort to make Christianity relevant to the business-oriented culture of the 1920s, Barton wrote a biography of Jesus. In it he derided what he saw as the Sunday school picture of Jesus as "meek and mild." In his book, *The Man Nobody Knows,* he portrays him as the prototype of the modern business executive. This selection is from the beginning of the book, in which Barton describes "How It Came to Be Written." As you read it, notice the characteristics Barton assigns to Jesus. How does this portrayal reflect 1920s attitudes toward business?

The Man Nobody Knows

Bruce Barton

How It Came to Be Written

The little boy's body sat bolt upright in the rough wooden chair, but his mind was very busy. This was his weekly hour of revolt. The kindly lady who could never seem to find her glasses would have been terribly shocked if she had known what was going on inside the little boy's mind.

"You must love Jesus," she said every Sunday, "and God."

. . . Jesus was the "lamb of God." The little boy did not know what that meant, but it sounded like Mary's little lamb.

Something for girls—sissified. Jesus was also "meek and lowly," a "man of sorrows and acquainted with grief." He went around for three years telling people not to do things. . . .

Years went by and the boy grew up and became a business man

He began to wonder about Jesus.

He said to himself: "Only strong magnetic men inspire great enthusiasm and build great organizations. Yet Jesus built the greatest organization of all. It is extraordinary." The more sermons the man heard and the more books he read the more mystified he became.

One day he decided to wipe his mind clean of books and sermons.

He said. "I will read what the men who knew Jesus personally said about him. I will read about him—as though he were a new historical character, about whom I had never heard, anything at all."

The man was amazed.

A physical weakling! Where did they get that idea? Jesus pushed a plane and swung an adze; he was a successful carpenter. He slept outdoors and spent his days walking around his favorite lake. His muscles were so strong that when he drove the moneychangers out, nobody dared to oppose him.

A kill-joy! He was the most popular dinner guest in Jerusalem! The criticism which proper people made was that he spent too much time with publicans and sinners (very good fellows, on the whole, the man thought) and enjoyed society too much. They called him a "wine bibber and a gluttonous man."

A failure! He picked up twelve men from the bottom ranks of business and forged them into an organization that conquered the world.

When the man had finished his reading he exclaimed. "This is a man nobody knows."

"Some day," said he, "someone will write a book about Jesus. Every business man will read it and send it to his partners and his salesmen. For it will tell the story of the founder of modern business."

So the man waited for someone to write this book, but no one did. Instead, more books were published about the "lamb of God" who was weak and unhappy and glad to die.

The man became impatient. One day he said, "I believe I will try to write that book, myself."

And he did.

Document 18.3 The Ku Klux Klan's Fight for Americanism (1926)

By 1900 the original Ku Klux Klan, which had used terror to help reestablish white control in the post-Civil War South, had almost died out. In the 1920s, however, the Klan made a comeback. This time its strength was not restricted to the South but it spread rapidly in the North, with its largest membership in Indiana. To its original animosity toward blacks, it added hostility to Jews, Catholics, and foreigners. It saw its role as defending old-stock Americans from the supposed threat of non-whites, newer immigrants, and new cultural developments, which thrived in the Twenties. This selection is from an article written by the Klan's president, Hiram W. Evans.

The Ku Klux Klan's Fight for Americanism (1926)

Hiram W. Evans

The Klan, therefore, has now come to speak for the great mass of Americans of the old pioneer stock. We believe that it does fairly and faithfully represent them, and our proof lies in their support. To understand the Klan, then, it is necessary to understand the character and present mind of the mass of old-stock Americans. The mass, it must be remembered, as distinguished from the intellectually mongrelized "Liberals."

These are, in the first place, a blend of various peoples of the so-called Nordic race, the race which, with all its faults, has given the world almost the whole of modern civilization. The Klan does not try to represent any people but these. . . .

These Nordic Americans for the last generation have found themselves increasingly uncomfortable, and finally deeply distressed. There appeared first confusion in thought and opinion, a groping and hesitancy about national affairs and private life alike, in sharp contrast to the clear, straightforward purposes of our earlier years. There was futility in religion, too, which was in many ways even more distressing. Presently we began to find that we were dealing with strange ideas; policies that always sounded well but somehow always made us still more uncomfortable.

Finally came the moral breakdown that has been going on for two decades. One by one all our traditional moral standards went by the boards or were so disregarded that they ceased to be binding. The sacredness of our Sabbath, of our homes, of chastity, and finally even of our right to teach our own children in our own schools fundamental facts and truths were torn away from us. Those who maintained the old standards did so only in the face of constant ridicule. . . .

The old-stock Americans are learning, however. They have begun to arm themselves for this new type of warfare. Most important, they have broken away from the fetters of the false ideals and philanthropy which put aliens ahead of their own children and their own race. . . .

One more point about the present attitude of the old-stock American: he has revived and increased his long-standing distrust of the Roman Catholic Church. It is for this that the native Americans, and

---

the Klan as their leader, are most often denounced as intolerant and prejudiced. . . .

The Ku Klux Klan, in short, is an organization which gives expression, direction and purpose to the most vital instincts, hopes, and resentments of the old-stock Americans, provides them with leadership, and is enlisting and preparing them for militant, constructive action toward fulfilling their racial and national destiny . . . The Klan literally is once more the embattled American farmer and artisan, coordinated into a disciplined and growing army, and launched upon a definite crusade for Americanism! . . .

Thus the Klan goes back to the American racial instincts, and to the common sense which is their first product, as the basis of its beliefs and methods. . . .

There are three of these great racial instincts, vital elements in both the historic and the present attempts to build an America which shall fulfill the aspirations and justify the heroism of the men who made the nation. These are the instincts of loyalty to the white race, to the traditions of America, and to the spirit of Protestantism, which has been an essential part of Americanism ever since the days of Roanoke and Plymouth Rock. They are condensed into the Klan slogan: "Native, white, Protestant supremacy."

Document 18.4 Speech in the House of Representatives in Support of Prohibition, April 19, 1926

Agitation for the prohibition of alcoholic beverages began before the Civil War. During the first decades of the twentieth century it led to demands for nationwide prohibition. In 1914 a measure to enact Prohibition with a Constitutional amendment received a majority in the House of Representatives, but fell short of the two-thirds necessary to send the proposed amendment to the states for their approval. By 1920, however, the movement had gained even greater support, and the Eighteenth Amendment to the Constitution was adopted. Congress then passed the Volstead Act, which provided the mechanism for enforcing the Amendment.

Prohibition sprang out of a typical American belief in the possibility of reforming long-standing abuses, which went back to the Puritans. But it also played a part in a cultural struggle, which often followed religious lines. By the beginning of the twentieth century, many Protestant denominations—Baptists, Methodists, Presbyterians—opposed the use of alcoholic beverages. Other denominations—Catholics, Jews, Eastern Orthodox, and some Lutherans (who were Protestants)—believed in moderate drinking. Many members of the second group consisted largely of recent immigrants, who had mostly settled in cities. For many of them the neighborhood bar or tavern was a center of social activity. They therefore saw Prohibition as an attack on their way of life. In fact, many Prohibition advocates saw it in much the same way—as a means of reforming and Americanizing these new immigrants. During the First World War the movement gained momentum fueled by animosity toward the largely German-American brewers and a desire to protect the health of American soldiers. In the 1920s, after the enactment of Prohibition, the new urban culture, which celebrated new fashions, dances, and music, was linked in many minds with drinking in illegal speakeasies and night clubs. Proponents of older, more conservative values continued to see Prohibition as a weapon against this culture. Two speeches in Congress in 1926 illustrate the opposing arguments.

Speech in the House of Representatives in Support of Prohibition, April 19, 1926

Prohibition, the Constitution, the Enforcement of Prohibition, and Its Effect

Mr. GREEN of Florida. Mr. Speaker, I ask unanimous consent to extend my remarks in the Record on the subject of law enforcement.

The SPEAKER. Is there objection? [After a pause.] The Chair hears none.

Mr. GREEN of Florida. Mr. Speaker and fellow Members of the House, a great deal has recently been said relative to prohibition, its enforcement, and the lack of same, and I assure you that it gives me pleasure to at this time have the opportunity to express to you my views on this timely and all-important subject. It is always a pleasure to me to defend laws and to advocate their rigid and full enforcement. The fact is, as an officer of our Government and as a private citizen I am for the rigid enforcement of each and every law, both Federal and State, because without law and its strict enforcement our Government surely could not long exist.

Inasmuch as our Federal prohibition laws are based upon the eighteenth amendment to the Constitution, I think it well to briefly discuss the Constitution, which is a written instrument declaring the powers granted by the people of the United States for the establishment of the Federal Government; dividing the machinery of government into legislative, judicial, and executive branches; defining the power and duty of each and asserting certain principles by which they are to be governed. It was drafted by representatives selected by the original thirteen States, with the exception of Rhode Island, in a convention held at Philadelphia in the year 1787, written, of course, by Thomas Jefferson.

The Constitution was submitted to and ratified by the conventions of the thirteen States and became effective March 4, 1789, at which time Washington was made President; and, may I say in passing, that the original Constitution had opposers of its ratification; notably among them were such men as the eloquent Patrick Henry, Benjamin Harrison, John Tyler, Richard Henry Lee, Elbridge Gerry, Thomas Sumter, the then Governor of South Carolina, George Clinton, Governor of New York, and many others. Incidentally, their main force of attack was that it was destructive of the rights of the States just as the wet forces are to-day arguing that the eighteenth amendment is destructive of State rights; and, my friends, when I see the distinguished gentlemen of this House from such States as Maryland, New Jersey, New York, Massachusetts, and Rhode Island to-day defending so strongly the rights of the States I wonder how they and their predecessors stood during the years from 1840 to 1870, when the real rights of States were in jeopardy and when the States of my fair Southland suffered their almost every right to be confiscated. We from the South know and thoroughly appreciate what is meant by State rights and have no sympathy with those from the great wet centers when they cry State rights because it interferes with their pocketbook or their vicious appetites.

The Constitution may be amended by a vote of two-thirds of a quorum in the House of Representatives and in the Senate voting for said amendment; this vote offers it to the conventions or legislatures of the various States and must in turn be ratified by three-fourths of these legislatures. The eighteenth amendment, which prohibits the manufacture, sale, and transportation of intoxicating liquor within, the importation thereof into, or the exportation thereof from, the United States and all territories subject to the jurisdiction thereof for beverage purposes was passed by the United States Senate August 1, 1917, and by the House of Representatives December 17, 1917. It was then submitted to the legislatures of the several States, and by January 16, 1919, the legislatures of the necessary three-fourths of the states had ratified the amendment; it was then proclaimed by the Secretary of State and became an integral part of the Constitution, to take effect one year thereafter, going into effect January 16, 1920.

It is singular, Mr. Speaker, that 46 of the 48 States, all States except Rhode Island and Connecticut, ratified the eighteenth amendment. It is also interesting to note that the amendment was submitted by a vote of 282 to 128 in the House of Representatives, and by a vote of 65 to 20 in the United States Senate, in each branch more than the necessary two-thirds. Since the adoption of the eighteenth

---

Congressional Record, 69th Congress, 1st Session

amendment, measures bearing upon prohibition and its enforcement have repeatedly come before Congress, and it is interesting to note that every time, the dry vote has increased and the wet vote decreased.

Seven years' time was allowed for the various States to ratify the eighteenth amendment, but, Mr. Speaker, only 12 months were required. The total vote in the lower house of the legislatures of the States ratifying the eighteenth amendment was 3,782 votes for, to 1,035 votes against, or 78.5 per cent affirmative. The total vote in the senates of the respective legislatures was 1,310 for, to 237 against ratification, or 84.6 per cent affirmative; and it is also interesting to note that 98.2 per cent of the population of the United States resided in the 46 States which ratified the eighteenth amendment.

The enemies of prohibition should forget the erroneous idea that prohibition came in overnight, so to speak, by the adoption of the eighteenth amendment; the fact is, prohibition has been a live issue in all of the States for years and years, and only thorough ardent efforts of the drys and the religious and moral workers was it possible to adopt this amendment. Thirty-three States had adopted State prohibition prior to the date upon which national prohibition became effective.

These States and the date of adoption are as follows: Alabama in 1915; Arizona in 1914; Arkansas in 1915; Colorado in 1914; Florida in 1918; Georgia in 1907; Idaho in 1915; Indiana in 1917; Iowa in 1915; Kansas in 1880; Kentucky in 1919; Maine in 1851; Michigan in 1916; Mississippi in 1908; Montana in 1916; Nebraska in 1916; Nevada in 1918; New Hampshire in 1917; New Mexico in 1917; North Carolina in 1908; North Dakota in 1889; Ohio in 1918; Oklahoma in 1907; Oregon in 1914; South Carolina in 1915; South Dakota in 1916; Tennessee in 1909; Texas in 1918; Utah in 1917; Virginia in 1914; Washington in 1914; West Virginia in 1912; Wyoming in 1918.

By adding the area of these, you will find that 95.4 per cent of the total area of the United States and that 68.3 per cent of the total population of the United States lived in no-license territory at the time that the eighteenth amendment became effective, and yet we still have those wet advocates who cry State rights and who would force alcoholic liquors and all of its iniquities over this vast dry territory and this large majority of American citizens. I am sure that since this date, dry area and dry population census percentage has increased. In fact, I do not believe that more than 15 per cent of the peoples of the United States are wet, and this meager minority in their selfish and vicious beliefs would undertake to force intoxicating liquors upon the other 85 per cent.

This meager wet minority, which advocates the modification of the Volstead law, contend that crime and drunkenness have increased and that prohibition has failed. Permit me to say, Mr. Speaker, that the latest official refutation of the charge that prohibition has failed, that drunkenness has increased, and that crimes related to drinking have gone upward is given by the preliminary report of the United States Census Bureau's count of prisoners for the year 1923. Comparing that year with 1910, a year uncomplicated with war, unusual economic conditions, or saloon restriction, the figures in this census report show a remarkable decrease.

There were 121.2 prisoners in penal institutions January 1, 1910, for each 100,000 persons in the country. On January 1, 1923, this had dropped to 99.7, a decrease of 17.7 per cent. The number of commitments per 100,000 population showed an even greater relative decrease, falling from 521.7 per 100,000 in 1910 to 325.1 per 100,000 in 1923, a reduction of 37.7 per cent.

The decrease in drunkenness commitments is especially significant. There were 170,941 such commitments in 1910, but only 91,367 in 1923, the ratio in 1910 being 185.9 per 100,000, and in 1923, 83.1, a decrease of 55.2 per cent. Disorderly-conduct cases dropped 51.5 per cent, assault commitments 53.1 per cent, prostitution cases 28.8 per cent, and other offenses generally related to intemperance and drunkenness in equal degree.

The decrease in the number of commitments to jails and workhouses is more significant in relation to the liquor question than the decrease in the total number of commitments.

The total commitments would have been much lower if "violations of city ordinances," had not risen 67.3 per cent in the ratio per 100,000.

That drink-caused crime has greatly decreased since the eighteenth amendment closed the saloon, the most prolific source of crime and misery, is proven beyond refutation by these Government figures.

I have tables bearing out these statements, but they are rather lengthy and I shall not ask permission to place them in the RECORD, but will be glad to show them to anyone who may doubt the veracity of the above statements.

The wets claim, I believe, among other things, that the health of the country is worse now than it was before prohibition, but statistics reveal the opposite, as will be seen by the crude death rates issued by the Bureau of the Census for the following years:

1913	14.1	1918	18.1
1914	13.6	1919	12.9
1915	13.6	1920	13.1
1916	14.0	1921	11.6
1917	14.3	1922	11.8

I do not have the 1923 statistics officially. Reports from 65 cities, received each week during 1922 and 1923, show a death rate of 13 for 52 weeks of 1923, as compared with 12.5 for the same period in 1922. On the basis of the ratio between the death rate of these cities and the Nation in 1922, the death rate for 1923 may be estimated at 12.2 per 1,000 population. The average annual death rate from 1913 to 1917 was 13.92 per 1,000. Since the influenza epidemic made the 1915 rate abnormal, it may be ignored, although the greater mortality among users of alcohol definitely increased the toll of death. Had the average rate of the five wet years prevailed in the years of prohibition, 873,975 more deaths would have been recorded. Prohibition did not save all of these lives, but no other single factor affecting the entire people did so much to reduce mortality.

The decrease in the death rate from tuberculosis of all forms is significant. This was between 140 and 150 per 100,000 in the years before prohibition, the lowest figure recorded in the wet years being 14.2 in 1916. The following figures, as issued by the Bureau of the Census, show the continuous decrease since alcohol was outlawed as a beverage:

1919	125.9	1921	99.4
1920	114.2	1922	97.0

One might quote like decrease in the death rate in other diseases in which the use of alcohol depresses vitality and breaks protective barriers.

The decrease in deaths from alcoholism under prohibition appears in the following figures:

Alcoholism death rates per 100,000 policyholders in the Metropolitan Life Insurance Co., industrial department:

1912	5.3	1918	1.8
1913	5.2	1919	1.4
1914	4.7	1920	.6
1915	4.1	1921	.9
1916	5.1	1922	2.1
1917	4.9		

Alcoholism death rate, United States Census Bureau:

1912	5.3	1918	2.7
1913	5.9	1919	1.6
1914	4.9	1920	1.0
1915	4.4	1921	1.8
1916	5.8	1922	2.6
1917	5.2		

The increase for 1922 is marked, due probably to the propaganda of opponents of prohibition, but is still far below the lowest recorded for the license era. This is the more significant, since the intoxicants obtainable are usually poisonous. If any considerable fraction of the former quantities of liquor was now being used, the dangerous beverages of the bootlegger would send the alcoholism death rates soaring. That these rates continue to fall is good evidence of the effectiveness of prohibition in greatly decreasing liquor consumption.

It has also been contended by the wets that the morality and spiritual life of the Nation is lower since the adoption of the eighteenth amendment, but to the contrary, statistics reveal that the opposite is altogether the case. I shall not place in the RECORD tables showing the great improvement on the morals of our country, as I believe it is too evident to be stressed.

Mr. Speaker, to my great surprise there are those who will contend that prohibition is unsound economically. After all, these great issues resolve themselves in to an economic status, and statistics show that since the advent of national prohibition, America has grown financially by leaps and bounds. America, in reality, was a dry Nation long before the adoption of the eighteenth amendment, because, I say it was dry from the time a majority of its area and a majority of its citizens lived in license free territory; and it is interesting to note this vast and enormous business, economic, and financial growth in the past 20 years has been phenomenal. America's manufactured products have increased from $15,000,000,000 to over $60,000,000,000, her food products have increased from less than $3,000,000,000 to over $10,000,000,000 her mineral products have increased from about one and one-third billion dollars to $6,000,000,000, her imports and exports amounted to $2,450,000,000 and reports for 1924 showed increase to $8,200,000,000; the bank clearings were, $438,000,000 for 1924, or four times that of 20 years ago, and bank deposits have increased in like proportion and $43,000,000,000 were deposited in the banks of the United States in 1924.

Now, my friends, is there anything which speaks better for prohibition than this great financial steadiness and growth; why, America to-day is the world's banker. Financial experts like Herbert Hoover, Judge Gary, Henry Ford, Roger Babson, R. H. Scott, and others, attribute our prosperity in part to prohibition; you probably know how long drunken employees would be permitted to work for Henry Ford, America's greatest financial wizard. The foreign nations which are jealous of us and envy our prosperity under prohibition criticize us extremely for having adopted prohibition, but when they want money, they come to America after it. And we can not forget that during the great World War America was the only dry nation which had soldiers on the firing line, and their record is known too well by each of you for me to stress it here, and I would have you bear in mind also, that when the time for peace came, the peace terms were dictated by a dry nation's president, Woodrow Wilson, President of the United States of America. It seems to me that this alone should be argument enough for prohibition and for its strict enforcement.

No nation is so prominent to-day in world affairs as is the United States. It leads in invention, education, diplomacy, jurisprudence, and finance, and this great lead and prosperity among the nations of the world is strengthened by its being the only dry nation.

Those who are trying so hard to modify the Volstead Act would have us to believe that more alcohol is consumed now than was consumed before the adoption of the eighteenth amendment, but for your information, I desire to read here a short statement by Hon. Wayne B. Wheeler, superintendent of the Anti-Saloon League of America:

> The consumption of intoxicants has dropped to a small fraction of its former total. The records show that prior to prohibition we consumed 84,825,000 gallons of pure alcohol annually in 1,880,000,000 gallons of beer; 83,000,000 gallons of pure alcohol in 167,000,000 gallons of whisky and distilled spirits; over 6,000,000 gallons of pure alcohol in 42,000,000 gallons of wine, a total of over 174,000,000 gallons of pure alcohol. This is more than twice the total production of denatured alcohol total.
>
> Under prohibition 6,000,000 gallons of specially denatured alcohol was diverted to beverage use, and the best estimate is that less than 10,000,000 gallons of alcohol is made or consumed in smuggled liquor, moonshine, and home brew, exclusive of permitted beverages. This is less than 10 per cent of the former beverage consumption.
>
> The newly issued census figures show a 55 per cent decrease in drunkenness commitments in 1923 compared with 1910. Later figures show this decrease continued through 1925.
>
> America's sobriety is far ahead of European nations cited by the wets as evidence of the superiority of license. The ratio of drunkenness convictions in England and Wales was 200 per 100,000 population in 1923. The ratio of such convictions in the United States was 83.1 in the same year, 1923, according to the Census Bureau. London arrests three and a half times as many for intoxication per year as New York, and Paris twice as many, in spite of the greater severity of our police. One hundred and ninety-three thousand registered home distilleries in France contribute to the intoxication of that nation. With bread lines, unemployment doles, debt dodging, and hands outstretched for American loans, the wet nations of Europe may profit by America's example of new freedom from alcohol's rule.
>
> * * *
>
> Pauperism and the slums that clustered around their creator, the saloon, have gone with it. Our pauperism ratio to-day, according to the latest census estimate, is the lowest in our history.

A great deal has been said relative to the cost of enforcing prohibition, but, Mr. Speaker, I am always willing to vote to expend money when the investment is so good. Money spent to enforce prohibition is a wise investment. I voted for the appropriation to enforce prohibition, and would have voted for had it carried twice the amount. The cost of prohibition enforcement through the Prohibition Bureau amounts to about $9,000,000 annually. The total appropriation of $9,250,000 covers the enforcement of the law against narcotics as well as intoxicating liquor. The returns to the Government through penalties, seized property, and so forth, is shown by the following report for the fiscal year ending June 30, 1922:

Court fines, exclusive of Alaska	$2,824,685.01
Taxes and penalties for illegal manufacture and sale of	239,964.14
Amounts paid in compromise	1,739,662.80
Total	4,804,271.95

Action has been taken on the forfeiture of bonds of $3,000,000.

Over $130,000,000 of special assessed taxes have been placed on the tax list, a considerable portion of which will be collected.

As a matter of fact, it is costing the Government practically nothing to enforce prohibition. Bootleggers, rum runners, and illicit dealers are paying for their lawlessness through these fines and penalties. Even if $5,000,000 more were added, if the internal-revenue collectors and other Federal officers would use the power they have to impose penalties upon these illicit dealers, it would bring back in dollars to the Government twice as much as it costs. If the income-tax division and the revenue collectors would do their whole duty, the Government would collect $5 for every $1 it costs to enforce the law, even though the alleged added amount spent by the Justice Department were all counted in.

In Ohio the State prohibition commissioner, under the State law, made his report for 22 months, showing that with 1 commissioner and 22 assistants it cost the State $216,000 to enforce prohibition. There was returned to the State, county, and local treasuries $2,000,000 which bootleggers and rum runners paid for their experiment in lawlessness.

But even if there were no compensation and the Government did not get $1 back, it would furnish no good reason why the law should not be enforced. To spend $9,000,000 to enforce prohibition for 110,000,000 people means about 8 cents per head.

For an average family of five this is 40 cents.

Mr. Speaker, I hold in my hand remarks by the Attorney General of the United States, recently made before the Womens' National Committee for Law Enforcement, Hotel Washington, Washington, D. C. I shall not read it, as I have been given unanimous consent to include it in the RECORD in my remarks. It will follow my remarks in the RECORD.

Those who are asking for a modification of the Volstead Act, cry liberty and freedom, but when personal liberty and personal freedom is corruption, vice, financial greed, immorality at the distress, injustice, and expense to others, then it ceases to be liberty and freedom; particularly is this true when it would be so called liberty and freedom for the meager minority at the peril of the great majority. Why, they have brought witnesses from foreign countries to testify that we should modify our prohibition laws, and I for one do not need foreigners from Canada or from any other country to come to Washington to tell me what laws are needed for the American people.

My experience, Mr. Speaker, is that we have too many foreigners interfering with the administration of American laws, and all foreigners, whether they be rich or poor, humble or high, pauper, foreign minister, or diplomat, should be compelled to abide by our laws when they are within our bounds, and surely no foreign nation should expect their subjects, even though they be foreign ministers or diplomats, to openly and notoriously violate our laws when they are within our bounds.

Mr. Speaker, we need dry men to enforce dry laws; so long as the powers that be, which are given authority to enforce our prohibition laws are not in full sympathy with their enforcement, you may expect graft, greed, corruption, and unlawful acts in prohibition enforcement to continue. Only recently, I read in a paper where at Tampa, Fla., on April 17, $15,000 worth of imported liquor and alcohol had been stolen from the Government warehouse. Now, were the officers in charge performing their full duty? I say they were not. So long as wet men are placed in charge of enforcing a dry law, you may expect warehouses to leak. And I hope the time will soon come when prohibition officers will be instantly fired when they go before committees and say that the sale of beer or wine would strengthen prohibition. Men who believe the sale of light wine or beer would strengthen prohibition are wet to the core, and should never be permitted to occupy a dry berth.

I am proud to say, Mr. Speaker, that I came from a dry State. Florida is a dry State and is enforcing her prohibition laws. While I was on the bench before I came to Congress, I sentenced law violators to months in the jail for having in their possession less than one pint of intoxicating liquor. But, Mr. Speaker, we need the cooperation and full service of dry Federal prohibition enforcement agents.

I hold in my hand a clipping from a newspaper of my State; it is an article written by a small school boy, Elmer McMillan, a boy in his early teens, who resides in my home city; I shall not take the time to read it, but it concludes as follows:

> Why should we degrade our country to satisfy the thirst of some degraded men who do not think of the American homes but of the money they will make in the liquor traffic. If this is all the respect we have for our country, I do not think we should have the right to be protected by the American flag and to call ourselves American citizens. For

the main thought of every American citizen under Old Glory should be to raise the flag to higher places and not lower it.

Now, Mr. Speaker, this is a typical American boy, raised by a mother who is a total invalid, but a sweet Christian character, and in spite of her affliction has regularly gone with her family to church, and raised by an honest, plain father, who works daily for the support of his several children, and so long as steady American fathers raise patriotic sons like Elmer McMillan, America shall be a dry Nation.

Remarks by the Attorney General of the United States at Luncheon of Women's National Committee for Law Enforcement, Hotel Washington, Washington, D. C., April 13, 1926

Madame the President and members of the Women's Committee on Law Enforcement, in approaching the subject before you at this social gathering of the representatives of your great body, I am somewhat at a loss how to begin.

To me, the matter of having the law observed, in a country under a Government like ours, seems a very simple thing. All that is necessary is that each member of each family in each community in each State shall go about his and her business each day with the purpose in mind to obey the rules made by society for its own guidance. But it happens that there are here and there among us persons who do not have such purpose; persons who, instead of trying to earn an honest living, by honest toil, undertake to get the means of living in what they think and hope will be an easier way.

We must remember that a living for all must be earned by all, and each member of society who does not by some useful action earn his keep, increases the burden of the rest who have to earn it for them.

With those who are a burden from being mere drones, shirks, we need not further concern ourselves here; with those who by active preying on their fellow members of the social body undertake to get a living, or more than a living—the means of luxury—we are here very much concerned.

With those who undertake to set aside the rules of life which we ourselves have made, and satisfy their cravings of lust, of appetite, of revenge, of malice by reprisals on individuals, on the community, we are very much concerned.

We make law governing the relations of individuals to each other and their property, and we provide courts in which individuals may seek redress for violations of their legal rights by other individuals.

We make law governing the relations of individuals to the community, and provide by law penalties for infraction of such law. The community as a body can not well impose such penalties, and so we provide courts to pass on the question of whether there has been an infraction of the law, and provide representatives of the community to present in such courts charges against persons accused of infractions of the law—prosecuting officers.

What is the duty of such a representative of the community toward its laws?

It seems to me that a prosecuting officer, while and so long as he holds his place as the representative of the law, ought not to take the position that the law as it is ought not to be the law.

The law is the will of the body politic, and we are in our places by the will of the body politic, put there to execute that will; and if we go about declaring in speech and in print that the law ought to be changed, so that acts which are offenses against the law will not be offenses, we thereby weaken our causes in the minds of the tribunals before whom we must try them.

I notice on the letterheads of this committee that the purpose of the organizations it represents is to encourage the enforcement of all the law, with especial emphasis on the eighteenth amendment and the Volstead Act, and I have been informed by some of your officers that you are particularly anxious for an expression of my views on that subject.

Let me say that what my views are is not, as I see it, of much greater importance than what your views are. I can keep the machinery of prosecution of violators of the law in motion, but you can make the results of such work effective, or to a considerable extent impair its effectiveness.

At the risk of being accused of having a single-track mind, I wish to repeat here in substance a few observations I have before publicly made on this subject.

In this country, under our system of government, the will of the people expressed by their vote becomes and is the rule of conduct which all citizens are bound to observe and which all citizens or aliens must be compelled to observe. That rule of conduct creates the duty of every inhabitant of the jurisdiction doing the voting.

The eighteenth amendment is the law of the land.

The Volstead Act is the law of the land.

Both by constitutional command of the whole people and by legislative enactment of their representatives in Congress it has been decreed that traffic in intoxicating liquor shall cease.

There is no room for discussion as to what the voters of the country have said.

There is no halfway place in the command they have laid upon their servants chosen and appointed to administer the law.

But notwithstanding that the law is as it is, notwithstanding the will of the people is that this traffic, and, of course, the drinking of alcohol, shall cease, a considerable number of persons insist they will not obey the law and persist in the traffic to supply drink for themselves and others who are willing to reward them for the chances they take.

Those who engage in the business, those who furnish the business by buying its wares, and some who do not wish to either sell or buy liquor, undertake to excuse the violators by saying over and over that this law is an infringement of personal liberty.

They declare that since the prohibition law went into effect it has never been practically in effect.

That it has been a disastrous, tragic failure.

That the Federal Government is powerless to enforce it, because, they say, "The instinct of personal liberty is very strong." "Man can not be made over by law," and "thousands of the best citizens of the country have been brought into contact with the bootlegger, and have no compunction whatever about violating the law."

Let us examine these propositions briefly.

Though some of those who make these claims and arguments may not, do not, have in mind a purpose to make the thing prohibited easier to procure and less dangerous to make and sell by those who would provide it, nevertheless such is the effect upon the execution of the law.

Personal liberty to do what? Anything except to facilitate the making, sale, and use of intoxicants? Why? Any reason, except that the use of them may not be interfered with?

What other result can follow the constant declaration that the law is not binding on the consciences of those who do not favor its provisions, because they say it interferes with personal liberty and the instinct of personal liberty is very strong. What other result can follow than that juries will hesitate to convict on charges of violation of the law?

What other result can follow than that those contemplating engaging in the traffic will be encouraged by the thought that probably, even if detected and arrested, conviction will not follow?

No compunction about violating the law? Violating it how? What for? Anything except to provide intoxicants for somebody to drink?

No.

Such contentions, when made by those who do not want liquor for themselves, who would not intentionally put obstacles in the way of enforcement of the law, must be made without realization of the effect of their position.

That effect can be and is only to weaken public sentiment in favor of any law enforcement and to encourage violation of all law.

It is only a step—and an easy one—for the man of loose moral fiber who hears and reads that men of education, of standing and influence, aver and urge that he is not in conscience bound to give allegiance to one provision of the Constitution, is not in conscience bound to observe one statute because it interferes with his liberty to do as he pleases in that matter, to come to the conclusion that he is not in conscience bound to observe another law, and then another, which interferes with the liberty he would have to do some other act but for the law; and when he is told that many of the best citizens violate a part of the law without compunction, what conclusion can he reach but that he may violate any part of it without compunction?

The difference between civilization and barbarism is in the presence or absence of law.

The very idea of law in a community carries with it the surrender of individual freedom of action for the good of the whole body.

In a state of barbarism one may walk or drive where he please, unless the "personal liberty" of another stronger than he interferes.

In Washington one must drive on the right-hand side of the street. Why? Because the community has decided that the welfare of the whole, of which he is a part, demands that he be deprived of liberty to drive where he please and compelled to go on the right-hand side.

Does anyone contend that "man can not be made over by law" in this matter?

Does anyone contend that because "the instinct of personal liberty is very strong" he has a right to endanger the safety of everyone in the street, including himself, by asserting his personal liberty and driving on the left-hand side?

What is the difference between insuring the safety of travel by depriving men of their personal liberty through compelling them to drive on the right side and compelling them to be sober when driving through depriving them of the means of getting drunk?

The real source of the embarrassment to the enforcement of the law is, not that the law interferes with personal liberty—any law which has any effect upon the conduct of the individuals composing society does that—must do that—but that so many well-intentioned persons, thoughtlessly, or following some process of unsound reasoning, join hands with those who intentionally violate the law and give them aid and comfort in attempting to justify their unlawful conduct.

There is no right of personal liberty to perpetuate an institution which the law condemns.

In this country that the liquor traffic shall be exterminated is established by solemn resolution of the electorate.

That it ought not to exist is admitted by those making the arguments and claims I have been discussing when they say either by way of preface or conclusion to every discussion, "We do not desire to bring back intoxicating liquor"; "There is no intention ever to bring back the saloon." Those who say this honestly surely can not have thought out the result to which their arguments tend.

The rest "do protest too much."

Again, if it be true that "the prohibitory law has never been practically in effect," that "it has been a disastrous, tragic failure," that "the Government is powerless to enforce it," in what way does it interfere with the personal liberty of those who would drink intoxicants?

The answer is, as everybody knows, that by reason of the existence of national prohibition, by reason of its practical effect, by reason of the exertion of the power of the Federal Government, the traffic in liquor is becoming day by day more and more difficult and dangerous to carry on.

An the application of the Federal power grows more strict, and the manufacture within the country and importation from without become more restricted, as the business becomes more difficult and dangerous, the price of the goods dealt in rises, and right there is where the shoe pinches; right there is the evidence which can not be controverted, that the Federal Government is not "powerless to enforce" the law.

I maintain that to show the law, any law, is violated is not to show that it is not being enforced, or that it can not be enforced.

If that argument were sound, then, because crimes of murder, rape, robbery, smuggling, stealing, embezzlement, continue to be committed, we must say the penalties against them can not be imposed.

No one likes that.

As the amount of liquor available for consumption decreases and the price of liquor rises and the profit per quart or per gallon increases, new and keener wits and ingenuity are attracted to the business; new and complicated and skillful schemes are devised for evading the law and constantly increasing watchfulness, activity, and study required for their detection; many of them go on for a long time without detection. But ways of meeting and overcoming them are found and can be found for all of them.

Recently some one made an argument that the great increase of cases in court for violation of the prohibitory law is an indication that the law is not being and can not be enforced.

hibit, but rather breeds defiance, and in addition leaves in its wake a rapidly broadening trail of misery and corruption?

In discussing the colossal failure of the Volstead Act I seldom refer to the stupendous expense to the taxpayers. Were real results accomplished, no one would question the cost.

However, when a Federal officer sworn to enforce the law frankly exposes the situation, as did United States District Attorney Buckner in New York a few days ago, it is time to sit up and take notice. The district attorney disturbed those who decline to admit failure by claiming with present Federal appropriations, which according to Attorney General Sargent amount now to $30,000,000 a year, he was unable to more than make an effort to cover one-fifth of the violations.

If District Attorney Buckner's estimate is correct that it requires $30,000,000 to pursue one-fifth of the violations and then fail, it would apparently require $150,000,000 annually to conduct anything like a complete campaign of enforcement.

This is entirely apart from the millions States and municipalities are spending and the millions it costs to maintain the courts of the country, both State and Federal, whose work to-day is almost exclusively confined to violations of the prohibition act. Just think of it! One hundred and fifty million dollars a year from the taxpayers. Why, do you realize that the last Federal appropriation for the great Department of Agriculture, with all its ramifications in every State in the Union, was less than this amount? Can't you imagine when the American people actually realize this situation they will arise en masse and demand a termination of the bluff which instead of bringing about temperance is demoralizing the public service of the country?

O fellow citizens, the time has passed for stubbornness and politics, for impugning motives and misrepresenting facts. This intolerable situation in which we find ourselves must be remedied. A solution can not be reached through vilification. The facts are with us and we can no longer evade them.

I will quote but one statistic. It should be convincing. The Federal Bureau of the Census recently issued a table showing the combined death rate in the country from all causes as gradually decreasing, while during the same period the deaths from alcoholic poisoning have increased without exception in every single State in the Union. Is that sectional? And yet defenders of the Volstead Act claim progress. There has been progress, but the trouble is it has been in the wrong direction.

I have always admitted modifying the Volstead Act, while greatly helping the situation, will not solve the entire problem.

We can well afford to heed the much better moral and social condition prevailing in the various so-called wet Provinces of our neighbor on the north, Canada.

Most of the Canadian Provinces tried our experiment and, following us, voted dry. All but one—Ontario—has returned to some form of wetness. Surveys and reviews of the results have clearly and positively demonstrated generally improved conditions.

These countries have apparently decided governmental distribution of pure and legalized liquors was preferable to the bootleggers' distribution of poisonous substitutes. That's what we have to-day.

We could profit through their experience and some day we will, but it is appalling to contemplate the havoc in the meantime.

The bootleggers and the extreme drys are together resisting all efforts for modification. Public opinion, however, as now daily expressed from pulpit and forum, is demanding action and freely admitting the error we have made. Only pure, unadulterated stubbornness maintains otherwise.

I earnestly hope the demand for modification, now so manifest, will grow stronger and stronger, in order that cooperative action can be assured and respect for law renewed.

Is it not significant when prominent educators, like Dean Gauss, of Princeton, and President Butler, of Columbia, demand modification? They are in daily contact with those approaching manhood. They unhesitatingly admit the calamity of the present situation.

Only to-day an association of the powerful Episcopal Church, through Doctor Empringham, secretary of the Church Temperance Society, came out flatly for modification. Certainly no sane man would question their sincerity.

The common-sense result of modification would be a lower consumption of hard liquors. That's true temperance.

We are not enlisted in an effort to tear down but rather to build up. To amend an unworkable law is not to violate it, but rather to make it worthy of the great Republic in which we live. We can and will no longer perpetuate a lie.

[Senator DILL followed, whose address appeared in the proceedings of the Senate of Saturday, February 6 (legislative day of Monday, February 1), 1926.]

Rebuttal by Senator Edge

My friends, as I anticipated, and yet with every good feeling to my colleague, he has adopted the usual old tactics, fallen back on the same old worn-out claims which I have on previous occasions completely punctured and disproved.

He asked me two questions, and in the limited time I have I don't want him to have the opportunity to say I have evaded anything. I will answer both of them.

He asked if I really am in favor of 2.75 per cent beer or some other voltage of beer, or whether I believed that the eighteenth amendment should stand, or if it should be amended or repealed.

When he attempts to minimize the inconsistencies and the discriminations of the present Volstead Act by using the expression that the cider and wine privilege of that act was for a few housewives to make fruit juices, then I must accuse him of evasion. Does he know that in the State of California alone over 45,000 permits were asked for and issued to enable citizens of that State to make what he calls fruit juices—in reality to make, of course, wine, and to make wine as intoxicating as 90 per cent of them could make it? They would not have bothered with permits otherwise. And when I contend that the Volstead Act, unless it be fair to all classes of citizens, invites the protest and challenge we now know exists, I simply repeat what every citizen knows and will admit if he wants to admit the facts.

Why should there be any objection to at least making the Volstead Act consistent in this regard? The Senator admits that we can not amend the Constitution through an act of Congress. I absolutely agree with him. Any amendment we add to the Volstead Act allowing 2.75 beer or whatever voltage that is not proven intoxicating as now allowed wines, the Supreme Court will have the final say. Why should Congress refuse this privilege? In refusing the privilege they invite the protest which is evident over all this country, and naturally so.

In his second question, as I recall it, he claimed a large quantity of beer was drunk before prohibition went into effect. I agree with him. And this is one of the main arguments I present. I say this because of the great number of people to-day who are drinking all kinds of substitute poisonous concoctions of every character. Our Nation was 100—yes, 1,000 per cent better off when they were drinking beer than when they are drinking the concoctions of to-day. My dear Senator, I think you made the statement that you looked forward to the day when the use of alcohol will have passed. We look forward to the day when we, at least, can be temperate, but you can not look forward to impossibilities. We are facing an issue we can not evade, and we should admit it is the duty of Congress to meet the issue. Perhaps my solution is not the best, but I want to see the time when both sides are free from bias and not extreme either way, when they will sit around a table recognizing the problem and solve it fair to the rights of all American citizens.

Document 18.6 The Real Reasons for Prohibition

In his book published in 1915 during the nation-wide debate over Prohibition, Percy Andreae argued that Prohibition was really an attempt by certain Protestant churches to impose their beliefs on the whole country. What are Andreae's arguments? How valid are they? How do Andreae's arguments fit into the culture clash?

The Real Reasons for Prohibition

Percy Andreae

I have met many active prohibitionists . . . all of them thoroughly in earnest. In some instances I have found that their allegiance to the cause of prohibition took its origin in the fact that some near relative or friend had succumbed to overindulgence in liquor. In one or two cases the man himself had been the victim of this weakness, and had come to the conclusion, firstly, that every one else was constituted as he was; and secondly, that unless one were prevented from drinking, he would not be secure from the temptation to do so himself.

This is one class of prohibitionists. The other, and by far the larger class, is made up of religious zealots, to whom prohibition is a word having at bottom a far wider application than that which is generally attributed to it. The liquor question . . . is merely put forth by them as a means to an end, an incidental factor in a fight which has for its object the supremacy of a certain form of religious faith. The belief of many of these people is that the Creator frowns upon enjoyment of any and every kind, and that he has merely endowed us with certain desires and capacities for pleasure in order to give us an opportunity to please Him by resisting them. They are, of course, perfectly entitled to this belief. . . . But are they privileged to force that belief on their fellow beings? That, in substance, is the question that is involved in the present-day prohibition movement. . . .

Prohibition is merely the title of the movement. Its real purpose is of a religious, sectarian character. . . .

If any one doubts the truth of the statement, let me put this to him: How many Roman Catholics are prohibitionists? How many Jews, the most temperate race on earth, are to be found in the ranks of prohibition? Or Lutherans? Or German Protestants generally? What is the proportion of Episcopalians to that of Methodists, Baptists, and Presbyterians, and the like, in the active prohibition army? The answer to these questions will, I venture to say, prove conclusively the assertion that the fight for prohibition is synonymous with the fight of a certain religious sect, or group of sects, for the supremacy of its ideas. In England it is the Nonconformists, which is in that country the generic name for the same sects, who are fighting the fight, and the suppression of liquor there is no more the ultimate end they have in view than it is here in America. It is the fads and restrictions that are part and parcel of their lugubrious notion of Godworship [sic] which they eventually hope to impose upon the rest of humanity; a Sunday without a smile, no games, no recreation, no pleasures, no music, card-playing tabooed, dancing anathematized, the beauties of art decried as impure—in short, this world reduced to a barren, forbidding wilderness in which we, its inhabitants, are to pass our time contemplating the joys of the next. . . .

What a strange reversal of conditions! The intolerants of a few hundred years ago are the upholders of liberty to-day, while those they once persecuted, having multiplied by grace of the very liberty that has so long sheltered them here, are now planning to impose the tyranny of their narrow creed, upon the descendants of their persecutors of yore.

Let the greater public, which is, after all, the arbiter of the country's destinies, pause and ponder these things before they are allowed to progress too far. Prohibition, though it must cause, and is already causing, incalculable damage, may never succeed in this country; but that which is behind it, as the catapults and the cannon were behind the battering rams in the battles of olden days, is certain to succeed unless timely measures of prevention are resorted to; and if it does succeed, we shall witness the enthronement of a monarch in this land of liberty compared with whose autocracy the autocracy of the Russian Czar is a mere trifle.

The name of this monarch is Religious Intolerance.

The Prohibition Movement in its Broader Bearings upon Social Commercial and Religious Liberties, Chicago: Felix Mendelsohn, 1915.

Module XVIII

Questions for Study and Critical Thinking

1. What are the key ideas in the selection from Purinton?

2. Do you agree with these ideas?

3. What characteristics of Jesus does Bruce Barton see as important for business executives?

4. Based on what you know about Jesus, do you agree that he had these characteristics?

5. In what ways does Barton's work reflect the values of the 1920s?

6. What groups did Evans claim the Klan protected? What groups did the Klan oppose?

7. What values does he endorse? Which ones does he oppose?

8. What are the main ideas in the selection by Evans?

9. How do these ideas fit into the 1920s?

10. What are principal arguments of the Congressman favoring Prohibition?

11. How valid are they? Would they convince you that prohibition of alcohol would be a good idea now?

12. If you found these arguments unconvincing, do you think many drugs prohibited today ought to be legalized?

13. What arguments did the Senator make against Prohibition? How valid are these arguments?

14. What are Andreae's arguments? How valid are they?

15. How do Andreae's arguments fit into the culture clash?

Module XIX

Surviving the Great Depression

Introduction

The Great Depression of the late 1920s and the 1930s was one of the greatest catastrophes in American history. At the Depression's depths, one quarter of the entire workforce was unemployed. People lost their savings and their homes. Men traveled from place to place searching for some improvement, hitching rides on freight trains, hitchhiking, or walking. Many people suffered from feelings of hopelessness and depression.

In November 1932, after Herbert Hoover's administration had failed for over two years to make any appreciable improvements in the situation, the voters elected the Democrat, Franklin D. Roosevelt, in a landslide. But what would Roosevelt do? Herbert Hoover had established limits to what he was willing to have the Federal government do. While Roosevelt did not have any clear ideas about how to curb the depression, he proposed, in a very American way, simply to experiment to see what worked. The Federal government would, therefore, be much more active and would do things it had never done before. In his speech to the Commonwealth Club in San Francisco, excerpted in this chapter, Roosevelt described this approach.

One of Roosevelt's most important accomplishments was raising the spirits of the nation. In doing this, his vibrant, sunny disposition played a major part, as did speeches expressing his optimism. His first inaugural address, in which he declared that, "we have nothing to fear but fear itself," is one of the most famous examples.

Roosevelt enjoyed tremendous trust from many Americans, who saw him as a man who understood them and wanted to help them personally. His wife, Eleanor, who became one of the most active First Ladies, also aroused great trust (as well as great hostility from those who disliked the New Deal).

Despite the unparalleled expansion of the Federal government under Roosevelt, however, the economy failed to emerge from the Depression until after World War II began. Roosevelt, therefore, was politically vulnerable to those on both the left and right who proposed more radical programs. One of his most formidable potential rivals was Huey Long, a populist senator from Louisiana, who proposed a massive redistribution of income from the rich to those less well off. Long, however, was assassinated before he could run for the presidency, and other radical leaders also failed to raise significant electoral support.

Document 19.1 The Philosophy of the New Deal

In 1932 in the midst of the presidential campaign Franklin Roosevelt outlined his emerging theory of government in a speech to the Commonwealth Club in San Francisco. He began by recalling the great debate between Alexander Hamilton and Thomas Jefferson in the first years of the nation's history. He then traced the rise of industry and big business. Finally, he asserted that the new conditions of an economy dominated by large industrial corporations required a new philosophy of government, to protect the rights of the people as a whole—especially during the Depression.

The Philosophy of the New Deal

Franklin D. Roosevelt

Speech to the Commonwealth Club of San Francisco

Sometimes, my friends, particularly in years such as these, the hand of discouragement falls upon us. It seems that things are in a rut, fixed, settled, that the world has grown old and tired and very much out of joint. This is the mood of depression, of dire and weary depression.

But then we look around us in America, and everything tells us that we are wrong. America is new. It is in the process of change and development. It has the great potentialities of youth, and particularly is this true of the great West, and of this coast, and of California. . . .

The issue of Government has always been whether individual men and women will have to serve some system of Government or economics, or whether a system of Government and economics exists to serve individual men and women. . . .

There were those who because they had seen the confusion which attended the years of war for American independence surrendered to the belief that popular Government was essentially dangerous and essentially unworkable. They were honest people, my friends, and we cannot deny that their experience had warranted some measure of fear. The most brilliant, honest and able exponent of this point of view was Hamilton. . . . Fundamentally he believed that the safety of the republic lay in the autocratic strength of its Government, that the destiny of individuals was to serve that Government, and that fundamentally a great and strong group of central institutions, guided by a small group of able and public spirited citizens, could best direct all Government.

But Mr. Jefferson, in the summer of 1776, after drafting the Declaration of Independence turned his mind to the same problem and took a different view. . . . "[A] Government must so order its functions as not to interfere with the individual." But . . . Jefferson realized that the exercise of the property rights might so interfere with the rights of the individual that the Government, without whose assistance the property rights could not exist, must intervene, not to destroy individualism, but to protect it.

You are familiar with the great political duel which followed; and how Hamilton, and his friends, building toward a dominant centralized power, were at length defeated in the great election of 1800, by Mr. Jefferson's party. Out of that duel came the two parties, Republican and Democratic, as we know them today.

So began, in American political life, the new day, the day of the individual against the system, the day in which individualism was made the great watchword of American life. The happiest of economic conditions made that day long and splendid. . . .

It was in the middle of the nineteenth century that a new force was released and a new dream created. The force was what is called the industrial revolution, the advance of steam and machinery and the rise of the forerunners of the modern industrial plant. The dream was the dream of an economic machine, able to raise the standard of living for everyone; to bring luxury within the reach of the humblest; to annihilate distance by steam power and later by electricity, and to release everyone from the drudgery of the heaviest manual toil. It was to be expected that this would necessarily affect Government. Heretofore, Government had merely been called upon to produce conditions within which people could live happily, labor peacefully, and rest secure. Now it was called upon to aid in the consummation of this new dream. There was, however, a shadow over the dream. To be made real, it required use of the talents of men of tremendous will and tremendous ambition, since by no other force could the problems of financing and engineering and new developments be brought to a consummation.

So manifest were the advantages of the machine age, however, that the United States fearlessly, cheerfully, and, I think, rightly, accepted the bitter with the sweet. It was thought that no price was too high to pay for the advantages which we could draw from a finished industrial system. The history of the last half century is accordingly in large measure a history of a group of financial Titans, whose meth-

---

From *The Public Papers and Addresses of Franklin D. Roosevelt.*

ods were not scrutinized with too much care, and who were honored in proportion as they produced the results, irrespective of the means they used. The financiers who pushed the railroads to the Pacific were always ruthless, often wasteful, and frequently corrupt; but they did build railroads, and we have them today. . . . As long as we had free land; as long as population was growing by leaps and bounds; as long as our industrial plants were insufficient to supply our own needs, society chose to give the ambitious man free play and unlimited reward provided only that he produced the economic plant so much desired.

During this period of expansion, there was equal opportunity for all and the business of Government was not to interfere but to assist in the development of industry. This was done at the request of business men themselves. The tariff was originally imposed for the purpose of "fostering our infant industry." . . . The railroads were subsidized, sometimes by grants of money, oftener by grants of land. . . . Some of my friends tell me that they do not want the Government in business. With this I agree; but I wonder whether they realize the implications of the past. For while it has been American doctrine that the Government must not go into business in competition with private enterprises, still it has been traditional, particularly in Republican administrations, for business urgently to ask the Government to put at private disposal all kinds of Government assistance. The same man who tells you that he does not want to see the Government interfere in business—and he means it, and has plenty of good reasons for saying so—is the first to go to Washington and ask the Government for a prohibitory tariff on his product. . . . Each group has sought protection from the Government for its own special interests, without realizing that the function of Government must be to favor no small group at the expense of its duty to protect the rights of personal freedom and of private property of all its citizens.

In retrospect we can now see that the turn of the tide came with the turn of the century. We were reaching our last frontier; there was no more free land and our industrial combinations had become great uncontrolled and irresponsible units of power within the State. Clear-sighted men saw with fear the danger that opportunity would no longer be equal; that the growing corporation, like the feudal baron of old, might threaten the economic freedom of individuals to earn a living. . . .

A glance at the situation today only too clearly indicates that equality of opportunity as we have known it no longer exists. Our industrial plant is built; the problem just now is whether under existing conditions it is not overbuilt. Our last frontier has long since been reached, and there is practically no more free land. More than half of our people do not live on the farms or on lands and cannot derive a living by cultivating their own property. There is no safety valve in the form of a Western prairie to which those thrown out of work by the Eastern economic machines can go for a new start. We are not able to invite the immigration from Europe to share our endless plenty. We are now providing a drab living for our own people. . . .

Just as freedom to farm has ceased, so also the opportunity in business has narrowed. It still is true that men can start small enterprises, trusting to native shrewdness and ability to keep abreast of competitors; but area after area has been preempted altogether by the great corporations, and even in the fields which still have no great concerns, the small man starts under a handicap. The unfeeling statistics of the past three decades show that the independent business man is running a losing race.

Perhaps he is forced to the wall; perhaps he cannot command credit; perhaps he is "squeezed out" . . . by highly organized corporate competitors, as your corner grocery man can tell you. Recently a careful study was made of the concentration of business in the United States. It showed that our economic life was dominated by some six hundred odd corporations who controlled two-thirds of American industry. Ten million small business men divided the other third. . . . Put plainly, we are steering a steady course toward economic oligarchy, if we are not there already.

Clearly, all this calls for a re-appraisal of values. A mere builder of more industrial plants, a creator of more railroad systems, an organizer of more corporations, is as likely to be a danger as a help. The day of the great promoter or the financial Titan, to whom we granted anything if only he would build, or develop, is over. Our task now is not discovery or exploitation of natural resources, or necessarily producing more goods. It is the soberer, less dramatic business of administering resources and plants already in hand, of seeking to reestablish foreign markets for our surplus production, of meeting the problem of underconsumption, of adjusting production to consumption, of distributing wealth and products more equitably, of adapting existing economic organizations to the service of the people. The day of enlightened administration has come. . . .

As I see it, the task of Government in its relation to business is to assist the development of an economic declaration of rights, an economic constitutional order. This is the common task of statesman and business man. It is the minimum requirement of a more permanently safe order of things.

Happily, the times indicate that to create such an order not only is the proper policy of Government, but it is the only line of safety for our economic structures as well. We know, now, that these economic units cannot exist unless prosperity is uniform, that is, unless purchasing power is well distributed throughout every group in the Nation. That is why even the most selfish of corporations for its own interest would be glad to see wages restored and unemployment ended and to bring the Western farmer back to his accustomed level of prosperity and to assure a permanent safety to both groups. That is why some enlightened industries themselves endeavor to limit the freedom of action of each man and business group within the industry in the common interest of all; why business men everywhere are asking a form of organization which will bring the scheme of things into balance, even though it may in some measure qualify the freedom of action of individual units within the business. . . .

I feel that we are coming to a view through the drift of our legislation and our public thinking in the past quarter century that private economic power is, to enlarge an old phrase, a public trust as well. I hold that continued enjoyment of that power by an individual or group must depend upon the fulfillment of that trust. The men who have reached the summit of American business life know this best; happily, many of these urge the binding quality of this greater social contract.

The terms of that contract are as old as the Republic, and as new as the new economic order.

Every man has a right to life; and this means that he has also a right to make a comfortable living. He may by sloth or crime decline to exercise that right; but it may not be denied him. We have no actual famine or dearth; our industrial and agricultural mechanism can produce enough and to spare. Our Government formal and informal, political and economic, owes to everyone an avenue to possess himself of a portion of that plenty sufficient for his needs, through his own work.

Every man has a right to his own property; which means a right to be assured, to the fullest extent attainable, in the safety of his savings. By no other means can men carry the burdens of those parts of life which, in the nature of things, afford no chance of labor; childhood, sickness, old age. In all thought of property, this right is paramount; all other property rights must yield to it. If, in accord with this principle, we must restrict the operations of the speculator, the manipulator, even the financier, I believe we must accept the restriction as needful, not to hamper individualism but to protect it.

These two requirements must be satisfied, in the main, by the individuals who claim and hold control of the great industrial and financial combinations which dominate so large a part of our industrial life. They have undertaken to be, not business men, but princes of property. I am not prepared to say that the system which produces them is wrong. I am very clear that they must fearlessly and competently assume the responsibility which goes with the power. So many enlightened business men know this that the statement would be little more than a platitude, were it not for an added implication.

This implication is, briefly, that the responsible heads of finance and industry instead of acting each for himself, must work together to achieve the common end. They must, where necessary, sacrifice this or that private advantage; and in reciprocal self-denial must seek a general advantage. It is here that formal Government—political Government, if you choose—comes in. Whenever in the pursuit of this objective the lone wolf, the unethical competitor, the reckless promoter . . . whose hand is against every man's, declines to join in achieving an end recognized as being for the public welfare, and threatens to drag the industry back to a state of anarchy, the Government may properly be asked to apply restraint. Likewise, should the group ever use its collective power contrary to the public welfare, the Government must be swift to enter and protect the public interest.

The Government should assume the function of economic regulation only as a last resort, to be tried only when private initiative, inspired by high responsibility, with such assistance and balance as Government can give, has finally failed. As yet there has been no final failure, because there has been no attempt; and I decline to assume that this Nation is unable to meet the situation.

The final term of the high contract was for liberty and the pursuit of happiness. We have learned a great deal of both in the past century. We know that individual liberty and individual happiness mean nothing unless both are ordered in the sense that one man's meat is not another man's poison. We know that the old "rights of personal competency," the right to read, to think, to speak, to choose and live a mode of life, must be respected at all hazards. We know that liberty to do anything which deprives others of those elemental rights is outside the protection of any compact; and that Government in this regard is the maintenance of a balance, within which every individual may have a place if he will take it; in which every individual may find safety if he wishes it; in which every individual may attain such power as his ability permits, consistent with his assuming the accompanying responsibility. . . .

Faith in America, faith in our tradition of personal responsibility, faith in our institutions, faith in ourselves demand that we recognize the new terms of the old social contract. We shall fulfill them. . . . We must do so, lest a rising tide of misery, engendered by our common failure, engulf us all. But failure is not an American habit; and in the strength of great hope we must all shoulder our common load.

Document 19.2 "We Have Nothing to Fear But Fear Itself," First Inaugural Address

Roosevelt began this address by denouncing fear that prevented action to deal with the Depression. But he was not just calling for positive thinking; he was announcing that his administration would take whatever action was necessary to fight the depression. What does Roosevelt say are the most important problems the new administration faces? To what lengths does he say he is willing to go to combat them?

"We Have Nothing to Fear But Fear Itself," First Inaugural Address

Franklin D. Roosevelt

This is a day of national consecration, and I am certain that my fellow Americans expect that on my induction into the Presidency I will address them with a candor and a decision which the present situation of our nation impels. This is pre-eminently the time to speak the truth, the whole truth, frankly and boldly. Nor need we shrink from honestly facing conditions in our country today. This great nation will endure as it has endured, will revive and will prosper.

So first of all let me assert my firm belief that the only thing we have to fear is fear itself—nameless, unreasoning, unjustified terror which paralyzes needed efforts to convert retreat into advance. In every dark hour of our national life a leadership of frankness and vigor has met with that understanding and support of the people themselves which is essential to victory. I am convinced that you will again give that support to leadership in these critical days.

In such a spirit on my part and on yours we face our common difficulties. They concern, thank God, only material things. Values have shrunken to fantastic levels; taxes have risen; our ability to pay has fallen; government of all kinds is faced by serious curtailment of income; the means of exchange are frozen in the currents of trade; the withered leaves of industrial enterprise lie on every side; farmers find no markets for their produce; the savings of many years in thousands of families are gone.

More important, a host of unemployed citizens face the grim problem of existence, and an equally great number toil with little return. Only a foolish optimist can deny the dark realities of the moment.

Yet our distress comes from no failure of substance. We are stricken by no plague of locusts. Compared with the perils which our forefathers conquered because they believed and were not afraid, we have still much to be thankful for. Nature still offers her bounty and human efforts have multiplied it. Plenty is at our doorstep, but a generous use of it languishes in the very sight of the supply. Primarily, this is because the rulers of the exchange of mankind's goods have failed through their own stubbornness and their own incompetence, have admitted their failure and abdicated. Practices of the unscrupulous money changers stand indicted in the court of public opinion, rejected by the hearts and minds of men.

True, they have tried, but their efforts have been cast in the pattern of an outworn tradition. Faced by failure of credit, they have proposed only the lending of more money. Stripped of the lure of profit by which to induce our people to follow their false leadership, they have resorted to exhortations,

---

First Inaugural Address, Franklin D. Roosevelt

pleading tearfully for restored confidence. They know only the rules of a generation of self-seekers. They have no vision, and when there is no vision the people perish.

The money changers have fled from their high seats in the temple of our civilization. We may now restore that temple to the ancient truths. The measure of the restoration lies in the extent to which we apply social values more noble than mere monetary profit.

Happiness lies not in the mere possession of money; it lies in the joy of achievement, in the thrill of creative effort. The joy and moral stimulation of work no longer must be forgotten in the mad chase of evanescent profits. These dark days will be worth all they cost us if they teach us that our true destiny is not to be ministered unto but to minister to ourselves and to our fellow men.

Recognition of the falsity of material wealth as the standard of success goes hand in hand with the abandonment of the false belief that public office and high political position are to be valued only by the standards of pride of place and personal profit; and there must be an end to a conduct in banking and in business which too often has given to a sacred trust the likeness of callous and selfish wrongdoing. Small wonder that confidence languishes, for it thrives only on honesty, on honor, on the sacredness of obligations, on faithful protection, on unselfish performance. Without them it cannot live.

Restoration calls, however, not for changes in ethics alone. This nation asks for action, and action now.

Our greatest primary task is to put people to work. This is no unsolvable problem if we face it wisely and courageously. It can be accomplished in part by direct recruiting by the Government itself, treating the task as we would treat the emergency of war, but at the same time, through this employment, accomplishing greatly needed projects to stimulate and reorganize the use of our natural resources.

Hand in hand with this, we must frankly recognize the overbalance of population in our industrial centers and, by engaging on a national scale in the redistribution, endeavor to provide a better use of the land for those best fitted for the land. The task can be helped by definite efforts to raise the values of agricultural products and with this the power to purchase the output of our cities. It can be helped by preventing realistically the tragedy of the growing loss, through foreclosure, of our small homes and our farms. It can be helped by insistence that the Federal, State and local governments act forthwith on the demand that their cost be drastically reduced. It can be helped by the unifying of relief activities which today are often scattered, uneconomical and unequal. It can be helped by national planning for a supervision of all forms of transportation and of communications and other utilities which have a definitely public character. There are many ways in which it can be helped, but it can never be helped merely by talking about it. We must act, and act quickly. . . .

This I propose to offer, pledging that the larger purposes will bind upon us all as a sacred obligation with a unity of duty hitherto evoked only in the time of armed strife.

With this pledge taken, I assume unhesitatingly the leadership of this great army of our people, dedicated to a disciplined attack upon our common problems.

Action in this image and to this end is feasible under the form of government which we have inherited from our ancestors. Our Constitution is so simple and practical that it is possible always to meet extraordinary needs by changes in emphasis and arrangement without loss of essential form. That is why our constitutional system has proved itself the most superbly enduring political mechanism the modern world has produced. It has met every stress of vast expansion of territory, of foreign wars, of bitter internal strife, of world relations.

It is to be hoped that the normal balance of executive and legislative authority may be wholly adequate to meet the unprecedented task before us. But it may be that an unprecedented demand and need for undelayed action may call for temporary departure from that normal balance of public procedure.

I am prepared under my constitutional duty to recommend the measures that a stricken nation in the midst of a stricken world may require. These measures, or such other measures as the Congress may build out of its experience and wisdom, I shall seek, within my constitutional authority, to bring to speedy adoption.

But in the event that the Congress shall fail to take one of these two courses, and in the event that the national emergency is still critical, I shall not evade the clear course of duty that will then confront me. I shall ask the Congress for the one remaining instrument to meet the crisis—broad Executive power to wage a war against the emergency as great as the power that would be given me if we were in fact invaded by a foreign foe.

For the trust reposed in me I will return the courage and the devotion that befit the time. I can do no less . . .

Document 19.3 The Second Fireside Chat of 1934

Among Roosevelt's talents was the ability to explain his policies in clear, simple, and persuasive ways. To do this, he inaugurated a series of radio programs, which he termed "fireside chats," in which he addressed his audience like a friendly neighbor sitting down with people in their homes. When he began these talks, the radio was less than fifteen years old, and these talks were among the most effective uses of the this new electronic medium so far, as well as one of the most effective means of communication by any president in American history.

The Second Fireside Chat of 1934

Franklin D. Roosevelt

Three months have passed since I talked with you shortly after the adjournment of the Congress. Tonight I continue that report, though, because of the shortness of time, I must defer a number of subjects to a later date.

Recently the most notable public questions that have concerned us all have had to do with industry and labor, and with respect to these, certain developments have taken place which I consider of importance. I am happy to report that after years of uncertainty, culminating in the collapse of the spring of 1933, we are bringing order out of the old chaos with a greater certainty of the employment of labor at a reasonable wage and of more business at a fair profit. These governmental and industrial developments hold promise of new achievements for the Nation.

Men may differ as to the particular form of governmental activity with respect to industry and business, but nearly all are agreed that private enterprise in times such as these cannot be left without assistance and without reasonable safeguards lest it destroy not only itself but also our processes of civilization. The underlying necessity for such activity is indeed as strong now as it was years ago when Elihu Root said the following very significant words:

> Instead of the give and take of free individual contract, the tremendous power of organization has combined great aggregations of capital in enormous industrial establishments working through vast agencies of commerce and employing great masses of men in movements of production and transportation and trade, so great in the mass that each individual concerned in them is quite helpless by himself. The relations between the employer and the employed, between the owners of aggregated capital and the units of organized labor, between the small producer, the small trader, the consumer, and the great transporting and manufacturing and distributing agencies, all present new questions for the solution of which the old reliance upon the free action of individual wills appears quite inadequate. And in many directions, the intervention of that organized control which we call government seems necessary to produce the same result of justice and right conduct which obtained through the attrition of individuals before the new conditions arose.

It was in this spirit thus described by Secretary Root that we approached our task of reviving private enterprise in March, 1933. Our first problem was, of course, the banking situation because, as you know, the banks had collapsed. Some banks could not be saved, but the great majority of them, either through their own resources or with Government aid, have been restored to complete public confidence. This has given safety to millions of depositors in these banks. Closely following this great constructive effort we have, through various Federal agencies, saved debtors and creditors alike in many other fields of enterprise, such as loans on farm mortgages

---

The Second Fireside Chat of 1934.

and home mortgages; loans to the railroads and insurance companies and, finally, help for home owners and industry itself.

In all of these efforts the Government has come to the assistance of business and with the full expectation that the money used to assist these enterprises will eventually be repaid. I believe it will be.

The second step we have taken in the restoration of normal business enterprise has been to clean up thoroughly unwholesome conditions in the field of investment. In this we have had assistance from many bankers and business men, most of whom recognize the past evils in the banking system, in the sale of securities, in the deliberate encouragement of stock gambling, in the sale of unsound mortgages and in many other ways in which the public lost billions of dollars. They saw that without changes in the policies and methods of investment there could be no recovery of public confidence in the security of savings. The country now enjoys the safety of bank savings under the new banking laws, the careful checking of new securities under the Securities Act and the curtailment of rank stock speculation through the Securities Exchange Act. I sincerely hope that as a result people will be discouraged in unhappy efforts to get rich quick by speculating in securities. The average person almost always loses. Only a very small minority of the people of this country believe in gambling as a substitute for the old philosophy of Benjamin Franklin that the way to wealth is through work.

In meeting the problems of industrial recovery the chief agency of the Government has been the National Recovery Administration. Under its guidance, trades and industries covering over 90 percent of all industrial employees have adopted codes of fair competition, which have been approved by the President. Under these codes, in the industries covered, child labor has been eliminated. The work day and the work week have been shortened. Minimum wages have been established and other wages adjusted toward a rising standard of living. The emergency purpose of the N.R.A. was to put men to work, and since its creation more than four million persons have been reemployed, in great part through the cooperation of American business brought about under the codes.

Benefits of the Industrial Recovery Program have come, not only to labor in the form of new jobs, in relief from overwork and in relief from underpay, but also to the owners and managers of industry because, together with a great increase in the payrolls, there has come a substantial rise in the total of industrial profits—a rise from a deficit figure in the first quarter of 1933 to a level of sustained profits within one year from the inauguration of N.R.A.

Now it should not be expected that even employed labor and capital would be completely satisfied with present conditions. Employed workers have not by any means all enjoyed a return to the earnings of prosperous times, although millions of hitherto underprivileged workers are today far better paid than ever before. Also, billions of dollars of invested capital have today a greater security of present and future earning power than before. This is because of the establishment of fair, competitive standards and because of relief from unfair competition in wage cutting which depresses markets and destroys purchasing power. But it is an undeniable fact that the restoration of other billions of sound investments to a reasonable earning power could not be brought about in one year. There is no magic formula, no economic panacea, which could simply revive overnight the heavy industries and the trades dependent upon them.

Nevertheless the gains of trade and industry, as a whole, have been substantial. In these gains and in the policies of the Administration there are assurances that hearten all forward-looking men and women with the confidence that we are definitely rebuilding our political and economic system on the lines laid down by the New Deal—lines which as I have so often made clear, are in complete accord with the underlying principles of orderly popular government which Americans have demanded since the white man first came to these shores. We count, in the future as in the past, on the driving power of individual initiative and the incentive of fair profit, strengthened with the acceptance of those obligations to the public interest which rest upon us all. We have the right to expect that this driving power will be given patriotically and whole-heartedly to our Nation. . . .

Closely allied to the N.R.A. is the program of public works provided for in the same Act and designed to put more men back to work, both directly on the public works themselves, and indirectly in the industries supplying the materials for these public works. To those who say that our expenditures for public works and other means for recovery are a waste that we cannot afford, I answer that no country, however rich, can afford the waste of its human resources. Demoralization caused by vast unemployment is our greatest extravagance. Morally, it is the greatest menace to our social order. Some people try to tell me that we must make up our minds that for the future we shall permanently have millions of unemployed just as other countries have had them for over a decade. What may be necessary for those countries is not my responsibility to determine. But as for this country, I stand or fall by my refusal to accept as a necessary condition of our future a permanent army of unemployed. On the contrary, we must make it a national principle that we will not tolerate a large army of unemployed and that we will arrange our national economy to end our present unemployment as soon as we can and then to take wise measures against its return. I do not want to think that it is the destiny of any American to remain permanently on relief rolls. . . .

In our efforts for recovery we have avoided, on the one hand, the theory that business should and must be taken over into an all-embracing Government. We have avoided, on the other hand, the equally untenable theory that it is an interference with liberty to offer reasonable help when private enterprise is in need of help. The course we have followed fits the American practice of Government, a practice of taking action step by step, or regulating only to meet concrete needs, a practice of courageous recognition of change. I believe with Abraham Lincoln, that "The legitimate object of Government is to do for a community of people whatever they need to have done but cannot do at all or cannot do so well for themselves in their separate and individual capacities."

I am not for a return to that definition of liberty under which for many years a free people were being gradually regimented into the service of the privileged few. I prefer and I am sure you prefer that broader definition of liberty under which we are moving forward to greater freedom, to greater security for the average man than he has ever known before in the history of America.

Document 19.4 Share Our Wealth

Huey Long was a Louisiana politician who through populist appeals and a colorful political persona built a political organization that dominated the state. In 1932 he supported Franklin D. Roosevelt for the presidency, but soon set his own course. He announced a radical program to redistribute wealth, which he eventually called the Share-Our-Wealth plan. This would have taken money from the wealthy and provided each family a "homestead" of $5,000 and a guaranteed income of $2,500 per year. Most analysts believed this plan made no economic sense, but Long formed a national Save-Our-Wealth Society with many local affiliates. Many Democrats thought Long would constitute a threat to Roosevelt in the 1936 presidential election, but in 1935 Long was assassinated in the Louisiana capitol. In the following selection Long summarizes his plan.

Share Our Wealth

Huey Long

. . . Here is what we stand for in a nutshell:

1. We propose that every family in America shall at least own a homestead equal in value to not less than one-third the average family wealth. The average family wealth of America, at normal values, is approximately $16,000. So our first proposition means that every family shall have a home and the comforts of a home up to a value of not less than $5,000.
2. We propose that no family shall own more than 300 times the average family wealth, which means that no family shall possess more than a wealth of $5,000,000. And we think that is too much. The two propositions together mean that no family shall own less than one-third of the average family wealth, nor shall any family own more than 300 times the average family wealth. That is to say that none should be so poor as to have less than one-third of the average, and none should be so rich as to have more than 300 times the average.
3. We next propose that every family shall have an income equal to at least one-third of the average family income in America. If all were allowed to work, according to our statistics, there would

Congressional Record, 74th Congress, 1st Session.

be an average family income of from $5,000 to $10,000 per year. So, therefore, in addition to the home which every family would own and the comforts of life which every family would enjoy, every family would make not less than $2,000 to $3,000 per year upon which to live and educate their children.

4. We propose that no family shall have an income of more than 300 times the average family income. Less the income taxes, this would mean an annual income of $1,000,000 would be the maximum allowed any one family in 1 year. The third and fourth propositions simply mean that no family should earn less than one-third the average, and no family should earn more than 300 times the average; none to make too much, none to make too little. Everyone to have the things required for life; every man a king.
5. We propose a pension to the old people. Under our proposal taxes would not be levied upon the sons and daughters, nor the working people to support their aged fathers and mothers. But on the contrary, such support as would be given for old-age pensions would be borne solely by the surplus money which the Government would rake off the big fortunes and big inheritances.
6. We propose to care for the veterans of our wars, including the immediate cash payment of a soldier's bonus, and last, but not least, we propose that every child in America have a right to education and training, not only through grammar and high school, but also through colleges and universities. And this education and training would be of such extent as will equip each child to battle on fair terms in the work which it is compelled to perform throughout life. We would not have it that a child could go to college or university provided his parents had the money on which to send him, but it would be the right of every child under our plan to the costs, including living expenses of college and university training, which could be done by our country at a cost considerably less than is required for the military training which has been given our youth in the past. . . .

Let no one tell you that it is difficult to redistribute the wealth of this land; it matters not how rich or great one may be, when he dies his wealth must be redistributed anyway. The law of God shows how it has been throughout time. Nothing is more sensible or better understood than the redistribution of property. The laws of God command it. It is required of all nations that live. . . .

So let us be about our work. It is simple. Why lie ye here idle? There is enough for all. Let there be peace in the land. Let our children be happy. . . .

How wonderful, how great, how fruitful to all this great land of ours can be. We only have to eliminate useless greed, provide that none shall be too big and none too small. Beautiful America can rise to the opportunity before it. It means to us all:

Every man a king.

Document 19.5 Letters to New Deal Officials

Although ordinary Americans have probably always written letters to high government officials, Franklin D. Roosevelt and the New Deal established an unusual sense of intimacy with common people. The following letters show the confidence ordinary Americans had in referring their problems to New Deal officials. The writers often express confidence that the FDR administration was on the side of ordinary workers as opposed to business owners and managers. These letters also reveal the conflicts between classes and ethnic groups. Frances Perkins, to whom several of the letters were addressed, was the secretary of labor.

Letters to New Deal Officials

30. I have not got any work are no where to put my thing

[April 5, 1934]

Mr Norma Tohmas

Dear Sir

in regard to condition I am in I have Not got any work are No where to put My thing I have got My house hold setting in a wood shed and the rain is runing ever thing I have got I thought I would write you and see if you help me get Me a tent are some place to take my wife and thing

Your E. W. [male]
[Tyronza, Arkansas]

31. He got half of every thing

April 6, 1934

Dear Mr Norman Tohmas

there is a man Live clost he get $4.50. Every 2 weeks he has to trade at Brown Store and Brown Charge him 50¢ for letting him traid there I live on Brown place he Says I haft to move For he going to tear this Old house there no place I can find to move to I ask him for a garden he Said no Mr Spirun Shear crop for him he him he got half of Every thing he rais the paople that get orders Just haft to trade at Sertin Stores and they our Charge for their products there are me and my to Babys and mother and her little Boy no one Elce would turn Brown in So I thought I would

Miss L. B.
Leachville, Ark.

32. If you would send me some of the clothes that is of no longer use to you

Waterburg, Vt.
Jan 19 1934

Dear Mrs. Roosevelt:

I am write you to ask you if you would send me some of the clothes that is of no longer use to you

I have a family of nine children It would be if grate helf of you would send me some clothes witch I could fix over for them.

I would be very grateful

I remain

Your respectfully
Mrs. A. M.
Waterburg Vermont

33. For the first time of my lifetime I am asking a favor

Goff Kansas
May 10–1935

Mrs Franklin D. Roosevelt:

My Dear Friend:

For the first time of my lifetime I am asking a favor and this one I am needing very badly and I am coming to you for help.

Among your friends do you know of one who is discarding a spring coat for a new one. If so could you beg the old one for me. I wear a size 40 to 42 I have not had a spring coat for six years and last Sunday when getting ready to go to church I see my winter coat had several very thin places in the back that is very noticeable My clothes are very plain so I could wear only something plain. we were hit very hard by the drought and every penny we can save goes for feed to put in crop.

Hoping for a favorable reply.

Your friend Mrs. J. T.
Goff. Ks

---

73. We have no one to give us a Christmas prestns.

Warren, Ohio
Dec. 22, 1935

Dear President Roosevelt,

Please help us, my mother is sick three year and was in the hospital three month and she came out but she is not better and my Father is peralised and can not work and we are poor and the Cumunity fun gives us six dollars an we are six people four children three boy 15, 13, 12, an one gril 10, and to parents. We have no one to give us a Chrismas presents, and if you want to buy a Christmas present please buy us a stove to do our cooking and to make good bread.

Please excuse me for not writing it so well because the little girl 10 year old is writing.

Merry Christmas
[Anonymous]

74. My friends at school have skates and laugh because I dont have some

Blacksburg S.C.
January 19. [1934]

Dear Mrs. Roosevelt,

Mrs. Roosevelt will you send me and my sister, Ruth, a pair of ball bearing roller skates? Our friens have skates and we are not able to buy them. We sure will thank you if you will.

yours trully,
L. L. [female]

P.S. I am twelve years old and in the sixth grade at Blacksburg Grammar school. My friends at school have skates and laugh because I dont have some.

your's trully
L.

75. All the time he's crying because he can't find work

[February, 1936]

Mr. And Mrs. Roosevelt.
Wash. D.C.

Dear Mr. President:

I'm a boy of 12 years. I want to tell you about my family. My father hasn't worked for 5 months. He went plenty times to relief, he filled out application. They won't give us anything. I don't know why. Please you do something. We haven't paid 4 months rent, Everyday the landlord rings the door bell, we don't open the door for him. We are afraid that will be put out, been put out before, and don't want to happen again. We haven't paid the gas bill, and the electric bill, haven't paid grocery bill for 3 months. My brother goes to Lane Tech. High School. he's eighteen years old, hasn't gone to school for 2 weeks because he got no carfare. I have a sister she's twenty years, she can't find work. My father he staying home. All the time he's crying because he can't find work. I told him why are you crying daddy, and daddy said why shouldn't I cry when there is nothing in the house. I feel sorry for him. That night I couldn't sleep. The next morning I wrote this letter to you. in my room. Were American citizens and were born in Chicago, Ill. I and I don't know why they don't help us Please answer right away because, we need it. will starve Thank you.

God bless you.

[Anonymous]
Chicago, M.

76. I do hope that President Roosevelt can make those big money guys loosen up the money

Moorhead, Minn.,
March 26, 1934

Dear Mrs Franklin D. Roosevelt,

I have been very interested in you because I read in the papers how much you are doing for the poor children and crippled children. I want to thank you for doing so much good for those little children cause I know how tough it is now.

111. All else has failed

Cambridge
May 16, 1934

[Dear President Roosevelt:]

I am now at the point of despration. But as I have 19 grandchildren all under 14 years of age 9 of whom are boys, to do anything desperette now they would never live down the disgrace. I was always a hard worker saved money invested in the auto business and lost. Am 55 years old. . . . I would not wish at the cost of my life that any one should know I wrote you this letter [seeking a loan]. All shall be returned in do All I want is a chance. . . . It is my last hope and effort All else has failed.

[Initials omitted because of writer's request]

112. Please help me please

High Point N C
Dec 15. 1935

Mr Roosevelte I am In nead Bad Please help me I have 7 children and is Sick all the time one of my children is Sick and has Ben for a lone time and I have No under clothes for none of the famiely we cant harly hide I Self with top cloths I ned Milk and my Boy need milk Please give my childrens and my Self Some under cloths or we will freze to Deth this cold wethr we can not Make it pay Rent get Something to Eat and get wood and coal no one work But my husBan he make $6.75 per week no way way I can get any under cloths for the famely please help me I have not a teeth in My head wen I Eat I nely Dieys no way to get any please help me please.

[Anonymous]

113. Which would be the most human way to dispose of my self and family

Latrobe, Pa.
April 4, 1934

Mr. Bruce McClure*

Dear Sir:

In regards to relief and NRA, I wish to call attention to my case, I was forced onto relief by the Latrobe Borough Council. I had been employed as Patrolman of the Borough until Jan. 8–34, then without any just cause whatsoever, I was let go. Just to satisfy Mr. William McCafferty and Mr. V. B. Stader, two of the Honorable Council of said Boro, they replaced me with a man who was working 5 days a week at Latrobe Electric Steel Co. and sent me out on the mercy of the relief with 6 children and a wife to support. Now I am forced with proposition of being set out of my home because I cannot pay my rent. I have 10 day to get another house, no job, no means of paying rent. Can you be so kind as to advise me as to which would be the most human way to dispose of my self and family, as this is about the only thing that I see left to do. No home, no work, no money. We cannot go along this way. They have shut the water supply from us. No means of sanitation. We cannot keep the children clean and tidy as they should be. They are all 6 in school but will soon haft to take them out if something is not done. I want work and money enough to support this family. I am getting relief to partly feed them but where is the shelter and water coming from and clothes. I lost my work through no fault of mine and for no just reason whatsoever and I feel I am entitle to some consideration. Thanking you in advance for any help, I remain

Yours truly,
J. S. H. [male],
Latrobe, Pa.

*Secretary, Civil Works Administration.

Module XIX
Questions for Study and Critical Thinking

1. In his Commonwealth Club speech, what does Roosevelt say was responsible for the Depression?

2. According to this speech, what should be done to deal with the Depression?

3. What new role for government does Roosevelt's conception imply?

4. In his first inaugural address whom does Roosevelt blame for the nation's desperate situation?

5. According to Roosevelt in his first inaugural address, what is the greatest task facing his administration?

6. In his second Fireside Chat, what did Franklin D. Roosevelt say should be the relationship between government and business at that time?

7. Do you agree? Why?

8. What did Roosevelt say to those who claimed public works programs to employ the unemployed were wasteful? Do you agree?

9. What did Huey Long propose in his Save-Our-Wealth proposal?

10. How practical do you think this plan was? Why?

11. In the letters to New Deal officials, what kinds of problems do people write about?

12. What do the writers want government officials to do?

Module XX

The American People in World War II

Introduction

For many Americans, the Second World War was the most significant event in their lives. They sensed a danger to the nation itself. The enemies represented palpable evil, and few doubted the justice of the cause. For those reasons some historians have dubbed it "the good war." The following selections reveal a range of experiences from diverse Americans, both servicemen and civilians.

Document 20.1 "A Date Which Will Live in Infamy"

One of the most famous speeches given by a U.S. president was Franklin D. Roosevelt's address to Congress the day after the Japanese attacked Pearl Harbor. Throughout the United States Americans were rivetted by this speech, uttered in Roosevelt's distinctive words and voice.

So memorable to a shocked and frightened nation was this address that the phrase "a date that will live in infamy" became part of the general vocabulary. As indicated by this phrase, in this speech Roosevelt emphasized the treachery he attributed to actions of the Japanese.

"A Date Which Will Live In Infamy" FDR Asks for a Declaration of War

Franklin D. Roosevelt

Speech to Congress, December 8, 1941

Yesterday, December 7, 1941—a date which will live in infamy—the United States of America was suddenly and deliberately attacked by naval and air forces of the Empire of Japan.

The United States was at peace with that Nation and, at the solicitation of Japan, was still in conversation with its Government and its Emperor looking toward the maintenance of peace in the Pacific. Indeed, one hour after Japanese air squadrons had commenced bombing in Oahu, the Japanese Ambassador to the United States and his colleague delivered to the Secretary of State a formal reply to a recent American message. While this reply stated that it seemed useless to continue the existing diplomatic negotiations, it contained no threat or hint of war or armed attack.

It will be recorded that the distance of Hawaii from Japan makes it obvious that the attack was deliberately planned many days or even weeks ago. During the intervening time the Japanese Government has deliberately sought to deceive the United States by false statements and expressions of hope for continued peace.

Speech to Congress, 77th Congress, 1st session.

The attack yesterday on the Hawaiian Islands has caused severe damage to American naval and military forces. Very many American lives have been lost. In addition, American ships have been reported torpedoed on the high seas between San Francisco and Honolulu.

Yesterday the Japanese Government also launched an attack against Malaya.

Last night Japanese forces attacked Hong Kong.

Last night Japanese forces attacked Guam.

Last night Japanese forces attacked the Philippine Islands.

Last night the Japanese attacked Wake Island.

This morning the Japanese attacked Midway Island.

Japan has, therefore, undertaken a surprise offensive extending throughout the Pacific area. The facts of yesterday speak for themselves. The people of the United States have already formed their opinions and well understand the implications to the very life and safety of our Nation

As Commander in Chief of the Army and Navy I have directed that all measures be taken for our defense.

Always will we remember the character of the onslaught against us.

No matter how long it may take us to overcome this premeditated invasion, the American people in their righteous might will win through to absolute victory.

I believe I interpret the will of the Congress and of the people when I assert that we will not only defend ourselves to the uttermost but will make very certain that this form of treachery shall never endanger us again.

Hostilities exist. There is no blinking at the fact that our people, our territory, and our interests are in grave danger.

With confidence in our armed forces—with the unbounded determination of our people—we will gain the inevitable triumph—so help us God.

I ask that the Congress declare that since the unprovoked and dastardly attack by Japan on Sunday, December 7, a state of war has existed between the United States and the Japanese Empire.

Document 20.2 The Bataan Death March

On December 7, 1941, the same day they attacked Pearl Harbor, Japanese forces also attacked the Philippines. This island nation had become independent but was still protected by treaty with the United States. The United States had two airbases there, a naval base, and troops. In addition, General Douglas MacArthur, a retired U.S. Army chief of staff, had been asked by the Philippine government to train and command its army. American forces were unprepared, and the initial Japanese onslaught destroyed most of aircraft in the Philippines. In Washington, Franklin Roosevelt and his military commanders decided to concentrate available forces to Europe, where they perceived the threat to be greater than in Asia, including the Philippines. After landing troops in the Philippines, the Japanese army forced the combined American and Philippine forces into retreat. MacArthur ordered a withdrawal onto Bataan, a peninsula on the west of Manilla Bay. As the Japanese began overrunning his troops' positions, MacArthur evacuated as many troops as possible to Corregidor, a fortified island in the bay. After his superiors ordered MacArthur to leave the Philippines for Australia, the outnumbered and surrounded American troops surrendered to the Japanese.

After their surrender, American and Filipino soldiers were lined up and marched to prisoner of war camps. In the process, victorious Japanese soldiers brutalized their captives, often beating them savagely and killing them. After the war a shocked United States tried and punished some of the soldiers implicated for war crimes. The accounts here were recorded by American soldiers after the war.

The Bataan Death March

Pfc. Blair Robinett
Company, 803d Engineers

My group came up the road from Mariveles another half mile or so when a Jap soldier stepped out, came across, and took my canteen out of its cover. He took a drink, filled his canteen out of mine, poured the rest of my water on the ground, and dropped the canteen at my feet. I thought he was going to walk back to the line of Jap troops standing across the road, so I bent over to pick up my canteen. But he turned around and hit me on the head with his rifle butt. Put a crease in the top of my head that I still have. I fell face down on the cobblestones. I crawled back up to my knees, debating whether to pick up the canteen again. I figured the best course of action was to stand up and leave the canteen alone. Soon as the Jap troops moved off, I squatted down and picked it up. A little later a Jap soldier came over to one of the lieutenants out of our company, and when he found out his canteen was empty he beat the lieutenant to his knees with the canteen. Just kept slapping him back and forth across the face.

We moved down the ridge a ways when we saw this GI. He was sick. I figured he had come out of the hospital that was in tents out under the trees. He was wobbling along, uneasy on his feet. There were Japanese infantry and tanks coming down the road alongside us. One of these Jap soldiers, I don't know whether he was on our side or if he deliberately came across the road, but he grabbed this sick guy by the arm and guided him to the middle of the road. Then he just flipped him out across the road. The guy hit the cobblestone about five feet in front of a tank and the tank pulled on across him. Well, it killed him quick. There must have been ten tanks in that column, and every one of them came up there right across the body. When the last tank left there was no way you could tell there'd ever been a man there. But his uniform was embedded in the cobblestone. The man disappeared, but his uniform had been pressed until it had become part of the ground.

Now we knew, if there had been any doubts before, we were in for a bad time.

Capt. Marion Lawton
1st Battalion, 31st Regiment, Philippine Army

When we had marched several kilometers, we came to a large group of prisoners who were all Americans. My little group had increased to about fifty by then. There I found my commanding officer, Colonel Erwin. He was a large fellow, a little over six feet tall and weighed probably 240 pounds. He was the type who believed in having an abundance of everything. I noticed he had a heavy barracks bag with him. I'd thrown away everything except a change of socks, underwear, and toilet articles, because I knew I couldn't carry a lot of stuff. Knowing how heavy Colonel Erwin's bag was, I volunteered to help him, but I warned him that I felt it was a mistake to carry that much. "Oh, no," he said, "I might need this gear." He had extra shoes and uniforms and who knows what else. Hadn't been looted either.

The Japs put us in groups of a hundred, columns of four, and marched us out by groups. I managed to stick with Colonel Erwin. This was April 9, the actual day of surrender. It was as hot as the dickens. The Jap trucks started coming in. And there was just clouds of dust. We started marching. I can't remember hours or specific days, but as we moved on it got hotter and we got more fatigued. After a couple of hours people started faltering. Thirsty, tired, some, like me, already sick. Most everyone was suffering from malaria and diarrhea, all hungry. I'd been pretty well fed, but a lot of these fellows had been on half rations since January and, on top of that, in the confusion of the last few days they had eaten nothing at all. So we were hungry, plus being under pressure of combat. We were emotionally spent, so horribly frightened and depressed and distressed, not knowing what was going to happen to us.

About midday Colonel Erwin, still holding his bag, started slowing down and gradually dropping back. Soon I lost sight of him. I got reports later of what happened. He finally dropped back to the tail of the column and the guards back there started prodding him. He drifted on back further still, until one of the guards stuck him with a bayonet. I guess

---

he was delirious and fevered and exhausted. Finally, a guard pushed him to the side of the road and put his rifle muzzle to his back and pulled the trigger. He was one of the early casualties.

With this exception I didn't see many atrocities, other than people being hit or bayonet prodded. See, I was among the first groups out and all the killings and beatings took place in the later groups, those who were one to three days hungrier and weaker.

Cpl. Hubert Cater
200th Coast Artillery (AA)

Suddenly the hill rocked under us. There was a roar to the left, to the right, and then several back to our rear. The Japs had moved their field guns into position around us on Cabcaben Field.

"Why the dirty bastards!" the man next to me said. "They're using us as a shield to fire on Corregidor." It was true. We should have realized then what to expect as their prisoners.

A flight of Jap bombers were flying over Corregidor. Our officers cautioned us not to watch them because if our anti-aircraft fire hit any of them we would cheer in spite of ourself.

Our chief worry was, would Corregidor return fire on the guns that surrounded us?

Corregidor didn't, but a gunboat out in the Bay did. I don't know the size of the shells; they were some smaller than our 3-inch. The first shell was to our right. Apparently, a dud. It skidded through the grass and set it on fire. Some of the men flattened out; others stood up ready to run to cover. Our officers motioned us down. There were a lot of Japs around us now.

The second shell burst to the rear and center of us. At the time I thought it had hit some of our men. A Jap soldier got part of his chin tore off. He was a terrible looking sight running around, evidently half out of his mind. From chin to waist he was covered with blood.

A young Jap officer who had been silently watching us motioned with his hand for us to take cover. About 300 of us ran across Cabcaben Field to get behind a hill. The rest ran the other way, up the road.

Night came. We had moved across the road into a rice field. Jap soldiers, tanks, big field guns, and horses went by in a steady stream. Occasionally, a Jap would run out and hit one of us with his rifle. No one slept. Most of the night Corregidor was firing their big guns. The only way to describe it—it sounded like freight trains going through the air over our heads. They were firing into the area that the Japanese would use to invade Bataan. During the night a man was sent with some canteens for water. The canteens were taken and he was beat up.

The next morning a steady stream of Filipino civilians began to go by, moving out of Bataan. Old and young, many were evidently sick. I didn't realize so many of them had been trapped on Bataan.

Sgt Ralph Levenberg
17th Pursuit Squadron

Eventually they started to systematically put us in groups of about 100 or so and marched us off. There were one, two, sometimes four guards, you never knew.

I was fortunate in two respects. First, I had a new pair of shoes, and second, I had some chlorine pills. The shoes I had kept with me ever since we left the barracks outside Manila, and the chlorine I had just managed to pick up. I don't know why, maybe because of my upbringing, I was taught to be protective of my physical being. I was therefore able from time to time, when we stopped near a creek which had dead bodies and horses floating in it, to get some water and purify it with the chlorine.

One of the tricks the Japs played on us—thought it was funny, too—was when they would be riding on the back of a truck, they would have these long black snake whips, and they'd whip that thing out and get some poor bastard by the neck or torso and drag him behind their truck. 'Course if one of our guys was quick enough he didn't get dragged too far. But, if the Japs got a sick guy. . . .

Capt. Mark Wohlfeld
27th Bombardment Group (L)

We were all mixed up—privates, officers, Scout officers, 31st Infantry, 192d Tank Battalion, 200th New Mexico Coast Artillery—just a jumbled mass of humanity.

My group stopped at a small bridge up above Cabcaben to let some Jap horse artillery through. They were in a real hurry to get these guns in place and start on Corregidor. Right behind the artillery there arrived a great big 1942 Cadillac equipped with a freshly cut wooden camera platform attached to the roof. As soon as they saw us they stopped and the cameraman jumped out and placed his tripod and camera on the platform. He had his big box camera which he looked down into. A white-shirted Japanese interpreter staged us for the cameraman. He told us to line up and put our hands over our heads.

We should look depressed and dejected. That wasn't hard. The cameraman took his pictures and started back down the road in his Cadillac towards Corregidor, while we started marching in the other direction. That picture eventually appeared in *Life* magazine.

An hour or so later we halted and fell out near a ditch where there were about five dead Filipinos lying around. They looked like swollen rag dolls. I used a handkerchief knotted at the four corners to keep the sun from my head. I asked the Japanese guard, part talk, part pantomime, "Can I have a helmet? Dead, Filipino. Sun, hot, hot." He finally gave in, but I wondered whether he'd shoot me when I got as far as the ditch: "Fuck it, I'll try it." There was this dead Filipino lying there, and because his face was so puffed up I could only barely manage to get the chin strap off. He was full of maggots and flies. I finally got the helmet off and wiped out the inside with a part of his uniform that wasn't soiled. Then I hung it from my belt so it would dry. Who cared for germs at a time like that? I came back from the ditch and sat next to Major Small. "Boy," he said, "could I stand a Coca-Cola now." I started thinking about my girlfriend then. She worked in Grand Central Station in a real estate office, and I knew she used to go downstairs on her break and get a nice Coke with lots of ice chips in it. I started to take the helmet off my belt and put it on my head, when I noticed the dead Filipino had scratched the name Mary in his helmet liner. The amazing thing was my girlfriend's name was also Mary

After a column of trucks carrying landing craft passed us, we resumed our march. We fell in behind another group marching out. We'd gone a little farther when we pulled off to the side of the road again to let some trucks roll by. Some of our young guys started asking the Japs whether they could have a drink of water. I looked to my right and saw a buffalo wallow about fifty yards off the road. It looked like green scum. The guards started to laugh and said. "O.K., O.K." So all these kids, eighteen or nineteen year old enlisted men, run for the water and began drowning each other trying to get a drink. The Japs thought it was hilarious. I noticed at the end of the scum some others drinking through handkerchiefs, thinking that would filter the bacteria out.

Finally, a Japanese officer came along and began shouting at the men in the water. There must have been fifty of them, and they scattered and ran back for the road. That wasn't the end of it. This officer found some Jap soldiers who had been watching us and ordered them to pull out of the line any Americans who had water stains on their uniforms. When we marched out, after a short while we heard shooting behind us.

That night when we stopped, most of us had had no water all day. Our tongues were thick with dust. We had come into this abandoned barrio and were now sitting in a field. My small group was made up of some senior officers, even a few full colonels. I noticed one, Col. Edmund Lillie, who had been my reserve unit instructor back in the States ten years before. I went up to him, but of course he didn't remember me. We started to talk and began wondering how we could get some water. There was an artesian well near us that had water dribbling out of it, but we were afraid that we'd be shot if we went to get any. Desperate as we were, Colonel Lillie asked a guard whether we could go and get water. The Jap agreed. Most of these officers did not have canteens, but I spotted an old pail, and since I was only a captain, I went over to get it. Inside the pail, stuck to the bottom, was some dried manure. "Maybe I can rinse it out," I said. Lillie told me, "Don't waste the water rinsing it just fill it up." When I got to the well, one of the Jap guards kept urging me to hurry up. As soon as I got as much as I could, without running the risk of being bayoneted, I came back to the group. There wasn't much water in the pail, but it was something. Lillie told us we could each have only one full mouthful before we passed the pail to the next man. In those days an officer's word meant something, so that's just what we did. Each of us took one full gulp. That way there was enough for everyone.

Capt. Loyd Mills
Company C, 57th Infantry, Philippine Scouts

The nights were the worst times for me. We walked all day, from early morning until dusk. Then we were put into barbed-wire enclosures in which the conditions were nearly indescribable. Filth and defecation all over the place. The smell was terrible. These same enclosures had been used every night, and when my group got to them, they were covered by the filth of five or six nights.

I had dysentery pretty bad, but I didn't worry about it because there wasn't anything you could do about it. You didn't stop on "the March" because you were dead if you did. They didn't mess around with you. You didn't have time to pull out and go over and squat. You would just release wherever you were. Generally right on yourself, or somebody else if they happened to be in your way. There was nothing else to do. Without food it was water more than anything. It just went through me . . . bang.

I was in a daze: One thing I knew was that I had to keep going. I was young, so I had that advantage over some of the older men. I helped along the way. If someone near you started stumbling and looked like he was going to fall, you would try to literally pick him up and keep him going. You always talked to them. Tried to make them understand that if they fell they were gone. 'Course, there was nothing you could do about the people who fell in the back.

Staff Sgt Harold Feiner 17th Ordnance Company, Provisional Tank Group

I don't know if the guards were Korean or Taiwanese. I was so miserable on that Death March that I couldn't tell you what they were. I know one thing about them, though—they were mean, sadistic, brutal. And yet, on "the March" I was befriended.

I had been hit at Cabcaben and had a piece of Corregidor shrapnel in my leg. It was the size of a piece of pencil lead and was laying along my shinbone. I had wrapped an old white towel around it and had managed to walk about fifteen miles, but I was getting weaker and more feverish the further I went. I was in bad shape. Guys had to help me. They would kind of hold onto me. If you fell, you were dead. They bayoneted you right away. No bullshit! If you fell, bingo, you were dead.

We finally stopped for the night near a small stream and I laid down. About an hour later this guy comes crawling along. He looked like an Italian, swarthy, kind of muscular. "Hey, fellows, any of you guys need any help?" he was whispering. "I'm a doctor." Didn't give us his name. When he got to me, he stopped and I told him about my leg. Just then a young guard saw us and came over. The first thing they did was hit you with their rifle butts. He spoke atrocious English and he yelled for us to separate. The doctor kept talking, and asked him would it be all right if he took the shrapnel out of my leg. "Wait, wait, wait," and he ran out into the road to see if anyone was coming. Then he came back and said, "Hurry, hurry." I remember the doctor saying, "Soldier, this is going to hurt. If you can take it, I'll get it out." He never had to worry about me hurting. As soon as he touched it, bam, I passed out. He took it out and wrapped a hand towel around my shin. When he left he said, "Yeah, well, I hope to God you make it. God bless you." He disappeared and I never got to know his name.

The Jap guard came up to me during the night and gave me a cup of sweetened chocolate, tasted like milk. I hadn't had any food and no water for days. I didn't speak one single word of Japanese then, but he could speak a little English, but with a really horrible accent. "Someday me go Hollywood, me going to be movie star." That's the way he talked. He made me laugh. All through the night he gave me something, because he knew I needed strength. In the morning he was gone. His squad had been replaced by another. The orders were given, "Everybody up, up, up." We got in line and I found I couldn't walk. My leg hurt so much. Some guys held me up and I was carried about 100 feet to the road. There we were told to stop and sit down. Then we were told to get up. We waited about a half an hour before we were permitted to sit down again. Then we were turned around and marched back to where we started. Wait . . . rest . . . wait . . . march . . . turn around . . . go back. We did this the whole day. I never had to walk, and by the time we started out the next day I had enough strength to limp along on my own. I'm not a religious man, but God said keep those men there, we want to save that man. I don't know what it was. I wouldn't have made it if I had to march that day.

Maybe a day or so later we came to a river. I was still in fairly bad shape. There were a lot of little rivers, and because it was the dry season, they were shallow. The bridge had been knocked out and the Japanese had reconstructed an engineering bridge. Since their troops were crossing it when we arrived, we were made to march down the bank, cross the river, and march up the other side. Sounds simple. We were told not to touch the water. Some of the guys managed to drag their towels in the water and got some water that way. One man, however, reached over and tried to cup his hands and drink some. He was twelve feet from me. They shot him. Some guards on the bridge just popped him off. Going up the other side was hard for me with my leg. I kept sliding. Going up on the slimy clay. Finally some guys helped me up.

When we got to the top of the bank, there was a little bend in the road before it crossed the bridge. At that point some Jap sentries were stationed and they were laughing at our struggles. When I got to the top—mind you, I was still crippled—for some reason, maybe because I needed help, one of the sentries took his rifle by the barrel and swung it at me and broke the ribs on my right side. Then I walked with broken ribs and a wounded leg. But I got to San Fernando. Had lots of help. But, hell, guys got there with less than me.

Document 20.3 An African-American Becomes a "Rosie the Riveter"

The Second World War opened up new employment opportunities for both women and African-Americans. As an African-American woman, Fanny Christina Hill found unprecedented job opportunities during the war, although she continued to encounter prejudice. In this selection she recounts her early life and then her experience working during the war at North American Aviation in Los Angeles building bombers.

An African-American Becomes a "Rosie the Riveter"

Fanny Christina Hill

I'll never forget, my grandmother on my father's side was telling me that she was a little girl when the slaves was freed. The master's wife told her mother, which was my great-grandmother, "Nancy, now you come in the house and you get you some of the dishes and things because you're going to have to be keeping house of your own and I want you to have something that you're familiar with." She gave my great-grandmother that bowl. That thing is over a hundred years old, passed down from one family to the other. My great-grandmother gave it to her girl, which was my grandmother; my father was next and then I'm next; then Beverly and then the little baby. . . .

My great-grandfather was named Crawford and he went by his own name; he didn't use the master's name. He was working as a carpenter during the slavery time, and he did all the building around the plantation. He had saved enough money to buy his freedom and he had half enough to buy his wife's freedom and then he was going to buy his little girl's freedom, which was my grandmother. But then they came along and freed the slaves, so he didn't have to buy them. He took that money and bought seventy acres of land right off of the plantation. He built them a house and they farmed that little seventy acres. . . .

My mother didn't come from this same group of people. I don't know too much about her parents because she doesn't know too much about them herself. She said they was cousins to the ones up there where my grandmother lived. The white people was almost like the Negroes: if they wasn't kin by marriage, they was kin by blood. So they were sort of the same kin in there somehow or the other. My mother was a very light-skinned woman and I know she got a lot of favors just by being that. From the black people, as well. She was almost as light as my grandbaby. And you see how dark I am? Because my father was dark.

She married my father when she was about sixteen, so from about sixteen until, oh, about thirty—I think that's how old she was when my father died. Then she was out there on her own with five children: one boy and four girls. I'm the youngest. I was born January 9, 1918. . . .

I decided I wanted to make more money, and I went to a little small town, Tyler, Texas. . . . And the only thing I could do there for a living was domestic work and it didn't pay very much. So I definitely didn't like it. . . .

. . . I left Tyler. I was saying, "I don't like it here because you can't make any money." I discovered I didn't have any trade. I had nothing I could do other than just that, and that wasn't what I wanted. So I decided I'd better get out of this town. I didn't like Dallas because that was too rough. Then someone told me, "Well, why don't you try California?" So then I got Los Angeles in my mind. I was twenty and I saved my money till I was twenty-one. In August 1940, I came here. . . .

When I first came, when my aunt met me down at the station, I had less than ten dollars. I went on to her house and stayed. In less than ten days I had found a job living on the place doing domestic work. I stayed there from some time in August until Christmas. I was making thirty-five dollars a month. That was so much better than what I was making at home, which was twelve dollars a month. I saved my money and I bought everybody a Christmas present and sent it. Oh, I was the happiest thing in the world! . . .

[She then returned to Texas to get married.] I stayed there for about nine months until he [her husband] went into the service. Then I came to Los Angeles. I told my sister, "Well, I better get me a good job around here working in a hotel or motel or something. I want to get me a good job so when the war is over, I'll have it." And she said, "No, you just come on out and go in the war plants and work and maybe you'll make enough money where you won't have to work in the hotels or motels." . . .

I don't remember what day of the week it was, but I guess I must have started out pretty early that morning. When I went there, the man didn't hire me. They had a school down here on Figueroa and he told me to go to the school. I went down and it was almost four o'clock and they told me they'd hire me. You had to fill out a form. They didn't bother too much about your experience because they knew you didn't have any experience in aircraft. Then they give you some kind of little test where you put the pegs in the right hole.

There were other people in there, kinda mixed. I assume it was more women than men. Most of the men was gone, and they weren't hiring too many men unless they had a good excuse. Most of the women was in my bracket, five or six years younger or older. I was twenty-four. There was a black girl that hired in with me. I went to work the next day, sixty cents an hour. I think I stayed at the school for about four weeks. They only taught you shooting and bucking rivets and how to drill the holes and to file. You had to use a hammer for certain things. After a couple of whiles, you worked on the real thing. But you were supervised so you didn't make a mess.

When we went into the plant, it wasn't too much different than down at the school. It was the same amount of noise; it was the same routine. One difference was there was just so many more people, and when you went in the door you had a badge to show and they looked at your lunch. I had gotten accustomed to a lot of people and I knew if it was a lot of people, it always meant something was going on. I got carried away: "As long as there's a lot of people here, I'll be making money." That was all I could ever see.

I was a good student, if I do say so myself. But I have found out through life, sometimes even if you're good, you just don't get the breaks if the color's not right. I could see where they made a difference in placing you in certain jobs. They had fifteen or twenty departments, but all the Negroes went to Department 17 because there was nothing but shooting and bucking rivets. You stood on one side of the panel and your partner stood on this side, and he would shoot the rivets with a gun and you'd buck them with the bar. That was about the size of it. I just didn't like it. I didn't think I could stay there with all this shooting and a'bucking and a'jumping and a'bumping. I stayed in it about two or three weeks and then I just decided I did not like that. I went and told my foreman and he didn't do anything about it, so I decided I'd leave.

While I was standing out on the railroad track, I ran into somebody else out there fussing also. I went over to the union and they told me what to do. I went back inside and they sent me to another department where you did bench work and I liked that much better. You had a little small jig that you would work on and you just drilled out holes. Sometimes you would rout them or you would scribe them and then you'd cut them with a cutters.

I must have stayed there nearly a year, and then they put me over in another department, "Plastics." It was the tail section of the B-Bomber, the Billy Mitchell Bomber. I put a little part in the gunsight. You had a little ratchet set and you would screw it in there. Then I cleaned the top of the glass off and put a piece of paper over it to seal it off to go to the next section. I worked over there until the end of the war. Well, not quite the end, because I got pregnant, and while I was off having the baby the war was over. . . .

Some weeks I brought home twenty-six dollars, some weeks sixteen dollars. Then it gradually went up to thirty dollars, then it went up a little bit more and a little bit more. And I learned somewhere along the line that in order to make a good move you gotta make some money. You don't make the same amount every day. You have some days good, sometimes bad. Whatever you make you're supposed to save some. I was also getting that fifty dollars a month from my husband and that was just saved right away. I was planning on buying a home and a car. And I was going to go back to school. My husband came back, but I never was laid off, so I just never found it necessary to look for another job or to go to school for another job.

I was still living over on Compton Avenue with my sister in this small little back house when my husband got home. Then, when Beverly was born, my sister moved in the front house and we stayed in the back house. When he came back, he looked for a job in the cleaning and pressing place, which was just plentiful. All the people had left these cleaning and pressing jobs and every other job; they was going to the defense plant to work because they was paying good. But in the meantime he was getting the same thing the people out there was getting, $1.25 an hour. That's why he didn't bother to go out to North American. But what we both weren't thinking about was that they did have better benefits because they did have an insurance plan and a union to back you up. Later he did come to work there, in 1951 or 1952.

I worked up until the end of March and then I took off. Beverly was born the twenty-first of June. I'd planned to come back somewhere in the last of August. I went to verify the fact that I did come back, so that did go on my record that I didn't just quit. But they laid off a lot of people, most of them, because the war was over.

It didn't bother me much—not thinking about it job-wise. I was just glad that the war was over. I didn't feel bad because my husband had a job and he also was eligible to go to school with his GI bill. So I really didn't have too many plans—which I wish I had had. I would have tore out page one and fixed it differently; put my version of page one in there.

I went and got me a job doing day work. That means you go to a person's house and clean up for one day out of the week and then you go to the next one and clean up. I did that a couple of times and I discovered I didn't like that so hot. Then I got me a job downtown working in a little factory where you do weaving—burned clothes and stuff like that. I learned to do that real good. It didn't pay too much but it paid enough to get me going, seventy-five cents or about like that.

When North American called me back, was I a happy soul! I dropped that job and went back. That was a dollar an hour. So, from sixty cents an hour, when I first hired in there, up to one dollar. That wasn't traveling fast, but it was better than anything else because you had hours to work by and you had benefits and you come home at night with your family. So it was a good deal.

It made me live better. I really did. We always say that Lincoln took the bale off of the Negroes. I think there is a statue up there in Washington, D.C., where he's lifting something off the Negro. Well, my sister always said—that's why you can't interview her because she's so radical—"Hitler was the one that got us out of the white folks' kitchen."

Module XX

Questions for Study and Critical Thinking

1. What phrases in Roosevelt's speech are particularly memorable? Why?

2. How did the war affect the soldiers?

3. What did they think about the war?

4. What did they think about the enemy?

5. What did they think about their comrades?

6. What did the war do for Fanny Christina Hill?

7. What instances of discrimination does she describe?

America and the Cold War

Introduction

At the end of the Second World War relations between the United States and the Soviet Union quickly turned from wartime cooperation to Cold War suspicion and hostility. Beginning with sharp disagreement over Soviet refusal to permit free elections in Poland, hostility grew rapidly. By 1946, just one year after Germany's surrender, U.S. government officials were contemplating the adoption of a policy to prevent future expansions of Soviet influence. One of the most influential advocates of what came to be called containment was the American diplomat George F. Kennan. His "Long Telegram," which he sent from the U.S. embassy in Moscow, helped shape U.S. thinking that the Soviets posed a threat of expansion and that the United States must resist it. Kennan later published his views in a famous article in *Foreign Affairs* magazine under the pseudonym of Mr. X.

Kennan's was not, however, the only view. Secretary of Commerce Henry Wallace and others on the left vigorously opposed containment policy. Under President Truman, however, the government adopted containment, and, despite some criticism, it remained U.S. policy under both Democratic and Republican presidents until the fall of communism in the Soviet Union.

Much of the criticism directed against Truman and his policies, however, came not from the left but from the right. The House Un-American Activities Committee investigated alleged communists and communist activities. Many of the accused were or had been in the government. In February 1950 Republican Senator Joseph McCarthy of Wisconsin made a speech in Wheeling, West Virginia, in which he asserted his possession of a list of 205 communists employed in the State Department. In 1952, as chairman of a Senate committee, McCarthy held hearings, broadcast live throughout the country, in which he accused the United States Army of harboring traitors.

Some public officials dared to oppose McCarthy. One was Senator Margaret Chase Smith of Maine, who wrote an open letter to the New York Times, in which she implicitly attacked McCarthy's views and tactics. Eventually, the Senate Judiciary Committee conducted hearings on McCarthy's charges of disloyalty within the State Department. In a scathing report it concluded that McCarthy's charges were baseless. The Senate voted to censure McCarthy, and he died soon afterward.

Truman's conduct of the Korean War also came under criticism. After a Chinese invasion of Korea forced American forces into headlong retreat, Douglas MacArthur, the American commander, urged the president to broaden the war by bombing China and assisting an invasion of China by the Nationalists, who had recently retreated from the mainland to Taiwan. When Truman rejected this idea, MacArthur expressed his disagreement in a letter to several senators. Truman promptly fired MacArthur for insubordination. MacArthur returned to a hero's welcome in the United States and a speech to a joint session of Congress. Truman's Korea policy remained controversial and formed a campaign theme in the 1952 campaign, in which the Republicans gained control of the White House and Congress.

Document 21.1 The Necessity for Containment: The "Long Telegram" (1946)

One of the most influential thinkers in the development of U.S. Cold War policy was the American diplomat George C. Kennan. In 1946, while stationed at the U.S. embassy in Moscow, Kennan wrote an eight thousand word analysis of Soviet intentions and policy, which he sent to the State Department in Washington. This "Long Telegram" proved very influential in causing President Truman and his advisors to adopt what later became known as containment policy. Kennan later published these views in the influential magazine *Foreign Affairs* under the pseudonym of Mr. X.

The Necessity for Containment: The "Long Telegram"

George F. Kennan

The Chargé in the Soviet Union (Kennan) to the Secretary of State

SECRET

Moscow, February 22, 1946—9 p.m.
[Received February 22 3:52 p.m.]

511. Answer to Dept's 284, Feb 3 *[13]*** involves questions so intricate, so delicate, so strange to our form of thought, and so important to analysis of our international environment that I cannot compress answers into single brief message without yielding to what I feel would be dangerous degree of over-simplification. I hope, therefore, Dept will bear with me if I submit in answer to this question five parts, subjects of which will be roughly as follows:

(1) features of postwar Soviet outlook.
(2) Background of this outlook.
(3) Its projection in practical policy on official level.
(4) Its projection on unofficial level.
(5) Practical deductions from standpoint of U.S. policy.

I apologize in advance for this burdening of telegraphic channel; but questions involved are of such urgent importance, particularly in view of recent events, that our answers to them, if they deserve attention at all, seem to me to deserve it at once. There follows

Part 1: Basic Features of Post War Soviet Outlook, as Put Forward by Official Propaganda Machine, Are as Follows:

(a) USSR still lives in antagonistic "capitalist encirclement" with which in the long run there can be no permanent peaceful coexistence. As stated by Stalin in 1927 to a delegation of American workers:

> "In course of further development of international revolution there will emerge two centers of world significance: a socialist center, drawing to itself the countries which tend toward socialism, and a capitalist center, drawing to itself the countries that incline toward capitalism. Battle between these two centers for command of world economy will decide fate of capitalism and of communism in entire world."

(b) Capitalist world is beset with internal conflicts, inherent in nature of capitalist society. These

---

*Not printed; in this telegram the Department informed the Chargé: "We should welcome receiving from you an interpretive analysis of what we may expect in the way of future implementation of these announced policies . . ." (861.00/2–1246). The policies referred to were those contained in the pre-election speeches of Stalin and his associates.

conflicts are insoluble by means of peaceful compromise. Greatest of them is that between England and U.S.

(c) Internal conflicts of capitalism inevitably generate wars. Wars thus generated may be of two kinds: intra-capitalist wars between two capitalist states, and wars of intervention against socialist world. Smart capitalists, vainly seeking escape from inner conflicts of capitalism, incline toward latter.

(d) Intervention against USSR, while it would be disastrous to those who undertook it, would cause renewed delay in progress of Soviet socialism and must therefore be forestalled at all costs.

(e) Conflicts between capitalist states, though likewise fraught with danger for USSR, nevertheless hold out great possibilities for advancement of socialist cause, particularly if USSR remains militarily powerful, ideologically monolithic and faithful to its present brilliant leadership.

(f) It must be borne in mind that capitalist world is not all bad. In addition to hopelessly reactionary and bourgeois elements, it includes (1) certain wholly enlightened and positive elements united in acceptable communistic parties and (2) certain other elements (now described for tactical reasons as progressive or democratic) whose reactions, aspirations and activities happen to be "objectively" favorable to interests of USSR. These last must be encouraged and utilized for Soviet purposes.

(g) Among negative elements of bourgeois-capitalist society, most dangerous of all are those whom Lenin called false friends of the people, namely moderate-socialist or social-democratic leaders (in other words, non-Communist left-wing). These are more dangerous than out-and-out reactionaries, for latter at least march under their true colors, whereas moderate left-wing leaders confuse people by employing devices of socialism to serve interests of reactionary capital.

So much for premises. To what deductions do they lead from standpoint of Soviet policy? To following:

(a) Everything must be done to advance relative strength of USSR as factor in international society. Conversely, no opportunity must be missed to reduce strength and influence, collectively as well as individually, of capitalist powers.

(b) Soviet efforts, and those of Russia's friends abroad, must be directed toward deepening and exploiting of differences and conflicts between capitalist powers. If these eventually deepen into an "imperialist" war, this war must be turned into revolutionary upheavals within the various capitalist countries.

(c) "Democratic-progressive" elements abroad are to be utilized to maximum to bring pressure to bear on capitalist governments along lines agreeable to Soviet interests.

(d) Relentless battle must be waged against socialist and social-democratic leaders abroad.

Part 2: Background of Outlook

Before examining ramifications of this party line in practice there are certain aspects of it to which I wish to draw attention.

First, it does not represent natural outlook of Russian people. Latter are, by and large, friendly to outside world, eager for experience of it, eager to measure against it talents they are conscious of possessing, eager above all to live in peace and enjoy fruits of their own labor. Party line only represents thesis which official propaganda machine puts forward with great skill and persistence to a public often remarkably resistant in the stronghold of its innermost thoughts. But party line is binding for outlook and conduct of people who make up apparatus of power—party, secret police and Government—and it is exclusively with these that we have to deal.

Second, please note that premises on which this party line is based are for most part simply not true. Experience has shown that peaceful and mutually profitable coexistence of capitalism and socialist states is entirely possible. Basic internal conflicts in advanced countries are no longer primarily those arising out of capitalist ownership of means of production, but are ones arising from advanced urbanism and industrialism as such, which Russia has thus far been spared not by socialism but only by her own backwardness. Internal rivalries of capitalism do not always generate wars; and not all wars are attributable to this cause. To speak of possibility of intervention against USSR today, after elimination of Germany and Japan and after example of recent war, is sheerest nonsense. If not provoked by forces of intolerance and subversion "capitalist" world of today is quite capable of living at peace with itself and with Russia. Finally, no sane person has reason to doubt sincerity of moderate socialist leaders in Western countries. Nor is it fair to deny success of their efforts to improve conditions for working population whenever, as in Scandinavia, they have been given chance to show what they could do.

Falseness of these premises, every one of which pre-dates recent war, was amply demonstrated by that conflict itself. Anglo-American differences did not turn out to be major differences of Western World. Capitalist countries, other than those of Axis, showed no disposition to solve their differences by joining in crusade against USSR. Instead of imperialist war turning into civil wars and revolution, USSR found itself obliged to fight side by side with capitalist powers for an avowed community of aims.

Nevertheless, all these theses, however baseless and disproven, are being boldly put forward again today. What does this indicate? It indicates that Soviet party line is not based on any objective analysis of situation beyond Russia's borders: that it has, indeed, little to do with conditions outside of Russia; that it arises mainly from basic inner-Russian necessities which existed before recent war and exist today.

At bottom of Kremlin's neurotic view of world affairs is traditional and instinctive Russian sense of insecurity. Originally, this was insecurity of a peaceful agricultural people trying to live on vast exposed plain in neighborhood of fierce nomadic peoples. To this was added, as Russia came into contact with economically advanced West, fear of more competent, more powerful, more highly organized societies in that area. But this latter type of insecurity was one which afflicted rather Russian rulers than Russian people; for Russian rulers have invariably sensed that their rule was relatively archaic in form, fragile and artificial in its psychological foundation, unable to stand comparison or contact with political systems of Western countries. For this reason they have always feared foreign penetration, feared direct contact between Western world and their own, feared what would happen if Russians learned truth about world without or if foreigners learned truth about world within. And they have learned to seek security only in patient but deadly struggle for total destruction of rival power, never in compacts and compromises with it.

It was no coincidence that Marxism, which had smouldered ineffectively for half a century in Western Europe, caught hold and blazed for first time in Russia. Only in this land which had never known a friendly neighbor or indeed any tolerant equilibrium of separate powers, either internal or international, could a doctrine thrive which viewed economic conflicts of society as insoluble by peaceful means. After establishment of Bolshevist regime, Marxist dogma, rendered even more truculent and intolerant by Lenin's interpretation, became a perfect vehicle for sense of insecurity with which Bolsheviks, even more than previous Russian rulers, were afflicted. In this dogma, with its basic altruism of purpose, they found justification for their instinctive fear of outside world, for the dictatorship without which they did not know how to rule, for cruelties they did not dare not to inflict, for sacrifices they felt bound to demand. In the name of Marxism they sacrificed every single ethical value in their methods and tactics. Today they cannot dispense with it. It is fig leaf of their moral and intellectual respectability. Without it they would stand before history, at best, as only the last of that long succession of cruel and wasteful Russian rulers who have relentlessly forced country on to ever new heights of military power in order to guarantee external security of their internally weak regimes. This is why Soviet purposes must always be solemnly clothed in trappings of Marxism, and why no one should underrate importance of dogma in Soviet affairs. Thus Soviet leaders are driven [by?] necessities of their own past and present position to put forward a dogma which [apparent omission] outside world as evil, hostile and menacing, but as bearing within itself germs of creeping disease and destined to be wracked with growing internal convulsions until it is given final *coup de grace* by rising power of socialism and yields to new and better world. This thesis provides justification for that increase of military and police power of Russian state, for that isolation of Russian population from outside world, and for that fluid and constant pressure to extend limits of Russian police power which are together the natural and instinctive urges of Russian rulers. Basically this is only the steady advance of uneasy Russian nationalism, a centuries old movement in which conceptions of offense and defense are inextricably confused. But in new guise of international Marxism, with its honeyed promises to a desperate and war torn outside world, it is more dangerous and insidious than ever before.

It should not be thought from above that Soviet party line is necessarily disingenuous and insincere on part of all those who put it forward. Many of them are too ignorant of outside world and mentally too dependent to question [apparent omission] self-hypnotism, and who have no difficulty making themselves believe what they find it comforting and convenient to believe. Finally we have the unsolved mystery as to who, if anyone, in this great land actually receives accurate and unbiased information about outside world. In atmosphere of oriental secretiveness and conspiracy which pervades this Government, possibilities for distorting or poisoning sources and currents of information are infinite. The very disrespect of Russians for objective truth—indeed, their disbelief in its existence—leads them to view all stated facts as instruments for furtherance of one ulterior purpose or another. There is good reason to suspect that this Government is actually a conspiracy within a conspiracy; and I for one am reluctant to believe that Stalin himself receives anything like an objective picture of outside world. Here there is ample scope for the type of subtle intrigue at which Russians are past masters. Inability of foreign governments to place their case squarely before Russian policy makers—extent to which they are delivered up in their relations with Russia to good graces of obscure and unknown advisers whom they never see and cannot influence—this to my mind is most disquieting feature of diplomacy in Moscow, and one which Western statesmen would do well to keep in mind if they would understand nature of difficulties encountered here.

Part 3: Projection of Soviet Outlook in Practical Policy on Official Level

We have now seen nature and background of Soviet program. What may we expect by way of its practical implementation?

Soviet policy, as Department implies in its query under reference, is conducted on two planes: (1) official plane represented by actions undertaken officially in name of Soviet Government; and (2) subterranean plane of actions undertaken by agencies for which Soviet Government does not admit responsibility.

Policy promulgated on both planes will be calculated to serve basic policies (a) to (d) outlined in part 1. Actions taken on different planes will differ considerably, but will dovetail into each other in purpose, time and effect.

On official plane we must look for following:

(a) Internal policy devoted to increasing in every way strength and prestige of Soviet state: intensive military-industrialization; maximum development of armed forces; great displays to impress outsiders; continued secretiveness about internal matters, designed to conceal weaknesses and to keep opponents in dark.

(b) Wherever it is considered timely and promising, efforts will be made to advance official limits of Soviet power. For the moment, these efforts are restricted to certain neighboring points conceived of here as being of immediate strategic necessity, such as Northern Iran, Turkey, possibly Bornholm. However, other points may at any time come into question, if and as concealed Soviet political power is extended to new areas. Thus a "friendly" Persian Government might be asked to grant Russia a port on Persian Gulf. Should Spain fall under Communist control, question of Soviet base at Gibraltar Strait might be activated. But such claims will appear on official level only when unofficial preparation is complete.

(c) Russians will participate officially in international organizations where they see opportunity of extending Soviet power or of inhibiting or diluting power of others. Moscow sees in UNO not the mechanism for a permanent and stable world society founded on mutual interest and aims of all nations, but an arena in which aims just mentioned can be favorably pursued. As long as UNO is considered here to serve this purpose, Soviets will remain with it. But if at any time they come to conclusion that it is serving to embarrass or frustrate their aims for power expansion and if they see better prospects for pursuit of these aims along other lines, they will not hesitate to abandon UNO. This would imply, however, that they felt themselves strong enough to split unity of other nations by their withdrawal, to render UNO ineffective as a threat to their aims or security, and to replace it with an international weapon more effective from their viewpoint. Thus Soviet attitude toward UNO will depend largely on loyalty of other nations to it, and on degree of vigor, decisiveness and cohesion with which these nations defend in UNO the peaceful and hopeful concept of international life, which that organization represents to our way of thinking. I reiterate, Moscow has no abstract devotion to UNO ideals. Its attitude to that organization will remain essentially pragmatic and tactical.

(d) Toward colonial areas and backward or dependent peoples, Soviet policy, even on official plane, will be directed toward weakening of power and influence and contacts of advanced Western nations, on theory that in so far as this policy is successful, there will be created a vacuum which will favor Communist-Soviet penetration. Soviet pressure for participation in trusteeship arrangements thus represents, in my opinion, a desire to be in a position to complicate and inhibit exertion of Western influence at such points rather than to provide major channel for exerting of Soviet power. Latter motive is not lacking, but for this Soviets prefer to rely on other channels than official trusteeship arrangements. Thus we may expect to find Soviets asking for admission everywhere to trusteeship or similar arrangements and using levers thus acquired to weaken Western influence among such people.

(e) Russians will strive energetically to develop Soviet representation in, and official ties with, countries in which they sense strong possibilities of opposition to Western centers of power. This applies to such widely separated points as Germany, Argentina, Middle Eastern countries, etc.

(f) In international economic matters, Soviet policy will really be dominated by pursuit of autarchy for Soviet Union and Soviet-dominated adjacent areas taken together. That, however, will be underlying policy. As far as official line is concerned, position is not yet clear. Soviet Government has shown strange reticence since termination hostilities on subject foreign trade. If large scale long term credits should be forthcoming, I believe Soviet Government may eventually again do lip service, as it did in 1930's to desirability of building up international economic exchanges in general. Otherwise I think it possible Soviet foreign trade may be restricted largely to Soviet's own security sphere, including occupied areas in Germany, and that, a cold official shoulder may be turned to principle of general economic collaboration among nations.

(g) With respect to cultural collaboration, lip service will likewise be rendered to desirability of deepening cultural contacts between peoples, but this will not in practice be interpreted in any way which could weaken security position of Soviet peoples. Actual manifestations of Soviet policy in this respect will be restricted to arid channels of closely shepherded official visits and functions, with superabundance of vodka and speeches and dearth of permanent effects.

(h) Beyond this, Soviet official relations will take what might be called "correct" course with individual foreign governments, with great stress being laid on prestige of Soviet Union and its representatives and with punctilious attention to protocol, as distinct from good manners.

Part 4: Following May Be Said as to What We May Expect by Way of Implementation of Basic Soviet Policies on Unofficial, or Subterranean Plane, i.e., on Plane for Which Soviet Government Accepts no Responsibility

Agencies utilized for promulgation of policies on this plane are following:

1. Inner central core of Communist Parties in other countries. While many of persons who compose this category may also appear and act in unrelated public capacities, they are in reality working closely together as an underground operating directorate of world communism, a concealed Comintern* tightly coordinated and directed by Moscow. It is important to remember that this inner core is actually working on underground lines, despite legality of parties with which it is associated.

2. Rank and file of Communist Parties. Note distinction is drawn between these and persons defined in paragraph 1. This distinction has become much sharper in recent years. Whereas formerly foreign Communist Parties represented a curious (and from Moscow's standpoint often inconvenient) mixture of conspiracy and legitimate activity, now the conspiratorial element has been neatly concentrated in inner circle and ordered underground, while rank and file—no longer even taken into confidence about realities of movement—are thrust forward as bona fide internal partisans of certain political tendencies within their respective countries, genuinely innocent of conspiratorial connection with foreign states. Only in certain countries where communists are numerically strong do they now regularly appear and act as a body. As a rule they are used to penetrate, and to influence or dominate, as case may be, other organizations less likely to be suspected of being tools of Soviet Government, with a view to accomplishing their purposes through [apparent omission] organizations, rather than by direct action as a separate political party.

3. A wide variety of national associations or bodies which can be dominated or influenced by such penetration. These include: labor unions, youth leagues, women's organizations, racial societies, religious societies, social organizations, cultural groups, liberal magazines, publishing houses, etc.

4. International organizations which can be similarly penetrated through influence over various national components. Labor, youth and women's organizations are prominent among them. Particular, almost vital, importance is attached in this connection to international labor movement. In this, Moscow sees possibility of sidetracking western governments in world affairs and building up international lobby capable of compelling governments to take actions favorable to Soviet interests in various countries and of paralyzing actions disagreeable to USSR.

5. Russian Orthodox Church, with its foreign branches, and through it the Eastern Orthodox Church in general.

6. Pan-Slav movement and other movements (Azerbaijan, Armenian, Turcoman, etc.) based on racial groups within Soviet Union.

7. Governments or governing groups willing to lend themselves to Soviet purposes in one degree or another, such as present Bulgarian and Yugoslav Governments, North Persian regime, Chinese Communists, etc. Not only propaganda machines but

*The Third (Communist) International, founded by the Bolsheviks at Moscow in March 1919, announced as having been dissolved in May 1943; see *Foreign Relations,* 1943, vol. III, pp. 531–532, and 542–543.

actual policies of these regimes can be placed extensively at disposal of USSR.

It may be expected that component parts of this far-flung apparatus will be utilized, in accordance with their individual suitability, as follows:

(a) To undermine general political and strategic potential of major western powers. Efforts will be made in such countries to disrupt national self confidence, to hamstring measures of national defense, to increase social and industrial unrest, to stimulate all forms of disunity. All persons with grievances, whether economic or racial, will be urged to seek redress not in mediation and compromise, but in defiant violent struggle for destruction of other elements of society. Here poor will be set against rich, black against white, young against old, newcomers against established residents, etc.

(b) On unofficial plane particularly violent efforts will be made to weaken power and influence of Western Powers of [*on*] colonial backward, or dependent peoples. On this level, no holds will be barred. Mistakes and weaknesses of western colonial administration will be mercilessly exposed and exploited. Liberal opinion in Western countries will be mobilized to weaken colonial policies. Resentment among dependent peoples will be stimulated. And while latter are being encouraged to seek independence of Western Powers, Soviet dominated puppet political machines will be undergoing preparation to take over domestic power in respective colonial areas when independence is achieved.

(e) Where individual governments stand in path of Soviet purposes pressure will be brought for their removal from office. This can happen where governments directly oppose Soviet foreign policy aims (Turkey, Iran), where they seal their territories off against Communist penetration (Switzerland, Portugal), or where they compete too strongly, like Labor Government in England, for moral domination among elements which it is important for Communists to dominate. (Sometimes, two of these elements are present in a single case. Then Communist opposition becomes particularly shrill and savage.

(d) In foreign countries Communists will, as a rule, work toward destruction of all forms of personal independence, economic, political or moral. Their system can handle only individuals who have been brought into complete dependence on higher power. Thus persons who are financially independent—such as individual businessmen, estate owners, successful farmers, artisans and all those who exercise local leadership or have local prestige, such as popular local clergymen or political figures, are anathema. It is not by chance that even in USSR local officials are kept constantly on move from one job to another, to prevent their taking root.

(e) Everything possible will be done to set major Western Powers against each other. Anti-British talk will be plugged among Americans, anti-American talk among British. Continentals, including Germans, will be taught to abhor both Anglo-Saxon powers. Where suspicions exist, they will be fanned; where not, ignited. No effort will be spared to discredit and combat all efforts which threaten to lead to any sort of unity or cohesion among other [apparent omission] from which Russia might be excluded. Thus, all forms of international organization not amenable to Communist penetration and control, whether it be the Catholic [apparent omission] international economic concerns, or the international fraternity of royalty and aristocracy, must expect to find themselves under fire from many, and often [apparent omission].

(f) In general, all Soviet efforts on unofficial international plane will be negative and destructive in character, designed to tear down sources of strength beyond reach of Soviet control. This is only in line with basic Soviet instinct that there can be no compromise with power and that constructive work can start only when Communist power is dominant. But behind all this will be applied insistent, unceasing pressure for penetration and command of key positions in administration and especially in police apparatus of foreign countries. The Soviet regime is a police regime par excellence, reared in the dim half world of Tsarist police intrigue, accustomed to think primarily in terms of police power. This should never be lost sight of in gauging Soviet motives.

Part 5: [Practical Deductions From Standpoint of U.S. Policy]

In summary, we have here a political force committed fanatically to the belief that with U.S. there can be no permanent *modus vivendi,* that it is desirable and necessary that the internal harmony of our society be disrupted, our traditional way of life be destroyed, the international authority of our state be broken, if Soviet power is to be secure. This political force has complete power of disposition over energies of one of world's greatest peoples and resources of world's richest national territory, and is borne along by deep and powerful currents of Russian nationalism. In addition, it has an elaborate and far flung apparatus for exertion of its influence in other countries, an apparatus of amazing flexibility and versatility, managed by people whose experience and skill in underground methods are presumably without parallel in history. Finally, it is seemingly inaccessible to considerations of reality in its basic reactions. For it, the vast fund of objective fact about human society is not, as with us, the measure against which outlook is constantly being tested and re-formed, but a grab bag from which individual items are selected arbitrarily and tendenciously to bolster an outlook already preconceived. This is admittedly not a pleasant picture. Problem of how to cope with this force in [*is*] undoubtedly greatest task our diplomacy has ever faced and probably greatest it will ever have to face. It should be point of departure from which our political general staff work at present juncture should proceed. It should be approached with same thoroughness and care as solution of major strategic problem in war, and if necessary, with no smaller outlay in planning effort. I cannot attempt to suggest all answers here. But I would like to record my conviction that problem is within our power to solve—and that without recourse to any general military conflict. And in support of this conviction there are certain observations of a more encouraging nature I should like to make:

(1) Soviet power, unlike that of Hitlerite Germany, is neither schematic nor adventuristic. It does not work by fixed plans. It does not take unnecessary risks. Impervious to logic of reason, and it is highly sensitive to logic of force. For this reason it can easily withdraw—and usually does—when strong resistance is encountered at any point. Thus, if the adversary has sufficient force and makes clear his readiness to use it, he rarely has to do so. If situations are properly handled there need be no prestige-engaging showdowns.

(2) Gauged against Western World as a whole, Soviets are still by far the weaker force. Thus, their success will really depend on degree of cohesion, firmness and vigor which Western World can muster. And this is factor which it is within our power to influence.

(3) Success of Soviet system, as form of internal power is not yet finally proven. It has yet to be demonstrated that it can survive supreme test of successive transfer of power from one individual or group to another. Lenin's death was first such transfer, and its effects wracked Soviet state for 15 years. After Stalin's death or retirement will be second. But even this will not be final test. Soviet internal system will now be subjected, by virtue of recent territorial expansions, to series of additional strains which once proved severe tax on Tsardom. We here are convinced that never since termination of civil war have mass of Russian people been emotionally farther removed from doctrines of Communist Party than they are today. In Russia, party has now become a great and—for the moment—highly successful apparatus of dictatorial administration, but it has ceased to be a source of emotional inspiration. Thus, internal soundness and permanence of movement, need not yet be regarded as assured.

(4) All Soviet propaganda beyond Soviet security sphere is basically negative and destructive. It should therefore be relatively easy to combat it by any intelligent and really constructive program.

For these reasons I think we may approach calmly and with good heart problem of how to deal with Russia. As to how this approach should be made, I only wish to advance, by way of conclusion, following comments:

(1) Our first step must be to apprehend, and recognize for what it is, the nature of the movement with which we are dealing. We must study it with same courage, detachment, objectivity, and same determination not to be emotionally provoked or unseated by it, with which doctor studies unruly and unreasonable individual.

(2) We must see that our public is educated to realities of Russian situation. I cannot over-emphasize importance of this. Press cannot do this alone. It must be done mainly by Government, which is necessarily more experienced and better informed on practical problems involved. In this we need not be deterred by [ugliness?] of picture. I am convinced that there would be far less hysterical anti-Sovietism in our country today if realities of this situation were better understood by our people. There is nothing as dangerous or as terrifying as the unknown. It may also be argued that to reveal more information on our difficulties with Russia would reflect unfavorably on Russian-American relations. I feel that if there is any real risk here involved, it is one which we should have courage to face, and sooner the better. But I cannot see what we would be risking. Our stake in this country, even coming on heels of tremendous demonstrations of our friendship for Russian people, is remarkably small. We have here no investments to guard, no actual trade to lose, virtually no citizens to protect, few cultural contacts to preserve. Our only stake lies in what we hope rather than what we have; and I am convinced we have better chance of realizing those hopes if our public is enlightened and if our dealings with Russians are placed entirely on realistic and matter-of-fact basis.

(3) Much depends on health and vigor of our own society. World communism is like malignant parasite which feeds only on diseased tissue. This is point at which domestic and foreign policies meet. Every courageous and incisive measure to solve internal problems of our own society, to improve self-confidence, discipline, morale and community spirit of our own people, is a diplomatic victory over Moscow worth a thousand diplomatic notes and joint communiqués. If we cannot abandon fatalism

and indifference in face of deficiencies of our own society, Moscow will profit—Moscow cannot help profiting by them in its foreign policies.

(4) We must formulate and put forward for other nations a much more positive and constructive picture of sort of world we would like to see than we have put forward in past. It is not enough to urge people to develop political processes similar to our own. Many foreign peoples, in Europe at least, are tired and frightened by experiences of past, and are less interested in abstract freedom than in security. They are seeking guidance rather than responsibilities. We should be better able than Russians to give them this. And unless we do, Russians certainly will.

(5) Finally we must have courage and self-confidence to cling to our own methods and conceptions of human society. After all, the greatest danger that can befall us in coping with this problem of Soviet communism, is that we shall allow ourselves to become like those with whom we are coping.

KENNAN

Document 21.2 Are We Only Paying Lip Service to Peace? (1946)

Henry A. Wallace had a long record of holding high office in the Roosevelt and Truman administrations, where he was known for his liberal views. He had been Secretary of Agriculture in Franklin D. Roosevelt's cabinet from 1933 to 1941. In 1944 party leaders persuaded Roosevelt to replace the liberal Wallace with Harry Truman as his vice presidential candidate. Wallace then served as Secretary of Commerce. After the war ended, Wallace grew increasingly critical of Truman's policy toward the Soviet Union, which he believed was unduly harsh and warlike. In September, 1946, after Wallace publicly opposed the administration's policy, Truman fired Wallace. In the 1948 election Wallace ran for the presidency against Truman (who won the election). The document below is excerpted from a letter Wallace wrote to President Truman in July, 1946.

Are We Only Paying Lip Service to Peace?

Henry A. Wallace

I have been increasingly disturbed about the trend of international affairs since the end of the war, and I am even more troubled by the apparently growing feeling among the American people that another war is coming and the only way that we can head it off is to arm ourselves to the teeth. Yet all of past history indicates that an armaments race does not lead to peace but to war. The months just ahead may well be the crucial period which will decide whether the civilized world will go down in destruction after the five or ten years needed for several nations to arm themselves with atomic bombs. Therefore, I want to give you my views on how the present trend toward conflict might be averted. . . .

How do American actions since VJ Day [Victory in Japan Day, i.e., the end of World War II] appear to other nations? I mean by actions the concrete things like $13 billion for the War and Navy Departments, the Bikini tests of the atomic bomb and continued production of bombs, the plan to arm Latin America with our weapons, production of B-29s and planned production of B-36s, and the effort to secure air bases spread over half the globe from which the other half of the globe can be bombed. I cannot but feel that these actions must make it look to the rest of the world as if we were only paying lip service to peace at the conference table.

These facts rather make it appear either (1) that we are preparing ourselves to win the war which we regard as inevitable or (2) that we are trying to build up a predominance of force to intimidate the rest of mankind. How would it look to us if Russia had the atomic bomb and we did not, if Russia had 10,000-

From *A History of Our Time* by Henry A. Wallace. Published by Oxford University Press, Inc.

mile bombers and air bases within a thousand miles of our coastlines, and we did not?

Some of the military men and self-styled "realists" are saying: "What's wrong with trying to build up a predominance of force? The only way to preserve peace is for this country to be so well armed that no one will dare attack us. We know that America will never start a war." The flaw in this policy is simply that it will not work. In a world of atomic bombs and other revolutionary new weapons, such as radioactive poison gases and biological warfare, a peace maintained by a predominance of force is no longer possible.

Why is this so? The reasons are clear:

FIRST. Atomic warfare is cheap and easy compared with old-fashioned war. Within a very few years several countries can have atomic bombs and other atomic weapons. Compared with the cost of large armies and the manufacture of old-fashioned weapons, atomic bombs cost very little and require only a relatively small part of a nation's production plant and labor force.

SECOND. So far as winning a war is concerned, having more bombs—even many more bombs—than the other fellow is no longer a decisive advantage. If another nation had enough bombs to eliminate all of our principal cities and our heavy industry, it wouldn't help us very much if we had ten times as many bombs as we needed to do the same to them.

THIRD. And most important, the very fact that several nations have atomic bombs will inevitably result in a neurotic, fear-ridden, itching-trigger psychology in all the peoples of the world, and because of our wealth and vulnerability we would be among the most seriously affected. Atomic war will not require vast and time-consuming preparations, the mobilization of large armies, the conversion of a large proportion of a country's industrial plants to the manufacture of weapons. In a world armed with atomic weapons, some incident will lead to the use of those weapons.

There is a school of military thinking which recognizes these facts, recognizes that when several nations have atomic bombs, a war which will destroy modern civilization will result and that no nation or combination of nations can win such a war. This school of thought, therefore, advocates a "preventive war," an attack on Russia now before Russia has atomic bombs.

This scheme is not only immoral, but stupid. If we should attempt to destroy all the principal Russian cities and her heavy industry, we might well succeed. But the immediate countermeasure which such an attack would call forth is the prompt occupation of all Continental Europe by the Red Army. Would we be prepared to destroy the cities of all Europe in trying to finish what we had started? This idea is so contrary to all the basic instincts and principles of the American people that any such action would be possible only under a dictatorship at home. . . .

Our basic distrust of the Russians, which has been greatly intensified in recent months by the playing up of conflict in the press, stems from differences in political and economic organization. For the first time in our history defeatists among us have raised the fear of another system as a successful rival to democracy and free enterprise in other countries and perhaps even our own. I am convinced that we can meet that challenge as we have in the past by demonstrating that economic abundance can be achieved without sacrificing personal, political and religious liberties. We cannot meet it as Hitler tried to by an anti-Comintern alliance.

It is perhaps too easy to forget that despite the deep-seated differences in our cultures and intensive anti-Russian propaganda of some twenty-five years' standing, the American people reversed their attitudes during the crisis of war. Today, under the pressure of seemingly insoluble international problems and continuing deadlocks, the tide of American public opinion is again turning against Russia. In this reaction lies one of the dangers to which this letter is addressed. I should list the factors which make for Russian distrust of the United States and of the Western world as follows. The first is Russian history, which we must take into account because it is the setting in which Russians see all actions and policies of the rest of the world. Russian history for over a thousand years has been a succession of attempts, often unsuccessful, to resist invasion and conquest—by the Mongols, the Turks, the Swedes, the Germans and the Poles. The scant thirty years of the existence of the Soviet Government has in Russian eyes been a continuation of their historical struggle for national existence. The first four years of the new regime, from 1917 through 1921, were spent in resisting attempts at destruction by the Japanese, British and French, with some American assistance, and by the several White Russian armies encouraged and financed by the Western powers. Then, in 1941, the Soviet State was almost conquered by the Germans after a period during which the Western European powers had apparently acquiesced in the rearming of Germany in the belief that the Nazis would seek to expand eastward rather than westward. The Russians, therefore, obviously see themselves as fighting for their existence in a hostile world.

Second, it follows that to the Russians all of the defense and security measures of the Western powers seem to have an aggressive intent. Our actions to expand our military security system—such steps as extending the Monroe Doctrine to include the arming of the Western Hemisphere nations, our present monopoly of the atomic bomb, our interest in outlying bases and our general support of the British Empire—appear to them as going far beyond the requirements of defense. I think we might feel the same if the United States were the only capitalistic country in the world, and the principal socialistic countries were creating a level of armed strength far exceeding anything in their previous history. From the Russian point of view, also, the granting of a loan to Britain and the lack of tangible results on their request to borrow for rehabilitation purposes may be regarded as another evidence of strengthening of an anti-Soviet bloc.

Finally, our resistance to her attempts to obtain warm-water ports and her own security system in the form of "friendly" neighboring states seems, from the Russian point of view, to clinch the case. After twenty-five years of isolation and after having achieved the status of a major power, Russia believes that she is entitled to recognition of her new status. Our interest in establishing democracy in Eastern Europe, where democracy by and large has never existed, seems to her an attempt to re-establish the encirclement of unfriendly neighbors which was created after the last war, and which might serve as a springboard of still another effort to destroy her.

If this analysis is correct, and there is ample evidence to support it, the action to improve the situation is clearly indicated. The fundamental objective of such action should be to allay any reasonable Russian grounds for fear, suspicion and distrust. We must recognize that the world has changed and that today there can be no "One World" unless the United States and Russia can find some way of living together. For example, most of us are firmly convinced of the soundness of our position when we suggest the internationalization and de-fortification of the Danube or of the Dardanelles, but we would be horrified and angered by any Russian counterproposal that would involve also the internationalizing and disarming of Suez or Panama. We must recognize that to the Russians these seem to be identical situations. . . .

We should make an effort to counteract the irrational fear of Russia, which is being systematically built up in the American people by certain individuals and publications. The slogan that communism and capitalism, regimentation and democracy, cannot continue to exist in the same world is, from a historical point of view, pure propaganda. Several religious doctrines, all claiming to be the only true gospel and salvation, have existed side by side with a reasonable degree of tolerance for centuries. This country was for the first half of its national life a democratic island in a world dominated by absolutist governments.

We should not act as if we too felt that we were threatened in today's world. We are by far the most powerful nation in the world, the only Allied nation which came out of the war without devastation and much stronger than before the war. Any talk on our part about the need for strengthening our defenses further is bound to appear hypocritical to other nations. . . .

This proposal admittedly calls for a shift in some of our thinking about international matters. It is imperative that we make this shift. We have little time to lose. Our postwar actions have not yet been adjusted to the lessons to be gained from experience of Allied cooperation during the war and the facts of the atomic age.

It is certainly desirable that, as far as possible, we achieve unity on the home front with respect to our international relations; but unity on the basis of building up conflict abroad would prove to be not only unsound but disastrous. I think there is some reason to fear that in our earnest efforts to achieve bipartisan unity in this country we may have given way too much to isolationism masquerading as tough realism in international affairs.

The real test lies in the achievement of international unity. It will be fruitless to continue to seek solutions for the many specific problems that face us in the making of the peace and in the establishment of an enduring international order without first achieving an atmosphere of mutual trust and confidence. The task admittedly is not an easy one.

There is no question, as the Secretary of State has indicated, that negotiations with the Russians are difficult because of cultural differences, their traditional isolationism, and their insistence on a visible quid pro quo in all agreements. But the task is not an insuperable one if we take into account that to other nations our foreign policy consists not only of the principles that we advocate but of the actions we take.

Fundamentally, this comes down to the point discussed earlier in this letter, that even our own security, in the sense that we have known it in the past, cannot be preserved by military means in a world armed with atomic weapons. The only type of security which can be maintained by our own military force is the type described by a military man before the Senate Atomic Energy Commission—a security against invasion after all our cities and perhaps 40 million of our city population have been destroyed by atomic weapons. That is the best that "security" on the basis of armaments has to offer us. It is not the kind of security that our people and the people of the other United Nations are striving for.

Document 21.3 The United States Must Be Firm (1946)

Clark Clifford was special counsel and a trusted advisor to President Truman. As the following selection shows, he vigorously supported firm policies toward the Soviet Union. Later he served as an advisor to Presidents Kennedy and Johnson and a member of President Johnson's cabinet. The following excerpt is from a private memorandum Clifford wrote for President Truman.

The United States Must Be Firm

Clark Clifford

It is perhaps the greatest paradox of the present day that the leaders of a nation, now stronger than it has ever been before, should embark on so aggressive a course because their nation is "weak." And yet Stalin and his cohorts proclaim that "monopoly capitalism" threatens the world with war and that Russia must strengthen her defenses against the danger of foreign attacks. The USSR, according to Kremlin propaganda, is imperilled so long as it remains within a "capitalistic encirclement." This idea is absurd when adopted by so vast a country with such great natural wealth, a population of almost 200 million and no powerful or aggressive neighbors. But the process of injecting this propaganda into the minds of the Soviet people goes on with increasing intensity.

The concept of danger from the outside is deeply rooted in the Russian people's haunting sense of insecurity inherited from their past. It is maintained by their present leaders as a justification for the oppressive nature of the Soviet police state. The thesis, that the capitalist world is conspiring to attack the Soviet Union, is not based on any objective analysis of the situation beyond Russia's borders. It has little to do, indeed, with conditions outside the Soviet Union, and it has risen mainly from basic inner-Russian necessities which existed before the Second World War and which exist today. . . .

The Kremlin acknowledges no limit to the eventual power of the Soviet Union, but it is practical enough to be concerned with the actual position of the USSR today. In any matter deemed essential to the security of the Soviet Union, Soviet leaders will prove adamant in their claims and demands. In other matters they will prove grasping and opportunistic, but flexible in proportion to the degree and nature of the resistance encountered.

Recognition of the need to postpone the "inevitable" conflict is in no sense a betrayal of the Communist faith. Marx and Lenin encouraged compromise and collaboration with non-Communists for the accomplishment of ultimate communistic purposes. The USSR has followed such a course in the past. In 1939 the Kremlin signed a nonaggression pact with Germany and in 1941 a neutrality pact with Japan. Soviet leaders will continue to collaborate whenever it seems expedient, for time is needed to build up Soviet strength and weaken the opposition. Time is on the side of the Soviet Union, since population growth and economic development will, in the Soviet view, bring an increase in its relative strength. . . .

A direct threat to American security is implicit in Soviet foreign policy which is designed to prepare the Soviet Union for war with the leading capitalistic nations of the world. Soviet leaders recognize that the United States will be the Soviet Union's most powerful enemy if such a war as that predicted by Communist theory ever comes about and therefore the United States is the chief target of Soviet foreign and military policy. . . .

The most obvious Soviet threat to American security is the growing ability of the USSR to wage an offensive war against the United States. This has

---

The United States Must be Firm by Clark Clifford, Secretary of Defense.

not hitherto been possible, in the absence of Soviet long-range strategic air power and an almost total lack of sea power. Now, however, the USSR is rapidly developing elements of her military strength which she hitherto lacked and which will give the Soviet Union great offensive capabilities. Stalin has declared his intention of sparing no effort to build up the military strength of the Soviet Union. Development of atomic weapons, guided missiles, materials for biological warfare, a strategic air force, submarines of great cruising range, naval mines and mine craft, to name the most important, are extending the effective range of Soviet military power well into areas which the United States regards as vital to its security. . . .

The primary objective of United States policy toward the Soviet Union is to convince Soviet leaders that it is in their interest to participate in a system of world cooperation, that there are no fundamental causes for war between our two nations, and that the security and prosperity of the Soviet Union, and that of the rest of the world as well, is being jeopardized by the aggressive militaristic imperialism such as that in which the Soviet Union is now engaged. However, these same leaders with whom we hope to achieve an understanding on the principles of international peace appear to believe that a war with the United States and the other leading capitalistic nations is inevitable. They are increasing their military power and the sphere of Soviet influence in preparation for the "inevitable" conflict, and they are trying to weaken and subvert their potential opponents by every means at their disposal. So long as these men adhere to these beliefs, it is highly dangerous to conclude that hope of international peace lies only in "accord," "mutual understanding," or "solidarity" with the Soviet Union.

Adoption of such a policy would impel the United States to make sacrifices for the sake of Soviet-U.S. relations, which would only have the effect of raising Soviet hopes and increasing Soviet demands, and to ignore alternative lines of policy, which might be much more compatible with our own national and international interests.

The Soviet government will never be easy to "get along with." The American people must accustom themselves to this thought, not as a cause for despair, but as a fact to be faced objectively and courageously. If we find it impossible to enlist Soviet cooperation in the solution of world problems, we should be prepared to join with the British and other Western countries in an attempt to build up a world of our own which will pursue its own objectives and will recognize the Soviet orbit as a distinct entity with which conflict is not predestined but with which we cannot pursue common aims.

As long as the Soviet government maintains its present foreign policy, based upon the theory of an ultimate struggle between communism and capitalism, the United States must assume that the USSR might fight at any time for the two-fold purpose of expanding the territory under Communist control and weakening its potential capitalist opponents. The Soviet Union was able to flow into the political vacuum of the Balkans, Eastern Europe, the Near East, Manchuria and Korea because no other nation was both willing and able to prevent it. Soviet leaders were encouraged by easy success, and they are now preparing to take over new areas in the same way. The Soviet Union, as Stalin euphemistically phrased it, is preparing "for any eventuality."

Unless the United States is willing to sacrifice its future security for the sake of "accord" with the USSR now, this government must, as a first step toward world stabilization, seek to prevent additional Soviet aggression. . . . This government should be prepared, while scrupulously avoiding any act which would be an excuse for the Soviets to begin a war, to resist vigorously and successfully any efforts of the USSR to expand into areas vital to American security.

The language of military power is the only language which disciples of power politics understand. The United States must use that language in order that Soviet leaders will realize that our government is determined to uphold the interests of its citizens and the rights of small nations. Compromise and concessions are considered, by the Soviets, to be evidences of weakness, and they are encouraged by our "retreats" to make new and greater demands. The main deterrent to Soviet attack on the United States, or to attack on areas of the world which are vital to our security, will be the military power of this country. It must be made apparent to the Soviet government that our strength will be sufficient to repel any attack and sufficient to defeat the USSR decisively if a war should start. The prospect of defeat is the only sure means of deterring the Soviet Union.

The Soviet Union's vulnerability is limited due to the vast area over which its key industries and natural resources are widely dispersed, but it is vulnerable to atomic weapons, biological warfare, and long-range power. Therefore, in order to maintain our strength at a level which will be effective in restraining the Soviet Union, the United States must be prepared to wage atomic and biological warfare. A highly mechanized army, which can be moved either by sea or by air, capable of seizing and holding strategic areas, must be supported by powerful naval and air forces. A war with the USSR would be "total" in a more horrible sense than any previous war, and there must be constant research for both offensive and defensive weapons.

Whether it would actually be in this country's interest to employ atomic and biological weapons against the Soviet Union in the event of hostilities is a question which would require careful consideration in the light of the circumstances prevailing at the time. The decision would probably be influenced by a number of factors, such as the Soviet Union's capacity to employ similar weapons, which can not now be estimated. But the important point is that the United States must be prepared to wage atomic and biological warfare if necessary. The mere fact of preparedness may be the only powerful deterrent to Soviet aggressive action and in this sense the only sure guaranty of peace.

The United States, with a military potential composed primarily of [highly] effective technical weapons, should entertain no proposal for disarmament or limitation of armament as long as the possibility of Soviet aggression exists. Any discussion on the limitation of armaments should be pursued slowly and carefully with the knowledge constantly in mind that proposals on outlawing atomic warfare and long-range offensive weapons would greatly limit United States strength, while only moderately affecting the Soviet Union. The Soviet Union relies primarily on a large infantry and artillery force, and the result of such arms limitation would be to deprive the United States of its most effective weapons without impairing the Soviet Union's ability to wage a quick war of aggression in Western Europe, the Middle East or the Far East. . . .

In addition to maintaining our own strength, the United States should support and assist all democratic countries which are in any way menaced or endangered by the USSR. Providing military support in case of attack is a last resort; a more effective barrier to communism is strong economic support. Trade agreements, loans and technical missions strengthen our ties with friendly nations and are effective demonstrations that capitalism is at least the equal of communism. The United States can do much to ensure that economic opportunities, personal freedom and social equality are made possible in countries outside the Soviet sphere by generous financial assistance. Our policy on reparations should be directed toward strengthening the areas we are endeavoring to keep outside the Soviet sphere. Our efforts to break down trade barriers, open up rivers and international waterways, and bring about economic unification of countries, now divided by occupation armies, are also directed toward the reestablishment of vigorous and healthy non-Communist economies.

In conclusion, as long as the Soviet government adheres to its present policy, the United States should maintain military forces powerful enough to restrain the Soviet Union and to confine Soviet influence to its present area. All nations not now within the Soviet sphere should be given generous economic assistance and political support in their opposition to Soviet penetration. Economic aid may also be given to the Soviet government and private trade with the USSR permitted provided the results are beneficial to our interests.

Even though Soviet leaders profess to believe that the conflict between Capitalism and Communism is irreconcilable and must eventually be resolved by the triumph of the latter, it is our hope that they will change their minds and work out with us a fair and equitable settlement when they realize that we are too strong to be beaten and too determined to be frightened.

Document 21.4 President Truman Announces the Truman Doctrine

In 1947 President Truman made a crucial decision which directed American policy for more than forty years. In Greece, communist forces were threatening the government. In Turkey, the Soviet Union sought to increase their power over the straits leading from their naval bases in the Black Sea into the Mediterranean. Confronted by economic problems in the wake of World War II, the British announced that they would no longer be able to support the Turkish and Greek governments. Under these circumstances President Truman decided that the United States would step into the gap. In addition, he determined to enunciate a new, more comprehensive policy: that in the future the United States would aid any country threatened by communists. This policy of containing the Soviet Union and its allies become known as containment policy and provided the foundation of Cold War American doctrine. President Truman announced this policy in the following speech, delivered to a joint session of Congress on March 12, 1947.

President Truman Announces the Truman Doctrine

Harry S. Truman

Mr. President, Mr. Speaker, Members of the Congress of the United States:

The gravity of the situation which confronts the world today necessitates my appearance before a joint session of the Congress.

The foreign policy and the national security of this country are involved.

One aspect of the present situation, which I wish to present to you at this time for your consideration and decision, concerns Greece and Turkey.

The United States has received from the Greek Government an urgent appeal for financial and economic assistance. Preliminary reports from the American Economic Mission now in Greece and reports from the American Ambassador in Greece corroborate the statement of the Greek Government that assistance is imperative if Greece is to survive as a free nation. I do not believe that the American people and the Congress wish to turn a deaf ear to the appeal of the Greek Government.

Greece is not a rich country. Lack of sufficient natural resources has always forced the Greek people to work hard to make both ends meet. Since 1940 this industrious and peace-loving country has suffered invasion, four years of cruel enemy occupation, and bitter internal strife. . . .

The very existence of the Greek state is today threatened by the terrorist activities of several thousand armed men, led by Communists, who defy the Government's authority at a number of points, particularly along the northern boundaries. A commission appointed by the United Nations Security Council is at present investigating disturbed conditions in northern Greece and alleged border violations along the frontier between Greece on the one hand and Albania, Bulgaria, and Yugoslavia on the other.

Meanwhile, the Greek Government is unable to cope with the situation. The Greek Army is small and poorly equipped. It needs supplies and equipment if it is to restore authority to the Government throughout Greek territory.

Greece must have assistance if it is to become a self-supporting and self-respecting democracy.

The United States must supply that assistance. We have already extended to Greece certain types of relief and economic aid, but these are inadequate.

There is no other country to which democratic Greece can turn.

No other nation is willing and able to provide the necessary support for a democratic Greek Government.

The British Government, which has been helping Greece, can give no further financial or economic aid after March 31. Great Britain finds itself under the necessity of reducing or liquidating its commitments in several parts of the world, including Greece.

We have considered how the United Nations might assist in this crisis. But the situation is an urgent one requiring immediate action, and the United Nations and its related organizations are not in a position to extend help of the kind that is required.

It is important to note that the Greek Government has asked for our aid in utilizing effectively the financial and other assistance we may give to Greece, and in improving its public administration. It is of the utmost importance that we supervise the use of any funds made available to Greece, in such a manner that each dollar spent will count toward making Greece self-supporting, and will help to build an economy in which a healthy democracy can flourish.

No government is perfect. One of the chief virtues of a democracy, however, is that its defects are always visible and under democratic processes can be pointed out and corrected. The Government of Greece is not perfect. Nevertheless it represents 85 percent of the members of the Greek Parliament who were chosen in an election last year. Foreign observers, including 692 Americans, considered this election to be a fair expression of the views of the Greek people. The Greek Government has been operating in an atmosphere of chaos and extremism. It has made mistakes. The extension of aid by this country does not mean that the United States condones everything that the Greek Government has done or will do. We have condemned in the past, and

The Truman Doctrine, Harry S. Truman.

we condemn now, extremist measures of the right or the left. We have in the past advised tolerance, and we advise tolerance now.

Greece's neighbor, Turkey, also deserves our attention.

The future of Turkey as an independent and economically sound state is clearly no less important to the freedom-loving peoples of the world than the future of Greece. The circumstances in which Turkey finds itself today are considerably different from those of Greece. Turkey has been spared the disasters that have beset Greece. And during the war the United States and Great Britain furnished Turkey with material aid.

Nevertheless, Turkey now needs our support.

Since the war Turkey has sought additional financial assistance from Great Britain and the United States for the purpose of effecting that modernization necessary for the maintenance of its national integrity.

That integrity is essential to the preservation of order in the Middle East.

The British Government has informed us that, owing to its own difficulties, it can no longer extend financial or economic aid to Turkey.

As in the case of Greece, if Turkey is to have the assistance it needs, the United States must supply it. We are the only country able to provide that help.

I am fully aware of the broad implications involved if the United States is involved in the creation of conditions in which we and other nations will be able to work out a way of life free from coercion. This was a fundamental issue in the war with Germany and Japan. Our victory was won over countries which sought to impose their will, and their way of life upon other nations. To insure the peaceful development of nations, free from coercion, the United States has taken a leading part in establishing the United Nations.

The United Nations is designed to make possible lasting freedom and independence for all its members. We shall not realize our objectives, however, unless we are willing to help free peoples to maintain their free institutions and their national integrity against aggressive movements that seek to impose upon them totalitarian regimes. This is no more than a frank recognition that totalitarian regimes imposed upon free peoples, by direct or indirect aggression, undermine the foundations of international peace and hence the security of the United States. The peoples of a number of countries of the world have recently had totalitarian regimes forced upon them against their will. The Government of the United States has made frequent protests against coercion and intimidation, in violation of the Yalta agreement, in Poland, Rumania, and Bulgaria. I must also state that in a number of other countries there have been similar developments.

At the present moment in world history nearly every nation must choose between alternative ways of life. The choice is too often not a free one.

One way of life is based upon the will of the majority, and is distinguished by free institutions, representative government, free elections, guaranties of individual liberty, freedom of speech and religion, and freedom from political oppression.

The second way of life is based upon the will of a minority forcibly imposed upon the majority. It relies upon terror and oppression, a controlled press and radio, fixed elections, and the suppression of personal freedoms.

I believe that it must be the policy of the United States to support free peoples who are resisting attempted subjugation by armed minorities or by outside pressures.

I believe that we must assist free peoples to work out their own destinies in their own way.

I believe that our help should be primarily through economic and financial aid which is essential to economic stability and orderly political processes.

The world is not static, and the *status quo* is not sacred. But we cannot allow changes in the *status quo* in violation of the Charter of the United Nations by such methods as coercion, or by such subterfuges as political infiltration. In helping free and independent nations to maintain their freedom, the United States will be giving effect to the principles of the Charter of the United Nations.

It is necessary only to glance at a map to realize that the survival and integrity of the Greek nation are of grave importance in a much wider situation. If Greece should fall under the control of an armed minority, the effect upon its neighbor, Turkey, would be immediate and serious. Confusion and disorder might well spread throughout the entire Middle East.

Moreover, the disappearance of Greece as an independent state would have a profound effect upon those countries in Europe whose peoples are struggling against great difficulties to maintain their freedoms and their independence while they repair the damages of war.

It would be an unspeakable tragedy if these countries, which have struggled so long against overwhelming odds, should lose that victory for which they sacrificed so much. Collapse of free institutions and loss of independence would be disastrous not only for them but for the world. Discouragement and possibly failure would quickly be the lot of neighboring peoples striving to maintain their freedom and independence.

Should we fail to aid Greece and Turkey in this fateful hour, the effect will be far-reaching to the West as well as to the East.

We must take immediate and resolute action.

I therefore ask the Congress to provide authority for assistance to Greece and Turkey in the amount of $400,000,000 for the period ending June 30, 1948. In requesting these funds, I have taken into consideration the maximum amount of relief assistance which would be furnished to Greece out of the $350,000,000 which I recently requested that the Congress authorize for the prevention of starvation and suffering in countries devastated by the war.

In addition to funds, I ask the Congress to authorize the detail of American civilian and military personnel to Greece and Turkey, at the request of those countries, to assist in the tasks of reconstruction, and for the purpose of supervising the use of such financial and material assistance as may be furnished. I recommend that authority also be provided for the instruction and training of selected Greek and Turkish personnel.

Finally, I ask that the Congress provide authority which will permit the speediest and most effective use, in terms of needed commodities, supplies, and equipment, of such funds as may be authorized.

If further funds, or further authority, should be needed for purposes indicated in this message, I shall not hesitate to bring the situation before the Congress. On this subject the Executive and Legislative branches of the Government must work together.

This is a serious course upon which we embark.

I would not recommend it except that the alternative is much more serious.

The United States contributed $341,000,000,000 toward winning World War II. This is an investment in world freedom and world peace.

The assistance that I am recommending for Greece and Turkey amounts to little more than one-tenth of one percent of this investment. It is only common sense that we should safeguard this investment and make sure that it was not in vain.

The seeds of totalitarian regimes are nurtured by misery and want. They spread and grow in the evil soil of poverty and strife. They reach their full growth when the hope of a people for a better life has died.

We must keep that hope alive.

The free peoples of the world look to us for support in maintaining their freedoms.

If we falter in our leadership, we may endanger the peace of the world and we shall surely endanger the welfare of our own Nation.

Great responsibilities have been placed upon us by the swift movement of events.

I am confident that the Congress will face these responsibilities squarely.

Document 21.5 The Marshall Plan

The Second World War left the economies of the European countries severely damaged. In these conditions many U.S. policymakers feared that communist parties in Western European countries would become so strong they would be able to seize power. In response, General George C. Marshall and other officials of the Truman administration decided to initiate a plan of U.S. aid to rebuild the economies of European countries. This program became known as the Marshall Plan. In 1947 Marshall announced this plan in a speech at Harvard University.

The Marshall Plan

George C. Marshall

I need not tell you, gentlemen, that the world situation is very serious. That must be apparent to all intelligent people. I think one difficulty is that the problem is one of such enormous complexity that the very mass of facts presented to the public by press and radio make it exceedingly difficult for the man in the street to reach a clear appraisement of the situation. Furthermore, the people of this country are distant from the troubled areas of the earth and it is hard for them to comprehend the plight and consequent reactions of the long-suffering peoples, and the effect of those reactions on their governments in connection with our efforts to promote peace in the world.

In considering the requirements for the rehabilitation of Europe, the physical loss of life, the visible destruction of cities, factories, mines, and railroads was correctly estimated, but it has become obvious during recent months that this visible destruction was probably less serious than the dislocation of the entire fabric of European economy. For the past ten years conditions have been highly abnormal. The feverish preparation for war and the more feverish maintenance of the war effort engulfed all aspects of national economies. Machinery has fallen into disrepair or is entirely obsolete. Under the arbitrary and destructive Nazi rule, virtually every possible enterprise was geared into the German war machine. Long-standing commercial ties, private institutions, banks, insurance companies, and shipping companies disappeared, through loss of capital, absorption through nationalization, or by simple destruction. In many countries, confidence in the local currency has been severely shaken. The breakdown of the business structure of Europe during the war was complete. Recovery has been seriously retarded by the fact that two years after the close of hostilities a peace settlement with Germany and Austria has not been agreed upon. But even given a more prompt solution of these difficult problems, the rehabilitation of the economic structure of Europe quite evidently will require a much longer time and greater effort than had been foreseen.

There is a phase of this matter which is both interesting and serious. The farmer has always produced the foodstuffs to exchange with the city dweller for the other necessities of life. This division of labor is the basis of modern civilization. At the present time it is threatened with breakdown. The town and city industries are not producing adequate goods to exchange with the food-producing farmer. Raw materials and fuel are in short supply. Machinery is lacking or worn out. The farmer or the peasant cannot find the goods for sale which he desires to purchase. So the sale of his farm produce for money which he cannot use seems to him an unprofitable transaction. He, therefore, has withdrawn many fields from crop cultivation and is using them for grazing. He feeds more grain to stock and finds for himself and his family an ample supply of food, however short he may be on clothing and the other ordinary gadgets of civilization. Meanwhile people in the cities are short of food and fuel. So the governments are forced to use their foreign money and credits to procure these necessities abroad. This process exhausts funds which are urgently needed for reconstruction. Thus a very serious situation is rapidly developing which bodes no good for the world. The modern system of the division of labor upon which the exchange of products is based is in danger of breaking down.

The truth of the matter is that Europe's requirements for the next three or four years of foreign food and other essential products—principally from America—are so much greater than her present ability to pay that she must have substantial additional help or face economic, social, and political deterioration of a very grave character.

The remedy lies in breaking the vicious circle and restoring the confidence of the European people in the economic future of their own countries and of Europe as a whole. The manufacturer and the farmer throughout wide areas must be able and willing to exchange their products for currencies the continuing value of which is not open to question.

Aside from the demoralizing effect on the world at large and the possibilities of disturbances arising as a result of the desperation of the people concerned, the consequences to the economy of the United States should be apparent to all. It is logical

---

The Marshall Plan by George C. Marshall.

that the United States should do whatever it is able to do to assist in the return of normal economic health in the world, without which there can be no political stability and no assured peace. Our policy is directed not against any country or doctrine but against hunger, poverty, desperation, and chaos. Its purpose should be the revival of a working economy in the world so as to permit the emergence of political and social conditions in which free institutions can exist. Such assistance, I am convinced, must not be on a piecemeal basis as various crises develop. Any assistance that this Government may render in the future should provide a cure rather than a mere palliative. Any government that is willing to assist in the task of recovery will find full cooperation, I am sure, on the part of the United States Government. Any government which maneuvers to block the recovery of other countries cannot expect help from us. Furthermore, governments, political parties, or groups which seek to perpetuate human misery in order to profit therefrom politically or otherwise will encounter the opposition of the United States.

It is already evident that, before the United States Government can proceed much further in its efforts to alleviate the situation and help start the European world on its way to recovery, there must be some agreement among the countries of Europe as to the requirements of the situation and the part those countries themselves will take in order to give proper effect to whatever action might be undertaken by this Government. It would be neither fitting nor efficacious for this Government to undertake to draw up unilaterally a program designed to place Europe on its feet economically. This is the business of the Europeans. The initiative, I think, must come from Europe. The role of this country should consist of friendly aid in the drafting of a European program and of later support of such a program so far as it may be practical for us to do so. The program should be a joint one, agreed to by a number, if not all, European nations.

An essential part of any successful action on the part of the United States is an understanding on the part of the people of America of the character of the problem and the remedies to be applied. Political passion and prejudice should have no part. With foresight, and a willingness on the part of our people to face up to the vast responsibility which history has clearly placed upon our country, the difficulties I have outlined can and will be overcome.

. . . This program will cost our country billions of dollars. It will impose a burden on the American taxpayer. It will require sacrifices today in order that we may enjoy security and peace tomorrow. Should the Congress approve the program for European recovery, as I urgently recommend, we Americans will have made an historic decision of our peacetime history.

A nation in which the voice of its people directs the conduct of its affairs cannot embark on an undertaking of such magnitude and significance for light or purely sentimental reasons. Decisions of this importance are dictated by the highest considerations of national interest. There are none higher, I am sure, than the establishment of enduring peace and the maintenance of true freedom for the individual. In the deliberations of the coming weeks I ask that the European Recovery Program be judged in these terms and on this basis. . . .

The program is not one of a series of piecemeal relief measures. I ask that you note this difference, and keep it in mind throughout our explanations. The difference is absolutely vital.

Document 21.6 The Korean War and the Dismissal of MacArthur

At the beginning of World War II Korea was a Japanese possession. At the end of the Second World War the United States and the Soviet Union agreed on the temporary division of Korea. As the Cold War developed, however, little progress was made on unifying the country, and separate Korean governments were established in both the north and the south, the Soviets supporting the northern regime and the United States the southern. In 1950 the north invaded the south. Initially, northern armies were overwhelmingly successful. They captured the capitol of Seoul and then pushed southward, forcing the south Koreans and the United States into an enclave at the southern end of the Korean peninsula.

As supreme military commander in Asia, General Douglas MacArthur became responsible for the conduct of the war. Under his command U.S. forces landed at Inchon, far behind the north Korean front lines and quickly cut North Korean forces off from their bases farther north. U.S. forces then proceeded north until they almost reached the Chinese border.

At that point a large contingent of the Chinese army entered the war, sweeping across the border and driving American troops back. General MacArthur then began urging the government to widen the war with attacks on China. He urged that the Nationalist Chinese forces, which had been driven off the mainland to the island of Taiwan, invade China and that the U.S. bomb Chinese targets. President Truman and his advisors rejected this policy. MacArthur then wrote to Republican senators, urging the widening of the war. At that point Truman fired MacArthur for insubordination. MacArthur returned to the United States, where he addressed a joint session of Congress and then became a candidate for the 1952 Republican nomination for the presidency. The first document below is Truman's statement of Korean policy and defense of firing MacArthur. The second document contains excerpts from MacArthur's speech to a joint session of Congress, which he delivered upon his return to the U.S.

The Korean War and the Dismissal of MacArthur

Harry S. Truman

In the simplest terms, what we are doing in Korea is this:

We are trying to prevent a third world war.

I think most people in this country recognized that fact last June. And they warmly supported the decision of the Government to help the Republic of Korea against the Communist aggressors. Now, many persons, even some who applauded our decision to defend Korea, have forgotten the basic reason for our action. . . .

The Communists in the Kremlin are engaged in a monstrous conspiracy to stamp out freedom all over the world. If they were to succeed, the United States would be numbered among their principal victims. It must be clear to everyone that the United States cannot—and will not—sit idly by and await foreign conquest. The only question is: When is the best time to meet the threat and how? . . .

The aggression against Korea is the boldest and most dangerous move the Communists have yet made.

The attack on Korea was part of a greater plan for conquering all of Asia. . . .

They want to control all of Asia from the Kremlin.

This plan of conquest is in flat contradiction to what we believe. We believe that Korea belongs to the Koreans. We believe that India belongs to the Indians. We believe that all the nations of Asia should be free to work out their affairs in their own way. This is the basis of peace in the Far East and it is the basis of peace everywhere else.

The whole Communist imperialism is back of the attack on peace in the Far East. It was the Soviet Union that trained and equipped the North Koreans for aggression. The Chinese Communists massed forty-four well-trained and well-equipped divisions on the Korean frontier. These were the troops they threw into battle when the North Korean Communists were beaten.

The question we have to face is whether the Communist plan of conquest can be stopped without general war. Our Government and other countries associated with us in the United Nations believe that the best chance of stopping it without general war is to meet the attack in Korea and defeat it there.

That is what we have been doing. It is a difficult and bitter task.

But so far it has been successful.

So far, we have prevented World War III.

So far, by fighting a limited war in Korea, we have prevented aggression from succeeding and bringing on a general war. And the ability of the whole free world to resist Communist aggression has been greatly improved. . . .

But you may ask: Why can't we take steps to punish the aggressor? Why don't we bomb Manchuria and China itself? Why don't we assist nationalist Chinese troops to land on the mainland of China?

If we were to do these things we would be running a very grave risk of starting a general war.

Department of State Bulletin 24.

If that were to happen, we would have brought about the exact situation we are trying to prevent. . . .

I believe that we must try to limit the war to Korea for these vital reasons: to make sure that the precious lives of our fighting men are not wasted; to see that the security of our country and the free world is not needlessly jeopardized; and to prevent a third world war.

A number of events have made it evident that General MacArthur did not agree with that policy. I have therefore considered it essential to relieve General MacArthur so that there would be no doubt or confusion as to the real purpose and aim of our policy.

It was with the deepest personal regret that I found myself compelled to take this action. General MacArthur is one of our greatest military commanders. But the cause of world peace is more important than any individual.

The change in commands in the Far East means no change whatever in the policy of the United States. We will carry on the fight in Korea with vigor and determination in an effort to bring the war to a speedy and successful conclusion.

The new commander, Lt. Gen. Matthew Ridgway, has already demonstrated that he has the great qualities of military leadership needed for this task. We are ready, at any time, to negotiate for a restoration of peace in the area. But we will not engage in appeasement. We are only interested in real peace. Real peace can be achieved through a settlement based on the following factors:

One: the fighting must stop.

Two: concrete steps must be taken to insure that the fighting will not break out again.

Three: there must be an end to the aggression. A settlement founded upon these elements would open the way for the unification of Korea and the withdrawal of all foreign forces.

In the meantime, I want to be clear about our military objective. We are fighting to resist an outrageous aggression in Korea. We are trying to keep the Korean conflict from spreading to other areas. But at the same time we must conduct our military activities so as to insure the security of our forces. This is essential if they are to continue the fight until the enemy abandons its ruthless attempt to destroy the Republic of Korea.

That is our military objective—to repel attack and to restore peace. In the hard fighting in Korea, we are proving that collective action among nations is not only a high principle but a workable means of resisting aggression. Defeat of aggression in Korea may be the turning point in the world's search for a practical way of achieving peace and security. . . .

We do not want to widen the conflict. We will use every effort to prevent that disaster. And in so doing, we know that we are following the great principles of peace, freedom, and justice.

Document 21.7 Address to Congress, April 19, 1951

After MacArthur's dismissal by Truman, he returned to the United States with his wife and son and made a triumphal tour of the country. Everywhere he went, people greeted him as a hero, including New York, where he received the traditional ticker tape parade reserved for national heroes. Congress then bestowed one of its highest honors by inviting him to address a joint session of the House and Senate. MacArthur's speech rapidly became famous, especially its closing lines: "Old soldiers never die; they just fade away."

MacArthur moved to New York City, where he worked to secure the Republican presidential nomination two years later, in 1952. At that convention the Republican National Committee invited him to give a major address. According to some observers, however, the long and ponderous speech hurt his chances. The nomination went to his former aide, Dwight D. Eisenhower, who was elected president.

Address to Congress, April 19, 1951

Douglas MacArthur

. . . I do not stand here as an advocate for any partisan cause, for the issues are fundamental and reach quite beyond the realm of partisan consideration. They must be resolved on the highest plane of national interest if our course is to prove sound and our future protected. . . . I address you with neither rancor nor bitterness in the fading twilight of life with but one purpose in mind, to serve my country.

The issues are global and so interlocked that to consider the problems of one sector oblivious to those of another is but to court disaster for the whole.

While Asia is commonly referred to as the gateway to Europe, it is no less true that Europe is the gateway to Asia, and the broad influence of the one cannot fail to have its impact upon the other. . . .

The Communist threat is a global one. Its successful advance in one sector threatens the destruction of every other sector. You cannot appease or otherwise surrender to communism in Asia without simultaneously undermining our efforts to halt its advance in Europe. . . .

I now turn to the Korean conflict. While I was not consulted prior to the President's decision to intervene in the support of the Republic of Korea, that decision from a military standpoint proved a sound one . . . as we hurled back the invaders and decimated his forces. Our victory was complete and our objectives within reach when Red China intervened with numerically superior ground forces. This created a new war and an entirely new situation, a situation not contemplated when our forces were committed against the North Korean invaders, a situation which called for new decisions in the diplomatic sphere to permit the realistic adjustment of military strategy. Such decisions have not been forthcoming.

While no man in his right mind would advocate sending our ground forces into continental China—and such was never given a thought—the new situation did urgently demand a drastic revision of strategic planning if our political aim was to defeat this new enemy as we had defeated the old. . . .

I felt that military necessity in the conduct of the war made necessary:

First, the intensification of our economic blockade against China.

Second, the imposition of a naval blockade against the China coast.

Third, removal of restrictions on air reconnaissance of China's coastal areas and of Manchuria.

Fourth, removal of restrictions on the forces of the Republic of China on Formosa with logistical support to contribute to their effective operation against the Chinese mainland.

For entertaining these views . . . I have been severely criticized in lay circles, principally abroad, despite my understanding that from a military standpoint the above views have been fully shared in the past by practically every military leader concerned with the Korean campaign, including our own Joint Chiefs of Staff.

I called for reinforcements, but was informed that reinforcements were not available. I made clear that if not permitted to utilize the friendly Chinese force of some 600,000 men on Formosa; if not permitted to blockade the China coast to prevent the Chinese Reds from getting succor from without; and if there were to be no hope for major reinforcements, the position of the command from the military standpoint forbade victory. We could hold in Korea . . . but we could hope at best for only an indecisive campaign, with its terrible and constant attrition upon our forces if the enemy utilized his full military potential. I have constantly called for the new political decisions essential to a solution. Efforts have been made to distort my position. It has been said in effect that I was a warmonger. Nothing could be further from the truth. I know war as few other men now living know it, and nothing to me is more revolting. . . .

But once war is forced upon us, there is no other alternative than to apply every available means to bring it to a swift end. War's very object is victory—not prolonged indecision. In war, indeed, there can be no substitute for victory.

There are some who for varying reasons would appease Red China. They are blind to history's clear lesson. For history teaches with unmistakable emphasis that appeasement but begets new and bloodier

Address to Congress, April 1951.

war. It points to no single instance where the end had justified the means—where appeasement has led to more than a sham peace. Like blackmail, it lays the basis for new and successively greater demands, until, as in blackmail, violence becomes the only other alternative. Why, my soldiers asked of me, surrender military advantages to an enemy in the field? I cannot answer. Some may say to avoid spread of the conflict into an all-out war with China; others, to avoid Soviet intervention. Neither explanation seems valid. For China is already engaging with the maximum power it can commit, and the Soviet will not necessarily mesh its actions with our moves. Like a cobra, any new enemy will more likely strike when ever it feels that relativity in military or other potential is in its favor on a world-wide basis. . . .

I have just left your fighting sons in Korea. They have met all the tests there and I can report to you without reservation that they are splendid in every way. It was my constant effort to preserve them and end this savage conflict honorably and with the least loss of time and a minimum sacrifice of life. Its growing bloodshed has caused me the deepest anguish and anxiety. Those gallant men will remain often in my thoughts and in my prayers always.

I am closing my fifty-two years of military service. When I joined the Army even before the turn of the century, it was the fulfillment of all my boyish hopes and dreams. The world has turned over many times since I took the oath on the Plain at West Point, and the hopes and dreams have long since vanished. But I still remember the refrain of one of the most popular barrack ballads of that day, which proclaimed most proudly that—

"Old soldiers never die, they just fade away."

And like the old soldier of that ballad, I now close my military career and just fade away—an old soldier who tried to do his duty as God gave him the light to see that duty.

Good-by.

Document 21.8 The Threat of Communism (1950)

One of the most prominent political figures of the early 1950s was Joseph R. McCarthy, U.S. senator from Wisconsin. In 1950, in the midst of anxieties about the Cold War, McCarthy made a speech in Wheeling, West Virginia, in which he declared that he had in his hand a list of over 200 known communists working in the United States government. Subsequently, as chairman of an important Senate committee, he conducted nationally broadcast public hearings into his allegations of communists in the army and elsewhere in the government. This campaign made McCarthy famous and powerful.

A reaction to McCarthy's activities and methods, however, gathered force. Margaret Chase Smith, a Republican senator from Maine, issued a "declaration of conscience," in which she attacked McCarthy's methods. The Senate Foreign Relations Committee investigated McCarthy's charges and declared them without foundation. Dwight D. Eisenhower, the Republican president, found McCarthy repulsive and made no effort to save him from his enemies. Eventually, the Senate censured him. McCarthy's political power was ended, and he died a few years later.

The Threat of Communism

Joseph R. McCarthy

Ladies and gentlemen, tonight as we celebrate the one hundred and forty-first birthday of one of the greatest men in American history, I would like to be able to talk about what a glorious day today is in the history of the world. As we celebrate the birth of this man who with his whole heart and soul hated war, I would like to be able to speak of peace in our time, of war being outlawed, and of world-wide disarma-

The Threat of Communism, 81st Congress, 1950.

ment. These would be truly appropriate things to be able to mention as we celebrate the birthday of Abraham Lincoln.

Five years after a world war has been won, men's hearts should anticipate a long peace, and men's minds should be free from the heavy weight that comes with war. But this is not such a period—for this is not a period of peace. This is a time of the "cold war." This is a time when all the world is split into two vast, increasingly hostile armed camps—a time of a great armaments race.

Today we can almost physically hear the mutterings and rumblings of an invigorated god of war. You can see it, feel it, and hear it all the way from the hills of Indochina, from the shores of Formosa, right over into the very heart of Europe itself.

The one encouraging thing is that the "mad moment" has not yet arrived for the firing of the gun or the exploding of the bomb which will set civilization about the final task of destroying itself. There is still a hope for peace if we finally decide that no longer can we safely blind our eyes and close our ears to those facts which are shaping up more and more clearly. And that is that we are now engaged in a show-down fight—not the usual war between nations for land areas or other material gains, but a war between two diametrically opposed ideologies.

The great difference between between our western Christian world and the atheistic Communist world is not political, ladies and gentlemen, it is moral. There are other differences, of course, but those could be reconciled. For instance, the Marxian idea of confiscating the land and factories and running the entire economy as a single enterprise is momentous. Likewise, Lenin's invention of the one-party police state as a way to make Marx's idea work is hardly less momentous.

Stalin's resolute putting across of these two ideas, of course, did much to divide the world. With only those differences, however, the East and the West could most certainly still live in peace.

The real, basic difference, however lies in the religion of immoralism—invented by Marx, preached feverishly by Lenin, and carried to unimaginable extremes by Stalin. This religion of immoralism, if the Red half of the world wins—and well it may—this religion of immoralism will more deeply wound and damage mankind than any conveivable economic or political system.

Karl Marx dismissed God as a hoax, and Lenin and Stalin have added in clear-cut, unmistakable language their resolve that no nation, no people who believe in a God, can exist side by side with their communistic state.

Karl Marx, for example, expelled people from his Communist Party for mentioning such things as justice, humanity, or morality. He called this soulful ravings and sloppy sentimentality.

While Lincoln was a relatively young man in his late thirties, Karl Marx boasted that the Communist specter was haunting Europe. Since that time, hundreds of millions of people and vast areas of the world have fallen under Communist domination. Today, less than 100 years after Lincoln's death, Stalin brags that this Communist specter is not only haunting the world, but is about to completely subjugate it.

Today we are engaged in a final, all-out battle between communistic atheism and Christianity. The modern champions of communism have selected this as the time. And, ladies and gentlemen, the chips are down—they are truly down.

Lest there be any doubt that the time has been chosen, let us go directly to the leader of communism today—Joseph Stalin. Here is what he said—not back in 1928, not before the war, not during the war—but two years after the last war was ended: "To think that the Communist revolution can be carried out peacefully, within the framework of a Christian democracy, means one has either gone out of one's mind and lost all normal understanding, or has grossly and openly repudiated the Communist revolution."

And this is what was said by Lenin in 1919, which was also quoted with approval by Stalin in 1947:

"We are living," said Lenin, "not merely in a state, but in a system of states, and the existence of the Soviet Republic side by side with Christian states for a long time is unthinkable. One or the other must triumph in the end. And before that end supervenes, a series of frightful collisions between the Soviet Republic and the Bourgeois states will be inevitable."

Ladies and gentlemen, can there be anyone here tonight who is so blind as to say that the war is not on? Can there be anyone who fails to realize that the Communist world has said, "The time is now"—that this is the time for the show-down between the democratic Christian world and the Communist atheistic world?

Unless we face this fact, we shall pay the price that must be paid by those who wait too long.

Six years ago, at the time of the first conference to map out the peace—Dumbarton Oaks—there was within the Soviet orbit 180,000,000 people. Lined up on the antitotalitarian side there were in the world at that time roughly 1,625,000,000 people. Today, only six years later, there are 800,000,000 people under the absolute domination of Soviet Russia—an increase of over 400 percent. On our side, the figure has shrunk to around 500,000,000. In other words, in less than six years the odds have changed from 9 to 1 in our favor to 8 to 5 against us. This indicated the swiftness of the tempo of Communist victories and American defeats in the cold war. As one of our outstanding historical figures once said, "When a great democracy is destroyed, it will not be because of enemies from without, but rather because of enemies from within."

The truth of this statement is becoming terrifyingly clear as we see this country each day losing on every front.

At war's end we were physically the strongest nation on earth and, at least potentially, the most powerful intellectually and morally. Ours could have been the honor of being a beacon in the desert of destruction, a shining living proof that civilization was not yet ready to destroy itself. Unfortunately, we have failed miserably and tragically to arise to the opportunity.

The reason why we find ourselves in a position of impotency is not because our only powerful potential enemy has sent men to invade our shores, but rather because of the traitorous actions of those who have been treated so well by this Nation. It has not been the less fortunate or members of minority groups who have been selling this Nation out, but rather those who have had all the benefits that the wealthiest nation on earth has had to offer—the finest homes, the finest college education, and the finest jobs in Government we can give.

This is glaringly true in the State Department. There the bright young men who are born with silver spoons in their mouths are the ones who have been worst.

Now I know it is very easy for anyone to condemn a particular bureau or department in general terms. Therefore, I would like to cite one rather unusual case—the case of a man who has done much to shape our foreign policy.

When Chiang Kai-shek was fighting our war, the State Department had in China a young man named John S. Service. His task, obviously, was not to work for the communization of China. Strangely, however, he sent official reports back to the State Department urging that we torpedo our ally Chiang Kai-shek and stating, in effect, that communism was the best hope of China.

Later, this man—John Service—was picked up by the Federal Bureau of Investigation for turning over to the Communists secret State Department information. Strangely, however, he was never prosecuted. However, Joseph Grew, the Under Secretary of State, who insisted on his prosecution, was forced to resign. Two days after Grew's successor, Dean Acheson, took over as Under Secretary of State, this man—John Service—who had been picked up by the FBI and who had previously urged that communism was the best hope of China, was not only reinstated in the State Department but promoted. And finally, under Acheson, placed in charge of all placements and promotions.

Today, ladies and gentlemen, this man Service is on his way to represent the State Department and Acheson in Calcutta—by far and away the most important listening post in the Far East.

Now, let's see what happens when individuals with Communist connections are forced out of the State Department. Gustave Duran, who was labeled as (I quote) "a notorious international Communist," was made assistant to the Assistant Secretary of State in charge of Latin American affairs. He was taken into the State Department from his job as a lieutenant colonel in the Communist International Brigade. Finally, after intense cogressional pressure and criticism, he resigned in 1946 from the State Department—and, ladies and gentlemen, where do you think he is now? He took over a high-salaried job as Chief of Cultural Activities Section in the office of the Assistant Secretary General of the United Nations.

Then there was a Mrs. Mary Jane Kenny, from the Board of Economic Warfare in the State Department, who was named in an FBI report and in a House committee report as a courier for the Communist Party while working for the Government. And where do you think Mrs. Kenny is—she is now an editor in the United Nations Document Bureau.

Another interesting case was that of Julian H. Wadleigh, economist in the Trade Agreements Section of the State Department for 11 years and was sent to Turkey and Italy and other countries as United States representative. After the statute of limitations had run so he could not be prosecuted for treason, he openly and brazenly not only admitted but proclaimed that he had been a member of the Communist Party * * * that while working for the State Department he stole a vast number of secret documents * * * and furnished these documents to the Russian spy ring of which he was a part.

You will recall last spring there was held in New York what was known as the World Peace Conference—a conference which was labeled by the State Department and Mr. Truman as the sounding board for Communist propaganda and a front for Russia. Dr. Harlow Shapley was the chairman of that conference. Interestingly enough, according to the new release put out by the Department in July, the Secretary of State appointed Shapley on a commission which acts as liaison between UNESCO and the State Department.

This, ladies and gentlemen, gives you somewhat of a picture of the type of individuals who have been helping to shape our foreign policy. In my opinion the State Department, which is one of the most important government departments, is thoroughly infested with Communists.

I have in my hand 57 cases of individuals who would appear to be either card carrying members or certainly loyal to the Communist Party, but who nevertheless are still helping to shape our foreign policy.

One thing to remember in discussing the Communists in our Government is that we are not dealing with spies who get 30 pieces of silver to steal the blueprints of a new weapon. We are dealing with a far more sinister type of activity because it permits the enemy to guide and shape our policy.

In that connection, I would like to read to you very briefly from the testimony of Larry E. Kerley, a man who was with the counter espionage section of the FBI for eight years. And keep in mind as I read this to you that at the time he is speaking, there was in the State Department Alger Hiss, the convicted Alger Hiss; John Service, the man whom the FBI picked up for espionage—

And for turning over secret documents—Julian Wadleigh, who brazenly admitted he was a spy and wrote newspaper articles in regard thereto, plus hundreds of other bad security risks.

The FBI, I may add, has done an outstanding job, as all persons in Washington, Democrats and Republicans alike, agree. If J. Edgar Hoover had a free hand, we would not be plagued by Hisses and Wadleighs in high positions of power in the State Department. The FBI has only power to investigate.

Here is what the FFI man said.

In accordance with instructions of the State Department to the FBI, the FBI was not even permitted to open an espionage case against any Russia suspect without State Department approval.

In other words they could not afford to let the whole ring which extended into the State Department be exposed.

This brings us down to the case of one Alger Hiss who is important not as an individual any more, but rather because he is so representative of a group in the State Department. It is unnecessary to go over the sordid events showing how he sold out the Nation which had given him so much. Those are rather fresh in all of our minds.

However, it should be remembered that the facts in regard to his connection with this international Communist spy ring were made known to the then Under Secretary of State Berle three days after Hitler and Stalin signed the Russo-German alliance pact. At that time one Whittaker Chambers—who was also part of the spy ring—apparently decided that with Russia on Hitler's side, he could no longer betray our Nation to Russia. He gave Under Secretary of State Berle—and this is all a matter of record—practically all, if not more, of the facts upon which Hiss's conviction was based.

Under Secretary Berle promptly contacted Dean Acheson and received word in return that Acheson (and I quote) "could vouch for Hiss absolutely"—at which time the matter was dropped. And this, you understand, was at a time when Russia was an ally of Germany. This condition existed while Russia and Germany were invading and dismembering Poland, and while the Communist groups here were screaming "warmonger" at the United States for their support of the allied nations.

Again in 1943, the FBI had occasion to investigate the facts surrounding Hiss's contacts with the Russian spy ring. But even after that FBI report was submitted, nothing was done.

Then late in 1948—on August 5—when the Un-American Activities Committee called Alger Hiss to give an accounting, President Truman at once issued a Presidential directive ordering all Government agencies to refuse to turn over any information whatsoever in regard to the Communist activities of any Government employee to a congressional committee.

Incidentally, even after Hiss was convicted . . . it is interesting to note that the President still labeled the exposé of Hiss as a "red herring."

If time permitted, it might be well to go into detail about the fact that Hiss was Roosevelt's chief adviser at Yalta when Roosevelt was admittedly in ill health and tired physically and mentally * * * and when, according to the Secretary of State, Hiss and Gromyko drafted the report on the conference.

According to the then Secretary of State Stettinius, here are some of the things that Hiss helped to decide at Yalta. (1) The establishment of a European High Commission; (2) the treatment of Germany—this you will recall was the conference at which it was decided that we would occupy Berlin with Russia occupying an area completely circling the city, which, as you know, resulted in the Berlin airlift which cost 31 American lives; (3) the Polish question; (4) the relationship between UNRRA and the Soviet; (5) the rights of Americans on control commissions of Rumania, Bulgaria, and Hungary; (6) Iran; (7) China—here's where we gave away Manchuria; (8) Turkish Straits question; (9) International trusteeships; (10) Korea.

Of the results of this conference, Arthur Bliss Lane of the State Department had this to say: "As I glanced over the document, I could not believe my eyes. To me, almost every line spoke of a surrender to Stalin."

As you hear this story of high treason, I know that you are saying to yourself, "Well, why doesn't the Congress do something about it?" Actually, ladies and gentlemen, one of the important reasons for the graft, the corruption, the dishonesty, the disloyalty, the treason in high Government positions—one of the most important reasons why this continues is a lack of moral uprising on the part of the 140,000,000 American people. In the light of history, however, this is not hard to explain.

It is the result of an emotional hang-over and a temporary moral lapse which follows every war. It is the apathy to evil which people who have been subjected to the tremendous evils of war feel. As the people of the world see mass murder, the destruction of defenseless and innocent people, and all of the crime and lack of morals which go with war, they become numb and apathetic. It has always been thus after war.

However, the morals of our people have not been destroyed. They still exist. This cloak of numbness and apathy has only needed a spark to rekindle them. Happily, this spark has finally been supplied.

As you know, very recently the Secretary of State proclaimed his loyalty to a man guilty of what has always been considered as the most abominable of all crimes—of being a traitor to the people who gave him a position of great trust. The Secretary of State in attempting to justify his continued devotion to the man who sold out the Christian world to the atheistic world, referred to Christ's Sermon on the Mount as a justification and reason therefor, and the reaction of the American people to this would have made the heart of Abraham Lincoln happy.

When this pompous diplomat in striped pants, with a phony British accent, proclaimed to the American people that Christ on the Mount endorsed communism, high treason, and betrayal of a sacred trust, the blasphemy was so great that it awakened the dormant indignation of the American people.

He has lighted the spark which is resulting in a moral uprising and will end only when the whole sorry mess of twisted, warped thinkers are swept from the national scene so that we may have a new birth of national honesty and decency in Government.

Document 21.9 Declaration of Conscience (1950)

Margaret Chase Smith was a Senator from Maine and like McCarthy a member of the Republican Party. In 1950, however, she wrote a public letter to the *New York Times* expressing her opposition to McCarthy's activities and tactics.

Declaration of Conscience

Margaret Chase Smith

I would like to speak briefly and simply about a serious national condition. It is a national feeling of fear and frustration that could result in national suicide and the end of everything that we Americans hold dear. It is a condition that comes from the lack of effective leadership in either the Legislative Branch or the Executive Branch of our Government.

That leadership is so lacking that serious and responsible proposals are being made that national advisory commissions be appointed to provide such critically needed leadership. . . .

I speak as a Republican. I speak as a woman. I speak as a United States Senator. I speak as an American. . . .

I think that it is high time that we remembered that we have sworn to uphold and defend the Constitution. I think that it is high time that we remembered that the Constitution, as amended, speaks not only of the freedom of speech but also of trial by jury instead of trial by accusation. . . .

Those of us who shout the loudest about Americanism in making character assassinations are all too frequently those who, by our own words and acts, ignore some of the basic principles of Americanism:

From *The New York Times*, June 2, 1950. Reprinted with permission.

The right to criticize;

The right to hold unpopular beliefs;

The right to protest;

The right of independent thought.

The exercise of these rights should not cost one single American citizen his reputation or his right to a livelihood nor should he be in danger of losing his reputation or livelihood merely because he happens to know someone who holds unpopular beliefs. Who of us doesn't? Otherwise none of us could call our souls our own. Otherwise thought control would have set in.

The American people are sick and tired of being afraid to speak their minds lest they be politically smeared as "Communists" or "Fascists" by their opponents. Freedom of speech is not what it used to be in America. It has been so abused by some that it is not exercised by others. . . .

Today our country is being psychologically divided by the confusion and the suspicions that are bred in the United States Senate to spread like cancerous tentacles of "know nothing, suspect everything" attitudes. Today we have a Democratic Administration that has developed a mania for loose spending and loose programs. History is repeating itself—and the Republican Party again has the opportunity to emerge as the champion of unity and prudence.

The record of the present Democratic Administration has provided us with sufficient campaign issues without the necessity of resorting to political smears. America is rapidly losing its position as leader of the world simply because the Democratic Administration has pitifully failed to provide effective leadership. . . .

Yet to displace it with a Republican regime embracing a philosophy that lacks political integrity or intellectual honesty would prove equally disastrous to this nation. The nation sorely needs a Republican victory. But I don't want to see the Republican Party ride to political victory on the Four Horsemen of Calumny—Fear, Ignorance, Bigotry, and Smear.

I doubt if the Republican Party could—simply because I don't believe the American people will uphold any political party that puts political exploitation above national interest. Surely we Republicans aren't that desperate for victory. . . .

As a United States Senator, I am not proud of the way in which the Senate has been made a publicity platform for irresponsible sensationalism. I am not proud of the reckless abandon in which unproved charges have been hurled from this side of the aisle. I am not proud of the obviously staged, undignified countercharges that have been attempted in retaliation from the other side of the aisle.

I don't like the way the Senate has been made a rendezvous for vilification, for selfish political gain at the sacrifice of individual reputations and national unity. I am not proud of the way we smear outsiders from the Floor of the Senate and hide behind the cloak of congressional immunity and still place ourselves beyond criticism on the Floor of the Senate.

As an American, I am shocked at the way Republicans and Democrats alike are playing directly into the Communist design of "confuse, divide, and conquer." As an American, I don't want a Democratic Administration "whitewash" or "cover-up" any more than I want a Republican smear or witch hunt.

As an American, I condemn a Republican "Fascist" just as much as I condemn a Democrat "Communist." I condemn a Democrat "fascist" just as much as I condemn a Republican "Communist." They are equally dangerous to you and me and to our country. As an American, I want to see our nation recapture the strength and unity it once had when we fought the enemy instead of ourselves.

It is with these thoughts that I have drafted what I call a "Declaration of Conscience." I am gratified that [six Republican senators] have concurred in that declaration and have authorized me to announce their concurrence.

Document 21.10 McCarthy's Charges Rebutted

In 1950, after McCarthy began making his charges, the Senate Foreign Relations Committee created a subcommittee to investigate these charges. The subcommittee was chaired by Senator Millard Tydings, a Democrat. Since McCarthy, a Republican, had charged that the Executive Branch under President Truman, a Democrat, was riddled with Communists, McCarthy's charges quickly became an issue between the parties. Tyding's committee released a report highly critical of McCarthy's tactics and his accusations.

McCarthy's Charges Rebutted

Senate Foreign Relations Committee

The Facts Behind the Charge of "Whitewash"

Seldom, if ever, in the history of congressional investigations has a committee been subjected to an organized campaign of vilification and abuse comparable to that with which we have been confronted throughout this inquiry. This campaign has been so acute and so obviously designed to confuse and confound the American people that an analysis of the factors responsible therefor is indicated.

The first of these factors was the necessity of creating the impression that our inquiry was not thorough and sincere in order to camouflage the fact that the charges made by Senator McCarthy were groundless and that the Senate and the American people had been deceived. No sooner were hearings started than the cry of "whitewash" was raised along with the chant "investigate the charges and not McCarthy." This chant we have heard morning, noon, and night for almost four months from certain quarters for readily perceptible motives. Interestingly, had we elected to investigate Senator McCarthy, there would have been ample basis therefor, since we have been reliably informed that at the time he made the charges initially he had no information whatever to support them, and, furthermore, it early appeared that in securing Senate Resolution 231 a fraud had been perpetrated upon the Senate of the United States.

From the very outset of our inquiry, Senator McCarthy has sought to leave the impression that the subcommittee has been investigating him and not "disloyalty in the State Department." The reason for the Senator's concern is now apparent. He had no facts to support his wild and baseless charges, and lived in mortal fear that this situation would be exposed.

Few people, cognizant of the truth in even an elementary way, have, in the absence of political partisanship, placed any credence in the hit-and-run tactics of Senator McCarthy. He has stooped to a new low in his cavalier disregard of the facts.

The simple truth is that in making his speech at Wheeling [West Virginia],** Senator McCarthy was talking of a subject and circumstances about which he knew nothing. His extreme and irresponsible statements called for emergency measures. As Senator Wherry told Emmanuel S. Larsen, "Oh, Mac has gone out on a limb and kind of made a fool of himself and we have to back him up now." Starting with nothing, Senator McCarthy plunged headlong forward, desperately seeking to develop some information, which colored with distortion and fanned by a blaze of bias, would forestall a day of reckoning.

Certain elements rallied to his support, particularly those who ostensibly fight communism by adopting the vile methods of the Communists themselves and in so doing actually hinder the fight of all right-minded people who detest and abhor communism in all its manifestations. We cannot, however, destroy one evil by the adoption of another. Senator McCarthy and McCarthyism have been exposed for what they are—and the sight is not a pretty one. . . .

Another consideration is the oft-repeated and natural reaction of many good people that goes something like this—"Well, there must be something to the charges, or a United States Senator would never have made them!" The simple truth now is apparent, that a conclusion based on this premise, while normally true, is here erroneous; for we have the amazing spectacle of a United States Senator having made such charges with no facts or with discredited allegations of fact to support them.

Still, a third consideration has been the readiness of many people to believe charges of disloyalty in the State Department by reason of the Alger Hiss case. In this regard, we have been appalled by the studied effort to inject Hiss's name into our proceedings without any basis whatsoever therefor. The Hiss case was indeed despicable. The facts are, however, that Alger Hiss was convicted for perjury in connection with his associations with Whittaker Chambers back in 1938. To seek to translate that case to a setting 12 years later and employ it as a basis for charges of widespread disloyalty today in

---

Senate Committee on Foreign Relations, 81st Congress, 1950.

*A famous speech where McCarthy claimed that the State Department had 205 known Communists as employees.

the State Department is not convincing of anything to thinking men and women.

A . . . final consideration has been the vague uneasiness of many Americans concerning the ascendancy of the Communists in China and the decline of the Nationalist Government. In such a setting, there was "fertile ground" to receive any charges to indicate that perhaps someone, somewhere in our own State Department may have been responsible for the Chinese situation. To those who would know the true facts concerning American diplomacy in China, we earnestly recommend to your reading the so-called white paper on China, being the story of our relations with China during the period 1944 to 1949, based on the files of the State Department. . . .

General Observations

In concluding our report, we are constrained to make observations which we regard as fundamental.

It is, of course, clearly apparent that the charges of Communist infiltration of and influence upon the State Department are false. This knowledge is reassuring to all Americans whose faith has been temporarily shaken in the security of their Government by perhaps the most nefarious campaign of untruth in the history of our Republic.

We believe, however, that this knowledge and assurance, while important, will prove ultimately of secondary significance in contemplating the salutary aspects of our investigation. For we believe that inherent in the charges that have been made and the sinister campaign to give them ostensible verity are lessons from which the American people will find inspiration for a rededication to the principles and ideals that have made this Nation great.

We have seen the technique of the "Big Lie," elsewhere employed by the totalitarian dictator with devastating success, utilized here for the first time on a sustained basis in our history. We have seen how, through repetition and shifting untruths, it is possible to delude great numbers of people.

We have seen the character of private citizens and of Government employees virtually destroyed by public condemnation on the basis of gossip, distortion, hearsay, and deliberate untruths. By the mere fact of their associations with a few persons of alleged questionable proclivities an effort has been made to place the stigma of disloyalty upon individuals, some of whom are little people whose only asset is their character and devotion to duty and country. This has been done without the slightest vestige of respect for even the most elementary rules of evidence or fair play or, indeed, common decency. Indeed, we have seen an effort not merely to establish guilt by association but guilt by accusation alone. The spectacle is one we would expect in a totalitarian nation where the rights of the individual are crushed beneath the juggernaut of statism and oppression; it has no place in America where government exists to serve our people, not to destroy them.

We have seen an effort to inflame the American people with a wave of hysteria and fear on an unbelievable scale in this free Nation. Were this campaign founded in truth it would be questionable enough; where it is fraught with falsehood from beginning to end, its reprehensible and contemptible character defies adequate condemnation.

We sincerely believe that charges of the character which have been made in this case seriously impair the efforts of our agencies of Government to combat the problem of subversion. Furthermore, extravagant allegations, which cannot be proved and are not subject to proof, have the inevitable effect of dulling the awareness of all Americans to the true menace of communism. . . .

Communism represents the most diabolical concept ever designed to enslave mankind. Its stock and trade are deception, falsehood, and hate. The one hope of communism's success is to divide our people at home and our allies abroad. The false charges made in this case have succeeded in accomplishing to a great degree what the Communists themselves have been unable to do. These charges have created distrust and suspicion at home and raised serious doubts abroad. We can never hope to preserve for posterity the American dream of freedom by adopting totalitarian methods as an excuse to preserve that freedom. Our greatest weapon against communism is truth. If we lose that weapon, we shall have gone far toward that fate which has already brought sorrow, death, and degradation to millions of people upon this earth.

Module XXI

Questions for Study and Critical Thinking

1. What does Kennan believe will be the basic relationship between the United States and the Soviet Union?

2. What Soviet beliefs determine its policy toward the outside world?

3. What does Kennan recommend that the United States do to counter the Soviet Union?

4. What, according to Wallace, will result from American policy toward the Soviet Union?

5. What, according to Wallace, will atomic weapons lead to? Why?

6. According to Wallace, what does Russian history teach Soviet leaders? How does Wallace's view of Russian history differ from Kennan's?

7. According to Wallace, what U.S. actions would lead the Soviets to believe that the United States has aggressive designs on the Soviet Union? Do you think he was right? Why, or why not?

8. What, according to Wallace, should American policy do? Was he correct?

9. What, according to Clifford, is the Soviet threat to the United States?

10. Why does Clifford maintain that it would be "dangerous to conclude that hope of international peace lies only in 'accord,' 'mutual understanding,' or 'solidarity' with the Soviet Union"?

11. According to Clifford, what should American policy be toward the Soviet Union? Why?

12. What, in your own words, is the Truman Doctrine?

13. In your opinion, who was right–Kennan, Clifford, and Truman, or Wallace?

14. What danger was the Marshall Plan designed to avert?

15. What, according to Truman, is the goal of communist forces in Asia?

16. What does Truman say the U.S. is trying to avoid? Why did he oppose the suggestions of bombing China and helping Chinese Nationalist forces invade China?

17. What recommendations had MacArthur made, which the administration rejected?

18. In retrospect, who do you think was right, MacArthur or Truman? Why?

19. According to McCarthy, what is the principal means by which the United States was currently being weakened?

20. Who were the key people, according to McCarthy, who were weakening the United States?

21. What does Margaret Chase Smith criticize among Republicans?

22. What did the Senate Judiciary Committee say about McCarthy's charges?

23. Who do you think was right, McCarthy or his critics?

Module XXII

1950s America

Introduction

For many people, the 1950s is a mythical period. To those who have watched reruns of family TV comedies from that decade, it often appears a long-gone but idyllic world, in which marriages stayed together, women stayed home, and men, after a hard day of providing for their families, gently guided everyone to peace and tranquility. Others look upon it as an age of conformity, boredom, and lack of creativity. Nothing, of course, is as simple as either of these stereotypes. Even at the time, different views collided. On one hand, some celebrated the new prosperity and the acceptance of traditional values. On the other, some denounced the period as oppressive, conformist, and unjust.

The Fifties were a period of unprecedented prosperity. After long years of depression and war, they offered an apparent return to normality, which Americans embraced. Many welcomed the new houses built in suburbs across the country. Buying these houses was easier than ever before thanks to the federal government, which guaranteed loans and lowered down payments through Federal Housing Administration (FHA) and Veterans Administration (VA) programs. The VA program, in fact, allowed veterans to get loans with no down payment. Most families were also able to afford a car, sometimes two, and new appliances such as television sets and garbage disposals.

But below the surface tensions troubled the decade. Despite injunctions to "togetherness," marriage and family life often failed to meet expectations. Many women felt vaguely restless in their roles as housewives, even though they felt guilty about feeling restless. Men working for large corporations often found their jobs stultifying. Rigid racial segregation continued in the South. And many critics claimed that this was a generation without a social conscience. The selections in this chapter will let you read both sides of these issues, in the hope that you will be able to form your own coherent view of this decade.

Document 22.1 Up from the Potato Fields

Almost everyone connects the 1950s with the huge tracts of "ranch" or Cape Cod style houses with which builders in the 1950s filled the rapidly-expanding suburbs. The most famous of these builders was William Levitt, and the most famous tract was his Levittown on Long Island, New York. The houses, and those of most other builders, were inexpensive but were separated from neighboring houses, providing front, back, and side yards. Even though they were monotonously similar, owners quickly began altering them to suit their own tastes. The selection below describes Levittown.

Up from the Potato Fields

Time Magazine

On 1,200 flat acres of potato farmland near Hicksville, Long Island, an army of trucks sped over new-laid roads. Every 100 feet, the trucks stopped and dumped identical bundles of lumber, pipes, bricks, shingles and copper tubing—nearly as neatly packaged as loaves from a bakery. Near the bundles, giant machines with an endless chain of buckets ate into the earth, taking just 13 minutes to dig a narrow, four-foot trench around a 25-by-32 ft. rectangle. Then came more trucks, loaded with cement, and laid a four-inch foundation for a house in the rectangle.

After the machines came the men. On nearby slabs already dry, they worked in crews of two and three, laying bricks, raising studs, nailing lath, painting, sheathing, shingling. Each crew did its special job, then hurried on to the next site. Under the skilled combination of men and machines, new houses rose faster than Jack ever built them; a new one was finished every 15 minutes.

Three years ago, little potatoes had sprouted from these fields. Now there were 10,600 houses inhabited by more than 40,000 people, a community almost as big as 96-year-old Poughkeepsie, N.Y., Plainfield, N.J., or Chelsea, Mass. Its name: Levittown.

Levittown is known largely for one reason: it epitomizes the revolution which has brought mass production to the housing industry. Its creator, Long Island's Levitt & Sons, Inc., has become the biggest builder of houses in the U.S.

Super-Selling. The houses in Levittown, which sell for a uniform price of $7,990, cannot be mistaken for castles. Each has a sharp-angled roof and a picture window, radiant heating in the floor, 12-by-16 ft. living room, bath, kitchen, two bedrooms on the first floor, and an "expansion attic" which can be converted into two more bedrooms and bath. The kitchen has a refrigerator, stove and Bendix washer; the living room a fireplace and a built-in Admiral television set.

The Great Change. To a man, Bill Levitt and all the other builders know exactly whom to thank for the boom and the steadily expanding market. Said one San Francisco builder last week: "If it weren't for the Government, the boom would end overnight."

At war's end, when the U.S. desperately needed 5,000,000 houses, the nation had two choices: the Federal Government could try to build the houses itself, or it could pave the way for private industry to do the job, by making available billions in credit. The U.S. wisely handed the job to private industry, got 4,000,000 new units built since the war, probably faster and cheaper than could have been done any other way.

The Government has actually spent little cash itself. But by insuring loans up to 95% of the value of a house, the Federal Housing Administration made it easy for a builder to borrow the money with which to build low-cost houses. The Government made it just as easy for the buyer by liberally insuring his mortgage. Under a new housing act signed three months ago, the purchase terms on low-cost houses with Government-guaranteed mortgages were so liberalized that in many cases buying a house is now as easy as renting it. The new terms: 5% down (nothing down for veterans) and 30 years to pay. Thus an ex-G.I. could buy a Levitt house with no down payment and installments of $56 a month.

The countless new housing projects made possible by this financial easy street are changing the way of life of millions of U.S. citizens, who are realizing for the first time the great American dream of owning their own home. No longer must young married couples plan to start living in an apartment, saving for the distant day when they can buy a house. Now they can do it more easily than they can buy a $2,000 car on the installment plan.

Fountain of Youth. Like its counterparts across the land, Levittown is an entirely new kind of community. Despite its size, it is not incorporated, thus has no mayor, no police force, nor any of the other traditional city officers of its own. It has no movies, no nightclubs and only three bars (all in the community shopping centers).

And Levittown has very few old people. Few of its more than 40,000 residents are past 35; of some 8,000 children, scarcely 900 are more than seven years old. In front of almost every house along Levittown's 100 miles of winding streets sits a tricycle or a baby carriage. In Levittown, all activity stops from 12 to 2 in the afternoon; that is nap time. Said one Levittowner last week, "Everyone is so young that sometimes it's hard to remember how to get along with older people."

The community has an almost antiseptic air. Levittown streets, which have such fanciful names as Satellite, Horizon, Haymaker, are bare and flat as hospital corridors. Like a hospital, Levittown has rules all its own. Fences are not allowed (though here and there a home-owner has broken the rule). The plot of grass around each house must be cut at least once a week; if not, Bill Levitt's men mow the grass and send the bill. Wash cannot be hung out to dry on an ordinary clothesline; it must be arranged on rotary, removable drying racks and then not on weekends or on holidays.

There are perquisites as well as rules. For the young children there are parks and countless playgrounds. For the old folks (the 5- to 35-year-olds) there are baseball diamonds, handball courts, six huge 75-by-125 ft. swimming pools, plus 25-by-75 ft. kiddy pools, shopping centers and 60-odd fraternal clubs and veterans' organizations.

"The Old Freeze." Actually, Levittown's uniformity is more apparent than real. Though most of the incomes are about the same (average: about \$3,800), Levittowners come from all classes, all walks of life. Eighty percent of the men commute to their jobs in Manhattan, many sharing their transportation costs through car pools. Their jobs, as in any other big community, range from baking to banking, from teaching to preaching. Levittown has also developed its own unique way of keeping up with the Joneses. Some Levittowners buy a new house every year, as soon as the new model is on the market. . . .

How Long? By 1951 Levitt & Sons expect to build another 10,000 Levittown houses. But whether the Levitts, or all of the other builders, will build as many houses as they plan depends on how long the housing shortage—and the housing boom—lasts. Last week, the Department of Commerce estimated that about two-thirds of the pent-up housing demand has already been filled. However, said the department, the "remaining backlog is still large and appears to be sufficient to warrant construction close to the recent yearly rates for [another] three years."

That seemed a conservative prediction, if the big builders like Levitt could keep on thinking up new mass-production tricks, and small merchant builders could adapt more of them to their operations, thus broadening the market for small, cheap houses. By stabilizing the construction industry, builders could offer more permanent work to labor, and thus eliminate the cause of the featherbedding that now adds so much to building costs. And as efficiency increased, the mass builders might also find they could economically supply some of the individuality that their houses now lack.

Document 22.2 What TV Is Doing to America

Television was the great symbol of the Fifties, the first decade in which most Americans had a television set. In many homes a television set, enclosed in massive pieces of wooden furniture, formed the focal point of the living room. TV, however, aroused conflicting opinions about its possible effects. Critics worried about the danger of spending hours a day in front of the set. And despite programs that fifty years later seem amazingly wholesome, the critics harbored concerns about their content. The following article from *U.S. News and World Report*, a conservative news magazine, illustrates this criticism.

What TV Is Doing to America

U.S. News and World Report

The impact of TV on this country has been so massive that Americans are still wondering what hit them. Has the effect been good or bad? What permanent effects on the American way of life may be expected? These and other questions are considered in this survey.

Probably there are some people in the U.S. who have never seen a television program, but you would have to go into the hills to find them. Two out of three U.S. families now own their own sets or are paying for them. In 32 million homes, the dials are flicked on and off, from channel to channel, at least 100 million times between 8 a.m. and midnight.

Everywhere, children sit with eyes glued to screens—for three to four hours a day on the average. Their parents use up even more time mesmerized by this new marvel—or monster. They have spent 15 billion dollars to look since 1946.

Now, after nearly 10 years of TV, people are asking: "What hath TV wrought? What is this thing doing to us?"

Solid answers to this question are very hard to get. Pollsters, sociologists, doctors, teachers, the TV people themselves come up with more contradictions than conclusions whenever they start asking.

But almost everybody has an opinion and wants to air it.

What do these opinions add up to? People have strong views. Here are some widely held convictions, both against and for television:

That TV has kept people from going places and doing things, from reading, from thinking for themselves. Yet it is said also that TV has taken viewers vicariously into strange and fascinating spots and situations, brought distinguished and enchanting people into their living rooms, given them a new perspective.

That TV has interfered with schooling, kept children from learning to read and write, weakened their eyesight and softened their muscles. But there are those who hold that TV has made America's youngsters more "knowing" about life, more curious, given them a bigger vocabulary. Teaching by TV, educators say, is going to be a big thing in the future.

That TV arouses morbid emotions in children, glorifies violence, causes juvenile crime—that it starts domestic quarrels, tends to loosen morals and make people lazy and sodden. However, it keeps families together at home, provides a realm of cheap entertainment never before available, stimulates new lines of conversation.

That TV is giving the U.S. an almost primitive language, made up of grunts, whistles, standardized wisecracks and cliches—that it is turning the average American into a stereotype. Yet it is breaking down regional barriers and prejudices, ironing out accents, giving people in one part of the country a better understanding of people in other parts. TV is [making] politics "a rich man's game," turning statesmanship into a circus, handing demagogues a new weapon. But it is giving Americans their first good look at the inside of their Government, letting them judge the people they elect by sight as well as by sound and fury.

That TV has distorted and debased salesmanship, haunting people with singing "commercials" and slogans. However, because or in spite of TV, people are buying more things they never before thought they needed or wanted.

These are just some of the comments that people are making about TV. The experts say that it probably will be another generation before there is a firm basis of knowledge about television's impact on America.

Today's TV child, the boy or girl who has a TV set in his home, is too young to analyze his feelings. Older people, despite their frequent vehemence about TV, are still far from sure whether they have an Aladdin's lamp or hold a bear by the tail, Goliath with tubes. One thing you can be sure about. TV, a giant at 10, continues to grow like nobody's business. Here are some figures and comparisons: The 15 billion dollars that the U.S. people have invested in TV sets and repairs since the war is 15 per cent more than the country spent for new school and college buildings. About a billion more has gone into TV stations and equipment.

TV-viewing time is going *up*, not down, latest surveys show. This explodes the theory that people would taper off on television "once they got used to it."

"Pull" of popular TV programs is believed to be very effective. Pollsters report that three times as many people will leave a meal to answer questions at the door as will get up to abandon "Dragnet."

The number of families holding out against TV is declining to a small fraction. There still are 16 million families without sets, but most of these families either can't pay for sets or else live out of range of TV signals.

On an average evening, twice as many set owners will be watching TV as are engaged in any other form of entertainment or leisure activity, such as movie-going, card playing, or reading. Seven out of 10 American children watch TV between 6 and 8 o'clock most evenings.

Analysts are intrigued by the evidence that adults, not children, are the real television fans. The newest trend in viewing habits is a rise in the number of housewives who watch TV in the morning. One out of five with a set now watches a morning show with regularity.

What is it? Why do people want TV? A $67.50-per-week shoe repairman in San Francisco puts it about as plainly as anyone can. "TV," he says, "is the only amusement I can afford." That was the reason he gave for paying four weeks' wages for his set.

The cobbler's comment explains TV's basic lure. It is free entertainment except for the cost of set, and repairs and electricity. It becomes so absorbing that a broken set is a family catastrophe. People will pay to have the set fixed before they will pay the milk bill, if necessary.

What does TV do to people? What do people do with TV? The researchers are digging into these questions all the time. In general, they come to theories, rather than conclusions. There are three main theories:

THEORY "A": This is widely held by people whose professions bring them into close contact with juveniles—judges, district attorneys, police officers, ministers. It assumes that TV is bound to be affecting the American mind and character because it soaks up one to five hours a day or more that used to be spent in outdoor play, in games requiring reasoning and imagination, or in reading, talking, radio listening, or movie-going.

Even the more passive of these pursuits, the theory runs, required more exercise of brain than does TV watching. Then, too, many TV programs, the theorists say, are violent or in questionable taste.

Net effect, according to these people, is a wasting away or steady decline in certain basic skills among American youngsters. Children lose the ability to read, forfeit their physical dexterity, strength and initiative.

Some see a definite connection between TV and juvenile delinquency. The Kefauver Subcommittee of the Senate Judiciary Committee has just explored this aspect. It stated: "Members of the subcommittee share the concern of a large segment of the thinking public for the implications of the impact of this medium [television] . . . upon the ethical and cultural standards of the youth of America. It has been unable to gather proof of a direct causal relationship between the viewing of acts of crime and violence and the actual performance of criminal deeds. It has not, however, found irrefutable evidence that young people may not be negatively influenced in their present-day behavior by the saturated exposure they now receive to pictures and drama based on an underlying theme of lawlessness and crime which depict human violence."

THEORY "B": Mainly held by sociologists, communications economists, pollsters. This is that television is changing the American mind and character, although nobody knows for sure just how. The evidence is too fragmentary. The analysts are disturbed by some aspects of TV's effect on viewers. Some think TV is conditioning Americans to be "other directed," that is, getting their ideas from someone else. The early American, by contrast, is supposed to have been "inner directed," a man who thought things out for himself on the basis of his own reasoning.

A fancy name for this suspected effect of TV is "narcotic dysfunction." This means that more and more men come home in the evening, drop into a chair in front of the TV set after supper and slip into a dream world of unreality.

However, the same researchers confess that TV can have a broadening influence, bringing to the masses a taste of the arts and sciences, a peek into government that they couldn't get any other way.

THEORY "C": This is what the TV people themselves like to think. It is that television is rapidly becoming "one more service" to the U.S. public, another medium such as newspapers, magazines, radio. Some people watch TV a lot, others very little. Most people want a set around, but some don't lean on it.

The TV people minimize the idea that TV is dominating American life. It is almost as if they were afraid their own baby is getting too big. What they usually say is that the people who allow their lives to be controlled by television were similarly dominated by radio and the movies—and that they are only a small minority.

The TV habit. What do the theorists base their theories on? What have they found out about the place of the TV set in American life?

Many studies have been made of the "TV habit." Latest of these indicates that TV viewing reaches a peak just after a set enters a home, then falls off rather sharply. Next, viewing begins to rise again in the average home, building up, evidently, toward a new peak that is not yet measured.

The A. C. Nielsen Company, a market research organization that attaches mechanical recorders to sets in private homes, finds this: During the 12 months ended in April, 1955, average use per day of TV sets was 4 hours and 50 minutes. That was up 4 per cent over the year before . . .

Other studies indicate that women watch TV more than men do. Children, contrary to general impression, watch TV less than adults in the average home. Persons low in income, education or job status as a rule spend more time in front of TV sets than those with more money and education.

What's on TV. What do people get on TV? What do they want? Three out of every four TV programs are entertainment shows. . . . In a typical week of the peak TV season, in January of last year, crime, comedy, variety and Western shows accounted for 42.7 per cent of all TV program time on New York City screens. News accounted for 6.1 per cent of TV time—about the same share of time as was taken by quiz, stunt and contest shows. Other informational types of TV shows, such as interviews, weather reports, travelogues, children's instructional programs and cooking classes, got 16.2 per cent of the time.

Rating figures tend to show that people are getting just about what they want, in the opinion of the broadcasting industry. According to the "popularity" ratings of top shows, comedy and drama and straight entertainment are outpulling everything else.

What about information? The popularity cards seem to indicate the reaction is a stifled yawn. In a two-week period last June, when two comedy programs, the "George Gobel Show" and "I Love Lucy," were at the top of the list, each reaching more than 13 million homes, the top-ranking informational programs were way down the line. The "March of Medicine," for example, was No. 62, reaching 6.57 million homes; "Meet the Press" was No. 150, getting to 1.14 million families.

Studies also have been made of how long various programs hold their audiences. Love and adventure performances, it develops, will keep about 85 per cent of the audience to the end. By contrast, the most gripping historical sketches hold only 65 per cent, and many hold less than one third of their starting viewers. Informational programs, again, rank near the bottom in "holding power."

Television critics, who write about TV programs in newspapers and magazines, are frequently harsh in their remarks about violence, sadism, bad taste on the screen. However, Dallas W. Smythe, a professor of communications economics at the University of Illinois, analyzed New York City programs for 1955 and concludes that programs which critics liked best seldom drew the biggest audiences.

The public is fickle. Top rating is hard to hold. The viewers tire rapidly of a particular show unless the producers manage to come up with fresh material, new appeals.

Document 22.3 The "Humble Role of Housewife"

Adlai Stevenson was the Democratic governor of Illinois, who ran for the presidency twice, in 1952 and 1956, losing both times to Dwight D. Eisenhower. An intelligent and witty man, many people considered him too intellectual to be elected president. In 1955 he delivered the graduation address at Smith College, an elite women's college. As an intellectual and a liberal, Stevenson enunciated the prevalent view of women's roles widely held by sophisticated Americans during the period.

The "Humble Role of Housewife"

Adlai Stevenson

I think there is much you can do about our crisis in the humble role of housewife. The peoples of the West are still struggling with the problems of a free society and just now are in dire trouble. For to create a free society is at all times a precarious and audacious experiment. Its bedrock is the concept of man as an end in himself. But violent pressures are constantly battering away at this concept, reducing man once again to subordinate status, limiting his range of choice, abrogating his responsibility and returning him to his primitive status of anonymity in the social group. I think you can be more helpful in identifying, isolating and combating these pressures, this virus, than you perhaps realize.

Let me put it this way: individualism has promoted technological advance, technology promoted increased specialization, and specialization promoted an ever closer economic interdependence between specialties.

As the old order disintegrated into this confederation of narrow specialties, each pulling in the direction of its particular interest, the individual person tended to become absorbed literally by his particular function in society. Having sacrificed wholeness of mind and breadth of outlook to the demands of their specialties, individuals no longer responded to social stimuli as total human beings; rather they reacted in partial ways as members of an economic class or industry or profession whose concern was with some limited self-interest.

Thus this typical Western man, or typical Western husband, operates well in the realm of means. . . . But outside his specialty, in the realm of ends, he is apt to operate poorly or not at all. And this neglect of the cultivation of more mature values can only mean that his life, and the life of the society he determines, will lack valid purpose, however busy and even profitable it may be.

And here's where you come in: to restore valid, meaningful purpose to life in your home; to beware of instinctive group reaction to the forces which play upon you and yours, to watch for and arrest the constant gravitational pulls to which we are all exposed—your workaday husband especially—in our specialized, fragmented society, that tend to widen the breach between reason and emotion, between means and ends.

And let me also remind you that you will live, most of you, in an environment in which "facts," the data of the senses, are glorified, and values—judgments—are assigned inferior status as mere "matters of opinion." It is an environment in which art is often regarded as an adornment of civilization rather than a vital element of it, while philosophy is not only neglected but deemed faintly disreputable because "it never gets you anywhere." Even religion, you will find, commands a lot of earnest allegiance that is more verbal than real, more formal than felt.

You may be hitched to one of these creatures we call "Western man" and I think part of your job is to keep him Western, to keep him truly purposeful, to keep him whole. In short—while I have had very little experience as a wife or mother—I think one of the biggest jobs for many of you will be to frustrate the crushing and corrupting effects of specialization, to integrate means and ends, to develop that balanced tension of mind and spirit which can be properly called "integrity."

This assignment for you, as wives and mothers, has great advantages. In the first place, it is home work—you can do it in the living-room with a baby in your lap or in the kitchen with a can opener in your hand. If you're really clever, maybe you can even practice your saving arts on that unsuspecting man while he's watching television!

And, secondly, it is important work worthy of you, whoever you are, or your education, whatever it is, because we will defeat totalitarian, authoritarian ideas only by better ideas; we will frustrate the evils of vocational specialization only by the virtues of intellectual generalization. Since Western rationalism and Eastern spiritualism met in Athens and that mighty creative fire broke out, collectivism in various forms has collided with individualism time and again. This twentieth-century collision, this "crisis" we are forever talking about, will be won at last not on the battlefield but in the head and heart.

So you see, I have some rather large notions about you and what you have to do to rescue us wretched slaves of specialization and group thinking from further shrinkage and contraction of mind and spirit. But you will have to be alert or you may get caught yourself—even in the kitchen or the nursery—by the steady pressures with which you will be surrounded. . . .

Women, especially educated women, have a unique opportunity to influence us, man and boy, and to play a direct part in the unfolding drama of our free society. But I am told that nowadays the young wife or mother is short of time for such subtle arts, that things are not what they used to be; that once immersed in the very pressing and particular problems of domesticity, many women feel frustrated and far apart from the great issues and stirring debates for which their education has given them understanding and relish. Once they read Baudelaire. Now it is the Consumers' Guide. Once they wrote poetry. Now it's the laundry list. Once they discussed art and philosophy until late in the night. Now they are so tired they fall asleep as soon as the dishes are finished. There is, often, a sense of contraction, of closing horizons and lost opportunities. They had hoped to play their part in the crisis of the age. But what they do is wash the diapers. (Or do they any longer?)

Now I hope I have not painted too depressing a view of your future, for the fact is that Western marriage and motherhood are yet another instance of the emergence of individual freedom in our Western society. Their basis is the recognition in women as well as men of the primacy of personality and individuality. I have just returned from sub-Saharan Africa where the illiteracy of the African mother is a formidable obstacle to the education and advancement of her child and where polygamy and female labor are still the dominant system.

The point is that whether we talk of Africa, Islam or Asia, women "never had it so good" as you do. And in spite of the difficulties of domesticity, you have a way to participate actively in the crisis in addition to keeping yourself and those about you straight on the difference between means and ends, mind and spirit, reason and emotion—not to mention keeping your man straight on the differences between Botticelli and Chianti. . . .

In modern America the home is not the boundary of a woman's life. There are outside activities aplenty. But even more important is the fact, surely, that what you have learned and can learn will fit you for the primary task of making homes and whole human beings in whom the rational values of freedom, tolerance, charity and free inquiry can take root.

Module XXII
Questions for Study and Critical Thinking

1. What features of Levittown seemed revolutionary?

2. What criticisms could be made of it and similar suburban housing developments?

3. What criticisms of TV does *U.S. News* describe?

4. In your view, are these criticisms justified?

5. What virtues does it say some people claim for TV?

6. Does TV really have these virtues? Why do you think the way you do?

7. What, according to Adlai Stevenson, is the housewife's most important job?

8. What do you think of that idea?

Module XXIII

The Civil Rights Struggle in the 1950s and 1960s

Introduction

In the 1950s, racial segregation, enforced by law in Southern states, finally came under serious attack. In 1954 in the case of *Brown v. Board of Education* the Supreme Court ruled unanimously that racial segregation in public schools was unconstitutional. In 1957, after mobs prevented the admission of black students to Central High School in Little Rock, Arkansas, President Eisenhower sent federal troops to enforce the court order for their admission.

In 1955 in Montgomery, Alabama, Rosa Parks, a black woman, defied a municipal bus driver's order to surrender her seat to a white man. Her refusal touched off a boycott of city buses by African-Americans and led to a full-scale campaign for black civil rights. The Montgomery bus boycott also produced a national leader for the new civil rights movement, Martin Luther King, Jr., a young Baptist minister. Under his leadership the movement adopted nonviolent disobedience of segregation laws as its primary tactic.

In 1960 the protests intensified. In February of that year black students in Greensboro, North Carolina began staging sit-ins at a segregated lunch counter in the local Woolworth store, in which they took all the available seats and refused to leave. The sit-ins rapidly spread to other places in the South. As a result, many merchants desegregated their lunch counters. In the next year the Congress of Racial Equality (CORE) organized "freedom rides," in which black students rode buses through the South and attempted to integrate the segregated bus stations. In some places this led to savage brutality from local white people. President Kennedy thereupon sent in federal marshals to keep order and also ordered all bus and railroad stations in the country desegregated. The next year a federal court ordered the University of Mississippi to admit James Meredith, a black student. Governor Ross Barnett of Mississippi, however, refused to allow Meredith to enroll. When a riot broke out, Kennedy sent in federal marshals to maintain law and order and help Meredith to enroll.

Finally, in 1963 Martin Luther King organized a series of nonviolent demonstrations in Birmingham, Alabama (the site of the bus boycott in 1955). The police commissioner, "Bull" Conner, responded by attacking the demonstrators, including even children, with police dogs, fire hoses, and electric cattle prods. All of this was televised to the nation, much of which watched in horror. Soon afterward, a federal court ordered black students to be admitted to the University of Alabama. In a gesture of defiance, the governor, George C. Wallace, pledged to stand personally in the "schoolhouse" door to prevent the students' enrollment. In secret negotiations Kennedy and his brother Robert, the attorney general, persuaded Wallace to move aside when federal marshals actually accompanied the students to the administration building.

In the wake of these events Kennedy delivered a nationally-televised address in which he called achieving integration a moral issue. In the summer 200,000 demonstrators staged a giant march to the Lincoln Memorial in Washington, D.C., where King gave his famous "I have a dream" speech.

In 1964, after Kennedy had been assassinated and Lyndon Johnson had become president, Johnson achieved the passage of the Civil Rights Act of 1964, prohibiting discrimination based on race, ethnicity, religion, or sex. Election officials in many places in the South, however, continued to obstruct blacks from registering and voting. Johnson, therefore, persuaded Congress to pass the Voting Rights Act of 1965. This provided for sending federal voting registrars to prevent discrimination in registration and voting.

Despite these legal landmarks, however, racial issues continued to trouble the country. In 1965 the Watts section of Los Angeles was subjected to three days of rioting. In 1968 a sniper murdered Martin Luther King. Riots thereupon broke out in many American cities. The civil rights movement itself was riven by internal disagreements. One branch stressed "black power," and many members of this group disavowed nonviolence. The documents in this section provide a selection of the voices heard in the United States during this struggle.

Document 23.1 96 Southern Congressmen and Senators Oppose Integration

When the Supreme Court announced its ban on segregation in *Brown v. Board of Education,* many Southern political leaders immediately announced their opposition to school integration and the *Brown* decision. Almost one hundred Southern Congressmen, including many powerful figures on the national scene, signed the following public letter denouncing the court and defending racial segregation.

. . . We regard the decision of the Supreme Court in the school cases as clear abuse of judicial power. It climaxes a trend in the Federal judiciary undertaking to legislate, in derogation of the authority of Congress, and to encroach upon the reserved rights of the states and the people.

The original Constitution does not mention education. Neither does the Fourteenth Amendment nor any other amendment. The debates preceding the submission of the Fourteenth Amendment clearly show that there was no intent that it should affect the systems of education maintained by the states. . . .

When the amendment was adopted in 1868, there were thirty-seven states of the Union. Every one of the twenty-six states that had any substantial racial differences among its people either approved the operation of segregated schools already in existence or subsequently established such schools by action of the same law-making body which considered the Fourteenth Amendment.

As admitted by the Supreme Court in the public school case (*Brown v. Board of Education*), the doctrine of separate but equal schools "apparently originated in *Roberts v. City of Boston* (1849), upholding school segregation against attack as being violative of a state constitutional guarantee of equality." This constitutional doctrine began in the North—not in the South—and it was followed not only in Massachusetts, but in Connecticut, New York, Illinois, Indiana, Michigan, Minnesota, New Jersey, Ohio, Pennsylvania and other northern states until they, exercising their rights as states through the constitutional processes of local self-government, changed their school systems.

In the case of *Plessy v. Ferguson* in 1896 the Supreme Court expressly declared that under the Fourteenth Amendment no person was denied any of his rights if the states provided separate but equal public facilities. This decision has been followed in many other cases. It is notable that the Supreme Court, speaking through Chief Justice Taft, a former President of the United States, unanimously declared in 1927 in *Lunt v. Rice* that the "separate but equal" principle is ". . . within the discretion of the state in regulating its public schools and does not conflict with the Fourteenth Amendment."

This interpretation, restated time and again, became a part of the life of the people of many of the states and confirmed their habits, customs, traditions and way of life. It is founded on elemental humanity and common sense, for parents should not be deprived by Government of the right to direct the lives and education of their own children.

Though there has been no constitutional amendment or act of Congress changing this established legal principle almost a century old, the Supreme Court of the United States, with no legal basis for such action, undertook to exercise their naked judicial power and substituted their personal political and social ideas for the established law of the land.

This unwarranted exercise of power by the court, contrary to the Constitution, is creating chaos and confusion in the states principally affected. It is destroying the amicable relations between the white

---

Text of the 96th Congressmen's Declaration on Integration.

and Negro races that have been created through ninety years of patient effort by the good people of both races. It has planted hatred and suspicion where there has been heretofore friendship and understanding.

Without regard to the consent of the governed, outside agitators are threatening immediate and revolutionary changes in our public school systems. If done, this is certain to destroy the system of public education in some of the states.

With the gravest concern for the explosive and dangerous condition created by this decision and inflamed by outside meddlers:

We reaffirm our reliance on the Constitution as the fundamental law of the land.

We decry the Supreme Court's encroachments on rights reserved to the states and to the people, contrary to established law and to the Constitution.

We commend the motives of those states which have declared the intention to resist forced integration by any lawful means. . . .

We pledge ourselves to use all lawful means to bring about a reversal of this decision which is contrary to the Constitution and to prevent the use of force in its implementation.

In this trying period, as we all seek to right this wrong, we appeal to our people not to be provoked by the agitators and troublemakers invading our states and to scrupulously refrain from disorder and lawless acts.

Document 23.2 President Eisenhower Speaks to the Nation about the Situation in Little Rock

In 1957, a federal court ordered the integration of Central High School in Little Rock, Arkansas. Local white people responded by blocking school entrances to prevent the black students from enrolling. In the midst of the riotous conditions, Orval Faubus, the governor of Arkansas, inflamed rather than soothed the situation. President Dwight D. Eisenhower then decided that it was his duty to ensure that the federal court was obeyed. He nationalized the Arkansas National Guard and ordered the 82nd Airborne Division to Little Rock to maintain order and make sure that the students could safely enter school. The following document is an excerpt from Eisenhower's speech to the nation announcing his decision.

President Eisenhower Speaks to the Nation about the Situation in Little Rock

Dwight D. Eisenhower

My Fellow Citizens. . . . I must speak to you about the serious situation that has arisen in Little Rock. . . . In that city, under the leadership of demagogic extremists, disorderly mobs have deliberately prevented the carrying out of proper orders from a federal court. Local authorities have not eliminated that violent opposition and, under the law, I yesterday issued a proclamation calling upon the mob to disperse.

This morning the mob again gathered in front of the Central High School of Little Rock, obviously for the purpose of again preventing the carrying out of the court's order relating to the admission of Negro children to that school.

Whenever normal agencies prove inadequate to the task and it becomes necessary for the executive branch of the federal government to use its powers and authority to uphold federal courts, the President's responsibility is inescapable.

In accordance with that responsibility, I have today issued an Executive Order directing the use of troops under federal authority to aid in the execution of federal law at Little Rock, Arkansas. This became necessary when my Proclamation of yesterday was

---

Address to the Nation about the situation in Little Rock, President Dwight D. Eisenhower.

not observed, and the obstruction of justice still continues. It is important that the reasons for my action be understood by all our citizens.

As you know, the Supreme Court of the United States has decided that separate public educational facilities for the races are inherently unequal and therefore compulsory school segregation laws are unconstitutional. . . .

During the past several years, many communities in our southern states have instituted public school plans for gradual progress in the enrollment and attendance of school children of all races in order to bring themselves into compliance with the law of the land.

They thus demonstrated to the world that we are a nation in which laws, not men, are supreme. I regret to say that this truth—the cornerstone of our liberties—was not observed in this instance. . . .

Here is the sequence of events in the development of the Little Rock school case. In May of 1955, the Little Rock School Board approved a moderate plan for the gradual desegregation of the public schools in that city. It provided that a start toward integration would be made at the present term in the high school, and that the plan would be in full operation by 1963. . . . Now this Little Rock plan was challenged in the courts by some who believed that the period of time as proposed in the plan was too long.

The United States Court at Little Rock, which has supervisory responsibility under the law for the plan of desegregation in the public schools, dismissed the challenge, thus approving a gradual rather than an abrupt change from the existing system. The court found that the school board had acted in good faith in planning for a public school system free from racial discrimination.

Since that time, the court has on three separate occasions issued orders directing that the plan be carried out. All persons were instructed to refrain from interfering with the efforts of the school board to comply with the law.

Proper and sensible observance of the law then demanded the respectful obedience which the nation has a right to expect from all its people. This, unfortunately, has not been the case at Little Rock. Certain misguided persons, many of them imported into Little Rock by agitators, have insisted upon defying the law and have sought to bring it into disrepute. The orders of the court have thus been frustrated.

The very basis of our individual rights and freedoms rests upon the certainty that the President and the Executive Branch of Government will support and insure the carrying out of the decisions of the federal courts, even, when necessary, with all the means at the President's command. . . .

Mob rule cannot be allowed to override the decisions of our courts.

Now, let me make it very clear that federal troops are not being used to relieve local and state authorities of their primary duty to preserve the peace and order of the community. . . .

The proper use of the powers of the Executive Branch to enforce the orders of a federal court is limited to extraordinary and compelling circumstances. Manifestly, such an extreme situation has been created in Little Rock. This challenge must be met and with such measures as will preserve to the people as a whole their lawfully protected rights in a climate permitting their free and fair exercise.

The overwhelming majority of our people in every section of the country are united in their respect for observance of the law—even in those cases where they may disagree with that law. . . . A foundation of our American way of life is our national respect for law.

In the South, as elsewhere, citizens are keenly aware of the disservice that has been done to the people of Arkansas in the eyes of the nation, and that has been done to the nation in the eyes of the world.

At a time when we face grave situations abroad because of the hatred that communism bears toward a system of government based on human rights, it would be difficult to exaggerate the harm that is being done to the prestige and influence, and indeed to the safety, of our nation and the world.

Our enemies are gloating over this incident and using it everywhere to misrepresent our whole nation. We are portrayed as a violator of those standards of conduct which the peoples of the world united to proclaim in the Charter of the United Nations. There they affirmed "faith in fundamental human rights" and "in the dignity and worth of the human person" and they did so "without distinction as to race, sex, language or religion."

And so, with deep confidence, I call upon the citizens of the State of Arkansas to assist in bringing to an immediate end all interference with the law and its processes. If resistance to the federal court orders ceases at once, the further presence of federal troops will be unnecessary and the City of Little Rock will return to its normal habits of peace and order and a blot upon the fair name and high honor of our nation in the world will be removed.

Thus will be restored the image of America and of all its parts as one nation, indivisible, with liberty and justice for all.

Document 23.3 Letter from the Birmingham City Jail

Beginning with the Montgomery bus boycott in 1955, the civil rights movement employed a strategy of nonviolent disobedience, developed by Martin Luther King, Jr., in which demonstrators intentionally disobeyed laws enforcing segregation while remaining nonviolent but unyielding. Some whites opposed these tactics, arguing that intentional violation of laws would lead to lawlessness, disorder, and chaos. Some whites also criticized the involvement of leaders from outside the local region. In 1963 several white ministers publicly criticized King's tactics. When King was imprisoned during demonstrations he led in Birmingham, Alabama, he responded to these ministers with a public "Letter from the Birmingham City Jail." Although ostensibly directed to the local ministers, King was using this letter to make a systematic defense of his tactics to the entire country.

Letter from the Birmingham City Jail

Martin Luther King, Jr.

My dear Fellow Clergymen,

While confined here in the Birmingham city jail, I came across your recent statement calling our present activities "unwise and untimely." . . . [S]ince I feel that you are men of genuine good will and your criticisms are sincerely set forth, I would like to answer your statement in what I hope will be patient and reasonable terms.

I think I should give the reason for my being in Birmingham, since you have been influenced by the argument of "outsiders coming in." I have the honor of serving as president of the Southern Christian Leadership Conference, an organization operating in every southern state, with headquarters in Atlanta, Georgia. We have some eighty-five affiliate organizations all across the South. . . . Several months ago our local affiliate here in Birmingham invited us to be on call to engage in a nonviolent direct action program if such were deemed necessary. . . .

Beyond this, I am in Birmingham because injustice is here. . . . I cannot sit idly by in Atlanta and not be concerned about what happens in Birmingham. Injustice anywhere is a threat to justice everywhere. . . .

You deplore the demonstrations that are presently taking place in Birmingham. But I am sorry that your statement did not express a similar concern for the conditions that brought the demonstrations into being. . . .

Birmingham is probably the most thoroughly segregated city in the United States. Its ugly record of police brutality is known in every section of this country. Its unjust treatment of Negroes in the courts is a notorious reality. There have been more unsolved bombings of Negro homes and churches in Birmingham than any city in this nation. These are the hard, brutal and unbelievable facts. . . .

You may well ask, "Why direct action? Why sit-ins, marches, etc.? Isn't negotiation a better path?" You are exactly right in your call for negotiation. Indeed, this is the purpose of direct action. Nonviolent direct action seeks to create such a crisis and establish such creative tension that a community that has constantly refused to negotiate is forced to confront the issue. It seeks so to dramatize the issue that it can no longer be ignored. . . . So the purpose of the direct action is to create a situation so crisis-packed that it will inevitably open the door to negotiation. . . .

One of the basic points in your statement is that our acts are untimely. . . . My friends, I must say to you that we have not made a single gain in civil rights without determined legal and nonviolent pressure. History is the long and tragic story of the fact that privileged groups seldom give up their privileges voluntarily. . . .

We know through painful experience that freedom is never voluntarily given by the oppressor; it must be demanded by the oppressed. Frankly, I have never yet engaged in a direct action movement that was "well timed," according to the timetable of those who have not suffered unduly from the disease of segregation. For years now I have heard the words "Wait!" It rings in the ear of every Negro with a piercing familiarity. This "Wait" has almost always meant "Never." . . . We have waited for more than 340 years for our constitutional and God-given rights. The nations of Asia and Africa are moving with jetlike speed toward the goal of political independence, and we still creep at horse and buggy pace toward the gaining of a cup of coffee at a lunch counter. I guess it is easy for those who have never felt the stinging darts of segregation to say, "Wait." But when you have seen vicious mobs lynch your mothers and fathers at will and drown your sisters and brothers at whim; when you have seen hate-filled policemen curse, kick, brutalize and even kill your black brothers and sisters with impunity; when you see the vast majority of your twenty million Negro brothers smothering in an airtight cage of poverty in the midst of an affluent society; when you suddenly find your tongue twisted and your speech stammering as you seek to explain to your six-year-old daughter why she can't go to the public amusement park that has just been advertised on television, and see tears welling up in her little eyes when she is told that Funtown is closed to colored children, and see the depressing clouds of inferiority begin to form in her little mental sky, and see her begin to distort her little personality by unconsciously developing a bitterness toward white people; when you have to concoct an answer for a five-year-old son asking in agonizing pathos: "Daddy, why do white people treat colored people so mean?"; when you take a cross-country drive and find it necessary to sleep night after night in the uncomfortable corners of your automobile because no motel will accept you; when you are humiliated day in and day out by nagging signs reading "white" and "colored"; when your first name becomes "nigger" and your middle name becomes "boy" (however old you are) and your last name becomes "John," and when your wife and mother are never given the respected title "Mrs."; when you are harried by day and haunted by night by the fact that you are a Negro, living constantly at tiptoe stance never quite knowing what to expect next, and plagued with inner fears and outer resentments; when you are forever fighting a degenerating sense of "nobodiness"; then you will understand why we find it difficult to wait. There comes a time when the cup of endurance runs over, and men are no longer willing to be plunged into an abyss of injustice where they experience the blackness of corroding despair. I hope, sirs, you can understand our legitimate and unavoidable impatience.

You express a great deal of anxiety over our willingness to break laws. This is certainly a legitimate concern. Since we so diligently urge people to obey the Supreme Court's decision of 1954 outlawing segregation in the public schools, it is rather strange and paradoxical to find us consciously breaking laws. One may well ask, "How can you advocate breaking some laws and obeying others?" The answer is found in the fact that there are two types of laws: there are just and there are unjust laws. I would agree with Saint Augustine that "An unjust law is no law at all."

Now what is the difference between the two? How does one determine when a law is just or unjust? A just law is a man-made code that squares with the moral law or the law of God. An unjust law is a code that is out of harmony with the moral law. To put it in the terms of Saint Thomas Aquinas, an unjust law is a human law that is not rooted in eternal and natural law. Any law that uplifts human personality is just. Any law that degrades human personality is unjust. All segregation statutes are unjust because segregation distorts the soul and damages the personality. It gives the segregator a false sense of superiority, and the segregated a false sense of inferiority. . . . So segregation is not only politically, economically and sociologically unsound, but it is morally wrong and sinful. . . . So I can urge men to disobey segregation ordinances because they are morally wrong. . . .

I hope you can see the distinction I am trying to point out. In no sense do I advocate evading or defying the law as the rabid segregationist would do. This would lead to anarchy. One who breaks an unjust law must do it openly, lovingly . . . and with a willingness to accept the penalty. I submit that an individual who breaks a law that conscience tells him is unjust, and willingly accepts the penalty by staying in jail to arouse the conscience of the community over its injustice, is in reality expressing the very highest respect for law.

Of course, there is nothing new about this kind of civil disobedience. . . . It was practiced superbly by the early Christians who were willing to face hungry lions and the excruciating pain of chopping blocks, before submitting to certain unjust laws of the Roman Empire.

I must make two honest confessions to you, my Christian and Jewish brothers. First, I must confess that over the last few years I have been gravely disappointed with the white moderate. I have almost reached the regrettable conclusion that the Negro's great stumbling block in the stride toward freedom is not the White Citizens' Councillor or the Ku Klux Klanner, but the white moderate who is more devoted to order than to justice; who prefers a negative peace which is the absence of tension to a positive peace which is the presence of justice; who constantly says, "I agree with you in the goal you seek, but I can't agree with your methods of direct action"; who paternalistically feels that he can set the timetable for another man s freedom; who lives by the myth of time and who constantly advised the Negro to wait until a "more convenient season." Shallow understanding from people of good will is more frustrating than absolute misunderstanding from people of ill will. Lukewarm acceptance is much more bewildering than outright rejection.

I had hoped that the white moderate would understand that law and order exist for the purpose of establishing justice, and that when they fail to do this they become dangerously structured dams that block the flow of social progress. I had hoped that the white moderate would understand that the present tension of the South is merely a necessary phase of the transition from an obnoxious negative peace, where the Negro passively accepted his unjust plight, to a substance-filled positive peace, where all men will respect the dignity and worth of human personality. Actually, we who engage in nonviolent direct action are not the creators of tension. We merely bring to the surface the hidden tension that is already alive. We bring it out in the open where it can be seen and dealt with. . . .

In your statement you asserted that our actions, even though peaceful, must be condemned because they precipitate violence. But can this assertion be logically made? Isn't this like condemning the robbed man because his possession of money precipitated the evil act of robbery?

You spoke of our activity in Birmingham as extreme. At first I was rather disappointed that fellow clergymen would see my nonviolent efforts as those of the extremist. I started thinking about the fact that I stand in the middle of two opposing forces in the Negro community. One is a force of complacency made up of Negroes who, as a result of long years of oppression, have been so completely drained of self-respect and a sense of "somebodiness" that they have adjusted to segregation, and, of a few Negroes in the middle class who, because of a degree of academic and economic security, and because at points they profit by segregation, have unconsciously become insensitive to the problems of the masses. The other force is one of bitterness and hatred, and comes perilously close to advocating violence. It is expressed in the various black nationalist groups that are springing up over the nation, the largest and best known being Elijah Muhammad's Muslim movement. This movement is nourished by the contemporary frustration over the continued existence of racial discrimination. It is made up of people who have lost faith in America, who have absolutely repudiated Christianity, and who have concluded that the white man is an incurable "devil." I have tried to stand between these two forces, saying that we need not follow the "do-nothingism" of the complacent or the hatred and despair of the black nationalist. There is the more excellent way of love and nonviolent protest. I'm grateful to God that, through the Negro church, the dimension of nonviolence entered our struggle. If this philosophy had not emerged, I am convinced that by now many streets of the South would be flowing with floods of blood. And I am further convinced that if our white brothers dismiss us as "rabble-rousers" and "outside agitators," those of us who are working through the channels of nonviolent direct action and refuse to support our nonviolent efforts, millions of Negroes, out of frustration and despair, will seek solace and security in black nationalist ideologies, a development that will lead inevitably to a frightening racial nightmare.

Oppressed people cannot remain oppressed forever. The urge for freedom will eventually come. This is what happened to the American Negro. . . .

But as I continued to think about the matter I gradually gained a bit of satisfaction from being considered an extremist. Was not Jesus an extremist in love—"Love your enemies, bless them that curse you, pray for them that despitefully use you." . . . Was not Abraham Lincoln an extremist? "This nation cannot survive half slave and half free." Was not Thomas Jefferson an extremist—"We hold these truths to be self-evident, that all men are created equal." So the question is not whether we will be extremist but what kind of extremist will we be. Will we be extremists for hate or will we be extremists for love? Will we be extremists for the preservation of injustice—or will we be extremists for the cause of justice? . . .

But before closing I am impelled to mention one other point in your statement that troubled me profoundly. You warmly commended the Birmingham police force for keeping "order" and "preventing violence." I don't believe you would have so warmly commended the police force if you had seen its angry violent dogs literally biting six unarmed, nonviolent Negroes. I don't believe you would so quickly commend the policemen if you would observe their ugly and inhuman treatment of Negroes here in the city jail; if you would watch them push and curse old Negro women and young Negro girls; if you would see them slap and kick old Negro men and young boys; if you will observe them, as they did on two occasions, refuse to give us food because we wanted to sing our grace together. I'm sorry that I can't join you in your praise for the police department. . . .

I wish you had commended the Negro sit-inners and demonstrators of Birmingham for their sublime courage, their willingness to suffer and their amazing discipline in the midst of the most inhuman provocation. One day the South will recognize its real heroes. They will be the James Merediths courageously and with a majestic sense of purpose facing jeering and hostile mobs and the agonizing loneliness that characterizes the life of the pioneer. They will be old, oppressed, battered Negro women, symbolized in a seventy-two-year-old woman of Montgomery, Alabama, who rose up with a sense of dignity and with her people decided not to ride the segregated buses, and responded to one who inquired about her tiredness with ungrammatical profundity: "My feet is tired, but my soul is rested." They will be the young high school and college students, young ministers of the gospel and a host of their elders courageously and nonviolently sitting-in at lunch counters and willingly going to jail for conscience's sake. One day the South will know that when these disinherited children of God sat down at lunch counters they were in reality standing up for the best in the American dream and the most sacred values in our Judeo-Christian heritage, and thusly, carrying our whole nation back to those great wells of democracy which were dug deep by the Founding Fathers in the formulation of the Constitution and the Declaration of Independence.

Document 23.4 "I Have a Dream"

Martin Luther King, Jr., delivered his most famous speech at a mass demonstration in 1963 in Washington, D.C. After the group of over 200,000 demonstrators marched down the Mall to the Lincoln Memorial, a series of speakers addressed them. In his speech King combined his vision for the future with the African-American past as he quoted from old spirituals in which slaves and their descendants looked forward to liberation.

"I Have a Dream"

Martin Luther King, Jr.

Delivered on the steps at the Lincoln Memorial in Washington D.C. on August 28, 1963

Five score years ago, a great American, in whose symbolic shadow we stand signed the Emancipation Proclamation. This momentous decree came as a great beacon light of hope to millions of Negro slaves who had been seared in the flames of withering injustice. It came as a joyous daybreak to end the long night of captivity.

But one hundred years later, we must face the tragic fact that the Negro is still not free. One hundred years later, the life of the Negro is still sadly crippled by the manacles of segregation and the chains of discrimination. One hundred years later, the Negro lives on a lonely island of poverty in the midst of a vast ocean of material prosperity. One hundred years later, the Negro is still languishing in the corners of American society and finds himself an exile in his own land. So we have come here today to dramatize an appalling condition.

In a sense we have come to our nation's capital to cash a check. When the architects of our republic wrote the magnificent words of the Constitution and the Declaration of Independence, they were signing a promissory note to which every American was to fall heir. This note was a promise that all men would be guaranteed the inalienable rights of life, liberty, and the pursuit of happiness.

It is obvious today that America has defaulted on this promissory note insofar as her citizens of color are concerned. Instead of honoring this sacred obligation, America has given the Negro people a bad check which has come back marked "insufficient funds." But we refuse to believe that the bank of justice is bankrupt. We refuse to believe that there are insufficient funds in the great vaults of opportunity of this nation. So we have come to cash this check — a check that will give us upon demand the riches of freedom and the security of justice. We have also come to this hallowed spot to remind America of the fierce urgency of now. This is no time to engage in the luxury of cooling off or to take the tranquilizing drug of gradualism. Now is the time to rise from the dark and desolate valley of segregation to the sunlit path of racial justice. Now is the time to open the doors of opportunity to all of God's children. Now is the time to lift our nation from the quicksands of racial injustice to the solid rock of brotherhood.

It would be fatal for the nation to overlook the urgency of the moment and to underestimate the determination of the Negro. This sweltering summer of the Negro's legitimate discontent will not pass until there is an invigorating autumn of freedom and equality. Nineteen sixty-three is not an end, but a beginning. Those who hope that the Negro needed to blow off steam and will now be content will have a rude awakening if the nation returns to business as usual. There will be neither rest nor tranquility in America until the Negro is granted his citizenship rights. The whirlwinds of revolt will continue to shake the foundations of our nation until the bright day of justice emerges.

But there is something that I must say to my people who stand on the warm threshold which leads into the palace of justice. In the process of gaining our rightful place we must not be guilty of wrongful deeds. Let us not seek to satisfy our thirst for freedom by drinking from the cup of bitterness and hatred.

We must forever conduct our struggle on the high plane of dignity and discipline. We must not allow our creative protest to degenerate into physical violence. Again and again we must rise to the majestic heights of meeting physical force with soul force. The marvelous new militancy which has engulfed the Negro community must not lead us to distrust of all white people, for many of our white brothers, as evidenced by their presence here today, have come to realize that their destiny is tied up with our destiny and their freedom is inextricably bound to our freedom. We cannot walk alone.

And as we walk, we must make the pledge that we shall march ahead. We cannot turn back. There are those who are asking the devotees of civil rights, "When will you be satisfied?" We can never be satisfied as long as our bodies, heavy with the fatigue of travel, cannot gain lodging in the motels of the highways and the hotels of the cities. We cannot be satisfied as long as the Negro's basic mobility is from a smaller ghetto to a larger one. We can never be satisfied as long as a Negro in Mississippi cannot vote and a Negro in New York believes he has nothing for which to vote. No, no, we are not satisfied, and we will not be satisfied until justice rolls down like waters and righteousness like a mighty stream.

I am not unmindful that some of you have come here out of great trials and tribulations. Some of you have come fresh from narrow cells. Some of you have come from areas where your quest for freedom left you battered by the storms of persecution and staggered by the winds of police brutality. You have been the veterans of creative suffering. Continue to work with the faith that unearned suffering is redemptive.

Go back to Mississippi, go back to Alabama, go back to Georgia, go back to Louisiana, go back to the slums and ghettos of our northern cities, knowing that somehow this situation can and will be changed. Let us not wallow in the valley of despair.

I say to you today, my friends, that in spite of the difficulties and frustrations of the moment, I still have a dream. It is a dream deeply rooted in the American dream.

I have a dream that one day this nation will rise up and live out the true meaning of its creed: "We hold these truths to be self-evident: that all men are created equal."

I have a dream that one day on the red hills of Georgia the sons of former slaves and the sons of former slaveowners will be able to sit down together at a table of brotherhood.

I have a dream that one day even the state of Mississippi, a desert state, sweltering with the heat of injustice and oppression, will be transformed into an oasis of freedom and justice.

I have a dream that my four children will one day live in a nation where they will not be judged by the color of their skin but by the content of their character.

I have a dream today.

I have a dream that one day the state of Alabama, whose governor's lips are presently dripping with the words of interposition and nullification, will be transformed into a situation where little black boys and black girls will be able to join hands with little white boys and white girls and walk together as sisters and brothers.

I have a dream today.

I have a dream that one day every valley shall be exalted, every hill and mountain shall be made low, the rough places will be made plain, and the crooked places will be made straight, and the glory of the Lord shall be revealed, and all flesh shall see it together.

This is our hope. This is the faith with which I return to the South. With this faith we will be able to hew out of the mountain of despair a stone of hope. With this faith we will be able to transform the jangling discords of our nation into a beautiful symphony of brotherhood. With this faith we will be able to work together, to pray together, to struggle together, to go to jail together, to stand up for freedom together, knowing that we will be free one day.

This will be the day when all of God's children will be able to sing with a new meaning, "My country, 'tis of thee, sweet land of liberty, of thee I sing. Land where my fathers died, land of the pilgrim's pride, from every mountainside, let freedom ring."

And if America is to be a great nation this must become true. So let freedom ring from the prodigious hilltops of New Hampshire. Let freedom ring from the mighty mountains of New York. Let freedom ring from the heightening Alleghenies of Pennsylvania!

Let freedom ring from the snowcapped Rockies of Colorado!

Let freedom ring from the curvaceous peaks of California!

But not only that; let freedom ring from Stone Mountain of Georgia!

Let freedom ring from Lookout Mountain of Tennessee!

Let freedom ring from every hill and every molehill of Mississippi. From every mountainside, let freedom ring.

When we let freedom ring, when we let it ring from every village and every hamlet, from every state and every city, we will be able to speed up that day when all of God's children, black men and white men, Jews and Gentiles, Protestants and Catholics, will be able to join hands and sing in the words of the old Negro spiritual, "Free at last! free at last! thank God Almighty, we are free at last!"

Document 23.5 What We Have Gone through for the Right to Vote

In 1964 a group of black civil rights activists challenged the Mississippi delegation to the Democratic National Convention, which was composed mostly of white segregationists. Calling themselves the Mississippi Freedom Democratic Party, they asked to be recognized as the legitimate Democratic delegation from Mississippi. One of the leaders of the dissident group was Fannie Lou Hamer, a Mississippi sharecropper.

What We Have Gone through for the Right to Vote

Fannie Lou Hamer

Mr. Chairman, and the Credentials Committee, my name is Mrs. Fannie Lou Hamer, and I live at 626 East Lafayette Street, Ruleville, Mississippi, Sunflower County, the home of Senator James O. Eastland, and Senator Stennis.

It was the 31st of August in 1962 that eighteen of us traveled twenty-six miles to the county courthouse in Indianola to try to register to try to become first-class citizens. We was met in Indianola by Mississippi men, highway patrolmen, and they only allowed two of us in to take the literacy test at the time. After we had taken this test and started back to Ruleville, we was held up by the City Police and the State Highway Patrolmen and carried back to

Indianola, where the bus driver was charged that day with driving a bus the wrong color.

After we paid the fine among us, we continued on to Ruleville, and Reverend Jeff Sunny carried me four miles in the rural area where I had worked as a timekeeper and sharecropper for eighteen years. I was met there by my children, who told me the plantation owner was angry because I had gone down to try to register. After they told me, my husband came, and said the plantation owner was raising cain because I had tried to register, and before he quit talking the plantation owner came, and said, "Fannie Lou, do you know—did Pap tell you what I said?"

I said, "Yes, Sir."

He said, "I mean that," he said. "If you don't go down and withdraw your registration, you have to leave," he said. "Then if you go down withdraw," he said. "You will—you might hate to go because we are not ready for that in Mississippi."

And I addressed him and told him and said, "I didn't try to register for you. I tried to register for myself." I had to leave that same night.

On the 10th of September, 1962, sixteen bullets was fired into the home of Mr. and Mrs. Robert Tucker for me. That same night two girls were shot in Ruleville, Mississippi. Also Mr. Joe McDonald's house was shot in.

And in June the 9th, 1963, I had attended a voter-registration workshop, was returning back to Mississippi. Ten of us was traveling by the Continental Trailway bus. When we got to Winona, Mississippi, which is Montgomery County, four of the people got off to use the washroom, and two of the people—to use the restaurant—two of the people wanted to use the washroom. The four people that had gone in to use the restaurant was ordered out. During this time I was on the bus. But when I looked through the window and saw they had rushed out, I got off of the bus to see what had happened, and one of the ladies said, "It was a state highway patrolman and a chief of police ordered us out."

I got back on the bus and one of the persons had used the washroom got back on the bus, too. As soon as I was seated on the bus, I saw when they began to get the four people in a highway patrolman's car. I stepped off the bus to see what was happening and somebody screamed from the car that the four workers was in and said, "Get that one there," and when I went to get in the car, when the man told me I was under arrest, he kicked me.

I was carried to the county jail, and put in the booking room. They left some of the people in the booking room and began to place us in cells. I was placed in a cell with a young woman called Miss Euvester Simpson. After I was placed in the cell I began to hear sounds of licks and screams. I could hear the sounds of licks and horrible screams, and I could hear somebody say, "Can you say, yes sir, nigger? Can you say yes, sir?"

And they would say other horrible names. She would say, "Yes, I can say yes, sir."

"So say it."

She says, "I don't know you well enough."

They beat her, I don't know how long, and after a while she began to pray, and asked God to have mercy on those people.

And it wasn't too long before three white men came to my cell. One of these men was a State Highway Patrolman and he asked me where I was from, and I told him Ruleville. He said, "We are going to check this." And they left my cell and it wasn't too long before they came back. He said "You are from Ruleville all right," and he used a curse word, and he said, "We are going to make you wish you was dead."

I was carried out of that cell into another cell where they had two Negro prisoners. The State Highway Patrolman ordered the first Negro to take the blackjack. The first Negro prisoner ordered me, by orders from the State Highway Patrolman for me, to lay down on a bunk bed on my face, and I laid on my face. The first Negro began to beat, and I was beat by the first Negro until he was exhausted, and I was holding my hands behind me at that time on my left side because I suffered from polio when I was six years old. After the first Negro had beat until he was exhausted, the State Highway Patrolman ordered the second Negro to take the blackjack.

The second Negro began to beat and I began to work my feet, and the State Highway Patrolman ordered the first Negro who had beat to set on my feet to keep me from working my feet. I began to scream and one white man got up and began to beat me in my head and tell me to hush. One white man—my dress had worked up high, he walked over and pulled my dress down—and he pulled my dress back, back up.

I was in jail when Medgar Evers was murdered.

. . .

All of this is on account we want to register, to become first-class citizens, and if the Freedom Democratic Party is not seated now, I question America, in this America, the land of the free and the home of the brave, where we have to sleep with our telephones off the hooks because our lives be threatened daily, because we want to live as decent human beings, in America?

"Thank you."

Document 23.6 Black Power

As the 1960s progressed, the voices of those impatient with the progress of nonviolent civil disobedience became more prominent. One of the spokesmen for the new idea of "black power" was Stokely Carmichael, who had previously worked in the Students' Nonviolent Coordinating Committee (SNCC), a leading organization practicing King's strategy of nonviolent civil disobedience. Black power meant different things to different people. Here, Carmichael explains his concept.

Black Power

Stokeley Carmichael

One of the tragedies of the struggle against racism is that up to now there has been no national organization which could speak to the growing militancy of young black people in the urban ghetto. There has been only a civil rights movement, whose tone of voice was adapted to an audience of liberal whites. It served as a sort of buffer zone between them and angry young blacks. None of its so-called leaders could go into a rioting community and be listened to. In a sense, I blame ourselves—together with the mass media—for what has happened in Watts, Harlem, Chicago, Cleveland, Omaha [where riots occurred in the 1960s]. Each time the people in those cities saw Martin Luther King get slapped, they became angry; when they saw four little black girls bombed to death, they were angrier; and when nothing happened, they were steaming. We had nothing to offer that they could see, except to go out and be beaten again. We helped to build their frustration.

For too many years, black Americans marched and had their heads broken and got shot. They were saying to the country, "Look, you guys are supposed to be nice guys and we are only going to do what we are supposed to do—why do you beat us up, why don't you give us what we ask, why don't you straighten yourselves out?" After years of this, we are at almost the same point because we demonstrated from a position of weakness. We cannot be expected any longer to march and have our heads broken in order to say to whites: come on, you're nice guys. For you are not nice guys. We have found you out.

An organization which claims to speak for the needs of a community—as does the Student Nonviolent Coordinating Committee—must speak in the tone of that community, not as somebody else's buffer zone. This is the significance of black power as a slogan. For once, black people are going to use the words they want to use—not just the words whites want to hear. And they will do this no matter how often the press tries to stop the use of the slogan by equating it with racism or separatism.

An organization which claims to be working for the needs of a community—as SNCC does—must work to provide that community with a position of strength from which to make its voice heard. This is the significance of black power beyond the slogan.

Black power can be clearly defined for those who do not attach the fears of white America to their questions about it. We should begin with the basic fact that black Americans have two problems: they are poor and they are black. All other problems arise from this two-sided reality: lack of education, the so-called apathy of black men. Any program to end racism must address itself to that double reality.

Almost from its beginning, SNCC sought to address itself to both conditions with a program aimed at winning political power for impoverished Southern blacks. We had to begin with politics because black Americans are a propertyless people in a country where property is valued above all. We had to work for power, because this country does not function by morality, love, and nonviolence, but by power. Thus we determined to win political power, with the idea of moving on from there into activity that would have economic effects. With power, the masses could make or participate in making the decisions which govern destinies, and thus create basic change in day-to-day lives. . . .

SNCC today is working in both North and South on programs of voter registration and independent political organizing. In some places, such as Alabama, Los Angeles, New York, Philadelphia, and New Jersey, independent organizing under the black panther symbol is in progress. The creation of a national "black panther party" must come about; it will take time to build, and it is much too early to predict its success. We have no infallible master plan and we make no claim to exclusive knowledge of how to end racism; different groups will work in their own different ways. SNCC cannot spell out the full logistics of self-determination but it can address itself to the problem by helping black communities define their needs, realize their strength, and go into action along a variety of lines which they must choose for themselves. . . .

Ultimately, the economic foundations of this country must be shaken if black people are to control their lives. The colonies of the United States—and this includes the black ghettoes within its borders, north and south—must be liberated. For a century, this nation has been like an octopus of exploitation, its tentacles stretching from Mississippi and Harlem to South America, the Middle East, southern Africa, and Vietnam; the form of exploitation varies from area to area but the essential result has been the same—a powerful few have been maintained and enriched at the expense of the poor and voiceless colored masses. This pattern must be broken. As its grip loosens here and there around the world, the hopes of black Americans become more realistic. For racism to die, a totally different America must be born.

This is what the white society does not wish to face; this is why that society prefers to talk about integration. But integration speaks not at all to the problem of poverty, only to the problem of blackness. Integration today means the man who "makes it," leaving his black brothers behind in the ghetto as fast as his new sports car will take him. It has no relevance to the Harlem wino or to the cotton picker making three dollars a day. . . .

Integration, moreover, speaks to the problem of blackness in a despicable way. As a goal, it has been based on complete acceptance of the fact that in order to have a decent house or education, blacks must move into a white neighborhood or send their children to a white school. This reinforces, among both black and white, the idea that "white" is automatically better and "black" is by definition inferior. This is why integration is a subterfuge for the maintenance of white supremacy. It allows the nation to focus on a handful of Southern children who get into white schools, at great price, and to ignore the 94 percent who are left behind in unimproved all-black schools. Such situations will not change until black people have power—to control their own school boards, in this case. Then Negroes become equal in a way that means something, and integration ceases to be a one-way street. Then integration doesn't mean draining skills and energies from the ghetto into white neighborhoods; then it can mean white people moving from Beverly Hills into Watts. . . . Then integration becomes relevant. . . .

Whites will not see that I, for example, as a person oppressed because of my blackness, have common cause with other blacks who are oppressed because of blackness. This is not to say that there are no white people who see things as I do, but that it is black people I must speak to first. It must be the oppressed to whom SNCC addresses itself primarily, not to friends from the oppressing group.

From birth, black people are told a set of lies about themselves. We are told that we are lazy—yet I drive through the Delta area of Mississippi and watch black people picking cotton in the hot sun for fourteen hours. We are told, "If you work hard, you'll succeed"—but if that were true, black people would own this country. We are oppressed because we are black—not because we are ignorant, not because we are lazy, not because we're stupid (and got good rhythm), but because we're black.

The need for psychological equality is the reason why SNCC today believes that blacks must organize in the black community. Only black people can convey the revolutionary idea that black people are able to do things themselves. Only they can help create in the community an aroused and continuing black consciousness that will provide the basis for political strength. In the past, white allies have furthered white supremacy without the whites involved realizing it—or wanting it, I think. Black people must do things for themselves; they must get poverty money they will control and spend themselves; they must conduct tutorial programs themselves so that black children can identify with black people. This is one reason Africa has such importance: The reality of black men ruling their own nations gives blacks elsewhere a sense of possibility, of power, which they do not now have.

This does not mean we don't welcome help, or friends. But we want the right to decide whether anyone is, in fact, our friend. In the past, black Americans have been almost the only people whom everybody and his momma could jump up and call their friends. We have been tokens, symbols, objects—as I was in high school to many young whites, who liked having "a Negro friend." We want to decide who is our friend, and we will not accept someone who comes to us and says: "If you do X, Y, and Z, then I'll help you." We will not be told whom we should choose as allies. We will not be isolated from any group or nation except by our own choice. We cannot have the oppressors telling the oppressed how to rid themselves of the oppressor. . . .

Black people do not want to "take over" this country. They don't want to "get whitey"; they just want to get him off their backs, as the saying goes. . . . The white man is irrelevant to blacks, except as an oppressive force. Blacks want to be in his place, yes, but not in order to terrorize and lynch and starve him. They want to be in his place because that is where a decent life can be had.

But our vision is not merely of a society in which all black men have enough to buy the good things of life. When we urge that black money go into black pockets, we mean the communal pocket. We want to see money go back into the community and used to benefit it. We want to see the cooperative concept applied in business and banking. We want to see black ghetto residents demand that an exploiting landlord or storekeeper sell them, at minimal cost, a building or a shop that they will own and improve cooperatively; they can back their demand with a rent strike, or a boycott, and a community so unified behind them that no one else will move into the building or buy at the store. The society we seek to build among black people, then, is not a capitalist one. It is a society in which the spirit of community and humanistic love prevail. The word love is suspect; black expectations of what it might produce have been betrayed too often. But those were expectations of a response from the white community, which failed us. The love we seek to encourage is within the black community, the only American community where men call each other "brother" when they meet. We can build a community of love only where we have the ability and power to do so: among blacks.

As for white America, perhaps it can stop crying out against "black supremacy," "black nationalism," "racism in reverse," and begin facing reality. The reality is that this nation, from top to bottom, is racist; that racism is not primarily a problem of "human relations" but of an exploitation maintained—either actively or through silence—by the society as a whole. . . .

We have found that they usually cannot condemn themselves, and so we have done it. But the rebuilding of this society, if at all possible, is basically the responsibility of whites—not blacks We won't fight to save the present society, in Vietnam or anywhere else. We are just going to work in the way we see fit, and on the goals we define, not for civil rights but for all our human rights.

Module XXIII

Questions for Study and Critical Thinking

1. What did the Southern Senators and Representatives say was wrong with the Supreme Court's decision?

2. What do you think of their logic?

3. Why did President Eisenhower say he was sending troops into Little Rock?

4. Why did Rosa Parks say she refused to give up her seat on the bus?

5. In his “Letter from Birmingham City Jail” how did King answer the charge that he was an “outside agitator,” who should not have been involved in demonstrations in Birmingham?

6. What reasons did King give for African-Americans’ unwillingness to “wait”?

7. How did King justify disobeying laws?

8. How did he say we can distinguish between just and unjust laws?

9. Do you agree or disagree with King? Why?

10. What happened to Fannie Lou Hamer as a result of her attempt to register to vote?

11. Fannie Lou Hamer gave her testimony in an attempt to persuade the Democratic convention credentials committee to recognize her group rather than the regular Mississippi Democratic Party. Why would this testimony tend to accomplish that purpose?

12. What, according to Stokely Carmichael, is black power?

13. What do you think of Carmichael's thinking on this subject?

Module XXIV

The Vietnam War and the Culture of Protest

Introduction

The 1960s began with an air of optimism. Although elected by a narrow margin, John F. Kennedy seemed a glamorous figure, who summoned Americans to lofty goals. Kennedy's assassination in November of 1963 stunned the country. It was the first in a shattering series of assassinations in a decade of violence.

While Kennedy's successor, Lyndon B. Johnson, lacked Kennedy's glamour, he dedicated himself to an aggressive program of liberal reforms, and succeeded in achieving the enactment of the first major piece of civil rights legislation since Reconstruction. The Civil Rights Act of 1964 outlawed discrimination on the basis of race, religion, national origin, or sex. Johnson also embarked on other ambitious reforms, including a war on poverty itself.

At the same time, however, Johnson continued U.S. military support of South Vietnam in its war with Viet Cong rebels and North Vietnamese troops. Unfortunately for Johnson, the situation in South Vietnam was deteriorating. Faced with a series of unappealing options, Johnson decided to increase the American military involvement. On 7 August 1964 at Johnson's urging, Congress passed the Gulf of Tonkin Resolution, which authorized the president to "take all necessary measures" to protect American forces and "prevent future aggression" in Southeast Asia. In March, at Johnson's direction, the United States began a massive bombing campaign of North Vietnam. In the same month two battalions of Marines landed in South Vietnam, at Da Nang. In the summer of that year Johnson announced a changed role for U.S. troops in Vietnam. From now on they would cease to perform merely defensive functions; instead, they would actively search for and attempt to destroy enemy forces. The number of troops also continued to grow. By the end of 1967 it had increased to over half a million.

As U.S. involvement grew, antiwar protests increased. By 1967 large demonstrations had become common. For many, the antiwar movement was part of a general protest against contemporary American society.

As the war and antiwar protests continued, some mainstream politicians joined the opposition. Among the most prominent was Eugene McCarthy, Democratic senator from Minnesota, who nearly defeated President Johnson in the 1968 New Hampshire presidential primary. Shortly thereafter Robert F. Kennedy, brother of the assassinated president, also entered the race, to the outrage of many McCarthy supporters. On 31 March 1965, to widespread astonishment, Johnson went on radio and television to announce a limited cessation of bombing in Vietnam—and his decision not to seek reelection.

During the race for the Democratic presidential nomination, which followed Johnson's withdrawal, Robert F. Kennedy was assassinated, and Eugene McCarthy was eventually defeated by Johnson's vice president and designated heir, Hubert Humphrey. In the general election, the Republican, Richard M. Nixon, narrowly defeated Humphrey

During the campaign Nixon announced that he had a secret plan to end American involvement in the Vietnam War. The plan attempted to diffuse opposition to the war while preventing South Vietnamese defeat. To minimize anxieties about the draft the new system exposed young men to the draft for only one year. For that year a lottery determined by birthday the order in which men would be drafted. Since a majority of draft-age men were not needed in any given year, they could determine immediately that they were permanently safe from induction.

Nixon also began the policy of "Vietnamization": pulling American troops out of Vietnam and turning the fighting over to the South Vietnamese. In the fall of 1969 he announced the withdrawal of 60,000 troops. The pull-outs continued, and by the fall of 1972 only 60,000 American servicemen remained.

At the same time Nixon tried to damage the capacity of the North Vietnamese to continue the war. Since they had built supply routes and staging areas just across the border from South Vietnam in Cambodia, Nixon ordered the bombing of those areas. In April 1970 he also announced that troops would cross into Cambodia to clean them out. Antiwar demonstrators responded with the largest demonstrations so far. In one, at Kent State University in Ohio on May 4, Ohio National Guard troops opened fire, killing four the demonstrators.

In March 1972, toward the end of Nixon's first term, the North Vietnamese mounted a major offensive. Nixon thereupon ordered bombing near Hanoi, the North Vietnamese capital, and Haiphong, its major port. He also sent his chief foreign policy advisor, Henry Kissinger, to negotiate in Paris with the North Vietnamese foreign minister, Le Doc Tho. In December 1972, when negotiations stalled, Nixon ordered the heaviest bombing of North Vietnam so far, the so-called "Christmas bombing," which ended on 30 January. The next month, on 27 January 1973, the United States and North Vietnam signed an agreement, which provided for hostilities to cease and American prisoners of war to be released. Other provisions, however, were less clear.

This agreement failed to create a permanent "peace with honor," which Nixon had sought. Over two years later, in April 1975, several months after Nixon had resigned during the Watergate scandal, the North Vietnamese launched another major offensive. They overran Saigon, the South Vietnamese capitol, as American and South Vietnamese officials fled, and occupied the entire country, ending American involvement and South Vietnamese independence.

The Vietnam War and American Vietnam policy has been controversial from the beginning of American involvement. The documents in this chapter provide a variety of viewpoints on the war. As you read make up your own mind. Was American policy right or wrong? What should the United States have done?

Document 24.1 President Johnson Asks for the Tonkin Gulf Resolution

In August 1964 Lyndon B. Johnson announced to Congress that North Vietnamese forces had attacked American naval vessels in international waters in the Gulf of Tonkin. He asked Congress to give him as president the authority to "protect our armed forces and to defend freedom and preserve peace in Southeast Asia." Although subsequent information cast doubt on the details of the reported attack, Congress swiftly responded with the Gulf of Tonkin Resolution, giving the president the powers he had asked. This resolution provided the legal basis for future U.S. military action in Vietnam.

Special Message to the Congress on U.S. Policy in Southeast Asia. August 5, 1964

Lyndon B. Johnson

To The Congress of the United States:

Last night I announced to the American people that the North Vietnamese regime had conducted further deliberate attacks against U.S. naval vessels operating in international waters, and that I had therefore directed air action against gun boats and supporting facilities used in these hostile operations. This air action has now been carried out with substantial damage to the boats and facilities. Two U.S. aircraft were lost in the action.

After consultation with the leaders of both parties in the Congress, I further announced a decision to ask the Congress for a Resolution expressing the unity and determination of the United States in supporting freedom and in protecting peace in Southeast Asia.

These latest actions of the North Vietnamese regime have given a new and grave turn to the already serious situation in Southeast Asia. Our commitments in that area are well known to the Congress. They were first made in 1954 by President Eisenhower. They were further defined in the Southeast Asia Collective Defense Treaty approved by the Senate in February 1955.

This Treaty with its accompanying protocol obligates the United States and other members to act in accordance with their Constitutional processes to meet Communist aggression against any of the parties or protocol states.

Our policy in Southeast Asia has been consistent and unchanged since 1954. I summarized it on June 2 in four simple propositions:

1. *America keeps her word.* Here as elsewhere, we must and shall honor our commitments.
2. *The issue is the future of Southeast Asia as a whole.* A threat to any nation in that region is a threat to all, and a threat to us.
3. *Our purpose is peace.* We have no military, political or territorial ambitions in the area.
4. *This is not just a jungle war, but a struggle for freedom on every front of human activity.* Our military and economic assistance to South Vietnam and Laos in particular has the purpose of helping these countries to repel aggression and strengthen their independence.

The threat to the free nations of Southeast Asia has long been clear. The North Vietnamese regime has constantly sought to take over South Vietnam and Laos. This Communist regime has violated the Geneva Accords for Vietnam. It has systematically conducted a campaign of subversion, which includes the direction, training, and supply of personnel and arms for the conduct of guerrilla warfare in South Vietnamese territory. In Laos, the North Vietnamese regime has maintained military forces, used Laotian territory for infiltration into South Vietnam, and most recently carried out combat operations—all in direct violation of the Geneva Agreements of 1962.

In recent months, the actions of the North Vietnamese regime have become steadily more threatening. In May, following new acts of Communist aggression in Laos, the United States undertook reconnaissance flights over Laotian territory, at the request of the Government of Laos. These flights had the essential mission of determining the situation in territory where Communist forces were preventing inspection by the International Control Commission. When the Communists attacked these aircraft, I responded by furnishing escort fighters with instructions to fire when fired upon. Thus, these latest North Vietnamese attacks on our naval vessels are not the first direct attack on armed forces of the United States.

As President of the United States I have concluded that I should now ask the Congress, on its part, to join in affirming the national determination that all such attacks will be met, and that the U.S. will continue in its basic policy of assisting the free nations of the area to defend their freedom.

As I have repeatedly made clear, the United States intends no rashness, and seeks no wider war. We must make it clear to all that the United States is united in its determination to bring about the end of Communist subversion and aggression in the area. We seek the full and effective restoration of

---

Special Message to Congress on U.S. Policy in Southeast Asia, President Lyndon B. Johnson.

the international agreements signed in Geneva in 1954, with respect to South Vietnam, and again in Geneva in 1962, with respect to Laos.

I recommend a Resolution expressing the support of the Congress for all necessary action to protect our armed forces and to assist nations covered by the SEATO Treaty. At the same time, I assure the Congress that we shall continue readily to explore any avenues of political solution that will effectively guarantee the removal of Communist subversion and the preservation of the independence of the nations of the area.

The Resolution could well be based upon similar resolutions enacted by the Congress in the past—to meet the threat to Formosa in 1955, to meet the threat to the Middle East in 1957, and to meet the threat in Cuba in 1962. It could state in the simplest terms the resolve and support of the Congress for action to deal appropriately with attacks against our armed forces and to defend freedom and preserve peace in Southeast Asia in accordance with the obligations of the United States under the southeast Asia Treaty. I urge the Congress to enact such a Resolution promptly and thus to give convincing evidence to the aggressive Communist nations, and to the world as a whole, that our policy in southeast Asia will be carried forward—and that the peace and security of the area will be preserved.

The events of this week would in any event have made the passage of a Congressional Resolution essential. But there is an additional reason for doing so at a time when we are entering on three months of political campaigning. Hostile nations must understand that in such a period the United States will continue to protect its national interests, and that in these matters there is no division among us.

Document 24.2 President Johnson's Vision for Vietnam

In 1965, just after sending the first official troops to Vietnam, Lyndon Johnson delivered a speech at Johns Hopkins University, in which he outlined a vision for Vietnam. In many ways this was a remarkable speech, in which he harkened back to the reclamation projects of the New Deal, like the Tennessee Valley Authority, and envisioned the United States transforming Southeast Asia with the same sort of ambitious programs.

President Johnson's Vision for Vietnam

Lyndon B. Johnson

Our objective is the independence of South Viet-Nam, and its freedom from attack. We want nothing for ourselves, only that the people of South Viet-Nam be allowed to guide their own country their own way.

In recent months attacks on South Viet-Nam were stepped up. Thus, it became necessary for us to increase our response and to make attacks by air. This is not a change of purpose. It is a change in what we believe that purpose requires. . . .

We hope that peace will come swiftly. But that is in the hands of others besides ourselves. And we must be prepared for a long continued conflict. It will require patience as well as bravery, the will to endure as well as the will to resist. . . .

These countries of southeast Asia are homes for millions of impoverished people. Each day these people rise at dawn and struggle through until the night to wrestle existence from the soil. They are often racked by disease, plagued by hunger, and death comes at the early age of 40.

Stability and peace do not come easily in such a land. Neither independence nor human dignity will ever be won, though, by arms alone. It also requires the work of peace. The American people have helped generously in past times. Now there must be a much more massive effort to improve the life of man in that conflict-torn corner of the world. . . .

American Goals in Vietnam, President Lyndon B. Johnson.

The task is nothing less than to enrich the hopes and existence of more than a hundred million people. And there is much to be done.

The vast Mekong River can provide food and water and power on a scale to dwarf even our own TVA.

The wonders of modern medicine can be spread through villages where thousands die every year from lack of care.

Schools can be established to train people in the skills that are needed to manage the process of development.

The ordinary men and women of North Viet-Nam, and South Viet-Nam . . . are brave people. They are filled with the same proportions of hate and fear, of love and hope. Most of them want the same things for themselves and their families. Most of them do not want their sons to die in battle, or to see their homes . . . destroyed.

Well, this can be their world yet. Man has the knowledge . . . to make this planet serve the real needs of the people who live on it.

Document 24.3 "Attention All Military Personnel"

The Vietnam Day Committee was an antiwar organization in Berkeley, California. Even before the beginning of the antiwar movement, the campus of the University of California at Berkeley had been a center of radical activity. Previously at Berkeley, students in the "The Free Speech Movement" had conducted large demonstrations against university regulation that they believed violated their right to free speech. Berkeley, therefore became a symbol of 1960s protest movements. In May 1965 the Vietnam Day Committee produced the following pamphlet for distribution to military personnel and potential draftees.

Attention All Military Personnel (Pamphlet, May 1965)

Vietnam Day Committee

You may soon be sent to Vietnam. You have heard about the war in the news; your officers will give you pep talks about it. But you probably feel as confused and uncertain as most Americans do. Many people will tell you to just follow orders and leave the thinking to others. But you have the right to know as much about this war as anyone. After all, it's you—not your Congressman—who might get killed.

Why Are We Fighting in Vietnam?

We are supposed to be fighting to protect democracy in Vietnam, and yet your own government admits that South Vietnam is run by a dictatorship. General Ky, the latest military dictator, is as bad as they come. In a recent interview he said: "People ask me who my heroes are. I have only one—Hitler. I admire Hitler because he pulled his country together when it was in a terrible state" (*London Sunday Mirror*, July 4, 1965).

General Ky doesn't mean much to us; we're not even sure how to pronounce his name, but the South Vietnamese have lived under men like him for years. As far as the Vietnamese are concerned, we are fighting on the side of Hitlerism: and they hope we lose.

Who Is the Enemy?

U.S. military spokesmen have often said that their greatest problem is finding the enemy. The enemy, they say, is everywhere. The old woman feeding her chickens may have a stock of hand grenades in her hut. The little boy who trails after the American soldiers during the day slips out to give information to the guerrillas at night. The washerwoman at the American air base brings a bomb to work one day. It is impossible, say the military, to tell which are the Viet Cong and which are the civilians.

And so, because the whole Vietnamese people seem to be the enemy, the military is taking no chances. They use tear gas—a weapon designed for use against civilians. They order American troops to fire at women and children—because women and children, after all, are firing at American troops. American fighter planes destroy civilian villages with napalm; American B-52s are flattening whole regions. That is why the war in Vietnam is so often called a "dirty war."

When the South Vietnamese people see you in your foreign uniform, they will think of you as their enemy. You are the ones bombing their towns. They don't know whether you're a draftee or a volunteer, whether you're for the war or against it; but they're not taking any chances either.

Free Elections

The Vietnamese would like to vote the foreigners out of their country, but they have been denied the chance. According to the Geneva Agreement of 1954, there were supposed to be elections throughout Vietnam in 1956. But the U.S. government was certain that our man in Vietnam, Premier Diem, would lose. So we decided not to allow any election until we were sure we could win. Diem set up a political police force and put all political opposition—Communist and anti-Communist—in jail. By 1959, it was clear there weren't going to be any elections, and the guerrillas known as the Viet Cong began to fight back. By 1963 our government was fed up with Diem, but still wasn't willing to risk elections. Our CIA helped a group of Vietnamese generals to overthrow Diem and kill him. Since then there have been a series of "better" military dictators. General Ky—the man who admires Hitler—is the latest one.

Fighting for Democracy

Your job as a soldier is supposed to be "to win the people of South Vietnam." Win them to what—democracy? No, we keep military dictators in power. What then? The American way of life? But why should they care any more about our way of life than we care about theirs? We can't speak their language or even pronounce their names. We don't know anything about their religion or even what it is. We never even heard of Vietnam until Washington decided to run it.

You are supposed to be fighting "to save the Vietnamese people from Communism." Certainly Communist influence is very strong in the National Liberation Front, the rebel government. Yet most of the people support the NLF. Why? Many of the same people who now lead the NLF led the Vietnamese independence movement against the Japanese during World II, and then went on to fight against French colonial rule. Most Vietnamese think of the NLF leaders as their country's outstanding patriots. In fact, many anti-Communists have joined the guerrilla forces in the belief that the most important thing is to get rid of foreign domination and military dictators. On the other hand, very few Vietnamese support the official government of General Ky. His army has low morale and a high desertion rate.

The Guerrillas

The newspapers and television have told us again and again what a tough fighter the Vietnamese guerrilla is. Short of ammunition and without any air cover, he can beat forces that outnumber him five or ten to one. Why do they have such high morale? They are not draftees; no draftees ever fight like that. They are not high-paid professional soldiers. Most of them are peasants who work their fields; they can't even spare the ammunition for target practice.

Their secret is that they know why they are fighting. They didn't hear about Vietnam in the newspapers; they've lived there all their lives. While we were in high school, they were living under the Diem regime and hating it. Now American planes are bombing their towns and strafing their fields; American troops have occupied their country; and if they complain out loud, an American-supported dictator sentences them to jail or the firing squad. Is it any wonder that they fight so fiercely?

Crushing the Resistance

The war in Vietnam is not being fought according to the rules. Prisoners are tortured. Our planes drop incendiary bombs on civilian villages. Our soldiers shoot at women and children. Your officers will tell you that it is all necessary, that we couldn't win the war any other way. *And they are right.* Americans are no more cruel than any other people; American soldiers don't enjoy this kind of war. But if you are going to wage war against an entire people, you have to become cruel.

The ordinary German soldier in occupied Europe wasn't especially cruel, either. But as the resistance movements grew, he *became* cruel. He shot at women and children because they were shooting at him; he never asked himself why they were shooting at him. When a certain town became a center of resistance activity, he followed his orders and destroyed the whole town. He knew that SS men were torturing captured resistance fighters, but it wasn't his business to interfere.

Following Orders

As a soldier you have been trained to obey orders, but as a human being you must take responsibility for your own acts. International and American law recognize that an individual soldier, even if acting under orders, must bear final legal and moral responsibility for what he does. This principle became a part of law after World War II, when the Allied nations, meeting in London, decided that German war criminals must be punished even if they committed war crimes under orders. This principle was the basis of the Nuremberg trials. We believe that the entire war in Vietnam is criminal and immoral. We believe that the atrocities which are necessary to wage this war against the people of Vietnam are inexcusable.

Oppose the War

We hope that you too find yourself, as a human being, unable to tolerate this nightmare war, and we hope that you will oppose it. We don't know what kind of risks we are taking in giving you this leaflet; you won't know what risk you will be taking in opposing the war. A growing number of GIs have already refused to fight in Vietnam and have been court-martialed. They have shown great courage. We believe that they, together with other courageous men who will join them, will have influence far out of proportion to their numbers.

There may be many other things you can do; since you are in the service, you know better than civilians what sorts of opposition are possible. But whatever you do, keep your eyes open. Draw your own conclusions from the things you see, read, and hear. At orientation sessions, don't be afraid to ask questions, and if you're not satisfied with the answers, keep asking. Take every chance you get to talk to your fellow soldiers about the war.

You may feel the war is wrong, and still decide not to face a court-martial. You may then find yourself in Vietnam under orders. You might be forced to do some fighting—but don't do any more than you have to. Good luck.

Document 24.4 U.S. Military Commander Announces Progress in the Vietnam War

As American military involvement in the Vietnam war increased, government leaders repeated attempts to assure the public that the war was going well and the U.S. would soon be successful. Influencing public opinion was actually an important part of the war. In 1967 the commander of American military forces in Vietnam, General William Westmoreland, gave a speech in which he attempted to persuade the public that the end was in sight. He announced that the U.S. had completed two phases of the war and was making excellent progress on the remaining two.

Progress Report on the War in Viet-Nam

General William C. Westmoreland

I would like to give you today a short progress report on some aspects of the war in Viet-Nam, because we in Viet-Nam are keenly aware of the genuine concern being expressed at home about the complex situation in that country.

The war in Viet-Nam eludes any precise numerical system of measurement or any easy portrayal of progress on battle maps. The war is unique and complicated in origin, in diversity of form, and in its diffusion throughout Viet-Nam. It is a war which probably could not have occurred in this pattern in any other country in these times. But if we had not met it squarely, it well could have been the precedent for countless more wars of a similar nature.

But we have confronted this challenge. We have found it to be like no other war we have fought before. There are no moving front lines—just a changing picture of small actions scattered over the country. Only a few of these actions are reported in detail. Even the trained observer is drawn to the unusual and the spectacular, and finds his attention shifting to another action before the significance or impact of the first can be analyzed.

I have been observing the war in South Viet-Nam at close hand for almost 4 years. During the first 1 1/2 years we were confined generally to an advisory role. In the past 2 1/2 years I have seen the progressive commitment of U.S. troops in support of the Vietnamese. I am absolutely certain that whereas in 1965 the enemy was winning, today he is certainly losing. There are indications that the Viet Cong and even Hanoi know this. However, the enemy may be operating from the delusion that political pressure here, combined with the tactical defeat of a major unit, might force the U.S. to "throw in the towel." If he does *not* believe this, there is very little logic to be found in his continuing the war in its present pattern.

Let me review with you the enemy's situation and our own, and let me offer my estimate of our relative positions.

Since 1925, when Ho Chi Minh arrived in Canton, China, he has actively sought to gain control of the area known as Indochina. In 1930 the Indochina Communist Party was created, with Ho Chi Minh as its chief. However, since that time the cause and methods have been similar to those of other Asian Communist parties.

Ho Chi Minh's party came to power amid the chaotic conditions at the end of World War II. Although the present government of North Viet-Nam has taken a facade of democracy, it has remained under tight control of the same small, determined group of Communists who served Ho Chi Minh in the Communist Party of the 1930's.

By 1954 it appeared to them that they had overcome the last major obstacle to the original goal. A million people had been displaced from the North, and although they were fleeing communism, they created a burden on the new government of South Viet-Nam. For the next few years the Communists believed that South Viet-Nam would succumb politically. These hopes were dashed by the vigor of the non-Communist government and by U.S. assistance.

In 1957 they reverted to terror, both indiscriminate and selective, with the assassination of teachers and local leaders. This terror rate went up every year. Despite that, it did not succeed. So, to guerrilla terror was added the military buildup of Viet Cong main-force units from 1959. Even this was not enough.

In 1963 and 1964 there started the military invasion from the North, when the first North Vietnamese regiments entered the South. This almost succeeded. By early 1965, the Vietnamese Government found its resolution exhausted by a decade of struggle and its last resources committed. It was at that point that the intervention of our Armed Forces restored a future to the long-suffering people of South Viet-Nam, who grasped the opportunity.

As you know, in the midst of war the South Vietnamese have in the past year held free elections and have turned out a larger percentage of the vote than we normally do in this country. The Viet Cong have tried desperately to stop these elections by terror and intimidation. But the Vietnamese voted despite the Viet Cong efforts. This mass disregard of Viet Cong initiatives killed the myth that the Viet

---

Department of State Bulletin, December 1967

Cong or the National Liberation Front speak for the people.

It is significant that the enemy has not won a major battle in more than a year. In general, he can fight his large forces only at the edges of his sanctuaries, as we have seen recently at Con Thien and along the DMZ, at Dak To opposite the Laotian border; at Song Be and Loc Ninh near the Cambodian border. His Viet Cong military units can no longer fill their ranks from the South but must depend increasingly on replacements from North Viet-Nam. His guerrilla force is declining at a steady rate. Morale problems are developing within his ranks.

Despite this, our enemy seeks to prolong the war, occasionally sallying forth from his sanctuaries and attempting by his countersweep operations to regain control of the population and to rebuild his guerrilla forces. Of essential importance is his desire to force us politically to stop, unconditionally, the bombing of his support base and his lines of communication. He appears to believe that he can defeat the Vietnamese forces, over 600,000 strong and getting stronger, reinforced by over 50,000 troops from free-world allies, and our commitment now approaching 500,000 men.

Buildup and Deployment of U.S. Forces

Our common plan with the Vietnamese has involved four distinct phases. In phase I we came to the aid of South Viet-Nam, prevented its collapse under the massive Communist thrust, built up our bases and began to deploy our foces. In phase I we planned and did the following:

Built ports, airfields, and supply and maintenance areas.
Set up a 10,000-mile-long supply pipeline.
Constructed an extensive communication system.
Brought in 400,000 men and several thousand aircraft.
Deployed troops throughout South Viet-Nam.
Learned to work alongside the Vietnamese Army, while encouraging development of a representative government.
Equipped and revitalized the Vietnamese Armed Forces, whose morale was low.
Expanded the Armed Forces of South Viet-Nam in quantitative terms.
Defended South Viet-Nam against defeat and against being cut in half.
Learned to cope with guerrilla tactics.
Set up an intelligence system for this new type of war.
Limited inflation.
Developed our own confidence that we could operate successfully in the environment of Southeast Asia.

We did all this by the middle of 1966. It was a tribute to U.S. organization, technology, and concerted diplomatic and military professionalism by many people.

Continuing Military and Economic Aid

At that point, during the summer of 1966, we moved into the second phase of our plan. In phase II we continued the pattern and did the following:

Drove the enemy divisions back to sanctuary or into hiding.
Trained, expanded, and improved the quality of the Vietnamese Armed Forces.
Assisted free-world forces of the Pacific area to join the battle against Communist aggression.
Entered enemy base areas and destroyed his supplies.
Raised enemy losses beyond his input capability.
Helped train the Vietnamese Army as a territorial security force.
Encouraged combined U.S.-Vietnamese operations.
Continued to help the Vietnamese Armed Forces in professional development.
Completed free elections within South Viet-Nam.
Saw an elected civilian government installed.
Stabilized prices—opening roads and canals.
Encouraged enemy defection and resettlement.
Discovered and thwarted the enemy's battle plans before they could be executed.
Unified the U.S. pacification assistance effort for better management of widespread resources.

We will complete this second phase by the end of this year. Before leaving my discussion of this phase, there is one other management aspect worthy of mention. Our rapid buildup 10,000 miles away in an undeveloped nation lacking in logistics support facilities has created many problems. Some units brought to Viet-Nam equipment that has not been needed. Some supplies were shipped automatically, based on experience in other wars, and have not been consumed in the quantities expected. At the same time, our magnificent fighting men have received what they needed to do their job. Now, at end of this second phase, we have been able to intensify logistical management and turn our attention to eliminating any excess items which may have developed. MACV has instituted an efficiency and economy program to which I have given the thrifty sounding name of Project MACONOMY.

Improving Vietnamese Effectiveness

With 1968, a new phase is now starting. We have reached an important point when the end begins to come into view. What is this third phase we are about to enter?

In phase III, in 1968, we intend to do the following:

Help the Vietnamese Armed Forces to continue improving their effectiveness.
Decrease our advisers in training centers and other places where the professional competence of Vietnamese officers makes this possible.
Increase our advisory effort with the younger brothers of the Vietnamese Army: the Regional Forces and Popular Forces.
Use U.S. and free-world forces to destroy North Vietnamese forays while we assist the Vietnamese to reorganize for territorial security.
Provide the new military equipment to revitalize the Vietnamese Army and prepare it to take on an ever-increasing share of the war.
Continue pressure on North to prevent rebuilding and to make infiltration more costly.
Turn a major share of frontline DMZ defense over to the Vietnamese Army.
Increase U.S. support in the rich and populated delta.
Help the Government of Viet-Nam single out and destroy the Communist shadow government.
Continue to isolate the guerrilla from the people.
Help the new Vietnamese government to respond to popular aspirations and to reduce and eliminate corruption.
Help the Vietnamese strengthen their police forces to enhance law and order.
Open more roads and canals.
Continue to improve the Vietnamese economy and standard of living.

The Final Phase

Now for phase IV—the final phase. That period will see the conclusion of our plan to weaken the enemy and strengthen our friends until we become progressively superfluous. The object will be to show the world that guerrilla warfare and invasion do not pay as a new means of Communist aggression.

I see phase IV happening as follows:

Infiltration will slow.
The Communist infrastructure will be cut up and near collapse.
The Vietnamese Government will prove its stability, and the Vietnamese Army will show that it can handle Viet Cong.
The Regional Forces and Popular Forces will reach a higher level of professional performance.
U.S. units can begin to phase down as the Vietnamese Army is modernized and develops its capacity to the fullest.
The military physical assets, bases and ports, will be progressively turned over to the Vietnamese.
The Vietnamese will take charge of the final mopping up of the Viet Cong (which will probably last several years). The U.S., at the same time, will continue the developmental help envisaged by the President for the community of Southeast Asia.

You may ask how long phase III will take, before we reach the final phase. We have already entered parts of phase III. Looking back on phases I and II, we can conclude that we have come a long way.

I see progress as I travel all over Viet-Nam.

I see it in the attitudes of the Vietnamese.

I see it in the open roads and canals.

I see it in the new crops and the new purchasing power of the farmer.

I see it in the increased willingness of the Vietnamese Army to fight North Vietnamese units and in the victories they are winning.

Parenthetically, I might say that the U.S. press tends to report U.S. actions; so you may not be as aware as I am of the victories won by South Vietnamese forces.

The enemy has many problems:

He is losing control of the scattered population under his influence.
He is losing credibility with the population he still controls.
He is alienating the people by his increased demands and taxes, where he can impose them.
He sees the strength of his forces steadily declining.
He can no longer recruit in the South to any meaningful extent; he must plug the gap with North Vietnamese.
His monsoon offensives have been failures.

He was dealt a mortal blow by the installation of a freely elected representative government.

And he failed in his desperate effort to take the world's headlines from the inauguration by a military victory.

Lastly, the Vietnamese Army is on the road to becoming a competent force. Korean troops in Viet-Nam provide a good example for the Vietnamese. Fifteen years ago the Koreans themselves had problems now ascribed to the Vietnamese. The Koreans surmounted these problems, and so can and will the Vietnamese.

The Vietnamese Armed Forces have accomplished much in a short time. Here are a few examples:

Career management for officers, particularly infantry officers, has been instituted.

Sound promotion procedures have been put into effect.

Discipline and conduct is being stressed.

Increased emphasis is being devoted to small unit tactics and leadership.

The promotion of enlisted men to the commissioned ranks is now commonplace (2,200 in 1966).

Officer candidates must now take basic training and prove that they have the leadership potential to be officers.

An Inspector General for the Vietnamese Armed Forces has been appointed and is now active in detailed inspections.

Corrupt and inefficient officials are being gradually eliminated.

The military school system has been revitalized.

The Military Academy has gone to a 4-year curriculum.

A school for battalion commanders has been established.

A 10-month National Defense College has been organized for selected senior officers.

The same personnel management programs which have been installed successfully in the Vietnamese Army are being expanded to the Regional Forces and Popular Forces.

We are making progress. We know you want an honorable and early transition to the fourth and last phase. So do your sons and so do I.

It lies within our grasp—the enemy's hopes are bankrupt. With your support we will give you a success that will impact not only on South Viet-Nam but on every emerging nation in the world.

Document 24.5 Vietnam Veterans Recount Their Experiences

While Americans at home might debate the Vietnam war, several hundred thousand young Americans actually went to Vietnam. While experiences varied, they had some things in common. In the following selection, three diverse Americans describe what they experienced.

Vietnam Veterans Recount Their Experiences

James R. Wilson

Richard C. Ensminger, Blowing Rock, North Carolina Marine Forward Observer, 1966–67, 1969

I guess I saw myself as another John Wayne for my first few weeks in Vietnam. I loaded myself down with extra grenades and ammo, but it didn't take me very long to learn that all that ammo was too heavy in the heat. On the other hand, it was an Article 15 offense to discard it in the field, so I finally worked myself down to one or two M-26 fragmentation grenades, eight to ten magazines for my M-14, and three or four canteens of water. Since I was a forward observer, I also carried a compass, a map case, a pair of binoculars, and at least one meal of C-rations. My helmet was decorated with bottles of Texas Pete hot sauce for the C-rats and bug juice to keep off the B-52 mosquitoes. We didn't wear underwear; it would rot off you because we were lucky to get a bath every two weeks.

My battalion ran a lot of short, sweeping combat operations along Highway 1 from Danang to Dong Ha. After a couple of months of that, I was sent out to a Fourth Marines firebase at Cam Lo, near the DMZ. The base had four tanks, four 105s, four 155s and two eight-inch howitzers, as well as two mortar units. Other than that, it was little more than red clay and heat. We lived in what we called lean-tos: two ponchos tied together. During the day we lived in what shade we could find or under the ponchos. They did double duty as body bags, too.

I worked on Operation Hastings as a forward observer, going out with units that had as many as forty men and as few as four or five. I called in harassing fire on Charlie. In Vietnam, a forward observer was supposed to have a radio operator with him, but most FOs carried their own radios. And we also preferred to carry our M-14s rather than M-16s because the 14 was more reliable and accurate. I learned a lot of things in Vietnam that hadn't been taught to me in the states. For instance, I loaded my own rounds. I used wire cutters to snip off the tip of M-14 bullets. You'd be surprised what a cutoff M-14 bullet can do to somebody—it will tear him a new you-know-what. Of course, the M-14 was a big, long-range infantry rifle that wasn't designed for close combat in the bush. Some marines cut off the barrels of their rifles to compensate for that. Whatever weapon a marine had, though—and some had .357 Magnum pistols—he kept it cleaned and in good working order because his life depended on it.

I was always humping, always on the move. All of us worried a lot about ambushes. For that reason, we never had a set time for a patrol to go out. Sometimes we'd go in the middle of the day or late evening. If we set a schedule, Charlie got to know about it. He would know when we were out, where we were, and whether we followed the same trail twice. You learned this from guys who had been over there for a while. They knew how to stay alive.

When I first got to Cam Lo, the old-timers who had been in Vietnam for a year wouldn't have anything to do with me. They knew I knew my job, but their attitude troubled me at first. We new guys stayed together and little by little moved into the group. It was an initiation. I had to prove to them that I wouldn't get them killed. It was something that everybody went through. One marine warned me, "I'll tell you once: you mess up and you're on your own. Mess up twice and I'll kill you." He was a lance corporal, the same rank as me.

"Are you kidding?" I said.

"No, I'm not. I'll kill you in a moment's notice. You're not gonna get me killed." I figured the best way not to screw up was to stay in the back and watch everybody else. New guys in the back of a line couldn't trip bouncing betties or step on mines. But if a new guy took the point, people started getting very nervous.

Most marine grunts were good for only six to eight months of combat. It took from three to six months to learn the basics of staying in one piece. Then, for the last couple of months before a guy's DEROS, we just left him alone for the most part because he had the short-timer's attitude. This was when most of our courts-martial and office hours came up. Short-timers didn't want to go out in the field; they were afraid some guy would screw up their chances of going home. Second lieutenants sometimes did that. They were a dime a dozen in the marines. A second lieutenant who screwed up twice was a dead man, and not necessarily because of the enemy. He might get killed by his own men.

A lieutenant who came in and said, "Hey, I don't know what's going on" and looked to his sergeants to help him along usually did all right. But one who marched in and announced that he was going to run the show, that he was the boss out there in the bush—if he made it, he was damn lucky. His sergeant might turn around to him and say, "Nobody can hear you. Stand up and tell 'em." Charlie would pick off that lieutenant as soon as he did that. The sergeants, now they were the ones we paid attention to. Some of those guys were amazingly brave: they would walk rice paddy dikes under fire and never get a scratch.

I could usually have gunfire coming in on Charlie within a minute or a minute and a half of asking for it. If gunfire had to be cleared through the Danang Intelligence Center because of friendly troops in the area, it might take half an hour, which was entirely too long. Sometimes Danang would even deny gunfire because friendly troops were out there. Of course they were. *We* were the friendlies who needed fire on an enemy position. When the first round slammed in, Charlie would always look around in surprise. If the round was close enough, he'd scramble around and try to scatter. If the second round was on target, I'd tell the gunners to fire for effect. Then I'd see bodies flying apart, vegetation being torn up, the earth just erupting, all hell in

---

one moment. I've been on the receiving end of it, so I know what the enemy's feelings must have been.

If a forward observer gets spotted by the enemy, his life expectancy is about fifteen seconds. The same is true for snipers and scouts. I knew that before I went to Vietnam. As soon as Charlie saw you, he was going to try to kill you. I had a close call like that on Operation Prairie. I caught some Charlies in the open, but I didn't know they had small flanking units all around them. When they passed by a firebase, I called in 81mm mortars, maybe a hundred rounds pumped out from four tubes. We started taking automatic weapons fire from the side while I was on the radio, telling the mortar crews what was happening. Before it was all over, my radio operator and three or four other grunts got hit. It was a damned scary business.

I got wounded nine months into my first tour, in February of 1967, when a firebase basically got overrun during Operation Independence. It was a shrapnel wound. Charlie mortared the place on a cold, rainy night, dropping maybe forty or fifty rounds before he came at us—I believe he knew that firebase backwards and forwards. Before it was over, I burned out the barrel of an M-60, the 60mm mortars ran out of ammunition, all the LAWs were fired and not one radio worked. I was down to fifteen rounds for my .45 pistol when Charlie finally pulled back. If he'd hit us again, all of us would have been dead.

We fired a lot of 60mm illumination rounds and pop-up flares during the attack. Everybody carried two or three pop-up flares. To fire one, you pulled the cap off and put it on the rear end. Then you hit the cap and a little parachute flare shot about two hundred feet in the air. The flares let us see the enemy fairly well; I could tell that some of them were moving quickly, but others, for some reason, weren't. They were firing their weapons mostly from the hip. I'll tell you, I was scared to hell and back, but I think I fought to the best of my ability. There was always some fear in my mind that I was going to screw up, that I would let down one or two guys that I'd gotten close to. It was like walking a log across a river: one wrong step and you're going to fall in. The fear of screwing up was there all the time.

There were always some guys who looked for any excuse to avoid combat. One of them lives here in Watauga County. The way he tells it, he would put on his flak vest, his helmet, and his body pants—which I never saw anybody wear in Vietnam—and then he'd drop an M-26 grenade on the ground and walk fifteen feet away. That gave him enough shrapnel wounds in his legs to get medevaced out. This guy never really got hurt, but he picked up three Purple Hearts. He boasted to me one day that's how he got out of Vietnam. Frankly, I don't talk to the man. The only legitimate way to get out of combat in Vietnam was heat exhaustion, but we could sometimes con the company commander into letting us go to the rear to pick up some supplies. We never knew what might come out on the resupply chopper. I remember one grunt who talked his way into going back to make sure we got some hot food. A note came back with the chopper: "I couldn't get the hot food, but here's two fifths of liquor." We needed liquor in the bush like we needed a hole in the head.

I stayed in Vietnam ten days longer than I was supposed to on my first tour. I was in the bush in March of 1967, still seeing guys getting killed, when I figured I'd have to take some action of my own. I got on the radio to regimental headquarters. They said, "You're still in the field, huh?" A couple of days later, a chopper came out to get me. Well, as luck would have it, 122mm rockets started coming into Danang just as I was getting on the freedom bird to Okinawa. The plane had made it to the end of the runway when the captain announced that he couldn't take off because a rocket had blown off the tail section. Still another delay while we transferred to a new plane. On this one, I discovered that I had come out of the bush so fast I still had forty rounds of M-14 ammo in some of my gear.

I came back to El Toro Marine Air Station in California, where I took a shower, picked up my seabag and gladly took thirty days' leave, with fifteen days of grace travel to my next duty station. When I went to Vietnam, I weighed 235 pounds. I weighed 175 pounds when I came back, all solid muscle and red clay dirt. I rode a military bus down to San Diego to catch a flight to Miami, where I planned to unwind for a while. I had on my short-sleeve khakis, which were very wrinkled because they had been in my seabag for thirteen months, and my combat boots. I had slapped some black polish on them, but I really didn't care what anybody said. I was home.

As I got off the bus and started to walk up a ramp at the San Diego airport, a woman who looked to be about fifty years old jumped out of the crowd and pointed a .22 pistol at a marine twenty guys in front of me.

"You woman and child killer!" she screamed. She put six rounds in that marine at point-blank range.

When I heard her first shot, I hit the ground and rolled back under the bus. It was an automatic reaction—I had to find a place to hide. The marine who was shot had wounds in his stomach and side, but none of them was fatal. The woman was lucky to live through what happened to her, too. Some of the other marines threw her over a fence eight feet high. I understand the fall broke both her legs and several ribs. All of us who witnessed the shooting were held up a day because we had to give statements to the police and navy criminal investigators about what had happened. I simply wrote that I crawled under a bus.

I believe in God and country. When I went to Vietnam, I believed it was my duty to go over there and fight for my country. I came back as a corporal E-4 with a Purple Heart and a couple of unit citations. I knew I had done something worthwhile, but I wasn't prepared for the demonstrations against the war here, for the people who downgraded me for being in the military. As I saw it, there were three groups of people in the United States: the older people who didn't care about the war, the kids who didn't understand it, and those who were totally against Vietnam, against everything we were doing over there. The situation eventually got so bad that we were told to stay away from the civilian population as much as possible to hold down friction.

I went on to Miami Beach to spend thirty days with a couple of sergeants, but I cut it short after only six days. I was twenty years old, but I was supposed to be twenty-one to walk into a bar. I was old enough to fight for my country, but I couldn't get a beer. That wasn't all. If I walked up to a girl and asked her to dance, she'd take one look at me, like I was something with a bad smell, and wouldn't have anything to do with me. I had been back from Vietnam for only a week and already I was feeling like an outsider. And I was getting angry. I let my weight shoot up to two hundred pounds, I wore all my campaign ribbons, and I let people know I was one mean mother. I remember walking in one bar in Miami and some people said they wanted me out of there. I told a dude who shoved me that if he did it one more time, I'd gladly take on him and everybody else in the place. Another veteran was in there, a fellow who had lost an arm in Korea.

"I'll be more than happy to back you up," he said. The place settled down fast.

I went on to my next duty station at Quantico Marine Base in Virginia for training in crowd and riot control. In the fall of 1967, a big antiwar demonstration was being planned at the Pentagon, and a bunch of us at Quantico were trucked up there for security. I was one of several marines put on top of the building. I had a pump shotgun, body armor, and a helmet. Our shells had rubber bullets in them, but somebody high up must have thought it would be a bad idea to issue ammo to men who had served in Vietnam. Maybe they were afraid we would get mad enough to shoot somebody.

I had to work one more big demonstration, this one in front of the Capitol. This time, about fifty marines were called up from Quantico. We were issued full riot gear: helmets with plastic face shields, body armor, gas masks, and shotguns with five rounds of rubber ammo. Some marines in the line behind me had tear gas guns for backup protection. The people in front of me called me a babykiller, they called my mother every name in the book, and they did the same for my sister. I didn't like crowd control duty and had asked to get out of it. I tried to make it clear to my sergeant that someday a protester would come up to me and say the wrong thing and I'd shoot the bastard.

"You can't do much harm with a rubber bullet," he said. Well, I stood in that line and took the verbal abuse, but when a man spit in my face, I showed him what a marine with a shotgun could do. I got an Article 15 for my trouble and a transfer to other duty.

I volunteered to go back to Vietnam after a little more than a year in the states. I didn't feel comfortable going outside a military base. Somehow, I felt I wasn't wanted in American society. And I was getting tired of the petty, spit-shined mentality of the stateside marines. In Vietnam, I could do what I was trained for. Maybe I was also getting a bit paranoid—officers and authority were making me nervous. When I got back to Danang in April of 1969, the base had grown tremendously. It was now a big city of metal buildings. Naturally, a few things hadn't changed. I still had to go through Dogpatch, two miles of whorehouses outside the base, to get to a staging area where I got orders for the 3/5th Marines.

As I see it now, I think I wanted another tour in Vietnam to help keep marines from getting killed. It had become more important to me to keep Americans alive than to kill NVA. I was a sergeant by this time, and I figured I would be sent out to a rifle company as a forward observer, which was a good way to accomplish what I wanted to do. But Vietnam had changed and the marines had, too. We had draftees now. On my first tour, we were all volunteers. Now there was a drug problem that I hadn't seen before. Marijuana grew in every creek bed in Vietnam. Grunts were getting stoned on it, on hash and other drugs—you name it, and you could buy it. I could see this was a different war from the first time around, and I made up my mind not to trust the men screwed up on drugs. I would do my duty, but I intended to come out alive.

When I flew out to my company near An Hoa, south of Danang, I jumped off the chopper in the middle of a firefight. In a way, my arrival was a sort of metaphor for my second tour. Lima company never stayed in one place; it was always on the move. No rest, no sleep. After only two weeks in the bush, I was numb, worn out. All I wanted was a hot meal and twenty-four hours of sleep. I saw a lot more killing and mutilation during my second tour. For one thing, I was closer to it. During my first tour, I spent some time with the Combined Action Platoon program on hamlet security, but now the war seemed like one endless search-and-destroy mission. Since I was one of the few forward observers in my battalion, I spent almost all my time in the bush. I would go back to the rear with a company, then turn right around and go back out with another one.

I was so tired I started to act by instinct alone. I was lucky to get four hours of sleep a night. I know now that I was doing a lot of stupid things: I'd see two VC running out there and call in a fire mission, instead of letting my snipers and scouts handle them. I'd just blow the hell out of an area. I was even calling in false reports. I was out for blood. The one mistake in my life that I'm sorry for, that I still have nightmares over, came one day I was with Lima company. We took some small-arms fire from a village. Right away, I called for mixed air and ground bursts of artillery fire that flattened the place in less than five minutes. . . . It was a godlike display of power. After it was all over, I walked through a burning, smoky ruin of straw and bamboo huts. I could see parts of human and animal bodies scattered all around, and I noticed that the air was saturated with a sharp smell of gunpowder and urine. At this time, every marine unit in my battalion was supposed to meet a quota in VC and NVA—it was a meat quota. A lot of civilians who got killed were called VC. In fact, the village that I shot up became a VC village: four hundred confirmed kills, women and children. Lima company met its meat quota for two months with that one village alone.

I justified what I had done by thinking about marines that I had seen get shot and lay wounded, unable to move to safety, while the VC kept shooting at them. Sometimes the VC would shoot at a grunt even after he was dead. Seeing such things had a hardening effect on all of us. I think a lot of marines felt we were still fighting for a reason in 1969, but we weren't sure what the reason was anymore. The war had become a sort of perpetual-motion killing machine. We killed them and they killed us, and nothing seemed to change.

In June of 1969, I was in the bush with Kilo company, which had a new lieutenant who didn't like artillery. I could see why—he wanted to prove himself by getting marines killed in senseless infantry assaults. He wanted to punch his ticket and win medals for fast promotion. The fact that he didn't like artillery meant nothing to me. If I wanted artillery, I called for it. Now, this lieutenant had been brought in to replace an officer wounded in a minor ambush. He wanted glory, but he was green and scared, and that led to a snap decision to put me in charge of an infantry platoon made up of two other platoons that had lost half their men. Well, I had forgotten my fire-team tactics a long time ago and I tried to tell him that. We stood ankle-deep in rice paddy water eleven clicks from An Hoa while he warned me I would be court-martialed if I refused to take over the platoon. He also ordered me to sign off the artillery radio net and get on the battalion net.

"That's strictly against orders," I said. Again, he said he was the commanding officer, he had authority to make decisions, and I was headed for a court-martial if I disobeyed him. I had questioned orders before but never disobeyed them. So, I took over the platoon of fifty-four marines and led them toward a hamlet a short distance away.

There was enough bamboo in the area to limit our line of sight to about a hundred meters. The NVA were waiting for us in a classic L-shaped ambush along a creek bed outside the hamlet. They let the point squad walk into the hamlet before opening up on the rest of us. I believe we were hit by an entire company of NVA supported by a weapons platoon because those people laid down some fire on us. I was one of the first men to get hit, in the back of my left leg, and I'm sure it was my radio operator who did it. I felt a sharp, burning pain in my leg and swung around and saw the RTO frozen to his rifle, which was still firing. His head was gone. A round had taken it off and blood was spurting up from his neck like a water fountain. He must have had his M-14 on automatic and his trigger finger touched it off when he was hit. It put seven bullets in my leg. To this day, I don't know who he was or where he was from.

I can remember somebody dragging me into a bomb crater or some other kind of hole. My leg felt like it was on fire. I reached for my backpack and got out a shot of morphine to get some relief from the pain. By that time in the war, almost everybody was carrying little tubes of morphine. I popped off the cap, squeezed a bit of the fluid out, and stuck the needle in my leg. I still had some idea of what was going on around me—all hell was breaking loose. About twenty feet away, a gook in a spider trap was popping up now and then to spray the area with his AK-47. I shot at him with my M-14. A lot of marines were getting hit. A corpsman jumped in the hole to give me another shot of morphine and fell back in when he tried to leave. His guts were blown out. I could hear men screaming for their mothers, for God, for death. Those who got up to help others got shot themselves.

The ambush probably lasted less than an hour, but it seemed like days. I heard choppers coming in and the next thing I knew, a marine was trying to help me. I was certain he was an NVA, so I pulled out my .45 pistol and tried to shoot him. I woke up in a hospital, thoroughly doped up on morphine, and somebody told me I was one of four survivors of the ambush. I still had my wounded leg, but my right arm was in traction. I was also in a body cast except for my right foot. I had dislocated my shoulder and still had four or five bullets inside of me, not to mention some four hundred tiny pieces of shrapnel.

Later, I was told that I was trying to operate the radio when I was in the hole. How it got there, I have no idea. Radio operators back at battalion headquarters heard me trying to call in artillery fire, but I wasn't giving the right coordinates. They couldn't talk to me because I never let go of the key on the microphone. According to what I was told, I was calling for variable time fuses, which would have thrown shrapnel down on me and everybody else. I figured three-fourths if not more of us were already dead and that I was going to die there, too. Why not take everybody out?

I was shipped out to a hospital in Japan for a while, and then on to Bethesda Naval Hospital. I kept my leg for twenty-two months. The doctors kept saying, "We'll save it. You're going to walk again." Then one day they walked in and said it had to come off four inches above the knee.

I prayed to the Lord that I wouldn't lose my leg, but for some reason I couldn't fight off the infections in my bones and blood. I was in a clean, isolated room at Bethesda with blood going into me, IVs and heart monitors hooked up to me, but the doctors didn't know why I wasn't healing. Anybody who came in to see me had to wear a bibbed gown and a face mask.

I was released from the marines after recovering from the loss of my leg. I was taking six shots of morphine a day until I left Bethesda, when they gave me a six-month prescription for 180 tablets of Demerol a month. The VA gave me Percodan, a sleep medication. I had so much painkiller I hardly knew what was going on. That was the start of a drug dependency that took years to get under control. I went to stay with my parents, who were living in Greensboro, North Carolina, at the time. They couldn't understand why I slept so much during the day. My father, in particular, was puzzled by my tendency to fly off the handle, why I couldn't stay in a room any length of time, why I was taking two or three showers a night to get the sweat off me.

A lot of my emotional and physical problems came out of my second tour in Vietnam. In my nightmares, I relive calling in artillery on the village and seeing my buddies get killed in the ambush. I know of one survivor who killed himself. If the others remember as much about it as I do, they would be better off dead, too. I've been in and out of hospitals maybe sixteen times with kidney, lung, liver, and prostate problems. I've developed diabetes, which means headaches, failing eyesight, and failing hearing. Something made me sterile in Vietnam and I believe it was Agent Orange. I sprayed Agent Orange around some of the firebases with a backpack pump like the ones used to fight forest fires. Choppers would come around and spray, too. A couple of days later, we would burn the dead vegetation to make a kill zone two or three hundred meters wide.

Sometimes, I think the VA has caused me more pain and aggravation than anything else. I go and sit in the VA hospital in Johnson City for hours on end just to hear somebody tell me all these problems are in my imagination. Maybe I shouldn't be surprised, because it took the VA twenty years to figure out I have 50 percent PTSD. There are days when I lock myself up in a room. Nancy understands that. She knows I need time to myself. She's gone through a lot of counseling herself at the Vet Center in Johnson City and she's learned that she's not the only woman trying to live with a Vietnam veteran. Twenty or thirty other wives around here are going through the same thing. With my stepchildren, it's been more difficult. I think my stepson Franklin understands me now more than he did, even though he lived away from home for three years because the courts said it was a bad idea for him to live under the same roof with me. I have a twenty-year-old stepdaughter who lives in Florida. She won't speak to me because she considers me too unpredictable.

I have been so depressed at times that I've thought of suicide. I'm a forty-two-year-old man living in the body of a sixty-year-old. I really believe my health is failing, that I am slowly dying. A couple of weeks ago, I was told that I have a bad blood flow from hardening of the arteries. No one in my family has ever had that. No one has had diabetes or a nervous condition.

I have very few friends. I don't make friends easily because I can't get close to people. I spent five months at the VA hospital in Augusta, Georgia, in 1985 for treatment of post-traumatic stress disorder, but I'm still described as somebody with "a nervous condition with bad personality disorders." Maybe so. I've had a lot of jobs and ended up getting fired from most of them. Probably the only people I can really relate to are the members of the Disabled American Veterans chapter in Boone.

You know, I believe the war started out as a just cause that ended up being a very political affair. A lot of people made a lot of money off it; some of them are still making money off it. In one way, I'm proud that I served. I'm a true marine who went and fought for my country and for a way of life and I'm proud of that. But I'm not proud of what I did over there. It sickens me now to see a child cry, a child hurt. I can't watch a war story or an operation on television without throwing my guts up and having nightmares that night.

Roosevelt Gore, Nichols, South Carolina Army Mortarman, 1967–1968

I finished Palmetto High School, a segregated school, in June of 1966. In August, I got my draft notice two weeks after I went to work for a factory in Mullins that made household furniture. I don't know how many whites was being drafted in Marion County at the time, but I do know a lot of blacks was being called. My father was very proud that I was going into the army. He wanted me to make a career out of it. I knew something was going on in Vietnam, but I didn't pay much attention to it. Two of my Palmetto High classmates had joined the marines and got killed over there, but Vietnam was still a long way off. I was more worried about my mother, who was very sick with heart disease at the time.

I went down to Fort Jackson for basic training and will never forget my drill instructor, a white guy who must have weighed two hundred pounds. He didn't like blacks. He always picked on blacks, maybe because we was from the South and he considered us to be illiterate. He used to kick us and spit on us, call us "niggers" and say, "All you black son-of-a-bitches are going to Vietnam." He liked to order me to get down on all fours and pick up cigarette butts with my mouth. Sometimes I've said, if I could see that guy again . . . but that's all in the past now.

He was a staff sergeant, big and intimidating with that Smokey the Bear hat that the DIs wore. Everybody in my outfit hated this guy but nobody knew what to do about him. We was so afraid we hardly even mentioned his name. As new as I was to the army, I thought all the sergeants and officers was going to be like him. All through basic, I kept wishing I'd never been drafted. AIT at Fort Jackson was much better, though. It was more professional and I don't remember any racial harassment. I got my MOS as a mortarman there and I liked it. I got to be pretty good with the 81mm mortars. I could set one up, adjust for elevation and deflection, and drop a round on the target within a couple of minutes.

I heard a lot of talk about Vietnam in AIT. It was obvious we was being trained for combat there, even though not everybody would be going. Quite a few of the guys I knew in AIT had brothers in Vietnam, which meant they couldn't get orders until their brothers came home. They liked to talk about Vietnam, maybe because they knew they wasn't going. I got my orders at the end of AIT. I came home to Mullins for thirty days, but there wasn't much to do except pull up cotton stalks. My daddy was more excited about Vietnam than I was. He thought it would make a man out of me. I didn't exactly see it that way because 1966 was one of the toughest times in Vietnam, and I was honestly afraid to go.

My mother never said much about Vietnam, but she broke down in tears the day I had to get on an airplane at Florence and fly up to Chicago. From there, I went on to Oakland Army Base for a couple of days of processing before going on to Vietnam. I didn't talk to very many people on the flight over. In fact, I spent most of my time writing a letter to my girlfriend back in Mullins. I had never been anyplace, so I told her about the Chicago airport, San Francisco, Oakland, our stopover in Anchorage, Alaska, and the time-zone changes.

We landed at Tan Son Nhut airport in Saigon at night and walked out into air so hot and sticky it was hard to breathe. Gosh, it had an odor—swampy like. It reminded me of the low country in the summer. I remember being very tired and wanting to lay down. I wondered if we would have a place to sleep that night, but before that could happen, we had to sign some papers at the airport and then load our duffel bags on a bus. I have no idea where we went to that night, only that it was a reception station out in the boondocks.

I got orders for the First Infantry Division while I was in AIT, so I didn't stay at the reception station very long. I flew out to Di An on a Huey the next day—my first ride in a helicopter. In fact, I knew so little about choppers that I didn't even buckle my seat belt during the flight; I thought I was going to fall out of that Huey the whole time. I was sent down to the weapons platoon of Charlie Company, 1/18th Infantry. I hardly had time to meet anybody, but I remember some short-timers saying, "Welcome to Vietnam. You can have it." The platoon sergeant told me to saddle up for a patrol with about twenty other guys that very night. Naturally, I had absolutely no idea of where I was or what was going on. But I do know that I almost drowned that night when we walked through a pond.

I stepped in a hole and went down like a rock. The guys walking behind me pulled me up. One of them said, "You can't swim?" The truth is, I didn't know how to swim. I was more concerned at the time that Charlie might open up on us, but thank God nothing happened.

I started to meet some of the other guys in my outfit after a couple of days at Di An. I could tell that a lot of them was from the South, but for some reason they didn't want to admit it. Not a single one of them would admit it. They wanted people to think they was from the North, and I can't tell you why. I told everybody I was from South Carolina. I didn't see any reason to make a secret of it, and neither did Dave Simpson, a medic who was from South Carolina, too, or Ted Burton, another medic from Tennessee.

Charlie Company had more blacks and Hispanics than it did whites. Most of the guys got along with each other pretty well, but there was a few blacks who liked to pick on the whites, especially when we was in Di An. Just the least little thing a white guy might say would set one of these black guys off and he would want to fight. The white might say "nigger" and that would be enough to cause trouble. I was never like that, though, and sometimes I felt the other blacks in the company resented me because I made friends with whites.

I saw my first real combat a couple of months after getting to Charlie Company. We was on a patrol when a VC hiding behind a tree with an AK-47 pinned down the whole company. My platoon sergeant got shot through the arm, and a medic, a white guy from Columbia, was killed with a round through his neck. Ted Burton was trying to put a bandage on the sergeant when I lobbed a hand grenade at the VC and flushed him out from behind the tree. A machinegunner killed him with a hundred rounds from his M-60. That VC looked like hamburger meat when he got through with him.

I was always the point man, maybe because I was black, until we went out on one patrol and set up for the night. We got attacked and the E-4 that was in charge of the squad, a white guy, cracked up. I got everybody back, no casualties, wounded, or nothing, because I was a pretty good soldier by then. I got my sergeant's stripes the next morning.

The worst time I had in Vietnam came on the night of November 2, 1967. I didn't know if I was going to make it or not. All three companies of the 1/18th was on Operation Shenandoah II in the rubber plantations around Loc Ninh. The intelligence people said a regiment of NVA and VC was in the area, so my company set up a perimeter in a field away from the rubber trees. The birds was so noisy after dark that I was sure somebody was moving out there. I tried to sleep, but I couldn't. About two o'clock in the morning, the birds got real quiet and that's when Charlie cut loose on us. A couple of patrols was run back to the perimeter by VC with flamethrowers. Rockets, mortars, and .50-caliber machine-gun fire started to come from everywhere.

I was in charge of the mortar squad and it didn't take us very long to start throwing it back at Charlie. They was about fifty yards away, so close we used only one or two charges on the mortar rounds. We was dropping them almost on the perimeter. We pumped a lot of rounds out there. Matter of fact, we fired so many illumination rounds we ran out of them for a while. When the illumination rounds was up, I could see the VC. They was dressed in green shirts and pants and helmets, and they was coming at us in a human wave.

I was standing up in a sandbag mortar pit directing fire. Another sergeant, a section leader named White, was outside the pit for some reason when a 82mm mortar round exploded about three feet in front of him. I heard the round that got him come whistling in. It was a real shame because White was scheduled to go to Hawaii on R&R to meet his wife. When the mortar round hit, I saw a flash of white light and felt a tremendous explosion, so loud that I have a ringing in my ears to this day. I felt something hit me in the stomach and butt, something that didn't hurt so much as burn.

I hollered, "Medic!" Dave Simpson came running up to me. He picked out some slivers of shrapnel and put bandages on my wounds. "You've got your Purple Heart," he said.

I went right back to directing mortar fire—I guess I was a gung-ho soldier. The attack went on most of the night. Before it was over, we had to call in airstrikes on the perimeter to help keep Charlie back. The jets dropped bombs so close to us some of our own people got hurt.

We didn't lose many people that night, but I counted 142 Vietnamese on the perimeter after the sun came up. They was about my age or younger. Most of them was torn apart and dead, but a few was still alive, moaning and groaning. I noticed that quite a few of them was carrying marijuana. The wounded ones tried to talk to us, but I didn't know what they was saying and I didn't care. They would look us in the face and stick out their arms, reach out to us, but I'll tell you I had no sympathy for them. None whatsoever. I wouldn't let them grab me or touch me in any way.

Somebody brought in a backhoe and scooped out a deep trench. We threw the Charlies into it, dead and alive. The wounded ones wasn't going to live very long, anyway. I knew it was a violation of the Geneva Convention, but what we did that morning has never bothered me. I wasn't in command. It was kill or be killed in Vietnam, and this time we had done the killing.

I didn't hear much news from the states while I was in Vietnam. To tell you the truth, I wasn't very concerned with civil rights and everything else that was going on back home. I was more concerned about staying alive.

After six months, though, I did begin to wonder what we were doing in Vietnam. It seemed like the more Viet Cong we killed, the more we had coming at us. I don't know how the Vietnamese civilians in our area felt about us, but some of the things I saw probably speak for themselves. The biggest thing that bothers me has to do with some of our soldiers who would use their rifle butts to hit Vietnamese kids on the side of the head. The kids was begging the GIs for food, asking for a piece of C-ration candy or whatever, and the guys, would just knock them out. I don't think anybody cared.

I told my folks about a lot of the things that was going on in my letters home, but it was a telegram that caused the most trouble. A day or two after the big attack in November, my mother got a telegram saying I'd been killed. She told me after I came back that the mailman got out of his car and walked up to the house with the telegram. He said he was sorry to have to deliver it. Of course, she knew right then what the telegram said. It was a big shock to her and she fell sick for a while, at least until the Red Cross could get the facts straight.

I finished my tour in February of 1968 and came back to Fort Hood, Texas, where I went into a ground-surveillance radar outfit for my last six months in the army. It was easy duty after Vietnam, but after a while I came to hate life in the states more than I had over there. There was a lot of reasons, I guess, but one of the biggest of them had to do with an incident at Fort Hood. A couple of white guys and me tried to go to a dance at the enlisted men's club one night. Well, some soldier had married a Vietnamese woman and brought her back here. She was taking up a cover charge at the door—I think it was a dollar—and when we walked up to her to pay our money to get in, she wouldn't take my dollar bill.

"Niggers can't come in here," she said, looking straight at me. Her remark almost tore me apart. I could hardly believe what that woman had said.

"I just spent a year over there trying to help you," I said, "and you're going to turn white on me?" I was angry, terribly angry. All three of us walked off. I didn't do a thing about it—but I should have.

Document 24.6 President Nixon Announces the "Vietnamization" of the War

Richard Nixon's policy was to withdraw American troops while trying at the same time to prevent a South Vietnamese military defeat. This strategy involved all of the following, preferably simultaneously: the use of American military power, reducing the exposure of Americans to duty in Vietnam, and reducing the number of U.S. troops in combat. In the following speech, which he made on nation-wide television in November 1969, Nixon explained his program.

President Nixon Announces the "Vietnamization" of the War

Richard M. Nixon

Let me briefly explain what has been described as the Nixon doctrine—a policy which not only will help end the war in Viet-Nam but which is an essential element of our program to prevent future Viet-Nams.

We Americans are a do-it-yourself people. We are an impatient people. Instead of teaching someone else to do a job, we like to do it ourselves. And this trait has been carried over into our foreign policy.

In Korea and again in Viet-Nam, the United States furnished most of the money, most of the arms, and most of the men to help the people of those

Department of State Bulletin, November 24, 1969.

countries defend their freedom against Communist aggression.

Before any American troops were committed to Viet-Nam, a leader of another Asian country expressed this opinion to me when I was traveling in Asia as a private citizen. He said: "When you are trying to assist another nation defend its freedom, U.S. policy should be to help them fight the war, but not to fight the war for them."

Well, in accordance with this wise counsel, I laid down in Guam three principles as guidelines for future American policy toward Asia:

- First, the United States will keep all of its treaty commitments.
- Second, we shall provide a shield if a nuclear power threatens the freedom of a nation allied with us or of a nation whose survival we consider vital to our security.
- Third, in cases involving other types of aggression, we shall furnish military and economic assistance when requested in accordance with our treaty commitments. But we shall look to the nation directly threatened to assume the primary responsibility of providing the manpower for its defense. . . .

The defense of freedom is everybody's business—not just America's business. And it is particularly the responsibility of the people whose freedom is threatened. In the previous administration we Americanized the war in Viet-Nam. In this administration we are Vietnamizing the search for peace.

The policy of the previous administration not only resulted in our assuming the primary responsibility for fighting the war but, even more significantly, did not adequately stress the goal of strengthening the South Vietnamese so that they could defend themselves when we left.

The Vietnamization plan was launched following Secretary [of Defense] Laird's visit to Viet-Nam in March. Under the plan, I ordered, first, a substantial increase in the training and equipment of South Vietnamese forces.

In July, on my visit to Viet-Nam, I changed General Abrams' orders so that they were consistent with the objectives of our new policies. Under the new orders, the primary mission of our troops is to enable the South Vietnamese forces to assume the full responsibility for the security of South Viet-Nam. . . .

We have adopted a plan which we have worked out in cooperation with the South Vietnamese for the complete withdrawal of all U.S. combat ground forces and their replacement by South Vietnamese forces on an orderly scheduled timetable. This withdrawal will be made from strength and not from weakness. As South Vietnamese forces become stronger, the rate of American withdrawal can become greater. . . .

If the level of infiltration or our casualties increase while we are trying to scale down the fighting, it will be the result of a conscious decision by the enemy.

Hanoi could make no greater mistake than to assume that an increase in violence will be to its advantage. If I conclude that increased enemy action jeopardizes our remaining forces in Viet-Nam, I shall not hesitate to take strong and effective measures to deal with that situation.

This is not a threat. This is a statement of policy which as Commander in Chief of our Armed Forces I am making in meeting my responsibility for the protection of American fighting men wherever they may be.

My fellow Americans, I am sure you can recognize from what I have said that we really only have two choices open to us if we want to end this war:

- I can order an immediate, precipitate withdrawal of all Americans from Viet-Nam without regard to the effects of that action.
- Or we can persist in our search for a just peace, through a negotiated settlement if possible or through continued implementation of our plan for Vietnamization if necessary—a plan in which we will withdraw all of our forces from Viet-Nam on a schedule in accordance with our program, as the South Vietnamese become strong enough to defend their own freedom.

I have chosen this second course. It is not the easy way. It is the right way. It is a plan which will end the war and serve the cause of peace, not just in Viet-Nam but in the Pacific and in the world.

In speaking of the consequences of a precipitate withdrawal, I mentioned that our allies would lose confidence in America.

Far more dangerous, we would lose confidence in ourselves. Oh, the immediate reaction would be a sense of relief that our men were coming home. But as we saw the consequences of what we had done, inevitable remorse and divisive recrimination would scar our spirit as a people . . .

If [this plan]] does succeed, what the critics say now won't matter. If it does not succeed, anything I say then won't matter.

I know it may not be fashionable to speak of patriotism or national destiny these days. But I feel it is appropriate to do so on this occasion.

Two hundred years ago this nation was weak and poor. But even then, America was the hope of millions in the world. Today we have become the strongest and richest nation in the world. The wheel of destiny has turned so that any hope the world has for the survival of peace and freedom will be determined by whether the American people have the moral stamina and the courage to meet the challenge of free-world leadership.

Let historians not record that when America was the most powerful nation in the world we passed on the other side of the road and allowed the last hopes for peace and freedom of millions of people to be suffocated by the forces of totalitarianism.

And so tonight—to you, the great silent majority of my fellow Americans—I ask for your support.

I pledged in my campaign for the Presidency to end the war in a way that we could win the peace. I have initiated a plan of action which will enable me to keep that pledge.

The more support I can have from the American people, the sooner that pledge can be redeemed; for the more divided we are at home, the less likely the enemy is to negotiate at Paris.

Let us be united for peace. Let us also be united against defeat. Because let us understand: North Viet-Nam cannot defeat or humiliate the United States. Only Americans can do that.

Module XXIV

Questions for Study and Critical Thinking

1. In his address to Congress on the Gulf of Tonkin incident, what reasons did Lyndon Johnson give for U.S. military involvement in Vietnam? What does he say American long-range goals are?

2. Do you find his statement convincing? Why or why not?

3. What, according to Johnson's Johns Hopkins speech, are the United States' main goals in Vietnam?

4. According to this speech, what part does U.S. military action have in fulfilling these goals?

5. What do you think Johnson's purposes were in delivering this speech?

6. How convincing do you think the speech was to the American public at the time? Explain. Do *you* find it persuasive today? Why or why not?

7. What did the Vietnam Day Committee advocate? What were their arguments?

8. What do you think of these arguments?

9. In his speech, what did General Westmoreland say the U.S. had already accomplished? What did he say still needed to be done? How long did he make it appear that this process would take?

10. What evidence did Westmoreland give for his optimistic assessment?

11. How believable do you think that Westmoreland's view was to the American public at that time?

12. In his memoir of Vietnam, what did Richard Ensminger learn about how to survive in the Vietnam War?

13. How did Americans in the U.S. treat him?

14. What can we learn about the Vietnam War from his account?

15. According to President Nixon, what new aspect did he introduce to American policy in Vietnam?

16. Do you think his strategy could have succeeded? Why, or why not?

17. What do you think the United States should have done regarding Vietnam?

Module XXV

Watergate

Introduction

One of the most traumatic events in recent American history was the Watergate scandal, which led to the only resignation of an American president in history—and a dramatic loss of confidence in the American political system. The scandal began with an apparently minor and little-noticed event. On June 17, 1972, several men were arrested for breaking into the headquarters of the Democratic National Committee in the Watergate building in Washington, D.C. Investigations by the *Washington Post* revealed that several of those arrested had previously worked for the Nixon reelection committee and one had even worked inside the White House. In November Richard Nixon was reelected president in a landslide, but shortly thereafter details of the Watergate break-in began to emerge. One of the defendants confessed and implicated others. The Senate formed a special committee under Senator Sam Ervin to investigate the matter. Testimony in the committee implicated high officials in the Nixon Administration, including the attorney general, John Mitchell; the counsel to the president, John Dean; and two of Nixon's top aides, John Ehrlichman and H. R. (Bob) Haldeman.

Nixon himself maintained that he had no advance knowledge of the break-in nor knowledge of the cover-up afterwards. However, testimony by Alexander Butterworth, a White House security aide, revealed that Nixon had ordered a tape recording system installed, which recorded everything spoken in the Oval Office. Nixon, however, refused to surrender the tapes to either the Senate committee or the special prosecutor he had appointed, Professor Archibald Cox of Harvard. When Cox filed suit to force him to hand over the tapes, the president ordered him fired. In the so-called Saturday Night Massacre, his attorney general and his chief aide resigned rather than fire Cox; one of their subordinates, Robert Bork, finally did.

To placate the public, Nixon appointed a new special prosecutor, Leon Jaworski, a prominent Texas Democrat, who continued to pursue evidence against Nixon. In addition, the House Judiciary Committee began hearings that might lead to impeachment. To stave off the demand for the tapes, the White House issued edited transcripts. While the transcripts contained no evidence implicating the president, they failed to help his reputation. They showed him and his aides as often crude and vindictive. And they didn't satisfy the demand for the tapes themselves.

Finally, in July 1974, the Supreme Court ruled unanimously that the president must give the tapes to the special prosecutor. When he did so, they revealed the "smoking gun"—conversations in which Nixon discussed the cover-up. Shortly thereafter the House Judiciary Committee voted three articles of impeachment, which it sent to the House of Representatives for action. Nixon, finding that he did not have the votes to prevent either impeachment by the House of Representatives or conviction by the Senate, resigned and flew to his home in California.

Document 25.1 Nixon Seeks to Avert Responsibility

On April 30, 1973, as more details of Watergate emerged, Richard Nixon gave a dramatic address on nationwide TV, in which he sought to reassure the nation. In this speech he announced the resignation of his two closest aides, John Erlichman and H. R. (Bob) Haldeman. He also announced the resignation of the attorney general and of John Dean, the White House counsel, whose responsibility was to provide legal advice to the president and his staff. In a bit of rhetorical sleight-of-hand, Nixon also announced that although he knew nothing of the Watergate planning or cover-up, as head of the administration, he accepted full responsibility.

Address to the Nation about the Watergate Investigations. April 30, 1973

Richard M. Nixon

Good evening:

I want to talk to you tonight from my heart on a subject of deep concern to every American.

In recent months, members of my Administration and officials of the Committee for the Re-Election of the President—including some of my closest friends and most trusted aides—have been charged with involvement in what has come to be known as the Watergate affair. These include charges of illegal activity during and preceding the 1972 Presidential election and charges that responsible officials participated in efforts to cover up that illegal activity.

The inevitable result of these charges has been to raise serious questions about the integrity of the White House itself. Tonight I wish to address those questions.

Last June 17, while I was in Florida trying to get a few days rest after my visit to Moscow, I first learned from news reports of the Watergate break-in. I was appalled at this senseless, illegal action, and I was shocked to learn that employees of the Re-Election Committee were apparently among those guilty. I immediately ordered an investigation by appropriate Government authorities. On September 15, as you will recall, indictments were brought against seven defendants in the case.

As the investigations went forward, I repeatedly asked those conducting the investigation whether there was any reason to believe that members of my Administration were in any way involved. I received repeated assurances that there were not. Because of these continuing reassurances, because I believed the reports I was getting, because I had faith in the persons from whom I was getting them, I discounted the stories in the press that appeared to implicate members of my Administration or other officials of the campaign committee.

Until March of this year, I remained convinced that the denials were true and that the charges of involvement by members of the White House Staff were false. The comments I made during this period, and the comments made by my Press Secretary in my behalf, were based on the information provided to us at the time we made those comments. However, new information then came to me which persuaded me that there was a real possibility that some of these charges were true, and suggesting further that there had been an effort to conceal the facts both from the public, from you, and from me.

As a result, on March 21, I personally assumed the responsibility for coordinating intensive new inquiries into the matter, and I personally ordered those conducting the investigations to get all the facts and to report them directly to me, right here in this office.

I again ordered that all persons in the Government or at the Re-Election Committee should cooperate fully with the FBI, the prosecutors, and the grand jury. I also ordered that anyone who refused to cooperate in telling the truth would be asked to

---

resign from Government service. And, with ground rules adopted that would preserve the basic constitutional separation of powers between the Congress and the Presidency, I directed that members of the White House Staff should appear and testify voluntarily under oath before the Senate committee which was investigating Watergate.

I was determined that we should get to the bottom of the matter, and that the truth should be fully brought out—no matter who was involved.

At the same time, I was determined not to take precipitate action and to avoid, if at all possible, any action that would appear to reflect on innocent people. I wanted to be fair. But I knew that in the final analysis, the integrity of this office—public faith in the integrity of this office—would have to take priority over all personal considerations.

Today, in one of the most difficult decisions of my Presidency, I accepted the resignations of two of my closest associates in the White House—Bob Haldeman, John Ehrlichman—two of the finest public servants it has been my privilege to know.

I want to stress that in accepting these resignations, I mean to leave no implication whatever of personal wrongdoing on their part, and I leave no implication tonight of implication on the part of others who have been charged in this matter. But in matters as sensitive as guarding the integrity of our democratic process, it is essential not only that rigorous legal and ethical standards be observed but also that the public, you, have total confidence that they are both being observed and enforced by those in authority and particularly by the President of the United States. They agreed with me that this move was necessary in order to restore that confidence.

Because Attorney General Kleindienst—though a distinguished public servant, my personal friend for 20 years, with no personal involvement whatever in this matter—has been a close personal and professional associate of some of those who are involved in this case, he and I both felt that it was also necessary to name a new Attorney General.

The Counsel to the President, John Dean, has also resigned.

As the new Attorney General, I have today named Elliot Richardson, a man of unimpeachable integrity and rigorously high principle. I have directed him to do everything necessary to ensure that the Department of Justice has the confidence and the trust of every law-abiding person in this country.

I have given him absolute authority to make all decisions bearing upon the prosecution of the Watergate case and related matters. I have instructed him that if he should consider it appropriate, he has the authority to name a special supervising prosecutor for matters arising out of the case.

Whatever may appear to have been the case before, whatever improper activities may yet be discovered in connection with this whole sordid affair, I want the American people, I want you to know beyond the shadow of a doubt that during my term as President, justice will be pursued fairly, fully, and impartially, no matter who is involved. This office is a sacred trust and I am determined to be worthy of that trust.

Looking back at the history of this case, two questions arise:

How could it have happened?

Who is to blame?

Political commentators have correctly observed that during my 27 years in politics I have always previously insisted on running my own campaigns for office.

But 1972 presented a very different situation. In both domestic and foreign policy, 1972 was a year of crucially important decisions, of intense negotiations, of vital new directions, particularly in working toward the goal which has been my overriding concern throughout my political career—the goal of bringing peace to America, peace to the world.

That is why I decided, as the 1972 campaign approached, that the Presidency should come first and politics second. To the maximum extent possible, therefore, I sought to delegate campaign operations, to remove the day-to-day campaign decisions from the President's office and from the White House. I also, as you recall, severely limited the number of my own campaign appearances.

Who, then, is to blame for what happened in this case?

For specific criminal actions by specific individuals, those who committed those actions must, of course, bear the liability and pay the penalty.

For the fact that alleged improper actions took place within the White House or within my campaign organization, the easiest course would be for me to blame those to whom I delegated the responsibility to run the campaign. But that would be a cowardly thing to do.

I will not place the blame on subordinates—on people whose zeal exceeded their judgment and who may have done wrong in a cause they deeply believed to be right.

In any organization, the man at the top must bear the responsibility. That responsibility, therefore, belongs here, in this office. I accept it. And I pledge to you tonight, from this office, that I will do everything in my power to ensure that the guilty are brought to justice and that such abuses are purged from our political processes in the years to come, long after I have left this office.

Some people, quite properly appalled at the abuses that occurred, will say that Watergate demonstrates the bankruptcy of the American political system. I believe precisely the opposite is true. Watergate represented a series of illegal acts and bad judgments by a number of individuals. It was the system that has brought the facts to light and that will bring those guilty to justice—a system that in this case has included a determined grand jury, honest prosecutors, a courageous judge, John Sirica, and a vigorous free press.

It is essential now that we place our faith in that system—and especially in the judicial system. It is essential that we let the judicial process go forward, respecting those safeguards that are established to protect the innocent as well as to convict the guilty. It is essential that in reacting to the excesses of others, we not fall into excesses ourselves.

It is also essential that we not be so distracted by events such as this that we neglect the vital work before us, before this Nation, before America, at a time of critical importance to America and the world.

Since March, when I first learned that the Watergate affair might in fact be far more serious than I had been led to believe, it has claimed far too much of my time and my attention.

Whatever may now transpire in the case, whatever the actions of the grand jury, whatever the outcome of any eventual trials, I must now turn my full attention—and I shall do so—once again to the larger duties of this office. I owe it to this great office that I hold, and I owe it to you—to my country.

I know that as Attorney General, Elliot Richardson will be both fair and he will be fearless in pursuing this case wherever it leads. I am confident that with him in charge, justice will be done.

There is vital work to be done toward our goal of a lasting structure of peace in the world—work that cannot wait, work that I must do.

Tomorrow, for example, Chancellor Brandt of West Germany will visit the White House for talks that are a vital element of "The Year of Europe," as I 973 has been called. We are already preparing for the next Soviet-American summit meeting later this year.

This is also a year in which we are seeking to negotiate a mutual and balanced reduction of armed forces in Europe, which will reduce our defense budget and allow us to have funds for other purposes at home so desperately needed. It is the year when the United States and Soviet negotiators will seek to work out the second and even more important round of our talks on limiting nuclear arms and of reducing the danger of a nuclear war that would destroy civilization as we know it. It is a year in which we confront the difficult tasks of maintaining peace in Southeast Asia and in the potentially explosive Middle East.

There is also vital work to be done right here in America: to ensure prosperity, and that means a good job for everyone who wants to work; to control inflation, that I know worries every housewife, everyone who tries to balance a family budget in America; to set in motion new and better ways of ensuring progress toward a better life for all Americans.

When I think of this office—of what it means—I think of all the things that I want to accomplish for this Nation, of all the things I want to accomplish for you.

On Christmas Eve, during my terrible personal ordeal of the renewed bombing of North Vietnam, which after 12 years of war finally helped to bring America peace with honor, I sat down just before midnight. I wrote out some of my goals for my second term as President.

Let me read them to you.

"To make it possible for our children, and for our children's children, to live in a world of peace.

"To make this country be more than ever a land of opportunity—of equal opportunity, full opportunity for every American.

"To provide jobs for all who can work, and generous help for those who cannot work.

"To establish a climate of decency and civility in which each person respects the feelings and the dignity and the God-given rights of his neighbor.

"To make this a land in which each person can dare to dream, can live his dreams—not in fear, but in hope—proud of his community, proud of his country, proud of what America has meant to himself and to the world."

These are great goals. I believe we can, we must work for them. We can achieve them. But we cannot achieve these goals unless we dedicate ourselves to another goal:

We must maintain the integrity of the White House, and that integrity must be real, not transparent. There can be no whitewash at the White House.

We must reform our political process—ridding it not only of the violations of the law but also of the ugly mob violence and other inexcusable campaign tactics that have been too often practiced and too readily accepted in the past, including those that may have been a response by one side to the excesses or expected excesses of the other side. Two wrongs do not make a right.

I have been in public life for more than a quarter of a century. Like any other calling, politics has good people and bad people. And let me tell you, the great majority in politics—in the Congress, in the

Federal Government, in the State government—are good people. I know that it can be very easy, under the intensive pressures of a campaign, for even well-intentioned people to fall into shady tactics—to rationalize this on the grounds that what is at stake is of such importance to the Nation that the end justifies the means. And both of our great parties have been guilty of such tactics in the past.

In recent years, however, the campaign excesses that have occurred on all sides have provided a sobering demonstration of how far this false doctrine can take us. The lesson is clear: America, in its political campaigns, must not again fall into the trap of letting the end, however great that end is, justify the means.

I urge the leaders of both political parties, I urge citizens, all of you, everywhere, to join in working toward a new set of standards, new rules and procedures to ensure that future elections will be as nearly free of such abuses as they possibly can be made. This is my goal. I ask you to join in making it America's goal.

When I was inaugurated for a second time this past January 20, I gave each member of my Cabinet and each member of my senior White House Staff a special 4-year calendar, with each day marked to show the number of days remaining to the Administration. In the inscription on each calendar, I wrote these words: "The Presidential term which begins today consists of 1,461 days—no more, no less. Each can be a day of strengthening and renewal for America; each can add depth and dimension to the American experience. If we strive together, if we make the most of the challenge and the opportunity that these days offer us, they can stand out as great days for America, and great moments in the history of the world."

I looked at my own calendar this morning up at Camp David as I was working on this speech. It showed exactly 1,361 days remaining in my term. I want these to be the best days in America's history, because I love America. I deeply believe that America is the hope of the world. And I know that in the quality and wisdom of the leadership America gives lies the only hope for millions of people all over the world that they can live their lives in peace and freedom. We must be worthy of that hope, in every sense of the word. Tonight, I ask for your prayers to help me in everything that I do throughout the days of my Presidency to be worthy of their hopes and of yours.

God bless America and God bless each and every one of you.

NOTE: The President spoke at 9:01 p.m. from the Oval Office at the White House. His address was broadcast live on nationwide radio and television.

Document 25.2 The "Smoking Gun" Tape of Conversation in the Oval Office, June 30, 1972

During the hearings conducted by the Senate select committee, the question that remained at the center of attention was one framed by Republican Senator Howard Baker: What did the President know and when did he know it? During the televised House and Senate committee hearings, many people increasingly suspected that Nixon had known about the break-in in either advance or shortly thereafter. In either case, he would be guilty of obstruction of justice, since he had not turned the perpetrators over to the proper authorities. Despite the suspicions, direct evidence of Nixon's knowledge—the so-called "smoking gun"—remained lacking. But when the tapes were turned over to the special prosecutor, this one—of a conversation between Nixon and his aides on June 30, 1972—was discovered.

The "Smoking Gun" Tape of Conversation in the Oval Office, June 30, 1972

One of the subjects of the June 30, 1972, discussion among the President, Haldeman and Mitchell was Mitchell's resignation as head of CRP:

"HALDEMAN, Well, there maybe is another facet. The longer you wait the more risk each hour brings. You run the risk of more stuff, valid or invalid, surfacing on the Watergate caper—type of thing—

"MITCHELL. You couldn't possibly do it if you got into a—

"HALDEMAN.—the potential problem and then you are stuck—

"PRESIDENT. Yes, that's the other thing, if something does come out, but we won't—we hope nothing will. It may not. But there is always the risk.

"HALDEMAN. As of now there is no problem there. As, as of any moment in the future there is at least a potential problem.

"PRESIDENT. Well, I'd cut the loss fast. I'd cut it fast. If we're going to do it I'd cut it fast. That's my view, generally speaking. And I wouldn't—and I don't think, though, as a matter of fact, I don't think the story, if we, if you put it in human terms—I think the story is, you're positive rather than negative, because as I said as I was preparing to answer for this press conference, I just wrote it out, as I usually do, one way—terribly sensitive [unintelligible]. A hell of a lot of people will like that answer. They would. And it'd make anybody else who asked any other question on it look like a selfish son-of-a-bitch, which I thoroughly intended them to look like."

* * *

"MITCHELL. [Unintelligible] Westchester Country Club with all the sympathy in the world.

"PRESIDENT. That's great. That's great.

"MITCHELL. (Unintelligible] don't let—

"HALDEMAN. You taking this route—people won't expect you to—be a surprise.

"PRESIDENT. No, if it's a surprise. Otherwise, you're right, it will be tied right to Watergate. [Unintelligible]—tighter if you wait too long, till it simmers down.

"HALDEMAN. You can't if other stuff develops on Watergate. The problem is, it's always potentially the same thing.

"PRESIDENT. Well if it does, don't just hardline.

"HALDEMAN. [Unintelligible] That's right. In other words, it'd be hard to hard-line Mitchell's departure under—

"PRESIDENT. That's right. You can't do it. I just want it to be handled in a way Martha's not hurt.

"MITCHELL. Yeah, okay." (Book II, 515–516)

"H. Now, on the investigation, you know the Democratic break-in thing, we're back in the problem area because the FBI is not under control, because Gray doesn't exactly know how to control it and they have—their investigation is now leading into some productive areas—because they've been able to trace the money—not through the money itself—but through the bank sources—the banker. And, and it goes in some directions we don't want it to go. Ah, also there have been some things—like an informant came in off the street to the FBI in Miami who was a photographer or has a friend who is a photographer who developed some films through this guy Barker and the films had pictures of Democratic National Committee letterhead documents and things. So it's things like that that are filtering in. Mitchell came up with yesterday, and John Dean analyzed very carefully last night and concludes, concurs now with Mitchell's recommendation that the only way to solve this, and we're set up beautifully to do it, ah, in that and that—the only network that paid any attention to it last night was NBC—they did a massive story on the Cuban thing.

"P. That's right.

"H. That the way to handle this now is for us to have Walters call Pat Gray and just say, 'Stay to hell out of this—this is ah, business here we don't want you to go any further on it.' That's not an unusual development, and ah, that would take care of it.

"P. What about Pat Gray—you mean Pat Gray doesn't want to?

"H. Pat does want to. He doesn't know how to, and he doesn't have . . . any basis for doing it. Given this, he will then have the basis. He'll call Mark Felt in . . .

Hearings before the Committee on the Judiciary, House of Representatives, 93rd Congress, 2nd session.

"P. Yeah.

"H. He'll call him and say, 'We've got the signal from across the river to put the hold on this.' And that will fit rather well because the FBI agents who are working on the case, at this point, feel that's what it is. . . .

"H. And you seem to think the thing to do is get them to stop?

"P. Right, fine." (WHT, June 23 , 1972, 10.04–11:39 a.m., 2–5)

Document 25.3 Articles of Impeachment

In July 1973, the Judiciary Committee of the House of Representatives began debate on proposed articles of impeachment. If the committee adopted these, they would go to the full House of Representatives for debate and a vote. If the House adopted them, the President would be impeached and then tried before the Senate, which could find him either not guilty or guilty. In the latter case he would be removed from office. On July 27 the committee approved the articles and sent them to the full House. A few days later Nixon resigned.

Articles of Impeachment

House Judiciary Committee

Article I

In his conduct of the office of President of the United States, Richard M. Nixon, in violation of his constitutional oath faithfully to execute the office of President of the United States and, to the best of his ability, preserve, protect, and defend the Constitution of the United States, and in violation of his constitutional duty to take care that the laws be faithfully executed, has prevented, obstructed, and impeded the administration of justice, in that:

On June 17, 1972, and prior thereto, agents of the Committee for the Reelection of the President committed unlawful entry of the headquarters of the Democratic National Committee in Washington, District of Columbia, for the purpose of securing political intelligence. Subsequent thereto, Richard M. Nixon, using the powers of his high office, engaged personally and through his close subordinates and agents, in a course of conduct or plan designed to delay, impede, and obstruct the investigation of such unlawful entry; to cover up, conceal and protect those responsible; and to conceal the existence and scope of other unlawful covert activities.

The means used to implement this course of conduct or plan included one or more of the following:

1. making false or misleading statements to lawfully authorized investigative officers and employees of the United States;
2. withholding relevant and material evidence or information from lawfully authorized investigative officers and employees of the United States;
3. approving, condoning, acquiescing in, and counseling witnesses with respect to the giving of false or misleading statements to lawfully authorized investigative officers and employees of the United States and false or misleading testimony in duly instituted judicial and congressional proceedings;
4. interfering or endeavoring to interfere with the conduct of investigations by the Department of Justice of the United States, the Federal Bureau of Investigation, the Office of Watergate Special Prosecution Force, and Congressional Committees;
5. approving, condoning, and acquiescing in, the surreptitious payment of substantial sums of

money for the purpose of obtaining the silence or influencing the testimony of witnesses, potential witnesses or individuals who participated in such unlawful entry and other illegal activities;

6. endeavoring to misuse the Central Intelligence Agency, an agency of the United States;
7. disseminating information received from officers of the Department of Justice of the United States to subjects of investigations conducted by lawfully authorized investigative officers and employees of the United States, for the purpose of aiding and assisting such subjects in their attempts to avoid criminal liability.
8. making or causing to be made false or misleading public statements for the purpose of deceiving the people of the United States into believing that a thorough and complete investigation had been conducted with respect to allegations of misconduct on the part of personnel of the executive branch of the United States and personnel of the Committee for the Re-election of the President, and that there was no involvement of such personnel in such misconduct; or
9. endeavoring to cause prospective defendants, and individuals duly tried and convicted, to expect favored treatment and consideration in return for their silence or false testimony, or rewarding individuals for their silence or false testimony.

In all of this, Richard M. Nixon has acted in a manner contrary to his trust as President and subversive of constitutional government, to the great prejudice of the cause of law and justice and to the manifest injury of the people of the United States.

Wherefore Richard M. Nixon, by such conduct, warrants impeachment and trial, and removal from office.

Article II

Using the powers of the office of President of the United States, Richard M. Nixon, in violation of his constitutional oath faithfully to execute the office of President of the United States and, to the best of his ability, preserve, protect, and defend the Constitution of the United States, and in disregard of his constitutional duty to take care that the laws be faithfully executed, has repeatedly engaged in conduct violating the constitutional rights of citizens, impairing the due and proper administration of justice and the conduct of lawful inquiries, or contravening the laws governing agencies of the executive branch and the purposes of these agencies.

This conduct has included one or more of the following:

1. He has, acting personally and through his subordinates and agents, endeavored to obtain from the Internal Revenue Service, in violation of the constitutional rights of citizens, confidential information contained in income tax returns for purposes not authorized by law, and to cause, in violation of the constitutional rights of citizens, income tax audits or other income tax investigations to be initiated or conducted in a discriminatory manner.
2. He misused the Federal Bureau of Investigation, the Secret Service, and other executive personnel, in violation or disregard of the constitutional rights of citizens, by directing or authorizing such agencies or personnel to conduct or continue electronic surveillance or other investigations for purposes unrelated to national security, the enforcement of laws, or any other lawful function of his office; he did direct, authorize, or permit the use of information obtained thereby for purposes unrelated to national security, the enforcement of laws, or any other lawful function of his office; and he did direct the concealment of certain records made by the Federal Bureau of Investigation of electronic surveillance.
3. He has, acting personally and through his subordinates and agents, in violation or disregard of the constitutional rights of citizens, authorized and permitted to be maintained a secret investigative unit within the office of the President, financed in part with money derived from campaign contributions, which unlawfully utilized the resources of the Central Intelligence Agency, engaged in covert and unlawful activities, and attempted to prejudice the constitutional right of an accused to a fair trial.
4. He has failed to take care that the laws were faithfully executed by failing to act when he knew or had reason to know that his close subordinates endeavored to impede and frustrate lawful inquiries by duly constituted executive, judicial, and legislative entities concerning the unlawful entry into the headquarters of the Democratic National Committee, and the cover up thereof, and concerning other unlawful activities including those relating to the confirmation of Richard Kleindienst as Attorney General of the United States, the electronic surveillance of private citizens, the break-in into the offices of Dr. Lewis Fielding and the campaign financing practices of the Committee to Re-elect the President.

5. In disregard of the rule of law, he knowingly misused the executive branch, including the Federal Bureau of Investigation, the Criminal Division, and the Office of Watergate Special Prosecution Force, of the Department of Justice, and the Central Intelligence Agency, in violation of his duty to take care that the laws be faithfully executed.

In all of this, Richard M. Nixon has acted in a manner contrary to his trust as President and subversive of constitutional government, to the great prejudice of the cause of law and justice and to the manifest injury of the people of the United States.

Wherefore Richard M. Nixon, by such conduct, warrants impeachment and trial, and removal from office.

—Adopted July 29 by a 28–10 vote

Article III

In his conduct of the office of President of the United States, Richard M. Nixon, contrary to his oath faithfully to execute the office of President of the United States and, to the best of his ability, preserve, protect, and defend the Constitution of the United States, and in violation of his constitutional duty to take care that the laws be faithfully executed, has failed without lawful cause or excuse to produce papers and things as directed by duly authorized subpoenas issued by the Committee on the Judiciary of the House of Representatives on April 11, 1974, May 15, 1974, May 30, 1974, and June 24, 1974, and willfully disobeyed such subpoenas. The subpoenaed papers and things were deemed necessary by the Committee in order to resolve by direct evidence fundamental, factual questions relating to Presidential direction, knowledge, or approval of actions demonstrated by other evidence to be substantial grounds for impeachment of the President. In refusing to produce these papers and things Richard M. Nixon, substituting his judgment as to what materials were necessary for the inquiry, interposed the powers of the Presidency against the lawful subpoenas of the House of Representatives, thereby assuming to himself functions and judgments necessary to the exercise of the sole power of impeachment vested by the Constitution in the House of Representatives.

In all of this, Richard M. Nixon has acted in a manner contrary to his trust as President and subversive of constitutional government, to the great prejudice of the cause of law and justice, and to the manifest injury of the people of the United States.

Wherefore, Richard M. Nixon by such conduct, warrants impeachment and trial, and removal from office.

—Adopted July 30 by a 21–17 vote

Document 25.4 The President Resigns

After the House Judiciary Committee approved the articles of impeachment, Richard Nixon spent several days considering the situation. Finally, Republican senators told him that if the case came for trial in the Senate, he would not have enough votes to avoid conviction and removal from office. Nixon decided to resign. On August 8, 1974, he delivered a nationally televised speech in which he announced his resignation. He and his family then flew to his home in California. His resignation became effective while he was in the air. Gerald Ford, the vice president, then became president. And Richard Nixon became the first American president ever to resign from office.

The President Resigns

Richard M. Nixon

Good evening:

This is the 37th time I have spoken to you from this office, where so many decisions have been made that shaped the history of this Nation. Each time I have done so to discuss with you some matter that I believe affected the national interest.

In all the decisions I have made in my public life, I have always tried to do what was best for the Nation. Throughout the long and difficult period of Watergate, I have felt it was my duty to persevere, to make every possible effort to complete the term of office to which you elected me.

In the past few days, however, it has become evident to me that I no longer have a strong enough political base in the Congress to justify continuing that effort. As long as there was such a base, I felt strongly that it was necessary to see the constitutional process through to its conclusion, that to do otherwise would be unfaithful to the spirit of that deliberately difficult process and a dangerously destabilizing precedent for the future,

But with the disappearance of that base, I now believe that the constitutional purpose has been served, and there is no longer a need for the process to be prolonged.

I would have preferred to carry through to the finish, whatever the personal agony it would have involved, and my family unanimously urged me to do so. But the interests of the Nation must always come before any personal considerations.

From the discussions I have had with Congressional and other leaders, I have concluded that because of the Watergate matter, I might not have the support of the Congress that I would consider necessary to back the very difficult decisions and carry out the duties of this office in the way the interests of the Nation will require.

I have never been a quitter. To leave office before my term is completed is abhorrent to every instinct in my body. But as President, I must put the interests of America first. America needs a full-time President and a full-time Congress, particularly at this time with problems we face at home and abroad.

To continue to fight through the months ahead for my personal vindication would almost totally absorb the time and attention of both the President and the Congress in a period when our entire focus should be on the great issues of peace abroad and prosperity without inflation at home.

Therefore, I shall resign the Presidency effective at noon tomorrow. Vice President Ford will be sworn in as President at that hour in this office.

As I recall the high hopes for America with which we began this second term, I feel a great sadness that I will not be here in this office working on your behalf to achieve those hopes in the next 2 1/2 years. But in turning over direction of the Government to Vice President Ford, I know, as I told the Nation when I nominated him for that office 10 months ago, that the leadership of America will be in good hands.

In passing this office to the Vice President, I also do so with the profound sense of the weight of responsibility that will fall on his shoulders tomorrow and, therefore, of the understanding, the patience, the cooperation he will need from all Americans.

As he assumes that responsibility, he will deserve the help and the support of all of us. As we look to the future, the first essential is to begin healing the wounds of this Nation, to put the bitterness and divisions of the recent past behind us and to rediscover those shared ideals that lie at the heart of our strength and unity as a great and as a free people.

By taking this action, I hope that I will have hastened the start of that process of healing which is so desperately needed in America.

I regret deeply any injuries that may have been done in the course of the events that led to this decision. I would say only that if some of my judgments were wrong—and some were wrong—they were made in what I believed at the time to be the best interest of the Nation.

To those who have stood with me during these past difficult months—to my family, my friends, to many others who joined in supporting my cause

---

Resignation Speech, Richard M. Nixon.

because they believed it was right—I will be eternally grateful for your support.

And to those who have not felt able to give me your support, let me say I leave with no bitterness toward those who have opposed me, because all of us, in the final analysis, have been concerned with the good of the country, however our judgments might differ.

So, let us all now join together in affirming that common commitment and in helping our new President succeed for the benefit of all Americans.

I shall leave this office with regret at not completing my term, but with gratitude for the privilege of serving as your President for the past 5 1/2 years. These years have been a momentous time in the history of our Nation and the world. They have been a time of achievement in which we can all be proud, achievements that represent the shared efforts of the Administration, the Congress, and the people.

But the challenges ahead are equally great, and they, too, will require the support and the efforts of the Congress and the people working in cooperation with the new Administration.

We have ended America's longest war, but in the work of securing a lasting peace in the world, the goals ahead are even more far-reaching and more difficult. We must complete a structure of peace so that it will be said of this generation, our generation of Americans, by the people of all nations, not only that we ended one war but that we prevented future wars.

We have unlocked the doors that for a quarter of a century stood between the United States and the People's Republic of China.

We must now ensure that the one quarter of the world's people who live in the People's Republic of China will be and remain not our enemies, but our friends.

In the Middle East, 100 million people in the Arab countries, many of whom have considered us their enemy for nearly 20 years, now look on us as their friends. We must continue to build on that friendship so that peace can settle at last over the Middle East and so that the cradle of civilization will not become its grave.

Together with the Soviet Union, we have made the crucial breakthroughs that have begun the process of limiting nuclear arms. But we must set as our goal not just limiting but reducing and, finally, destroying these terrible weapons so that they cannot destroy civilization and so that the threat of nuclear war will no longer hang over the world and the people.

We have opened the new relation with the Soviet Union. We must continue to develop and expand that new relationship so that the two strongest nations of the world will live together in cooperation rather than confrontation.

Around the world—in Asia, in Africa, in Latin America, in the Middle East—there are millions of people who live in terrible poverty, even starvation. We must keep as our goal turning away from production for war and expanding production for peace so that people everywhere on this Earth can at last look forward in their children's time, if not in our own time, to having the necessities for a decent life.

Here in America, we are fortunate that most of our people have not only the blessings of liberty but also the means to live full and good and, by the world's standards, even abundant lives. We must press on, however, toward a goal, not only of more and better jobs but of full opportunity for every American and of what we are striving so hard right now to achieve, prosperity without inflation.

For more than a quarter of a century in public life, I have shared in the turbulent history of this era. I have fought for what I believed in. I have tried, to the best of my ability, to discharge those duties and meet those responsibilities that were entrusted to me.

Sometimes I have succeeded and sometimes I have failed, but always I have taken heart from what Theodore Roosevelt once said about the man in the arena, "whose face is marred by dust and sweat and blood, who strives valiantly, who errs and comes short again and again because there is not effort without error and shortcoming, but who does actually strive to do the deed, who knows the great enthusiasms, the great devotions, who spends himself in a worthy cause, who at the best knows in the end the triumphs of high achievements and who at the worst, if he fails, at least fails while daring greatly."

I pledge to you tonight that as long as I have a breath of life in my body, I shall continue in that spirit. I shall continue to work for the great causes to which I have been dedicated throughout my years as a Congressman, a Senator, Vice President, and President, the cause of peace, not just for America but among all nations—prosperity, justice, and opportunity for all of our people.

There is one cause above all to which I have been devoted and to which I shall always be devoted for as long as I live.

When I first took the oath of office as President 5 1/2 years ago, I made this sacred commitment: to "consecrate my office, my energies, and all the wisdom I can summon to the cause of peace among nations."

I have done my very best in all the days since to be true to that pledge. As a result of these efforts, I am confident that the world is a safer place today, not only for the people of America but for the people of all nations, and that all of our children have a better chance than before of living in peace rather than dying in war.

This, more than anything, is what I hoped to achieve when I sought the Presidency. This, more than anything, is what I hope will be my legacy to you, to our country, as I leave the Presidency.

To have served in this office is to have felt a very personal sense of kinship with each and every American. In leaving it, I do so with this prayer: May God's grace be with you in all the days ahead.

Module XIV
Questions for Study and Critical Thinking

1. Where, according to Nixon's April 30 speech, did the blame for Watergate lie?

2. In this speech what techniques did Nixon use in seeking to avert blame from himself? Can you think of more recent examples of people using such tactics?

3. What criminal conduct does the "smoking gun" tape show Nixon committing?

4. In your own words, tell what the Articles of Impeachment accused Nixon of.

5. In your opinion, which of these (or all) are offenses meriting impeachment and removal from office? Why?

6. Why, in his resignation speech, did Nixon say that he had resigned? What is your assessment of that explanation?

Module XXVI

The New Conservatism

Introduction

In 1982 Ronald Reagan won a landslide victory in the presidential election and became the first of a new type of conservative to win the presidency. His victory represented a sharp shift to the right in American politics. It was, in many respects, the greatest change in political ideology since the victory of Franklin D. Roosevelt's New Deal in 1932.

Reagan was the most prominent and best known representative of a new conservative movement that began in the 1950s. This new movement centered around William F. Buckley, Jr., and his magazine the *National Review*. This conservative movement attempted to merge two ideological streams. One stream revered tradition, religion, and class structure and found its leading spokesman in Russell Kirk, a professor of literature. The other stream preached individualism, reverence for economic markets, and radical hostility to state action. It argued that the government should restrict itself to national defense, maintaining law and order, and providing only the most minimal public services. Although many saw these two views as contradictory, Buckley and his magazine announced that conservative writers had achieved a fusion, a synthesis, between them, united by anti-communism and a common revulsion at liberalism. Believing that liberalism dominated politics, they saw themselves as rebels, even revolutionaries, against the established order.

In the 1960s conservatives of this type seized control of the Republican Party. In 1964 they nominated Barry Goldwater for the presidency. At the convention that year they shouted down the representative of the party's liberal wing, Nelson Rockefeller, then governor of New York. Although Goldwater lost the election to Lyndon B. Johnson in a landslide, conservatives became even more determined to control the party and eventually elect one of their own to the presidency. The most prominent conservative to emerge from the wreck of 1964 was Ronald Reagan, an actor, who delivered a highly effective television address on behalf of Goldwater.

After establishing his celebrity in that campaign, Reagan ran for and won the governorship of California and was subsequently elected to a second term. In 1976 he challenged the incumbent Republican president, Gerald Ford, for the nomination. Although he lost, he continued to work in Republican circles. In 1980 he won the nomination and then the presidency.

Reagan was clear and unapologetic about the conservative ideas he intended to put into force. They included a desire to reduce the role of government, especially the Federal government. In particular, Reagan and other conservatives abhorred the attempt in the Federal income tax to redistribute wealth by exacting higher percentages of tax on higher incomes ("progressive" taxation). Reagan also believed the United States was too weak vis a vis the Soviet Union and its allies and aimed to increase American military strength. He and many other conservatives further believed that traditional religious values had weakened and wanted to strengthen them, using the government as much as possible. Reagan devoted his presidency to putting these conservative ideas into effect.

Since Reagan's presidential victory, conservatives have continued to control the Republican Party. In the 1988 election campaign, Reagan's vice president, George Bush, who had once denounced Reagan's conservative economic ideas as "voodoo economics," ran for the presidency on a conservative platform. Although Democrat Bill Clinton defeated Bush in 1992, two years later conservative Republicans under the leadership of Congressman Newt Gingrich captured control of Congress in a self-proclaimed conservative "revolution." Despite Bill Clinton's reelection to the presidency in 1996, the Republicans under the control of the conservative wing of the party maintained control of both Houses of Congress. In 2000, Bush's son, George W. Bush, also ran for the presidency as a "compassionate conservative" and defeated Al Gore by a narrow electoral vote margin. In this chapter writers propound and criticize modern American conservatism, especially as realized in the presidency of Ronald Reagan.

Document 26.1 A Conservative President's Inaugural Address, Ronald Reagan

Ronald Reagan was the most prominent American conservative and has remained the hero of the conservative movement. Known by friend and foe alike as "the Great Communicator," Reagan was an articulate spokesman for conservative ideas and policies. His first inaugural address, given in January 1981, clearly presented the conservative goals of his administration.

Inaugural Address, January 20, 1981

Ronald Reagan

Senator Hatfield, Mr. Chief Justice, Mr. President, Vice President Bush, Vice President Mondale, Senator Baker, Speaker O'Neill, Reverend Moomaw, and my fellow citizens:

To a few of us here today this is a solemn and most momentous occasion, and yet in the history of our nation it is a commonplace occurrence. The orderly transfer of authority as called for in the Constitution routinely takes place, as it has for almost two centuries, and few of us stop to think how unique we really are. In the eyes of many in the world, this every-4-year ceremony we accept as normal is nothing less than a miracle,

Mr. President, I want our fellow citizens to know how much you did to carry on this tradition. By your gracious cooperation in the transition process, you have shown a watching world that we are a united people pledged to maintaining a political system which guarantees individual liberty to a greater degree than any other, and I thank you and your people for all your help in maintaining the continuity which is the bulwark of our Republic.

The business of our nation goes forward. These United States are confronted with an economic affliction of great proportions. We suffer from the longest and one of the worst sustained inflations in our national history. It distorts our economic decisions, penalizes thrift, and crushes the struggling young and the fixed-income elderly alike. It threatens to shatter the lives of millions of our people.

Idle industries have cast workers into unemployment, human misery, and personal indignity. Those who do work are denied a fair return for their labor by a tax system which penalizes successful achievement and keeps us from maintaining full productivity.

But great as our tax burden is, it has not kept pace with public spending. For decades we have piled deficit upon deficit, mortgaging our future and our children's future for the temporary convenience of the present. To continue this long trend is to guarantee tremendous social, cultural, political, and economic upheavals.

You and I, as individuals, can, by borrowing, live beyond our means, but for only a limited period of time. Why, then, should we think that collectively, as a nation, we're not bound by that same limitation? We must act today in order to preserve tomorrow. And let there be no misunderstanding: We are going to begin to act, beginning today.

The economic ills we suffer have come upon us over several decades. They will not go away in days, weeks, or months, but they will go away. They will go away because we as Americans have the capacity now, as we've had in the past, to do whatever needs

Inaugural Address, Ronald Reagan.

to be done to preserve this last and greatest bastion of freedom.

In this present crisis, government is not the solution to our problem; government is the problem. From time to time we've been tempted to believe that society has become too complex to be managed by self-rule, that government by an elite group is superior to government for, by, and of the people. Well, if no one among us is capable of governing himself, then who among us has the capacity to govern someone else? All of us together, in and out of government, must bear the burden. The solutions we seek must be equitable, with no one group singled out to pay a higher price.

We hear much of special interest groups. Well, our concern must be for a special interest group that has been too long neglected. It knows no sectional boundaries or ethnic and racial divisions, and it crosses political party lines. It is made up of men and women who raise our food, patrol our streets, man our mines and factories, teach our children, keep our homes, and heal us when we're sick—professionals, industrialists, shopkeepers, clerks, cabbies, and truckdrivers. They are, in short, "We the people," this breed called Americans.

Well, this administration's objective will be a healthy, vigorous, growing economy that provides equal opportunities for all Americans, with no barriers born of bigotry or discrimination. Putting America back to work means putting all Americans back to work. Ending inflation means freeing all Americans from the terror of runaway living costs. All must share in the productive work of this "new beginning," and all must share in the bounty of a revived economy. With the idealism and fair play which are the core of our system and our strength, we can have a strong and prosperous America, at peace with itself and the world.

So, as we begin, let us take inventory. We are a nation that has a government—not the other way around. And this makes us special among the nations of the Earth. Our government has no power except that granted it by the people. It is time to check and reverse the growth of government, which shows signs of having grown beyond the consent of the governed.

It is my intention to curb the size and influence of the Federal establishment and to demand recognition of the distinction between the powers granted to the Federal Government and those reserved to the States or to the people. All of us need to be reminded that the Federal Government did not create the States; the States created the Federal Government.

Now, so there will be no misunderstanding, it's not my intention to do away with government. It is rather to make it work—work with us, not over us; to stand by our side, not ride on our back. Government can and must provide opportunity, not smother it; foster productivity, not stifle it.

If we look to the answer as to why for so many years we achieved so much, prospered as no other people on Earth, it was because here in this land we unleashed the energy and individual genius of man to a greater extent than has ever been done before. Freedom and the dignity of the individual have been more available and assured here than in any other place on Earth. The price for this freedom at times has been high, but we have never been unwilling to pay that price.

It is no coincidence that our present troubles parallel and are proportionate to the intervention and intrusion in our lives that result from unnecessary and excessive growth of government. It is time for us to realize that we're too great a nation to limit ourselves to small dreams. We're not, as some would have us believe, doomed to an inevitable decline. I do not believe in a fate that will fall on us no matter what we do. I do believe in a fate that will fall on us if we do nothing. So, with all the creative energy at our command, let us begin an era of national renewal. Let us renew our determination, our courage, and our strength. And let us renew our faith and our hope.

We have every right to dream heroic dreams. Those who say that we're in a time when there are not heroes, they just don't know where to look. You can see heroes every day going in and out of factory gates. Others, a handful in number, produce enough food to feed all of us and then the world beyond. You meet heroes across a counter, and they're on both sides of that counter. There are entrepreneurs with faith in themselves and faith in an idea who create new jobs, new wealth and opportunity. They're individuals and families whose taxes support the government and whose voluntary gifts support church, charity, culture, art, and education. Their patriotism is quiet, but deep. Their values sustain our national life.

Now, I have used the words "they" and "their" in speaking of these heroes. I could say "you" and "your," because I'm addressing the heroes of whom I speak—you, the citizens of this blessed land. Your dreams, your hopes, your goals are going to be the dreams, the hopes, and the goals of this administration, so help me God.

We shall reflect the compassion that is so much a part of your makeup. How can we love our country and not love our countrymen; and loving them, reach out a hand when they fall, heal them when they're sick, and provide opportunity to make them self-sufficient so they will be equal in fact and not just in theory?

Can we solve the problems confronting us? Well, the answer is an unequivocal and emphatic "yes." To paraphrase Winston Churchill, I did not take the oath I've just taken with the intention of presiding over the dissolution of the world's strongest economy.

In the days ahead I will propose removing the roadblocks that have slowed our economy and reduced productivity. Steps will be taken aimed at restoring the balance between the various levels of government. Progress may be slow, measured in inches and feet, not miles, but we will progress. It is time to reawaken this industrial giant; to get government back within its means, and to lighten our punitive tax burden. And these will be our first priorities, and on these principles there will be no compromise.

On the eve of our struggle for independence a man who might have been one of the greatest among the Founding Fathers, Dr. Joseph Warren, president of the Massachusetts Congress, said to his fellow Americans, "Our country is in danger, but not to be despaired of. . . . On you depend the fortunes of America. You are to decide the important questions upon which rests the happiness and the liberty of millions yet unborn. Act worthy of yourselves."

Well, I believe we, the Americans of today, are ready to act worthy of ourselves, ready to do what must be done to ensure happiness and liberty for ourselves, our children, and our children's children. And as we renew ourselves here in our own land, we will be seen as having greater strength throughout the world. We will again be the exemplar of freedom and a beacon of hope for those who do not now have freedom.

To those neighbors and allies who share our freedom, we will strengthen our historic ties and assure them of our support and firm commitment. We will match loyalty with loyalty. We will strive for mutually beneficial relations. We will not use our friendship to impose on their sovereignty, for our own sovereignty is not for sale.

As for the enemies of freedom, those who are potential adversaries, they will be reminded that peace is the highest aspiration of the American people. We will negotiate for it, sacrifice for it; we will not surrender for it, now or ever.

Our forbearance should never be misunderstood. Our reluctance for conflict should not be misjudged as a failure of will. When action is required to preserve our national security, we will act. We will maintain sufficient strength to prevail if need be, knowing that if we do so we have the best chance of never having to use that strength.

Above all, we must realize that no arsenal or no weapon in the arsenals of the world is so formidable as the will and moral courage of free men and women. It is a weapon our adversaries in today's world do not have. It is a weapon that we as Americans do have. Let that be understood by those who practice terrorism and prey upon their neighbors.

I'm told that tens of thousands of prayer meetings are being held on this day, and for that I'm deeply grateful. We are a nation under God, and I believe God intended for us to be free. It would be fitting and good, I think, if on each Inaugural Day in future years it should be declared a day of prayer.

This is the first time in our history that this ceremony has been held, as you've been told, on this West Front of the Capitol. Standing here, one faces a magnificent vista, opening up on this city's special beauty and history. At the end of this open mall are those shrines to the giants on whose shoulders we stand.

Directly in front of me, the monument to a monumental man, George Washington, father of our country. A man of humility who came to greatness reluctantly. He led America out of revolutionary victory into infant nationhood. Off to one side, the stately memorial to Thomas Jefferson. The Declaration of Independence flames with his eloquence. And then, beyond the Reflecting Pool, the dignified columns of the Lincoln Memorial. Whoever would understand in his heart the meaning of America will find it in the life of Abraham Lincoln.

Beyond those monuments to heroism is the Potomac River, and on the far shore the sloping hills of Arlington National Cemetery, with its row upon row of simple white markers bearing crosses or Stars of David. They add up to only a tiny fraction of the price that has been paid for our freedom.

Each one of those markers is a monument to the kind of hero I spoke of earlier. Their lives ended in places called Belleau Wood, The Argonne, Omaha Beach, Salerno, and halfway around the world on Guadalcanal, Tarawa, Pork Chop Hill, the Chosin Reservoir, and in a hundred rice paddies and jungles of a place called Vietnam.

Under one such marker lies a young man, Martin Treptow, who left his job in a small town barbershop in 1917 to go to France with the famed Rainbow Division. There, on the western front, he was killed trying to carry a message between battalions under heavy artillery fire.

We're told that on his body was found a diary. On the flyleaf under the heading, "My Pledge," he had written these words: "America must win this war. Therefore I will work, I will save, I will sacrifice, I will endure, I will fight cheerfully and do my utmost, as if the issue of the whole struggle depended on me alone."

The crisis we are facing today does not require of us the kind of sacrifice that Martin Treptow and so many thousands of others were called upon to make. It does require, however, our best effort and our willingness to believe in ourselves and to believe in our capacity to perform great deeds, to believe that together with God's help we can and will resolve the problems which now confront us.

And after all, why shouldn't we believe that? We are Americans.

God bless you, and thank you.

Document 26.2 Wealth and Poverty, George Gilder

In the 1980s the problem of poverty and how to escape it engaged several conservative writers. Among the most prominent was George Gilder. Gilder and other conservatives tried to show why some people were poor and others escaped poverty. Usually, liberals had argued that the most of the poor were trapped by circumstances beyond their control. The best, and usually only, way out was through government action. Gilder and other conservatives, on the other hand, maintained that the poor were usually trapped by their own patterns of behavior and lack of character. Accordingly, moreover, some of the poor actually got out of poverty—because they had different behavior patterns and better character. Such a view, of course, had been the dominant idea of the late nineteenth century, in which people believed the poor were poor because of their own failings.

If, therefore, the primary factor in making people either rich or poor was behavior and moral character, then government action was no longer called for. Government programs couldn't provide substitutes for behavior and character. In fact, they might actually have the opposite effect, causing the poor to become less diligent and resourceful and more dependent. And since government programs were ineffective and the behavior of the poor was the only way to get out of poverty, high levels of government action, which conservatives opposed, were unnecessary.

Implicit also in such explanations was the justification of wealth by those who already possessed it. For years modern liberals had advocated a redistribution of wealth. Greater equality was good, they argued, a value in its own right. In addition, the poor needed help, and the sector of society most able to provide the funds were the rich. Views such as Gilder's suggested that not only was redistribution unnecessary (because government efforts to reduce poverty were ineffective), but morally objectionable. If behavior and character were the keys to wealth, the rich had earned their money and deserved to keep it.

Wealth and Poverty

George Gilder

The only dependable route from poverty is always work, family, and faith. The first principle is that in order to move up, the poor must not only work, they must work harder than the classes above them. Every previous generation of the lower class has made such efforts. But the current poor, white even more than black, are refusing to work hard. Irwin Garfinkel and Robert Haveman, authors of an ingenious and sophisticated study of what they call *Earnings Capacity Utilization Rates,* have calculated the degree to which various income groups use their opportunities—how hard they work outside the home. This study shows that, for several understandable reasons, the current poor work substantially less, for fewer hours and weeks a year, and earn less in proportion to their age, education, and other credentials (even *after* correcting the figures for unemployment, disability, and presumed discrimination) than

---

either their predecessors in American cities or those now above them on the income scale. (The study was made at the federally funded Institute for Research on Poverty at the University of Wisconsin and used data from the census and the Michigan longitudinal survey.) The findings lend important confirmation to the growing body of evidence that work effort is the crucial unmeasured variable in American productivity and income distribution, and that current welfare and other subsidy programs substantially reduce work. The poor choose leisure not because of moral weakness, but because they are paid to do so.

A program to lift by transfers and preferences the incomes of less diligent groups is politically divisive—and very unlikely—because it incurs the bitter resistance of the real working class. In addition, such an effort breaks the psychological link between effort and reward, which is crucial to long-run upward mobility. Because effective work consists not in merely fulfilling the requirements of labor contracts, but in "putting out" with alertness and emotional commitment, workers have to understand and feel deeply that what they are given depends on what they give—that they must supply work in order to demand goods. Parents and schools must inculcate this idea in their children both by instruction and example. Nothing is more deadly to achievement than the belief that effort will not be rewarded, that the world is a bleak and discriminatory place in which only the predatory and the specially preferred can get ahead. Such a view in the home discourages the work effort in school that shapes earnings capacity afterward. As with so many aspects of human performance, work effort begins in family experiences, and its sources can be best explored through an examination of family structure.

Indeed, after work the second principle of upward mobility is the maintenance of monogamous marriage and family. Adjusting for discrimination against women and for child-care responsibilities, the Wisconsin study indicates that married men work between two and one-third and four times harder than married women, and more than twice as hard as female family heads. The work effort of married men increases with their age, credentials, education, job experience, and birth of children, while the work effort of married women steadily declines. Most important in judging the impact of marriage, husbands work 50 percent harder than bachelors of comparable age, education, and skills.

The effect of marriage, thus, is to increase the work effort of men by about half. Since men have higher earnings capacity to begin with, and since the female capacity-utilization figures would be even lower without an adjustment for discrimination, it is manifest that the maintenance of families is the key factor in reducing poverty.

Once a family is headed by a woman, it is almost impossible for it to greatly raise its income even if the woman is highly educated and trained and she hires day-care or domestic help. Her family responsibilities and distractions tend to prevent her from the kind of all-out commitment that is necessary for the full use of earning power. Few women with children make earning money the top priority in their lives.

A married man, on the other hand, is spurred by the claims of family to channel his otherwise disruptive male aggressions into his performance as a provider for a wife and children. These sexual differences alone, which manifest themselves in all societies known to anthropology, dictate that the first priority of any serious program against poverty is to strengthen the male role in poor families.

These narrow measures of work effort touch on just part of the manifold interplay between family and poverty. Edward Banfield's *The Unheavenly City* defines the lower class largely by its lack of an orientation to the future. Living from day to day and from hand to mouth, lower class individuals are unable to plan or save or keep a job. Banfield gives the impression that short-time horizons are a deep-seated psychological defect afflicting hundreds of thousands of the poor.

There is no question that Banfield puts his finger on a crucial problem of the poor and that he develops and documents his theme in an unrivaled classic of disciplined social science. But he fails to show how millions of men, equally present oriented, equally buffeted by impulse and blind to the future, have managed to become far-seeing members of the middle classes. He also fails to explain how millions of apparently future-oriented men can become dissolute followers of the sensuous moment, neglecting their jobs, dissipating their income and wealth, pursuing a horizon no longer than the most time-bound of the poor.

What Banfield is in fact describing in his lower-class category is largely the temperament of single, divorced, and separated men. The key to lower-class life in contemporary America is that unrelated individuals, as the census calls them, are so numerous and conspicuous that they set the tone for the entire community. Their congregation in ghettos, moreover, magnifies greatly their impact on the black poor, male and female (though, as Banfield rightly observes, this style of instant gratification is chiefly a male trait).

The short-sighted outlook of poverty stems largely from the breakdown of family responsibilities among fathers. The lives of the poor, all too often, are governed by the rhythms of tension and release that characterize the sexual experience of young single men. Because female sexuality, as it evolved over the millennia, is psychologically rooted in the bearing and nurturing of children, women have long horizons within their very bodies, glimpses of eternity within their wombs. Civilized society is dependent upon the submission of the short-term sexuality of young men to the extended maternal horizons of women. This is what happens in monogamous marriage; the man disciplines his sexuality and extends it into the future through the womb of a woman. The woman gives him access to his children, otherwise forever denied him; and he gives her the product of his labor, otherwise dissipated on temporary pleasures. The woman gives him a unique link to the future and a vision of it; he gives her faithfulness and a commitment to a lifetime of hard work. If work effort is the first principle of overcoming poverty, marriage is the prime source of upwardly mobile work.

It is love that changes the short horizons of youth and poverty into the long horizons of marriage and career. When marriages fail, the man often returns to the more primitive rhythms of singleness. On the average, his income drops by one-third and he shows a far higher propensity for drink, drugs, and crime. But when marriages in general hold firm and men in general love and support their children, Banfield's lower-class style changes into middle-class futurity.

The key to the intractable poverty of the hard-core American poor is the dominance of single and separated men in poor communities. Black "unrelated individuals" are not much more likely to be in poverty than white ones. The problem is neither race nor matriarchy in any meaningful sense. It is familial anarchy among the concentrated poor of the inner city, in which flamboyant and impulsive youths rather than responsible men provide the themes of aspiration. The result is that male sexual rhythms tend to prevail, and boys are brought up without authoritative fathers in the home to instill in them the values of responsible paternity: the discipline and love of children and the dependable performance of the provider role. "If she wants me, *she*'ll pay," one young stud assured me in prison, and perhaps, in the welfare culture, she can and will. Thus the pattern is extended into future generations.

In his concern with present and future orientation, Banfield was right about the role of time in upward mobility. "Capital," as the Austrian school of economists tells us, "*is* time"—the delay in consumption entailed by extended modes of production. In poor communities, it might be said, all time is present time, and capital—in its human form of work effort combined with education and savings—does not adequately accumulate to provide income and wealth. But a more fundamental way of defining the stagnant lower class is by its lack of family structure. The men's links to—children and future are too often insufficient to induce work and thrift.

Document 26.3 A Call to Return to Traditional Religious Morality, Jerry Falwell

In the 1970s Jerry Falwell, a Baptist minister from Lynchburg, Virginia, launched an organization called the Moral Majority. This organization sought to counter the liberal sexual values that had been developing during the 1960s and 1970s, as well as what many conservative Christians called "secular humanism," a rough grouping of secular values and beliefs held by some intellectuals and others in what conservative Christians perceived to be an elite group of opinion makers. Falwell's new organization attracted followers as well as critics. He and other conservative Christian leaders proved to be important new supporters of the conservative movement when Reagan was elected president in 1980. In this selection Falwell propounds his view of the state of contemporary America and what is needed to make it right.

A Call to Return to Traditional Religious Morality

Jerry Falwell

We must review our government and see where our leadership has taken us today and where our future leaders must take us tomorrow if we are to remain a free America. It is a sad fact today that Americans have made a god of government. They are looking to government rather than to God, who ordained government. The United States is a republic where laws rule. Although the people of the United States have a vote, America is not a democracy in the sense that the majority rules. Her citizens elect representatives who represent them and govern them by laws. I believe that God promoted America to a greatness no other nation has ever enjoyed because her heritage is one of a republic governed by laws predicated on the Bible.

America is facing a vacuum of leadership not only in regard to her elected officials, but also among her citizens who are not standing for what is right and decent. We need in America today powerful, dynamic, and godly leadership. Male leadership in our families is affecting male leadership in our churches, and it is affecting male leadership in our society. As we look across our nation today we find a tremendous vacuum of godly men who are willing to be the kind of spiritual leaders who are necessary not only to change a nation, but also to change the churches within our nation and the basic units of our entire society, our families.

If a man is not a student of the Word of God and does not know what the Bible says, I question his ability to be an effective leader. Whatever he leads, whether it be his family, his church, or his nation, will not be properly led without this priority. God alone has the wisdom to tell men and women where this world is going, where it needs to go, and how it can be redirected. Only by godly leadership can America be put back on a divine course. God will give national healing if men and women will pray and meet God's conditions, but we must have leadership in America to deliver God's message.

We must reverse the trend America finds herself in today. Young people between the ages of twenty-five and forty have been born and reared in a different world than Americans of years past. The television set has been their primary baby-sitter. From the television set they have learned situation ethics and immorality—they have learned a loss of respect for human life. They have learned to disrespect the family as God has established it. They have been educated in a public-school system that is permeated with secular humanism. They have been taught that the Bible is just another book of literature. They have been taught that there are no absolutes in our world today. They have been introduced to the drug culture. They have been reared by the family and by the public school in a society that is greatly void of discipline and character-building. These same young people have been reared under the influence of a government that has taught them socialism and welfarism. They have been taught to believe that the world owes them a living whether they work or not.

I believe that America was built on integrity, on faith in God, and on hard work. I do not believe that anyone has ever been successful in life without being willing to add that last ingredient—diligence or hard work. We now have second- and third-generation welfare recipients. Welfare is not always wrong. There are those who do need welfare, but we have reared a generation that understands neither the dignity nor the importance of work.

Every American who looks at the facts must share a deep concern and burden for our country. We are not unduly concerned when we say that there are some very dark clouds on America's horizon. I am not a pessimist, but it is indeed a time for truth. If Americans will face the truth, our nation can be turned around and can be saved from the evils and the destruction that have fallen upon every other nation that has turned its back on God.

There is no excuse for what is happening in our country. We must, from the highest office in the land right down to the shoe-shine boy in the airport, have a return to biblical basics. If the Congress of our United States will take its stand on that which is right and wrong, and if our President, our judiciary system, and our state and local leaders will take their stand on holy living, we can turn this country around.

I personally feel that the home and the family are still held in reverence by the vast majority of the American public. I believe there is still a vast number of Americans who love their country, are patriotic, and are willing to sacrifice for her. I remember the time when it was positive to be patriotic, and as far as I am concerned, it still is. I remember as a boy, when the flag was raised, everyone stood proudly and put his hand upon his heart and pledged allegiance with gratitude. I remember when the band struck up "The Stars and Stripes Forever," we stood and goose pimples would run all over me. I remember when I was in elementary school during World War II, when every report from the other shores meant something to us. We were not out demonstrating against our boys who were dying in Europe and Asia. We were praying for them and thanking God for them and buying war bonds to help pay for the materials and artillery they needed to fight and win and come back.

I believe that Americans want to see this country come back to basics, back to values, back to biblical morality, back to sensibility, and back to patriotism. Americans are looking for leadership and guidance. It is fair to ask the question, "If 84 per cent of the American people still believe in morality, why is America having such internal problems?" We must look for the answer to the highest places in every level of government. We have a lack of leadership in America. But Americans have been lax in voting in and out of office the right and the wrong people.

My responsibility as a preacher of the Gospel is one of influence, not of control, and that is the responsibility of each individual citizen. Through the ballot box Americans must provide for strong moral leadership at every level. If our country will get back on the track in sensibility and moral sanity, the crises that I have herein mentioned will work out in the course of time and with God's blessings.

It is now time to take a stand on certain moral issues, and we can only stand if we have leaders. We must stand against the Equal Rights Amendment, the feminist revolution, and the homosexual revolution. We must have a revival in this country. It can come if we will realize the danger and heed the admonition of God found in 2 Chronicles 7:14, "If my people, which are called by my name, shall humble themselves, and pray, and seek my face, and turn from their wicked ways; then will I hear from heaven, and will forgive their sin, and will heal their land."

As a preacher of the Gospel, I not only believe in prayer and preaching, I also believe in good citizenship. If a labor union in America has the right to organize and improve its working conditions, then I believe that the churches and the pastors, the priests, and the rabbis of America have a responsibility, not just the right, to see to it that the moral climate and conscience of Americans is such that this nation can be healed inwardly. If it is healed inwardly, then it will heal itself outwardly.

It is not easy to go against the tide and do what is right. This nation can be brought back to God, but there must first be an awareness of sin. The Bible declares, "Righteousness exalteth a nation: But sin is a reproach to any people." (Pr. 14:34) It is right living that has made America the greatest nation on earth, and with all of her shortcomings and failures, America is without question the greatest nation on the face of God's earth. We as Americans must recommit ourselves to keeping her that way. Our prayers must certainly be behind our President and our Congress. We are commissioned by Scripture (1. Tm. 2:1–3) to pray for those who are in authority, but we would also remind our leaders that the future of this great nation is in their hands. One day they will stand before God accountable with what they have done to ensure our future. God has charged us as Americans with great privileges, but to whom much is given "much is required." We are faced with great responsibilities. Today, more than at any time in history, America needs men and women of God who have an understanding of the times and are not afraid to stand up for what is right.

Americans have been silent much too long. We have stood by and watched as American power and influence have been systematically weakened in every sphere of the world.

We are not a perfect nation, but we are still a free nation because we have the blessing of God upon us. We must continue to follow in a path that will ensure that blessing. We must not forget the words of our national anthem, "Oh! thus be it ever, when free men shall stand/Between their loved homes and the war's desolation!/Blest with victory and peace, may the heav'n rescued land/Praise the Power that hath made and preserved us a nation./Then conquer we must, when our cause it is just,/And this be our motto: 'In God is our trust.'" We must not forget that it is God Almighty who has made and preserved us a nation.

Let us never forget that as our Constitution declares, we are endowed by our Creator with certain inalienable rights. It is only as we abide by those laws established by our Creator that He will continue to bless us with these rights. We are endowed our rights to freedom and liberty and the pursuit of happiness by the God who created man to be free and equal.

The hope of reversing the trends of decay in our republic now lies with the Christian public in America. We cannot expect help from the liberals. They certainly are not going to call our nation back to righteousness and neither are the pornographers, the smut peddlers, and those who are corrupting our youth. Moral Americans must be willing to put their reputations, their fortunes, and their very lives on the line for this great nation of ours. Would that we had the courage of our forefathers who knew the great responsibility that freedom carries with it. Patrick Henry said, "It is natural to man to indulge in the illusions of hope. We are apt to shut our eyes against a painful truth. . . . Is this the part of wise men, engaged in a great and arduous struggle for liberty? Are we disposed to be a number of those who, having eyes, see not, and having ears, hear not, the things which so nearly concern their temporal salvation? For my part, whatever anguish of spirit it may cost, I am willing to know the whole truth; to know the worst and to provide for it. . . . Is life so dear or peace so sweet, as to be purchased at the price of chains or slavery? Forbid it, Almighty God! I know not what course others may take, but as for me, give me liberty or give me death!"

More than ever before in the history of humanity, we must have heroes, those men and women who will stand for what is right and stand against what is wrong, no matter what it costs. Today we need men and women of character and integrity who will commit themselves to letting their posterity know the freedom that our Founding Fathers established for this nation. Let us stand by that statement in the Declaration of Independence that cost our forefathers so much: ". . . with a firm Reliance on the Protection of divine Providence, we mutually pledge to each other our lives, our Fortunes, and our sacred Honor."

Our Founding Fathers separated church and state in function, but never intended to establish a government void of God. As is evidenced by our Constitution, good people in America must exert an influence and provide a conscience and climate of morality in which it is difficult to go wrong, not difficult for people to go right in America.

I am positive in my belief regarding the Constitution that God led in the development of that document, and as a result, we here in America have enjoyed 204 years of unparalleled freedom. The most positive people in the world are people who believe the Bible to be the Word of God. The Bible contains a positive message. It is a message written by 40 men over a period of approximately 1,500 years under divine inspiration. It is God's message of love, redemption, and deliverance for a fallen race. What could be more positive than the message of redemption in the Bible? But God will force Himself upon no man. Each individual American must make His choice.

Peter Marshall knew that the choices of individuals determine the destiny of a nation. He immigrated to the United States as a young man and worked his way through seminary by digging ditches and doing newspaper work. His years in the ministry culminated with the pastorate of the historic New York Avenue Presbyterian Church in Washington, D.C. (Abraham Lincoln's church), located two blocks from the White House. Dr. Marshall became chaplain of the Senate in January 1947. He died suddenly in January 1949 while still holding office. He was a dynamic Christian and was called by many a reporter the "conscience of the Senate."

Peter Marshall summed it up well when in a sermon to the New York Presbyterian Church he challenged its members with these words: "Today, we are living in a time when enough individuals, choosing to go to hell, will pull the nation down to hell with them. The choices you make in moral and religious questions determine the way America will go. The choice before us is plain, Christ or chaos, conviction or compromise, discipline or disintegration. I am rather tired about hearing about our rights and privileges as American citizens. The time has come, it now is, when we ought to hear about the duties and responsibilities of our citizenship. America's future depends upon her accepting and demonstrating God's government. It is just as plain and clear as that."

Americans must no longer linger in ignorance and apathy. We cannot be silent about the sins that are destroying this nation. The choice is ours. We must turn America around or prepare for inevitable destruction. I am listening to the sounds that threaten to take away our liberties in America. And I have listened to God's admonitions and His direction—the only hopes of saving America. Are you listening too?

Document 26.4 The Importance of Religion, Speech to the National Association of Evangelicals, 1983, Ronald Reagan

Although some conservatives' primary goal was decreasing government intervention in the economy, one of the most important constituencies in the coalition of conservative voters in the 1980s and 1990s were those who wanted a greater role in national life for traditional religion. Among the leaders of this group were Jerry Falwell and Pat Robertson. The conservative program included demands for prayer in public schools, an emphasis on traditional sexual morality, and an end to abortion. Since the Supreme Court had ruled school-sponsored prayer and the prohibition of many abortions unconstitutional, the Republican platform called for Constitutional amendments to overturn the court's decision. In 1983 Reagan voiced support for the religious agenda of modern conservatism in a speech before the National Association of Evangelicals, a leading organization of theologically-conservative Protestants.

Remarks at the Annual Convention of the National Association of Evangelicals in Orlando, Florida

Ronald Reagan

March 8, 1983

Reverend clergy all, Senator Hawkins, distinguished members of the Florida congressional delegation, and all of you:

I can't tell you how you have warmed my heart with your welcome. I'm delighted to be here today.

Those of you in the National Association of Evangelicals are known for your spiritual and humanitarian work. And I would be especially remiss if I didn't discharge right now one personal debt of gratitude. Thank you for your prayers. Nancy and I have felt their presence many times in many ways. And believe me, for us they've made all the difference.

The other day in the East Room of the White House at a meeting there, someone asked me whether I was aware of all the people out there who were praying for the President. And I had to say, "Yes, I am. I've felt it. I believe in intercessionary prayer." But I couldn't help but say to that questioner after he'd asked the question that—or at least say to them that if sometimes when he was praying he got a busy signal, it was just me in there ahead of him. *[Laughter]* I think I understand how Abraham Lincoln felt when he said, "I have been driven many times to my knees by the overwhelming conviction that I had nowhere else to go."

From the joy and the good feeling of this conference, I go to a political reception. *[Laughter]* Now, I don't know why, but that bit of scheduling, reminds me of a story—*[laughter]*—which I'll share with you.

An evangelical minister and a politician arrived at Heaven's gate one day together. And St. Peter, after doing all the necessary formalities, took them in hand to show them where their quarters would be. And he took them to a small, single room with a bed, a chair, and a table and said this was for the clergyman. And the politician was a little worried about what might be in store for him. And he couldn't believe it then when St. Peter stopped in front of a beautiful mansion with lovely grounds, many servants, and told him that these would be his quarters.

And he couldn't help but ask, he said, "But wait, how—there's something wrong—how do I get this mansion while that good and holy man only gets a single room?" And St. Peter said, "You have to understand how things are up here. We've got thousands and thousands of clergy. You're the first politician who ever made it." *[Laughter]*

Speech to the National Association of Evangelicals, 1983.

But I don't want to contribute to a stereotype. *[Laughter]* So, I tell you there are a great many God-fearing, dedicated, noble men and women in public life, present company included. And, yes, we need your help to keep us ever mindful of the ideas and the principles that brought us into the public arena in the first place. The basis of those ideals and principles is a commitment to freedom and personal liberty that, itself, is grounded in the much deeper realization that freedom prospers only where the blessings of God are avidly sought and humbly accepted.

The American experiment in democracy rests on this insight. Its discovery was the great triumph of our Founding Fathers, voiced by William Penn when he said: "If we will not be governed by God, we must be governed by tyrants." Explaining the inalienable rights of men, Jefferson said, "The God who gave us life, gave us liberty at the same time." And it was George Washington who said that "of all the dispositions and habits which lead to political prosperity, religion and morality are indispensable supports."

And finally, that shrewdest of all observers of American democracy, Alexis de Tocqueville, put it eloquently after he had gone on a search for the secret of America's greatness and genius—and he said: "Not until I went into the churches of America and heard her pulpits aflame with righteousness did I understand the greatness and the genius of America. . . . America is good. And if America ever ceases to be good, America will cease to be great."

Well, I'm pleased to be here today with you who are keeping America great by keeping her good. Only through your work and prayers and those of millions of others can we hope to survive this perilous century and keep alive this experiment in liberty, this last, best hope of man.

I want you to know that this administration is motivated by a political philosophy that sees the greatness of America in you, her people, and in your families, churches, neighborhoods, communities—the institutions that foster and nourish values like concern for others and respect for the rule of law under God.

Now, I don't have to tell that this puts us in opposition to, or at least out of step with, a prevailing attitude of many who have turned to a modern-day secularism, discarding the tried and time-tested values upon which our very civilization is based. No matter how well intentioned, their value system is radically different from that of most Americans. And while they proclaim that they're freeing us from superstitions of the past, they've taken upon themselves the job of superintending us by government rule and regulation. Sometimes their voices are louder than ours, but they are not yet a majority.

An example of that vocal superiority is evident in a controversy now going on in Washington. And since I'm involved, I've been waiting to hear from the parents of young America. How far are they willing to go in giving to government their prerogatives as parents?

Let me state the case as briefly and simply as I can. An organization of citizens, sincerely motivated and deeply concerned about the increase in illegitimate births and abortions involving girls well below the age of consent, sometime ago established a nationwide network of clinics to offer help to these girls and, hopefully, alleviate this situation. Now, again, let me say, I do not fault their intent. However, in their well-intentioned effort, these clinics have decided to provide advice and birth control drugs and devices to underage girls without the knowledge of their parents.

For some years now, the Federal Government has helped with funds to subsidize these clinics. In providing for this, the Congress decreed that every effort would be made to maximize parental participation. Nevertheless, the drugs and devices are prescribed without getting parental consent or giving notification after they've done so. Girls termed "sexually active"—and that has replaced the word "promiscuous"—are given this help in order to prevent illegitimate birth or abortion.

Well, we have ordered clinics receiving Federal funds to notify the parents such help has been given. One of the Nation's leading newspapers has created the term "squeal rule" in editorializing against us for doing this, and we're being criticized for violating the privacy of young people. A judge has recently granted an injunction against an enforcement of our rule. I've watched TV panel shows discuss this issue, seen columnists pontificating on our error, but no one seems to mention morality as playing a part in the subject of sex.

Is all of Judeo-Christian tradition wrong? Are we to believe that something so sacred can be looked upon as a purely physical thing with no potential for emotional and psychological harm? And isn't it the parents' right to give counsel and advice to keep their children from making mistakes that may affect their entire lives?

Many of us in government would like to know what parents think about this intrusion in their family by government. We're going to fight in the courts. The right of parents and the rights of family take precedence over those of Washington-based bureaucrats and social engineers.

But the fight against parental notification is really only one example of many attempts to water down traditional values and even abrogate the original terms of American democracy. Freedom prospers when religion is vibrant and the rule of law under God is acknowledged. When our Founding Fathers passed the first amendment, they sought to protect churches from government interference. They never intended to construct a wall of hostility between government and the concept of religious belief itself.

The evidence of this permeates our history and our government. The Declaration of Independence mentions the Supreme Being no less than four times. "In God We Trust" is engraved on our coinage. The Supreme Court opens its proceedings with a religious invocation. And the Members of Congress open their sessions with a prayer. I just happen to believe the schoolchildren of the United States are entitled to the same privileges as Supreme Court Justices and Congressmen.

Last year, I sent the Congress a constitutional amendment to restore prayer to public schools. Already this session, there's growing bipartisan support for the amendment, and I am calling on the Congress to act speedily to pass it and to let our children pray.

Perhaps some of you read recently about the Lubbock school case, where a judge actually ruled that it was unconstitutional for a school district to give equal treatment to religious and nonreligious student groups, even when the group meetings were being held during the students' own time. The first amendment never intended to require government to discriminate against religious speech.

Senators Denton and Hatfield have proposed legislation in the Congress on the whole question of prohibiting discrimination against religious forms of student speech. Such legislation could go far to restore freedom of religious speech for public school students. And I hope the Congress considers these bills quickly. And with your help, I think it's possible we could also get the constitutional amendment through the Congress this year.

More than a decade ago, a Supreme Court decision literally wiped off the books of 50 States statutes protecting the rights of unborn children. Abortion on demand now takes the lives of up to 1 1/2 million unborn children a year. Human life legislation ending this tragedy will some day pass the Congress, and you and I must never rest until it does. Unless and until it can be proven that the unborn child is not a living entity, then its right to life, liberty, and the pursuit of happiness must be protected.

You may remember that when abortion on demand began, many, and, indeed, I'm sure many of you, warned that the practice would lead to a decline in respect for human life, that the philosophical premises used to justify abortion on demand would ultimately be used to justify other attacks on the sacredness of human life—infanticide or mercy killing. Tragically enough, those warnings proved all too true. Only last year a court permitted the death by starvation of a handicapped infant.

I have directed the Health and Human Services Department to make clear to every health care facility in the United States that the Rehabilitation Act of 1973 protects all handicapped persons against discrimination based on handicaps, including infants. And we have taken the further step of requiring that each and every recipient of Federal funds who provides health care services to infants must post and keep posted in a conspicuous place a notice stating that "discriminatory failure to feed and care for handicapped infants in this facility is prohibited by Federal law." It also lists a 24-hour, toll-free number so that nurses and others may report violations in time to save the infant's life.

In addition, recent legislation introduced in the Congress by Representative Henry Hyde of Illinois not only increases restrictions on publicly financed abortions, it also addresses this whole problem of infanticide. I urge the Congress to begin hearings and to adopt legislation that will protect the right of life to all children, including the disabled or handicapped.

Now, I'm sure that you must get discouraged at times, but you've done better than you know, perhaps. There's a great spiritual awakening in America, a renewal of the traditional values that have been the bedrock of America's goodness and greatness.

One recent survey by a Washington-based research council concluded that Americans were far more religious than the people of other nations: 95 percent of those surveyed expressed a belief in God and a huge majority believed the Ten Commandments had real meaning in their lives. And another study has found that an overwhelming majority of Americans disapprove of adultery, teenage sex, pornography, abortion, and hard drugs. And this same study showed a deep reverence for the importance of family ties and religious belief.

I think the items that we've discussed here today must be a key part of the nation's political agenda. For the first time the Congress is openly and seriously debating and dealing with the prayer and abortion issues—and that's enormous progress right there. I repeat: America is in the midst of a spiritual awakening and a moral renewal. And with your Biblical keynote, I say today, "Yes, let justice roll on like a river, righteousness like a never-failing stream."

Now, obviously, much of this new political and social consensus I've talked about is based on a positive view of American history, one that takes pride in our country's accomplishments and record. But we must never forget that no government schemes are going to perfect man. We know that living in this world means dealing with what philosophers would call the phenomenology of evil or, as theologians would put it, the doctrine of sin.

There is sin and evil in the world, and we're enjoined by Scripture and the Lord Jesus to oppose it with all our might. Our nation, too, has a legacy of evil with which it must deal. The glory of this land has been its capacity for transcending the moral evils of our past. For example, the long struggle of minority citizens for equal rights, once a source of disunity and civil war, is now a point of pride for all Americans. We must never go back. There is no room for racism, anti-Semitism, or other forms of ethnic and racial hatred in this country.

I know that you've been horrified, as have I, by the resurgence of some hate groups preaching bigotry and prejudice. Use the mighty voice of pulpits and the powerful standing of our churches to denounce and isolate these hate groups in our midst. The commandment given us is clear and simple: "Thou shalt love thy neighbor as thyself."

But whatever sad episodes exist in our past, any objective observer must hold a positive view of American history, a history that has been the story of hopes fulfilled and dreams made into reality. Espccially in this century, America has kept alight the torch of freedom, but not just for ourselves but for millions of others around the world.

And this brings me to my final point today. During my first press conference as President, in answer to a direct question, I pointed out that, as good Marxist-Leninists, the Soviet leaders have openly and publicly declared that the only morality they recognize is that which will further their cause, which is world revolution. I think I should point out I was only quoting Lenin, their guiding spirit, who said in 1920 that they repudiate all morality that proceeds from supernatural ideas—that's their name for religion—or ideas that are outside class conceptions. Morality is entirely subordinate to the interests of class war. And everything is moral that is necessary for the annihilation of the old, exploiting social order and for uniting the proletariat.

Well, I think the refusal of many influential people to accept this elementary fact of Soviet doctrine illustrates an historical reluctance to see totalitarian powers for what they are. We saw this phenomenon in the 1930's. We see it too often today.

This doesn't mean we should isolate ourselves and refuse to seek an understanding with them. I intend to do everything I can to persuade them of our peaceful intent, to remind them that it was the West that refused to use its nuclear monopoly in the forties and fifties for territorial gain and which now proposes 50-percent cut in strategic ballistic missiles and the elimination of an entire class of land-based, intermediate-range nuclear missiles.

At the same time, however, they must be made to understand we will never compromise our principles and standards. We will never give away our freedom. We will never abandon our belief in God. And we will never stop searching for a genuine peace. But we can assure none of these things America stands for through the so-called nuclear freeze solutions proposed by some.

The truth is that a freeze now would be a very dangerous fraud, for that is merely the illusion of peace. The reality is that we must find peace through strength.

I would agree to a freeze if only we could freeze the Soviets' global desires. A freeze at current levels of weapons would remove any incentive for the Soviets to negotiate seriously in Geneva and virtually end our chances to achieve the major arms reductions which we have proposed. Instead, they would achieve their objectives through the freeze.

A freeze would reward the Soviet Union for its enormous and unparalleled military buildup. It would prevent the essential and long overdue modernization of United States and allied defenses and would leave our aging forces increasingly vulnerable. And an honest freeze would require extensive prior negotiations on the systems and numbers to be limited and on the measures to ensure effective verification and compliance. And the kind of a freeze that has been suggested would be virtually impossible to verify. Such a major effort would divert us completely from our current negotiations on achieving substantial reductions.

A number of years ago, I heard a young father, a very prominent young man in the entertainment world, addressing a tremendous gathering in California. It was during the time of the cold war, and communism and our own way of life were very much on people's minds. And he was speaking to that subject. And suddenly, though, I heard him saying, "I love my little girls more than anything—" And I said to myself, "Oh, no, don't. You can't—don't say that." But I had underestimated him. He went on: "I would rather see my little girls die now, still believing in God, than have them grow up under communism and one day die no longer believing in God."

There were thousands of people in that audience. They came to their feet with shouts of joy.

They had instantly recognized the profound truth in what he had said, with regard to the physical and the soul and what was truly important.

Yes, let us pray for the salvation of all of those who live in that totalitarian darkness—pray they will discover the joy of knowing God. But until they do, let us be aware that while they preach the supremacy of the state, declare its omnipotence over individual man, and predict its eventual domination of all peoples on the Earth, they are the focus of evil in the modern world.

It was C. S. Lewis who, in his unforgettable "Screwtape Letters," wrote: "The greatest evil is not done now in those sordid 'dens of crime' that Dickens loved to paint. It is not even done in concentration camps and labor camps. In those we see its final result. But it is conceived and ordered (moved. seconded, carried and minuted) in clear, carpeted, warmed, and well-lighted offices, by quiet men with white collars and cut fingernails and smooth-shaven cheeks who do not need to raise their voice."

Well, because these "quiet men" do not "raise their voices," because they sometimes speak in soothing tones of brotherhood and peace, because, like other dictators before them, they're always making "their final territorial demand," some would have us accept them at their word and accommodate ourselves to their aggressive impulses. But if history teaches anything, it teaches that simple-minded appeasement or wishful thinking about our adversaries is folly. It means the betrayal of our past, the squandering of our freedom.

So, I urge you to speak out against those who would place the United States in a position of military and moral inferiority. You know, I've always believed that old Screwtape reserved his best efforts for those of you in the church. So, in your discussions of the nuclear freeze proposals, I urge you to beware the temptation of pride—the temptation of blithely declaring yourselves above it all and label both sides equally at fault, to ignore the facts of history and the aggressive impulses of an evil empire, to simply call the arms race a giant misunderstanding and thereby remove yourself from the struggle between right and wrong and good and evil.

I ask you to resist the attempts of those who would have you withhold your support for our efforts, this administration's efforts, to keep America strong and free, while we negotiate real and verifiable reductions in the world's nuclear arsenals and one day, with God's help, their total elimination.

While America's military strength is important, let me add here that I've always maintained that the struggle now going on for the world will never be decided by bombs or rockets, by armies or military might. The real crisis we face today is a spiritual one; at root, it is a test of moral will and faith.

Whittaker Chambers, the man whose own religious conversion made him a witness to one of the terrible traumas of our time, the Hiss-Chambers case, wrote that the crisis of the Western World exists to the degree in which the West is indifferent to God, the degree to which it collaborates in communism's attempt to make man stand alone without God. And then he said, for Marxism-Leninism is actually the second oldest faith, first proclaimed in the Garden of Eden with the words of temptation, "Ye shall be as gods."

The Western World can answer this challenge, he wrote, "but only provided that its faith in God and the freedom He enjoins is as great as communism's faith in Man."

I believe we shall rise to the challenge. I believe that communism is another sad, bizarre chapter in human history whose last pages even now are being written. I believe this because the source of our strength in the quest for human freedom is not material, but spiritual. And because it knows no limitation, it must terrify and ultimately triumph over those who would enslave their fellow man. For in the words of Isaiah: "He giveth power to the faint: and to them that have no might He increased strength. . . . But they that wait upon the Lord shall renew their strength; they shall mount up with wings as eagles; they shall run, and not be weary.

Yes, change your world. One of our Founding Fathers, Thomas Paine, said. "We have it within our power to begin the world over again." We can do it, doing together what no one church could do by itself.

God bless you, and thank you very much.

Document 26.5 The Failure of Communism, Ronald Reagan

Conservatives had long warned of the dangers of communism and had sometimes wanted to combat communist governments more aggressively than liberals. As president Ronald Reagan raised at least the rhetorical heat of the Cold War, calling the Soviet Union an "evil empire" and later at the Berlin War calling on the Soviet leader Mikhail Gorbachev to "tear this wall down." In this speech delivered to the British Parliament in London some seven years before the communist bloc in eastern Europe fell apart, Reagan made a systematic attack on communism.

Address to Members of the British Parliament

Ronald Reagan

June 8, 1982

My Lord Chancellor, Mr. Speaker:

The journey of which this visit forms a part is a long one. Already it has taken me to two great cities of the West, Rome and Paris, and to the economic summit at Versailles. And there, once again, our sister democracies have proved that even in a time of severe economic strain, free peoples can work together freely and voluntarily to address problems as serious as inflation, unemployment, trade, and economic development in a spirit of cooperation and solidarity.

Other milestones lie ahead. Later this week, in Germany, we and our NATO allies will discuss measures for our joint defense and America's latest initiatives for a more peaceful, secure world through arms reductions.

Each stop of this trip is important, but among them all, this moment occupies a special place in my heart and in the hearts of my countrymen—a moment of kinship and homecoming in these hallowed halls.

Speaking for all Americans, I want to say how very much at home we feel in your house. Every American would, because this is, as we have been so eloquently told, one of democracy's shrines. Here the rights of free people and the processes of representation have been debated and refined.

It has been said that an institution is the lengthening shadow of a man. This institution is the lengthening shadow of all the men and women who have sat here and all those who have voted to send representatives here.

This is my second visit to Great Britain as President of the United States. My first opportunity to stand on British soil occurred almost a year and a half ago when your Prime Minister graciously hosted a diplomatic dinner at the British Embassy in Washington. Mrs. Thatcher said then that she hoped I was not distressed to find staring down at me from the grand staircase a portrait of His Royal Majesty King George III. She suggested it was best to let bygones be bygones, and in view of our two countries' remarkable friendship in succeeding years, she added that most Englishmen today would agree with Thomas Jefferson that "a little rebellion now and then is a very good thing." *[Laughter]*

Well, from here I will go to Bonn and then Berlin, where there stands a grim symbol of power untamed. The Berlin Wall, that dreadful gray gash across the city, is in its third decade. It is the fitting signature of the regime that built it.

And a few hundred kilometers behind the Berlin Wall, there is another symbol. In the center of Warsaw, there is a sign that notes the distances to two capitals. In one direction it points toward Moscow. In the other it points toward Brussels, headquarters of Western Europe's tangible unity. The marker says that the distances from Warsaw to Moscow and Warsaw to Brussels are equal. The sign makes this point: Poland is not East or West. Poland is at the center of European civilization. It has contributed mightily to that civilization. It is doing so today by being magnificently unreconciled to oppression.

The Failure of Communism, President Ronald Reagan.

Poland's struggle to be Poland and to secure the basic rights we often take for granted demonstrates why we dare not take those rights for granted. Gladstone, defending the Reform Bill of 1866, declared, "You cannot fight against the future. Time is on our side." It was easier to believe in the march of democracy in Gladstone's day—in that high noon of Victorian optimism.

We're approaching the end of a bloody century plagued by a terrible political invention—totalitarianism. Optimism comes less easily today, not because democracy is less vigorous, but because democracy's enemies have refined their instruments of repression. Yet optimism is in order, because day by day democracy is proving itself to be a not-at-all-fragile flower. From Stettin on the Baltic to Varna on the Black Sea, the regimes planted by totalitarianism have had more than 30 years to establish their legitimacy. But none—not one regime—has yet been able to risk free elections. Regimes planted by bayonets do not take root.

The strength of the Solidarity movement in Poland demonstrates the truth told in an underground joke in the Soviet Union. It is that the Soviet Union would remain a one-party nation even if an opposition party were permitted, because everyone would join the opposition party. *[Laughter]*

America's time as a player on the stage of world history has been brief. I think understanding this fact has always made you patient with your younger cousins—well, not always patient. I do recall that on one occasion, Sir Winston Churchill said in exasperation about one of our most distinguished diplomats: "He is the only case I know of a bull who carries his china shop with him." *[Laughter]*

But witty as Sir Winston was, he also had that special attribute of great statesmen—the gift of vision, the willingness to see the future based on the experience of the past. It is this sense of history, this understanding of the past that I want to talk with you about today, for it is in remembering what we share of the past that our two nations can make common cause for the future.

We have not inherited an easy world. If developments like the Industrial Revolution, which began here in England, and the gifts of science and technology have made life much easier for us, they have also made it more dangerous There are threats now to our freedom, indeed to our very existence, that other generations could never even have imagined.

There is first the threat of global war. No President, no Congress, no Prime Minister, no Parliament can spend a day entirely free of this threat. And I don't have to tell you that in today's world the existence of nuclear weapons could mean, if not the extinction of mankind, then surely the end of civilization as we know it. That's why negotiations on intermediate-range nuclear forces now underway in Europe and the START talks—Strategic Arms Reduction Talks—which will begin later this month, are not just critical to American or Western policy; they are critical to mankind. Our commitment to early success in these negotiations is firm and unshakable, and our purpose is clear: reducing the risk of war by reducing the means of waging war on both sides.

At the same time there is a threat posed to human freedom by the enormous power of the modern state. History teaches the dangers of government that overreaches—political control taking precedence over free economic growth, secret police, mindless bureaucracy, all combining to stifle individual excellence and personal freedom.

Now, I'm aware that among us here and throughout Europe there is legitimate disagreement over the extent to which the public sector should play a role in a nation's economy and life. But on one point all of us are united—our abhorrence of dictatorship in all its forms, but most particularly totalitarianism and the terrible inhumanities it has caused in our time—the great purge, Auschwitz and Dachau, the Gulag, and Cambodia.

Historians looking back at our time will note the consistent restraint and peaceful intentions of the West. They will note that it was the democracies who refused to use the threat of their nuclear monopoly in the forties and early fifties for territorial or imperial gain. Had that nuclear monopoly been in the hands of the Communist world, the map of Europe—indeed, the world—would look very different today. And certainly they will note it was not the democracies that invaded Afghanistan or suppressed Polish Solidarity or used chemical and toxin warfare in Afghanistan and Southeast Asia.

If history teaches anything it teaches self-delusion in the face of unpleasant facts is folly. We see around us today the marks of our terrible dilemma—predictions of doomsday, antinuclear demonstrations, an arms race in which the West must, for its own protection, be an unwilling participant. At the same time we see totalitarian forces in the world who seek subversion and conflict around the globe to further their barbarous assault on the human spirit. What, then, is our course? Must civilization perish in a hail of fiery atoms? Must freedom wither in a quiet, deadening accommodation with totalitarian evil?

Sir Winston Churchill refused to accept the inevitability of war or even that it was imminent. He said, "I do not believe that Soviet Russia desires war. What they desire is the fruits of war and the indefinite expansion of their power and doctrines.

But what we have to consider here today while time remains is the permanent prevention of war and the establishment of conditions of freedom and democracy as rapidly as possible in all countries."

Well, this is precisely our mission today: to preserve freedom as well as peace. It may not be easy to see, but I believe we live now at a turning point.

In an ironic sense Karl Marx was right. We are witnessing today a great revolutionary crisis, a crisis where the demands of the economic order are conflicting directly with those of the political order. But the crisis is happening not in the free, non-Marxist West, but in the home of Marxist-Leninism, the Soviet Union. It is the Soviet Union that runs against the tide of history by denying human freedom and human dignity to its citizens. It also is in deep economic difficulty. The rate of growth in the national product has been steadily declining since the fifties and is less than half of what it was then.

The dimensions of this failure are astounding: A country which employs one-fifth of its population in agriculture is unable to feed its own people. Were it not for the private sector, the tiny private sector tolerated in Soviet agriculture, the country might be on the brink of famine. These private plots occupy a bare 3 percent of the arable land but account for nearly one-quarter of Soviet farm output and nearly one-third of meat products and vegetables. Overcentralized, with little or no incentives, year after year the Soviet system pours its best resource into the making of instruments of destruction. The constant shrinkage of economic growth combined with the growth of military production is putting a heavy strain on the Soviet people. What we see here is a political structure that no longer corresponds to its economic base, a society where productive forces are hampered by political ones.

The decay of the Soviet experiment should come as no surprise to us. Wherever the comparisons have been made between free and closed societies—West Germany and East Germany, Austria and Czechoslovakia, Malaysia and Vietnam—it is the democratic countries that are prosperous and responsive to the needs of their people. And one of the simple but overwhelming facts of our time is this: Of all the millions of refugees we've seen in the modern world, their flight is always away from, not toward the Communist world. Today on the NATO line, our military forces face east to prevent a possible invasion. On the other side of the line, the Soviet forces also face east to prevent their people from leaving.

The hard evidence of totalitarian rule has caused in mankind an uprising of the intellect and will. Whether it is the growth of the new schools of economics in America or England or the appearance of the so-called new philosophers in France, there is one unifying thread running through the intellectual work of these groups—rejection of the arbitrary power of the state, the refusal to subordinate the rights of the individual to the superstate, the realization that collectivism stifles all the best human impulses.

Since the exodus from Egypt, historians have written of those who sacrificed and struggled for freedom—the stand at Thermopylae, the revolt of Spartacus, the storming of the Bastille, the Warsaw uprising in World War II. More recently we've seen evidence of this same human impulse in one of the developing nations in Central America. For months and months the world news media covered the fighting in El Salvador. Day after day we were treated to stories and film slanted toward the brave freedom-fighters battling oppressive government forces in behalf of the silent, suffering people of that tortured country.

And then one day those silent, suffering people were offered a chance to vote, to choose the kind of government they wanted. Suddenly the freedom-fighters in the hills were exposed for what they really are—Cuban-backed guerrillas who want power for themselves, and their backers, not democracy for the people. They threatened death to any who voted, and destroyed hundreds of buses and trucks to keep the people from getting to the polling places. But on election day, the people of El Salvador, an unprecedented 1.4 million of them, braved ambush and gunfire, and trudged for miles to vote for freedom.

They stood for hours in the hot sun waiting for their turn to vote. Members of our Congress who went there as observers told me of a women who was wounded by rifle fire on the way to the polls, who refused to leave the line to have her wound treated until after she had voted. A grandmother, who had been told by the guerrillas she would be killed when she returned from the polls, and she told the guerrillas, "You can kill me, you can kill my family, kill my neighbors, but you can't kill us all." The real freedom-fighters of El Salvador turned out to be the people of that country—the young, the old, the in-between.

Strange, but in my own country there's been little if any news coverage of that war since the election. Now, perhaps they'll say it's—well, because there are newer struggles now.

On distant islands in the South Atlantic young men are fighting for Britain. And, yes, voices have been raised protesting their sacrifice for lumps of rock and earth so far away. But those young men aren't fighting for mere real estate. They fight for a cause—for the belief that armed aggression must not be allowed to succeed, and the people must participate in the decisions of government—*[applause]*—the decisions of government under the rule of law. If there had been firmer support for that principle some 45 years ago, perhaps our generation wouldn't have suffered the bloodletting of World War II.

In the Middle East now the guns sound once more, this time in Lebanon, a country that for too long has had to endure the tragedy of civil war, terrorism, and foreign intervention and occupation. The fighting in Lebanon on the part of all parties must stop, and Israel should bring its forces home. But this is not enough. We must all work to stamp out the scourge of terrorism that in the Middle East makes war an ever-present threat.

But beyond the troublespots lies a deeper, more positive pattern. Around the world today, the democratic revolution is gathering new strength. In India a critical test has been passed with the peaceful change of governing political parties. In Africa, Nigeria is moving into remarkable and unmistakable ways to build and strengthen its democratic institutions. In the Caribbean and Central America, 16 of 24 countries have freely elected governments. And in the United Nations, 8 of the 10 developing nations which have joined that body in the past 5 years are democracies.

In the Communist world as well, man's instinctive desire for freedom and self-determination surfaces again and again. To be sure, there are grim reminders of how brutally the police state attempts to snuff out this quest for self-rule—1953 in East Germany, 1956 in Hungary, 1968 in Czechoslovakia, 1981 in Poland. But the struggle continues in Poland. And we know that there are even those who strive and suffer for freedom within the confines of the Soviet Union itself. How we conduct ourselves here in the Western democracies will determine whether this trend continues.

No, democracy is not a fragile flower. Still it needs cultivating. If the rest of this century is to witness the gradual growth of freedom and democratic ideals, we must take actions to assist the campaign for democracy.

Some argue that we should encourage democratic change in right-wing dictatorships, but not in Communist regimes. Well, to accept this preposterous notion—as some well-meaning people have—is to invite the argument that once countries achieve a nuclear capability, they should be allowed an undisturbed reign of terror over their own citizens. We reject this course.

As for the Soviet view, Chairman Brezhnev repeatedly has stressed that the competition of ideas and systems must continue and that this is entirely consistent with relaxation of tensions and peace.

Well, we ask only that these systems begin by living up to their own constitutions, abiding by their own laws, and complying with the international obligations they have undertaken. We ask only for a process, a direction, a basic code of decency, not for an instant transformation.

We cannot ignore the fact that even without our encouragement there has been and will continue to be repeated explosions against repression and dictatorships. The Soviet Union itself is not immune to this reality. Any system is inherently unstable that has no peaceful means to legitimize its leaders. In such cases, the very repressiveness of the state ultimately drives people to resist it, if necessary, by force.

While we must be cautious about forcing the pace of change, we must not hesitate to declare our ultimate objectives and to take concrete actions to move toward them. We must be staunch in our conviction that freedom is not the sole prerogative of a lucky few, but the inalienable and universal right of all human beings. So states the United Nations Universal Declaration of Human Rights, which, among other things, guarantees free elections.

The objective I propose is quite simple to state: to foster the infrastructure of democracy, the system of a free press, unions, political parties, universities, which allows a people to choose their own way to develop their own culture, to reconcile their own differences through peaceful means.

This is not cultural imperialism, it is providing the means for genuine self-determination and protection for diversity. Democracy already flourishes in countries with very different cultures and historical experiences. It would be cultural condescension, or worse, to say that any people prefer dictatorship to democracy. Who would voluntarily choose not to have the right to vote, decide to purchase government propaganda handouts instead of independent newspapers, prefer government to worker-controlled unions, opt for land to be owned by the state instead of those who till it, want government repression of religious liberty, a single political party instead of a free choice, a rigid cultural orthodoxy instead of democratic tolerance and diversity?

Since 1917 the Soviet Union has given covert political training and assistance to Marxist-Leninists in many countries. Of course, it also has promoted the use of violence and subversion by these same forces. Over the past several decades, West European and other Social Democrats, Christian Democrats, and leaders have offered open assistance to fraternal, political, and social institutions to bring about peaceful and democratic progress. Appropriately, for a vigorous new democracy, the Federal

Republic of Germany's political foundations have become a major force in this effort.

We in America now intend to take additional steps, as many of our allies have already done, toward realizing this same goal. The chairmen and other leaders of the national Republican and Democratic Party organizations are initiating a study with the bipartisan American political foundation to determine how the United States can best contribute as a nation to the global campaign for democracy now gathering force. They will have the cooperation of congressional leaders of both parties, along with representatives of business, labor, and other major institutions in our society. I look forward to receiving their recommendations and to working with these institutions and the Congress in the common task of strengthening democracy throughout the world.

It is time that we committed ourselves as a nation—in both the pubic and private sectors—to assisting democratic development.

We plan to consult with leaders of other nations as well. There is a proposal before the Council of Europe to invite parliamentarians from democratic countries to a meeting next year in Strasbourg. That prestigious gathering could consider ways to help democratic political movements.

This November in Washington there will take place an international meeting on free elections. And next spring there will be a conference of world authorities on constitutionalism and self-government hosted by the Chief Justice of the United States. Authorities from a number of developing and developed countries—judges, philosophers, and politicians with practical experience—have agreed to explore how to turn principle into practice and further the rule of law.

At the same time, we invite the Soviet Union to consider with us how the competition of ideas and values—which it is committed to support—can be conducted on a peaceful and reciprocal basis. For example, I am prepared to offer President Brezhnev an opportunity to speak to the American people on our television if he will allow me the same opportunity with the Soviet people. We also suggest that panels of our newsmen periodically appear on each other's television to discuss major events.

Now, I don't wish to sound overly optimistic, yet the Soviet Union is not immune from the reality of what is going on in the world. It has happened in the past—a small ruling elite either mistakenly attempts to ease domestic unrest through greater repression and foreign adventure, or it chooses a wiser course. It begins to allow its people a voice in their own destiny. Even if this latter process is not realized soon, I believe the renewed strength of the democratic movement, complemented by a global campaign for freedom, will strengthen the prospects for arms control and a world at peace.

I have discussed on other occasions, including my address on May 9th, the elements of Western policies toward the Soviet Union to safeguard our interests and protect the peace. What I am describing now is a plan and a hope for the long term—the march of freedom and democracy which will leave Marxism-Leninism on the ashheap of history as it has left other tyrannies which stifle the freedom and muzzle the self-expression of the people. And that's why we must continue our efforts to strengthen NATO even as we move forward with our Zero-Option initiative in the negotiations on intermediate-range forces and our proposal for a one-third reduction in strategic ballistic missile warheads.

Our military strength is a prerequisite to peace, but let it be clear we maintain this strength in the hope it will never be used, for the ultimate determinant in the struggle that's now going on in the world will not be bombs and rockets, but a test of wills and ideas, a trial of spiritual resolve, the values we hold, the beliefs we cherish, the ideals to which we are dedicated.

The British people know that, given strong leadership, time and a little bit of hope, the forces of good ultimately rally and triumph over evil. Here among you is the cradle of self-government, the Mother of Parliaments. Here is the enduring greatness of the British contribution to mankind, the great civilized ideas: individual liberty, representative government, and the rule of law under God.

I've often wondered about the shyness of some of us in the West about standing for these ideals that have done so much to ease the plight of man and the hardships of our imperfect world. This reluctance to use those vast resources at our command reminds me of the elderly lady whose home was bombed in the Blitz. As the rescuers moved about, they found a bottle of brandy she'd stored behind the staircase, which was all that was left standing. And since she was barely conscious, one of the workers pulled the cork to give her a taste of it. She came around immediately and said, "Here now—there now, put it back. That's for emergencies." *[Laughter]*

Well, the emergency is upon us. Let us be shy no longer. Let us go to our strength. Let us offer hope. Let us tell the world that a new age is not only possible but probable.

During the dark days of the Second World War, when this island was incandescent with courage, Winston Churchill exclaimed about Britain's adversaries, "What kind of a people do they think we are?" Well, Britain's adversaries found out what extraordinary people the British are. But all the democracies paid a terrible price for allowing the dictators to underestimate us. We dare not make that mistake again. So, let us ask ourselves, "What kind of people do we think we are?" And let us answer, "Free people, worthy of freedom and determined not only to remain so but to help others gain their freedom as well."

Sir Winston led his people to great victory in war and then lost an election just as the fruits of victory were about to be enjoyed. But he left office honorably, and, as it turned out, temporarily, knowing that the liberty of his people was more important than the fate of any single leader. History recalls his greatness in ways no dictator will ever know. And he left us a message of hope for the future, as timely now as when he first uttered it, as opposition leader in the Commons nearly 27 years ago, when he said, "When we look back on all the perils through which we have passed and at the mighty foes that we have laid low and all the dark and deadly designs that we have frustrated, why should we fear for our future? We have," he said, "come safely through the worst."

Well, the task I've set forth will long outlive our own generation. But together, we too have come through the worst. Let us now begin a major effort to secure the best—a crusade for freedom that will engage the faith and fortitude of the next generation. For the sake of peace and justice, let us move toward a world in which all people are at last free to determine their own destiny.

Thank you.

Document 26.6 A Call for Common Ground and Common Sense

In the 1980s, Jesse Jackson, a former associate of Martin Luther King, Jr., and a Chicago minister, became a leading voice among African-Americans. At the same time Jackson also emerged as a national leader. In 1988 Jackson ran for the Democratic presidential nomination. He surprised many with the number votes he received, many from white Democrats. Nonetheless, however, he failed to get the nomination, which went to Massachusetts Governor Michael Dukakis. With his strong support among blacks and white liberals, Jackson was in a powerful position at the convention. The Democratic Party, hoping to inspire those voters to vote for Dukakis and other Democrats, invited Jackson to speak. His speech called for policies radically different from those advocated by Republican conservatives and is an important expression of liberal thought during this period.

Common Ground and Common Sense

Jesse Jackson, Candidate for Democratic Presidential Nomination

Delivered at the Democratic National Convention, Atlanta, Georgia, July 20, 1988

Tonight we pause and give praise and honor to God for being good enough to allow us to be at this place at this time. When I look out at this convention, I see the face of America, red, yellow, brown, black and white, we're all precious in God's sight—the real rainbow coalition. All of us, all of us who are here and think that, we are seated. But we're really standing on someone's shoulders. Ladies and gentlemen. Mrs. Rosa Parks.

The mother of the civil rights movement.

I want to express my deep love and appreciation for the support my family has given me over these past months.

They have endured pain, anxiety, threat and fear.

But they have been strengthened and made secure by a faith in God, in America and in you.

Your love has protected us and made us strong.

To my wife Jackie, the foundation of our family; to our five children whom you met tonight; to my mother Mrs. Helen Jackson, who is present tonight; and to my grandmother, Mrs. Maltilda Burns; my brother Chuck and his family; my mother-in-law,

Mrs. Gertrude Brown, who just last month at age 61 graduated from Hampton Institute, a marvelous achievement; I offer my appreciation to Mayor Andrew Young who has provided such gracious hospitality to all of us this week.

And a special salute to President Jimmy Carter.

President Carter restored honor to the White House after Watergate. He gave many of us a special opportunity to grow. For his kind words, for his unwavering commitment to peace in the world and the voters that came from his family, every member of his family, led by Billy and Amy, I offer him my special thanks, special thanks to the Carter family.

My right and my privilege to stand here before you has been won—in my lifetime—by the blood and the sweat of the innocent.

Twenty-four years ago, the late Fanny Lou Hamer and Aaron Henry—who sits here tonight from Mississippi—were locked out on the streets of Atlantic City, the head of the Mississippi Freedom Democratic Party.

But tonight, a black and white delegation from Mississippi is headed by Ed Cole, a black man, from Mississippi, 24 years later.

Many were lost in the struggle for the right to vote. Jimmy Lee Jackson, a young student, gave his life. Viola Luizzo, a white mother from Detroit, called nigger lover, and brains blown out at point blank range.

Schwerner, Goodman and Chaney—two Jews and a black—found in a common grave, bodies riddled with bullets in Mississippi. The four darling little girls in the church in Birmingham, Ala. They died that we might have a right to live.

Dr. Martin Luther King Jr. lies only a few miles from us tonight.

Tonight he must feet good as he looks down upon us. We sit here together, a rainbow, a coalition—the sons and daughters of slave masters and the sons and daughters of slaves sitting together around a common table, to decide the direction of our party and our country. His heart would be full tonight.

As a testament to the struggles of those who have gone before; as a legacy for those who will come after; as a tribute to the endurance, the patience, the courage of our forefathers and mothers; as an assurance that their prayers are being answered, their work has not been in vain, and hope is eternal; tomorrow night my name will go into nomination for the presidency of the United States of America.

We meet tonight at a crossroads, a point of decision.

Shall we expand, be inclusive, find unity and power; or suffer division and impotence.

We come to Atlanta, the cradle of the old South, the crucible of the new South.

Tonight there is a sense of celebration because we are moved, fundamentally moved, from racial battlegrounds by law, to economic common ground, tomorrow we will challenge to move to higher ground.

Common ground!

Think of Jerusalem—the intersection where many trails met. A small village that became the birthplace for three great religions—Judaism, Christianity and Islam.

Why was this village so blessed? Because it provided a crossroads where different people met, different cultures, and different civilizations could meet and find common ground.

When people come together, flowers always flourish and the air is rich with the aroma of a new spring.

Take New York, the dynamic metropolis. What makes New York so special?

It is the invitation of the Statue of Liberty—give me your tired, your poor, your huddled masses who yearn to breathe free.

Not restricted to English only.

Many people, many cultures, many languages—with one thing in common, the yearn to breathe free.

Common ground!

Tonight in Atlanta, for the first time in this century we convene in the South.

A state where governors once stood in school house doors. Where Julian Bond was denied his seat in the state legislature because of his conscientious objection to the Vietnam War.

A city that, through its five black universities, has graduated more black students than any city in the world.

Atlanta, now a modern intersection of the new South.

Common ground!

That is the challenge to our party tonight.

Left wing. Right wing. Progress will not come through boundless liberalism nor static conservatism, but at the critical mass of mutual survival. It takes two wings to fly.

Whether you're a hawk or a dove, you're just a bird living in the same environment, in the same world.

The Bible teaches that when lions and lambs lie down together, none will be afraid and there will be peace in the valley. It sounds impossible. Lions eat lambs. Lambs sensibly flee from lions. But even lions and lambs find common ground. Why?

Because neither lions nor lambs want the forest to catch on fire. Neither lions nor lambs want acid rain to fall. Neither lions nor lambs can survive nuclear war. If lions and lambs can find common ground, surely, we can as well, as civilized people.

The only time that we win is when we come together. In 1960, John Kennedy, the late John Kennedy, beat Richard Nixon by only 112,000 votes—less than one vote per precinct. He won by the margin of our hope. He brought us together. He reached out. He had the courage to defy his advisors and inquire about Dr. King's jailing in Albany, Georgia. We won by the margin of our hope, inspired by courageous leadership.

In 1964, Lyndon Johnson brought both wings together. The thesis, the antithesis and to create a synthesis and together we won.

In 1976, Jimmy Carter unified us again and we won. When we do not come together, we never win.

In 1968, division and despair in July led to our defeat in November.

In 1980, rancor in the spring and the summer led to Reagan in the fall. When we divide, we cannot win. We must find common ground as a basis for survival and development and change and growth.

Today when we debated, differed, deliberated, agreed to agree, agreed to disagree, when we had the good judgment to argue our case and then not self-destruct, George Bush was just a little further away from the White House and a little closer to private life.

Tonight, I salute Governor Michael Dukakis.

He has run a well-managed and a dignified campaign. No matter how tired or how tried, he always resisted the temptation to stoop to demagoguery.

I've watched a good mind fast at work, with steel nerves, guiding his campaign out of the crowded field without appeal to the worst in us. I've watched his perspective grow as his environment has expanded. I've seen his toughness and tenacity close up. I know his commitment to public service.

Mike Dukakis' parents were a doctor and a teacher; my parents, a maid, a beautician and a janitor.

There's a great gap between Brookline, Massachusetts and Haney Street, the Fieldcrest Village housing projects in Greenville, South Carolina.

He studied law; I studied theology. There are differences of religion, region, and race; differences in experiences and perspectives. But the genius of America is that out of the many, we become one.

Providence has enabled our paths to intersect. His foreparents came to America on immigrant ships; my foreparents came to America on slave ships. But whatever the original ships, we're in the same boat tonight.

Our ships could pass in the night if we have a false sense of independence, or they could collide and crash. We would lose our passengers. But we can seek a higher reality and a greater good apart. We can drift on the broken pieces of Reaganomics, satisfy our baser instincts, and exploit the fears of our people. At our highest, we can call upon noble instincts and navigate this vessel to safety. The greater good is the common good.

As Jesus said, "Not my will, but thine be done." It was his way of saying there's a higher good beyond personal comfort or position.

The good of our nation is at stake—its commitment to working men and women, to the poor and the vulnerable, to the many in the world. With so many guided missiles, and so much misguided leadership, the stakes are exceedingly high. Our choice, full participation in a Democratic government, or more abandonment and neglect. And so this night, we choose not a false sense of independence, not our capacity to survive and endure.

Tonight we choose interdependency in our capacity to act and unite for the greater good. The common good is finding commitment to new priorities, to expansion and inclusion. A commitment to expanded participation in the Democratic Party at every level. A commitment to a shared national campaign strategy and involvement at every level. A commitment to new priorities that ensure that hope will be kept alive. A common ground commitment for a legislative agenda by empowerment for the John Conyers bill, universal, on-site, same-day registration everywhere—and commitment to D.C. statehood and empower—D.C. deserves statehood. A commitment to economic set-asides, a commitment to the Dellums bill for comprehensive sanctions against South Africa, a shared commitment to a common direction.

Common ground. Easier said than done. Where do you find common ground at the point of challenge? This campaign has shown that politics need not be marketed by politicians, packaged by pollsters and pundits. Politics can be a marvel arena where people come together, define common ground.

We find common ground at the plant gate that closes on workers without notice. We find common ground at the farm auction where a good farmer loses his or her land to bad loans or diminishing markets. Common ground at the schoolyard where teachers cannot get adequate pay, and students cannot get a scholarship and can't make a loan. Common ground, at the hospital admitting room where somebody tonight is dying because they cannot afford to go upstairs to a bed that's empty, waiting for someone with insurance to get sick. We are a better nation than that. We must do better.

Common ground. What is leadership if not present help in a time of crisis? And so I met you at the point of challenge in Jay, Maine, where paper workers were striking for fair wages; in Greenfield, Iowa, where family farmers struggle for a fair price; in Cleveland, Ohio, where working women seek comparable worth; in McFarland, Calif., where the children of Hispanic farm workers may be dying from poison land, dying in clusters with cancer; in the AIDS hospice in Houston, Texas, where the sick support one another, 12 are rejected by their own parents and friends.

Common ground.

America's not a blanket woven from one thread, one color, one cloth. When I was a child growing up in Greenville, S.C., and grandmother could not afford a blanket, she didn't complain and we did not freeze. Instead, she took pieces of old cloth—patches, wool, silk, gabardine, crockersack on the patches—barely good enough to wipe off your shoes with.

But they didn't stay that way very long. With sturdy hands and a strong cord, she sewed them together into a quilt, a thing of beauty and power and culture.

Now, Democrats, we must build such a quilt. Farmers, you seek fair prices and you are right, but you cannot stand alone. Your patch is not big enough. Workers, you fight for fair wages. You are right. But your patch labor is not big enough. Women you seek comparable worth and pay equity. You are right. But your patch is not big enough. Women, mothers, who seek Head Start and day care and pre-natal care on the front side of life, rather than jail care and welfare on the back side of life, you're right, but your patch is not big enough.

Students, you seek scholarships. You are right. But your patch is not big enough. Blacks and Hispanics, when we fight for civil rights, we are right, but our patch is not big enough. Gays and lesbians, when you fight against discrimination and a cure for AIDS, you are right, but your patch is not big enough. Conservatives and progressives, when you fight for what you believe, right-wing, left-wing, hawk, dove—you are right, from your point of view, but your point of view is not enough.

But don't despair. Be as wise as my grandmama. Pool the patches and the pieces together, bound by a common thread. When we form a great quilt of unity and common ground we'll have the power to bring about health care and housing and jobs and education and hope to our nation.

We the people can win. We stand at the end of a long dark night of reaction. We stand tonight united in a commitment to a new direction. For almost eight years, we've been led by those who view social good coming from private interest, who viewed public life as a means to increase private wealth. They have been prepared to sacrifice the common good of the many to satisfy the private interest and the wealth of a few. We believe in a government that's a tool of our democracy in service to the public, not an instrument of the aristocracy in search of private wealth.

We believe in government with the consent of the governed of, for, and by the people. We must not emerge into a new day with a new direction. Reaganomics, based on the belief that the rich had too much money—too little money, and the poor had too much.

That's classic Reaganomics. It believes that the poor had too much money and the rich had too little money.

So, they engaged in reverse Robin Hood—took from the poor, gave to the rich, paid for by the middle class. We cannot stand four more years of Reaganomics in any version, in any disguise.

How do I document that case? Seven years later, the richest 1 percent of our society pays 20 percent less in taxes; the poorest 10 percent pay 20 percent more. Reaganomics.

Reagan gave the rich and the powerful a multibillion dollar party. Now, the party is over. He expects the people to pay for the damage. I take this principled position—convention, let us not raise taxes on the poor and the middle class, but those who had the party, the rich and the powerful must pay for the party!

I just want to take common sense to high places. We're spending $150 billion a year defending Europe and Japan 43 years after the war is over. We have more troops in Europe tonight than we had seven years ago, yet the threat of war is ever more remote. Germany and Japan are now creditor nations—that means they've got a surplus. We are a debtor nation—it means we are in debt.

Let them share more of the burden of their own defense—use some of that money to build decent housing!

Use some of that money to educate our children!

Use some of that money for long-term health care!

Use some of that money to wipe out these slums and put America back to work!

I just want to take common sense to high places. If we can bail out Europe and Japan, if we can bail out Continental Bank and Chrysler—and Mr. Iacocca makes $8,000 an hour, we can bail out the family farmer.

I just want to make common sense. It does not make sense to close down 650,000 family farms in this country while importing food from abroad subsidized by the U.S. government.

Let's make sense. It does not make sense to be escorting oil tankers up and down the Persian Gulf paying $2.50 for every $1.00 worth of oil we bring out while oil wells are capped in Texas, Oklahoma and Louisiana. I just want to make sense.

Leadership must meet the moral challenge of its day. What's the moral challenge of our day? We have public accommodations. We have the right to vote. We have open housing.

What's the fundamental challenge of our day? It is to end economic violence. Plant closing without notice, economic violence. Even the greedy do not profit long from greed. Economic violence. Most poor people are not lazy. They're not black. They're not brown. They're mostly white, and female and young.

But whether white, black or brown, the hungry baby's belly turned inside out is the same color. Call it pain. Call it hurt. Call it agony. Most poor people are not on welfare.

Some of them are illiterate and can't read the want-ad sections. And when they can, they can't find a job that matches their address. They work hard every day, I know. I live amongst them. I'm one of them.

I know they work. I'm a witness. They catch the early bus. They work every day. They raise other people's children. They work every day. They clean the streets. They work every day. They drive vans with cabs. They work every day. They change the beds you slept in these hotels last night and can't get a union contract. They work every day.

No more. They're not lazy. Someone must defend them because it's right, and they cannot speak for themselves. They work in hospitals. I know they do. They wipe the bodies of those who are sick with fever and pain. They empty their bedpans. They clean out their commode. No job is beneath them, and yet when they get sick, they cannot lie in the bed they made up every day. America, that is not right. We are a better nation than that. We are a better nation than that.

We need a real war on drugs. You can't just say no. It's deeper than that. You can't just get a palm reader or an astrologer; it's more profound than that. We're spending $150 billion on drugs a year. We've gone from ignoring it to focusing on the children. Children cannot buy $150 billion worth of drugs a year. A few high profile athletes—athletes are not laundering $150 billion a year—bankers are.

I met the children in Watts who are unfortunate in their despair. Their grapes of hope have become raisins of despair, and they're turning to each other and they're self-destructing—but I stayed with them all night long. I wanted to hear their case . They said, "Jesse Jackson, as you challenge us to say no to drugs, you're right. And to not sell them, you're right. And to not use these guns, you're right."

And, by the way, the promise of CETA—they displaced CETA. They did not replace CETA. We have neither jobs nor houses nor services nor training—no way out. Some of us take drugs as anesthesia for our pain. Some take drugs as a way of pleasure—both short-term pleasure and long-term pain. Some sell drugs to make money. It's wrong, we know. But you need to know that we know. We can go and buy the drugs by the boxes at the port. If we can buy the drugs at the port, don't you believe the federal government can stop it if they want to?

They say, "We don't have Saturday night specials any more." They say, "We buy AK-47s and Uzis, the latest lethal weapons. We buy them across the counter on Long Beach Boulevard." You cannot fight a war on drugs unless and until you are going to challenge the bankers and the gun sellers and those who grow them. Don't just focus on the children, let's stop drugs at the level of supply and demand. We must end the scourge on the American culture.

Leadership. What difference will we make? Leadership cannot just go along to get along. We must do more than change presidents. We must change direction. Leadership must face the moral challenge of our day. The nuclear war build-up is irrational. Strong leadership cannot desire to look tough, and let that stand in the way of the pursuit of peace. Leadership must reverse the arms race.

At least we should pledge no first use. Why? Because first use begat first retaliation, and that's mutual annihilation. That's not a rational way out. No use at all—let's think it out, and not fight it out, because it's an unwinnable fight. Why hold a card that you can never drop? Let's give peace a chance.

Leadership—we now have this marvelous opportunity to have a breakthrough with the Soviets. Last year, 200,000 Americans visited the Soviet Union. There's a chance for joint ventures into space, not Star Wars and the war arms escalation, but a space defense initiative. Let's build in space together, and demilitarize the heavens. There's a way out.

America, let us expand. When Mr. Reagan and Mr. Gorbachev met, there was a big meeting. They represented together one-eighth of the human race. Seven-eighths of the human race was locked out of that room. Most people in the world tonight—half are Asian, one-half of them are Chinese. There are 22 nations in the Middle East. There's Europe; 40 million Latin Americans next door to us; the Caribbean, Africa—a half-billion people. Most people in the world today are yellow or brown or black, non-

Christian, poor, female, young, and don't speak English—in the real world.

This generation must offer leadership to the real world. We're losing ground in Latin America, the Middle East, South Africa, because we're not focusing on the real world, that real world. We must use basic principles, support international law. We stand the most to gain from it. Support human rights; we believe in that. Support self-determination; we'll build on that. Support economic development; you know it's right. Be consistent, and gain our moral authority in the world.

I challenge you tonight, my friends, let's be bigger and better as a nation and as a party. We have basic challenges. Freedom in South Africa,—we've already agreed as Democrats to declare South Africa to be a terrorist state. But don't just stop there. Get South Africa out of Angola. Free Namibia. Support the front-line states. We must have a new, humane human rights assistance policy in Africa.

I'm often asked, "Jesse, why do you take on these touch issues? They're not very political. We can't win that way."

If an issue is morally right, it will eventually be political. It may be political and never be right. Fannie Lou Hamer didn't have the most votes in Atlantic City, but her principles have outlasted every delegate who voted to lock her out. Rosa Parks did not have the most votes, but she was morally right. Dr. King didn't have the most votes about the Vietnam war, but he was morally right.—If we're principled first, our politics will fall in place.

Jesse, why did you take these big bold initiatives? A poem by an unknown author went something like this: We mastered the air, we've conquered the sea, and anilihilated distance and prolonged life, we were not wise enough to live on this earth without war and without hate.

As for Jesse Jackson, I'm tired of sailing by little boat, far inside the harbor bar. I want to go out where the big ships float, out on the deep where the great ones are. And should my frail craft prove too slight, the waves that sweep those billows o'er, I'd rather go down in a stirring fight than drown to death in the sheltered shore.

We've got to go out, my friends, where the big boats are.

And then, for our children, young America, hold your head high now. We can win. We must not lose you to drugs and violence, premature pregnancy, suicide, cynicism, pessimism and despair. We can win.

Wherever you are tonight, I challenge you to hope and to dream. Don't submerge your dreams. Exercise above all else, even on drugs, dream of the day you're drug-free. Even in the gutter, dream of the day that you'll be up on your feet again. You must never stop dreaming. Face reality, yes. But don't stop with the way things are; dream of things as they ought to be. Dream. Face pain, but love, hope, faith, and dreams will help you rise above the pain.

Use hope and imagination as weapons of survival and progress, but you keep on dreaming, young America. Dream of peace. Peace is rational and reasonable. War is irrational in this age and unwinnable.

Dream of teachers who teach for life and not for living. Dream of doctors who are concerned more about public health than private wealth. Dream of lawyers more concerned about justice than a judgeship. Dream of preachers who are concerned more about prophecy than profiteering. Dream on the high road of sound values.

And in America, as we go forth to September, October and November and then beyond, America must never surrender to a high moral challenge.

Do not surrender to drugs. The best drug policy is a no first use. Don't surrender with needles and cynicism. Let's have no first use on the one hand, or clinics on the other. Never surrender, young America.

Go forward. America must never surrender to malnutrition. We can feed the hungry and clothe the naked. We must never surrender. We must go forward. We must never surrender to illiteracy. Invest in our children. Never surrender; and go forward.

We must never surrender to inequality. Women cannot compromise ERA or comparable worth. Women are making 60 cents on the dollar to what a man makes. Women cannot buy meat cheaper. Women cannot buy bread cheaper. Women cannot buy milk cheaper. Women deserve to get paid for the work that you do. It's right and it's fair.

Don't surrender, my friends. Those who have AIDS tonight, you deserve your compassion. Even with AIDS you must not surrender in your wheelchairs. I see you sitting here tonight in those wheelchairs. I've stayed with you. I've reached out to you across our nation. Don't you give up. I know it's tough sometimes. People look down on you. It took you a little more effort to get here tonight.

And no one should look down on you, but sometimes mean people do. The only justification we have for looking down on someone is that we're going to stop and pick them up. But even in your wheelchairs, don't you give up. We cannot forget 50 years ago when our backs were against the wall, Roosevelt was in a wheelchair. I would rather have Roosevelt in a wheelchair than Reagan and Bush on a horse. Don't you surrender and don't you give up.

Don't surrender and don't give up. Why can I challenge you this, way? Jesse Jackson, you don't understand my situation. You be on television. You don't understand. I see you with the big people. You don't understand my situation. I understand. You're seeing me on TV but you don't know the me that makes me, me. They wonder why does Jesse run, because they see me running for the White House. They don't see the house I'm running from.

I have a story. I wasn't always on television. Writers were not always outside my door. When I was born late one afternoon, October 8th, in Greenville, S.C., no writers asked my mother her name. Nobody chose to write down our address. My mama was not supposed to make it. And I was not supposed to make it. You see, I was born to a teen-age mother who was born to a teenage mother.

I understand. I know abandonment and people being mean to you, and saying you're nothing and nobody, and can never be anything. I understand. Jesse Jackson is my third name. I'm adopted. When I had no name, my grandmother gave me her name. My name was Jesse Burns until I was 12. So I wouldn't have a blank space, she gave me a name to hold me over. I understand when nobody knows your name. I understand when you have no name. I understand.

I wasn't born in the hospital. Mama didn't have insurance. I was born in the bed at home. I really do understand. Born in a three-room house, bathroom in the backyard, slop jar by the bed, no hot and cold running water. I understand. Wallpaper used for decoration? No. For a windbreaker. I understand. I'm a working person's person, that's why I understand you whether you're black or white.

I understand work. I was not born with a silver spoon in my mouth. I had a shovel programmed for my hand. My mother, a working woman. So many days she went to work early with runs in her stockings. She knew better, but she wore runs in her stockings so that my brother and I could have matching socks and not be laughed at at school.

I understand. At 3 o'clock on Thanksgiving Day we couldn't eat turkey because mama was preparing someone else's turkey at 3 o'clock. We had to play football to entertain ourselves and then around 6 o'clock she would get off the Alta Vista bus; then we would bring up the leftovers and eat our turkey—leftovers, the carcass, the cranberries around 8 o'clock at night. I really do understand.

Every one of these funny labels they put on you, those of you who are watching this broadcast tonight in the projects, on the corners, I understand. Call you outcast, low down, you can't make it, you're nothing, you're from nobody, subclass, underclass—when you see Jesse Jackson, when my name goes in nomination, your name goes in nomination.

I was born in the slum, but the slum was not born in me. And it wasn't born in you, and you can make it. Wherever you are tonight you can make it. Hold your head high, stick your chest out. You can make it. It gets dark sometimes, but the morning comes. Don't you surrender. Suffering breeds character. Character breeds faith. In the end faith will not disappoint.

You must not surrender. You may or may not get there, but just know that you're qualified and you hold on and hold out We must never surrender. America will get better and better. Keep hope alive. Keep hope alive. Keep hope alive. On tomorrow night and beyond, keep hope alive.

I love you very much. I love you very much.

Document 26.7 The "Contract with America"

Ronald Reagan left the presidency at the end of his two terms in 1989 and was succeeded by his vice president, George Bush. Bush was defeated by the Democrat Bill Clinton in 1992. As president, Clinton got off to a rocky start, and dissatisfaction with the operation of the political system and politicians remained widespread. In 1994, under the leadership of Republican Congressman Newt Gingrich of Georgia, the Republicans sought to win enough seats to control the House of Representatives. To that end, the House Republicans constructed a "Contract with America," incorporating Republican proposals vetted by public opinion polling. Standing in front of the Capitol, Republican candidates for the House signed the Contract. In the elections in November, the Republicans, to the surprise of many, scored an amazing victory and gained a majority of seats in both the House of Representatives and the Senate. This was the first time they had controlled both Houses of Congress since 1954. Under the leadership of Newt Gingrich, who became Speaker of the House, Republicans tried to put into law the provisions of the "Contract with America." In this effort their success was limited. Neverheless, the "Contract" was an important statement of conservative ideas in the mid-1990s.

The "Contract with America"

Thereafter, within the first hundred days of the 104th Congress, we shall bring to the House Floor the following bills, each to be given full and open debate, each to be given a clear and fair vote, and each to be immediately available this day for public inspection and scrutiny.

The Fiscal Responsibility Act

A balanced budget/tax limitation amendment and a legislative line-item veto to restore fiscal responsibility to an out-of-control Congress, requiring them to live under the same budget constraints as families and businesses.

The Taking Back Our Streets Act

An anti-crime package including stronger truth in sentencing, "good faith" exclusionary rule exemptions, effective death penalty provisions, and cuts in social spending from this summer's crime bill to fund prison construction and additional law enforcement to keep people secure in their neighborhoods and kids safe in their schools.

The Personal Responsibility Act

Discourage illegitimacy and teen pregnancy by prohibiting welfare to minor mothers and denying increased AFDC for additional children while on welfare, cut spending for welfare programs, and enact a tough two-years-and-out provision with work requirements to promote individual responsibility.

The Family Reinforcement Act

Child support enforcement, tax incentives for adoption, strengthening rights of parents in their children's education, stronger child pornography laws, and an elderly dependent care tax credit to reinforce the central role of families in American society.

The American Dream Restoration Act

A $500-per-child tax credit, begin repeal of the marriage tax penalty, and creation of American Dream Savings Accounts to provide middle-class tax relief.

The National Security Restoration Act

No U.S. troops under UN command and restoration of the essential parts of our national security funding to strengthen our national defense and maintain our credibility around the world.

The Senior Citizens Fairness Act

Raise the Social Security earnings limit, which currently forces seniors out of the workforce, repeal the 1993 tax hikes on Social Security benefits, and provide tax incentives for private long-term care insurance to let older Americans keep more of what they have earned over the years.

The Job Creation and Wage Enhancement Act

Small business incentives, capital gains cut and indexation, neutral cost recovery, risk assessment/cost-benefit analysis, strengthening of the Regulatory Flexibility Act and unfunded mandate reform to create jobs and raise worker wages.

The Common Sense Legal Reforms Act

"Loser pays" laws, reasonable limits on punitive damages, and reform of product liability laws to stem the endless tide of litigation.

Module XIV
Questions for Study and Critical Thinking

1. What policies did Ronald Reagan announce in his first inaugural address?

2. Do you agree or disagree with them? Why?

3. According to George Gilder, what are the only ways poor people can get out of poverty?

4. What are the strengths and weaknesses of his argument?

5. What does Falwell identify as the crucial problems of the United States? What does he say should be done about them?

6. Do you agree? Why or why not?

7. In his speech to the National Association of Evangelicals, what does Reagan say he will do about the conservative Christian's issues? What is your assessment of this response?

8. In his speech to the House of Commons, what criticisms did Reagan make of Communist regimes? What does he say American policy toward them should be

9. What is your assessment of these ideas?

10. What is your assessment of these proposals?

11. What were Jesse Jackson's criticisms of the Reagan Administration's policies?

12. Do you agree with these criticisms? Why or why not?

13. What policies did Jackson advocate? What do you think of them?

14. What policies did the Contract with America promise to enact?

15. Do you agree with these policies? Why or why not?

Travelers' Luggage

u will find at our store the largest assort-
nt of travelers' equipment to be found in the
y. Gladstone Bags, Over-Night Cases, fitted
plain, Hat Boxes, Steamer and Wardrobe
unks, Auto Touring Cases, Toilet Cases, and
well line of Ladies' Hand Purses and Bags,
all the new shades and grains of leather.
f you fail to inspect our display, you are
passing up the best

BLISS BROS.
AGS, TRUNKS, LEATHER GOODS
East Cortland St. Jackson, Mich.

"Hey There!
Wake Up!
You are blocking traffic—"

We let 'nothing interfere with the forward march of Dodge Brothers Motor Cars

We Sell 'em!

Gilbert Loomis Motors Co.
JACKSON

JACKSON'S ORIGINAL
BARBEQUE

Where Quality and Service are Unexcelled

Tasty - Tempting - Tummying
SANDWICHES
Using Original Kombak Sauce

RATCHFORD'S
BARBEQUE
East Michigan Avenue at Ganson

TOWNSEND & JOHNSON, Dealers in Real Estate and Mortgage
FIRE INSURANCE AND RENTAL AGENCY. Exchanges of Property a Specialty. Taxes Paid and Rents Carefully Looked A
Telephone 605. ROOM 20 DWIGHT BLOCK. Jackso

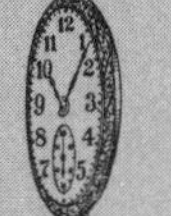

DIAMONDS
WATCHES
SILVERWARE
CHINA

DICKER & DOCKSE
QUALITY JEWELERS
128 W. Michigan Ave. Tel.

IN ACCOUNT WITH

FRANK GLINICKI
GROCERIES AND MEATS
9131 COR. PRINGLE & ELM

Field-Brundage
Company
Manufacturers of
Gasoline Engines
JACKSON, MICHIGAN

OUR LINE OF FISHING TACKLE is very complete. Come in and stock up before you go on your vacation.
FRANK McLEAN & COMPANY, 162 West Main Street.

ELECTRICAL

Bugg

Choicest Diamond Values

No one ever had a "kick" at our Diamond values—and we've sold plenty t
people of every walk of life. Such universal confidence must
be a real reflection of satisfaction.

IFTS THAT LAST

R JEWELRY features the marvelous
advances made in the
r's art in the last decade that places our
cts in the highest rank of modern, up-to-date
raft. By supplying your needs from the
t and artistic stock of jewelry offered by us,
e assured of upright dealing backed by our
ntee of quality and durability.

G. G. GASE
JACKSON'S OLDEST JEWELRY STORE
MAIN AND JACKSON STREETS

MRS. CLARA BROWN & CO.
FLORISTS
FLORAL DESIGNS. CUT FLOWERS. PARTY DECORATIONS.
BEDDING AND HOUSE PLANTS.
ORDERS FILLED PROMPTLY.
SALESROOM: 172 MAIN STREET WEST. Phone 173.
GREENHOUSES: OPP. MT. EVERGREEN CEMETERY. Both Phones 126.

SCHAFER'
ODORLESS
Dry Cleaning
Fully Covered by Insurance Until Returned to You
PHONE
4174
225
S. Mechanic
St.

MRS. KATE BATTAMS,
FINE MILLINERY.
class order work a specialty.
245 W. Main St.

SON
CO.,
acturers of
Grade
Hats,
Cortland St.
NE 975.

GEO. MEISTER, PIANOS, ORGANS, MUSICAL MERCHANDISE.

Professional Pharmacy
The Chemist Shop
253 WEST MICHIGAN AVENUE
Prescriptions—What You Need, When You Need It.

Prescriptions
Sick Room Supplies
Biologicals
Rubber Goods

Perfumes
Toilet Preparations
Surgical Supports
Drug Sundries

253 W. MICHIGAN AVE.
PHONE 2-1832

amsay's Candy
nk Ramsay's Soda
at Ramsay's Ice Cream

Happier Homes and Happier Wives with Modern Electric and Gas Labor Saving Appliances.

CONSUMERS POWER CO.
DIAL 8121

INTERNATIONAL
HARVESTER
TRUCKS
COMPANY
PLENTY OF WORK
FOR AN
INTERNATIONAL TRUCK

A load is just so many pounds or tons to an International, whether it be milk, livestock, grain, fruit, lumber or coal.

Body Styles for Every Need

Internationals are built in sizes meet every hauling need—from 1 to 10,000 pounds capacity.

Let Us Demonstrate One to You

INTERNATIONAL HARVESTER COMPAN
OF AMERICA
(Incorporated)
JACKSON, MICHIGAN
701 Michigan Ave., E.

SOLID JERSEY CREAM. HIGHLAND FARM. JACKSON, MICH.

J. E. SHORT,
Shoer of High Class
Coach Horses and
Gentlemen's Drivers
Expert in all matters pertaining to horse's feet.
Shop, 150 West Pearl Street. Jackson, Mich

THE REGENT CAFE
AIR CONDITIONED BY FRIGIDAIRE
FOR THE BENEFIT OF OUR PATRONS
OPEN 24 HOURS A DAY

S
Measure
West

nplete

DESIRABLE PATTERNS ALWAYS AVAILABLE AT LEADING STORES

MICHIGAN SEATING CO.
JACKSON, MICHIGAN
Sole Manufacturers of
Kaltex

Gilberts
PURITY

The Essence of Goodness

Gilbert's Chocolates aren't good just by chance, they're good on purpose, —by rule.

When you combine A grade materials with real candy making art an honest, intelligent desire to produce candy satisfaction, the result is inevitable—better candy.

Gilbert's Chocolates satisfy the most critical and bring them back for more. They have an appeal indescribable.

Try it once and you'll always buy it

PALMI
ART STUDIO

CARTER BUILDING DIAL 4036

Jackson
NO HILL TOO STEEP
NO SAND TOO DEEP

SILENCE
The True Indication of Mech
Perfection

Jackson Silence is valuable not only because of the freedom from noise annoyance. The silent operation of the car tells the complete story of smooth bearings, of perfect balance in moving parts, of a positive lubricating system, of expert workmanship and of excellence in design that 12 years' experience has brought to its present perfection.

On behalf of the Board of Directors, officers and employees
of City Bank & Trust Company, N.A., we are pleased to present this
limited edition of
The History of Business and Industry in Jackson, Michigan
Through its pages, Jackson's rich and vibrant history
comes alive and City Bank & Trust is proud to have played
a vital, long standing role in that heritage and growth.
City Bank & Trust dedicates this book to the people of Jackson,
past and present, whose faith, determination
and courage helped establish the foundation
of our city's growth.

Brian D. Bell
President and Chief Executive Officer
City Bank & Trust Company, N.A.

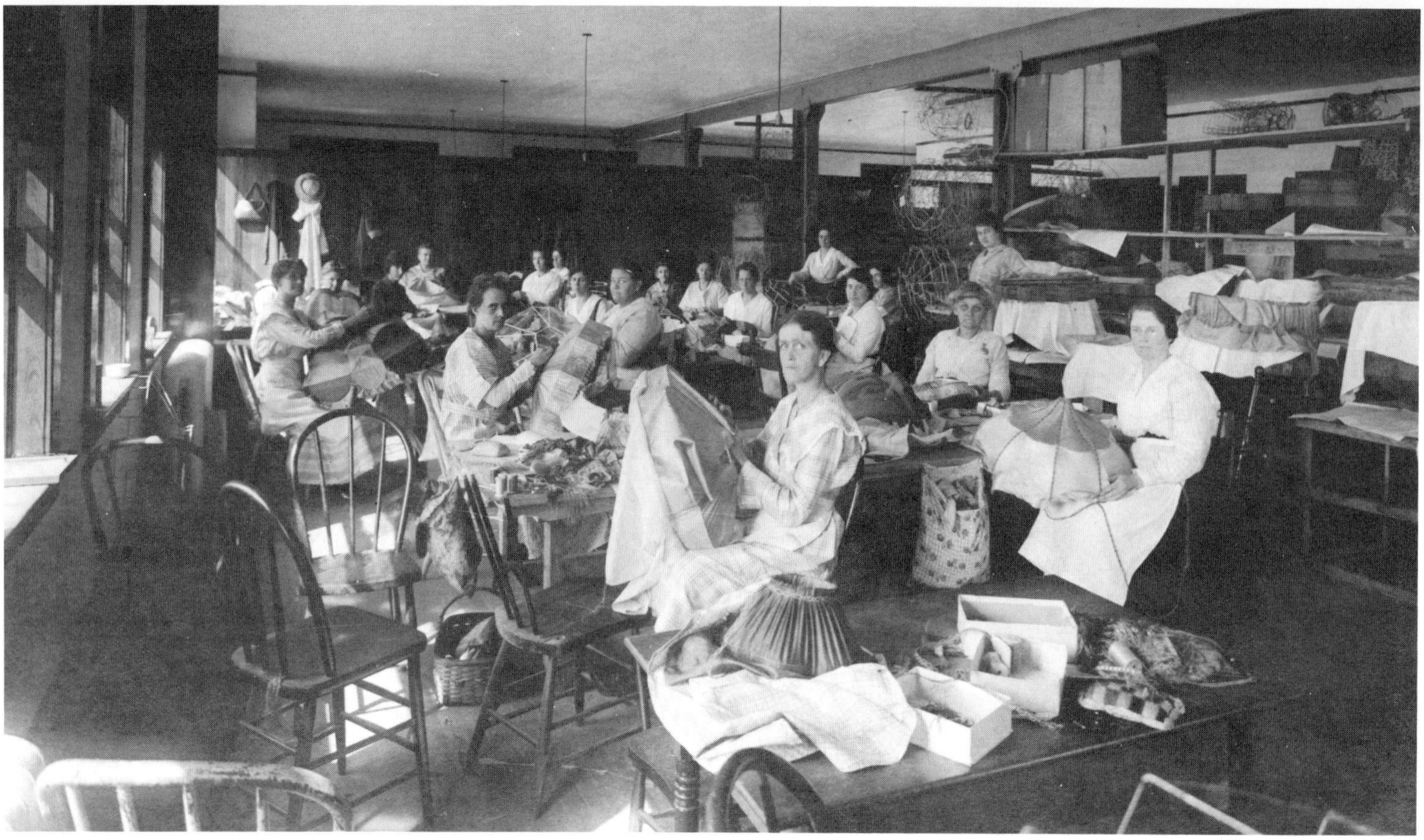